After Virtue

After Virtue

A Study in Moral Theory

By

ALASDAIR MACINTYRE

Second Edition

University of Notre Dame Press
Notre Dame, Indiana

Second edition 1984
University of Notre Dame Press
Notre Dame, Indiana

First edition 1981
University of Notre Dame Press
Notre Dame, Indiana

First Edition first published 1981 by
Gerald Duckworth & Co. Ltd.
The Old Piano Factory
43 Gloucester Crescent
London NW1

Library of Congress Cataloging in Publication Data

MacIntyre, Alasdair C.
    After virtue.

    Bibliography: p.
    Includes index.
    1. Ethics.   2. Virtues.   3. Virtue.   I. Title.
BJ1012.M325   1984   170'.42   83-40601
ISBN 0-268-00610-5
ISBN 0-268-00611-3 (pbk.)

Manufactured in the United States of America

TO THE MEMORY OF
MY FATHER AND HIS SISTERS AND BROTHERS

Gus am bris an la

Contents

Preface   ix
1. A Disquieting Suggestion   1
2. The Nature of Moral Disagreement Today
and the Claims of Emotivism   6
3. Emotivism: Social Content and Social Context   23
4. The Predecessor Culture and the
Enlightenment Project of Justifying Morality   36
5. Why the Enlightenment Project
of Justifying Morality Had to Fail   51
6. Some Consequences of the Failure
of the Enlightenment Project   62
7. 'Fact', Explanation and Expertise   79
8. The Character of Generalizations in Social Science
and their Lack of Predictive Power   88
9. Nietzsche or Aristotle?   109
10. The Virtues in Heroic Societies   121
11. The Virtues at Athens   131
12. Aristotle's Account of the Virtues   146
13. Medieval Aspects and Occasions   165
14. The Nature of the Virtues   181
15. The Virtues, the Unity of a Human Life
and the Concept of a Tradition   204
16. From the Virtues to Virtue and after Virtue   226
17. Justice as a Virtue: Changing Conceptions   244
18. After Virtue: Nietzsche *or* Aristotle,
Trotsky *and* St. Benedict   256
19. Postscript to the Second Edition   264
Bibliography   279
Index   283

Preface

This book emerged from extended reflection upon the inadequacies of my own earlier work in moral philosophy and from a growing dissatisfaction with the conception of 'moral philosophy' as an independent and isolable area of enquiry. A central theme of much of that earlier work (*A Short History of Ethics*, 1966; *Secularisation and Moral Change*, 1967; *Against the Self-Images of the Age*, 1971) was that we have to learn from history and anthropology of the variety of moral practices, beliefs and conceptual schemes. The notion that the moral philosopher can study *the* concepts of morality merely by reflecting, Oxford armchair style, on what he or she and those around him or her say and do is barren. *This* conviction I have found no good reason to abandon; and emigration to the United States has taught me that when the armchair is in Cambridge, Massachusetts, or in Princeton, New Jersey, it functions no better. But at the same time as I was affirming the variety and heterogeneity of moral beliefs, practices and concepts, it became clear that I was committing myself to evaluations of different particular beliefs, practices and concepts. I gave, or tried to give, for example, accounts of the rise and decline of different moralities; and it was as clear to others as it ought to have been to me that my historical and sociological accounts were, and could not but be, informed by a distinctive evaluative standpoint. More particularly I seemed to be asserting that the nature of moral community and moral judgment in distinctively modern societies was such that it was no longer possible to appeal to moral criteria in a way that had been possible in other times and places—*and* that this was a moral calamity! But to *what* could I be appealing, if my own analysis was correct?

At the same time, ever since the days when I was privileged to be a contributor to that most remarkable journal *The New Reasoner*, I had been preoccupied with the question of the basis for the moral rejection of Stalinism. Many of those who rejected Stalinism did so by reinvoking the principles of that liberalism in the criticism of which Marxism originated. Since I continued, and continue, to accept much of the substance of that criticism, this answer was not available to me. 'One cannot,' I wrote in responding to the positions then taken by Leszek Kolakowski, 'revive the moral content within Marxism by simply taking a Stalinist view of historical development and adding liberal morality to it' (*New Reasoner* 7, p. 100). Moreover I came to understand that Marxism itself has suffered from grave and harm-engendering moral impoverishment as much because of what it has inherited from liberal individualism as because of its departures from liberalism.

The conclusion which I reached and which is embodied in this book— although Marxism itself is only a marginal preoccupation—is that Marxism's moral defects and failures arise from the extent to which it, like liberal individualism, embodies the *ethos* of the distinctively modern and modernizing world, and that nothing less than a rejection of a large part of that ethos will provide us with a rationally and morally defensible standpoint from which to judge and to act—and in terms of which to evaluate various rival and heterogeneous moral schemes which compete for our allegiance. This drastic conclusion, I need scarcely add, is not to be attributed to those whose generous and just criticism of my earlier work enabled me to understand much, although perhaps as yet not all, of what is wrong with it: Eric John, J.M. Cameron and Alan Ryan. Nor should blame attach for that conclusion to those friends and colleagues whose influence has been continuous for a number of years and to whom I am exceptionally indebted: Heinz Lubasz and Marx Wartofsky.

Two of my colleagues at Boston University read large portions of my manuscript and made many helpful and illuminating suggestions. I owe a great debt of gratitude to Thomas McCarthy and Elizabeth Rapaport. Colleagues elsewhere to whom I am in debt in a variety of ways for similar suggestions are Marjorie Grene and Richard Rorty. For typing and retyping this book I am deeply grateful to Julie Keith Conley, and for several kinds of help in the production of the manuscript I have to thank Rosalie Carlson and Zara Chapin. I am also greatly indebted to the staffs of the Boston Athenaeum and the London Library.

Parts of this book have been read to various groups and their extended critical responses have been most valuable to me. In particular I must name the group that studied the Foundations of Ethics together for three years at the Hastings Center with the aid of a grant from the National Endowment for the Humanities—short passages from papers presented to that group in Volumes III and IV of the series on *The Foundations of Ethics and its Relationship to the Sciences* (1978 and 1980) reappear in Chapters 9 and 14 of this book and I am grateful to the Hastings Institute of Society, Ethics and the Life Sciences for permission to reprint them. I must also name with deep gratitude two other groups: the faculty members and graduate students of the Department of Philosophy of the University of Notre Dame, whose invitations to participate in their Perspectives Lecture

Series allowed me some of the most important opportunities to develop the ideas in this book, and the members of my N.E.H. Seminar at Boston University in the summer of 1978 whose collegial criticism of my work on the virtues played a very important part in my education. I must also therefore thank once more the National Endowment for the Humanities itself.

The dedication of this book expresses an indebtedness of a more fundamental order; if I had only recognized its fundamental character earlier, my progress towards the conclusions of this book could have been a good deal less tortuous. But I would not perhaps ever have been able to recognize it in a way that could help me towards these conclusions had it not been for what I owe to my wife, Lynn Sumida Joy — in this as in so much else *sine qua non*.

Watertown, Mass.   A.M.

1

A Disquieting Suggestion

Imagine that the natural sciences were to suffer the effects of a catastrophe. A series of environmental disasters are blamed by the general public on the scientists. Widespread riots occur, laboratories are burnt down, physicists are lynched, books and instruments are destroyed. Finally a Know-Nothing political movement takes power and successfully abolishes science teaching in schools and universities, imprisoning and executing the remaining scientists. Later still there is a reaction against this destructive movement and enlightened people seek to revive science, although they have largely forgotten what it was. But all that they possess are fragments: a knowledge of experiments detached from any knowledge of the theoretical context which gave them significance; parts of theories unrelated either to the other bits and pieces of theory which they possess or to experiment; instruments whose use has been forgotten; half-chapters from books, single pages from articles, not always fully legible because torn and charred. Nonetheless all these fragments are reembodied in a set of practices which go under the revived names of physics, chemistry and biology. Adults argue with each other about the respective merits of relativity theory, evolutionary theory and phlogiston theory, although they possess only a very partial knowledge of each. Children learn by heart the surviving portions of the periodic table and recite as incantations some of the theorems of Euclid. Nobody, or almost nobody, realizes that what they are doing is not natural science in any proper sense at all. For everything that they do and say conforms to certain canons of consistency and coherence and those contexts which would be needed to make sense of what they are doing have been lost, perhaps irretrievably.

In such a culture men would use expressions such as 'neutrino', 'mass', 'specific gravity', 'atomic weight' in systematic and often interrelated ways which would resemble in lesser or greater degrees the ways in which such expressions had been used in earlier times before scientific knowledge had been so largely lost. But many of the beliefs presupposed by the use of these expressions would have been lost and there would appear to be an element of arbitrariness and even of choice in their application which would appear very surprising to us. What would appear to be rival and competing premises for which no further argument could be given would abound. Subjectivist theories of science would appear and would be criticized by those who held that the notion of truth embodied in what they took to be science was incompatible with subjectivism.

This imaginary possible world is very like one that some science fiction writers have constructed. We may describe it as a world in which the language of natural science, or parts of it at least, continues to be used but is in a grave state of disorder. We may notice that if in this imaginary world analytical philosophy were to flourish, it would never reveal the fact of this disorder. For the techniques of analytical philosophy are essentially descriptive and descriptive of the language of the present at that. The analytical philosopher would be able to elucidate the conceptual structures of what was taken to be scientific thinking and discourse in the imaginary world in precisely the way that he elucidates the conceptual structures of natural science as it is.

Nor again would phenomenology or existentialism be able to discern anything wrong. All the structures of intentionality would be what they are now. The task of supplying an epistemological basis for these false simulacra of natural science would not differ in phenomenological terms from the task as it is presently envisaged. A Husserl or a Merleau-Ponty would be as deceived as a Strawson or a Quine.

What is the point of constructing this imaginary world inhabited by fictitious pseudo-scientists and real, genuine philosophy? The hypothesis which I wish to advance is that in the actual world which we inhabit the language of morality is in the same state of grave disorder as the language of natural science in the imaginary world which I described. What we possess, if this view is true, are the fragments of a conceptual scheme, parts which now lack those contexts from which their significance derived. We possess indeed simulacra of morality, we continue to use many of the key expressions. But we have—very largely, if not entirely—lost our comprehension, both theoretical and practical, of morality.

But how could this be so? The impulse to reject the whole suggestion out of hand will certainly be very strong. Our capacity to use moral language, to be guided by moral reasoning, to define our transactions with others in moral terms is so central to our view of ourselves that even to envisage the possibility of our radical incapacity in these respects is to ask for a shift in our view of what we are and do which is going to be difficult to achieve. But we do already know two things about the hypothesis which are initially important for us if we are to achieve such a shift in viewpoint. One is that philosophical analysis will not help us. In the real world the dominant philosophies of the present, analytical or phenomenological, will be as powerless to detect the disorders of moral thought and practice as they were impotent before the disorders of science in the imaginary world. Yet the powerlessness of this kind of philosophy does not leave us quite resourceless. For a prerequisite for understanding the present disordered state of the imaginary world was to understand its history, a history that had to be written in three distinct stages. The first stage was that in which the natural sciences flourished, the second that in which they suffered catastrophe and the third that in which they were restored but in damaged and disordered form. Notice that this history, being one of decline and fall, is informed by standards. It is not an evaluatively neutral chronicle. The form of the narrative, the division into stages, presuppose standards of achievement and failure, of order and disorder. It is what Hegel called philosophical history and what Collingwood took all successful historical writing to be. So that if we are to look for resources to investigate the hypothesis about morality which I have suggested, however bizarre and improbable it may appear to you now, we shall have to ask whether we can find in the type of philosophy and history propounded by writers such as Hegel and Collingwood—very different from each other as they are, of course—resources which we cannot find in analytical or phenomenological philosophy.

But this suggestion immediately brings to mind a crucial difficulty for my hypothesis. For one objection to the view of the imaginary world which I constructed, let alone to my view of the real world, is that the inhabitants of the imaginary world reached a point where they no longer realized the nature of the catastrophe which they had suffered. Yet surely an event of such striking world historical dimensions could not have been lost from view, so that it was both erased from memory and unrecoverable from historical records? And surely what holds of the fictitious world holds even more strongly of our own real world? If a catastrophe sufficient to throw the language and practice of morality into grave disorder had occurred, surely we should all know about it. It would indeed be one of the central facts of our history. Yet our history lies open to view, so it will be said, and no record of any such catastrophe survives. So my hypothesis must simply be abandoned. To this I must at the very least concede that it will have to be expanded, yet unfortunately at the outset expanded in such a way as to render it, if possible, initially even less credible than before. For the catastrophe will have to have been of such a kind that it was not and has not been—except perhaps by a very few—recognized as a catastrophe. We shall have to look not for a few brief striking events whose character is incontestably clear, but for a much longer, more complex and less easily identified process and probably one which by its very nature is open to rival interpretation. Yet the initial implausibility of this part of the hypothesis may perhaps be slightly lessened by another suggestion.

History by now in our culture means academic history, and academic history is less than two centuries old. Suppose it were the case that the catastrophe of which my hypothesis speaks had occurred before, or largely before, the founding of academic history, so that the moral and other evaluative presuppositions of academic history derived from the forms of the disorder which it brought about. Suppose, that is, that the standpoint of academic history is such that from its value-neutral viewpoint moral disorder must remain largely invisible. All that the historian—and what is true of the historian is characteristically true also of the social scientist— will be allowed to perceive by the canons and categories of his discipline will be one morality succeeding another: seventeenth-century Puritanism, eighteenth-century hedonism, the Victorian work-ethic and so on, but the very language of order and disorder will not be available to him. If this were to be so, it would at least explain why what I take to be the real world and its fate has remained unrecognized by the academic curriculum. For the forms of the academic curriculum would turn out to be among the symptoms of the disaster whose occurrence the curriculum does not acknowledge. Most academic history and sociology—the history of a Namier or a Hofstadter and the sociology of a Merton or a Lipset—are after all as far away from the historical standpoint of Hegel and Colling- wood as most academic philosophy is from their philosophical perspective.

It may seem to many readers that as I have elaborated my initial hypothesis I have step by step deprived myself of very nearly all possible argumentative allies. But is not just this required by the hypothesis itself? For if the hypothesis is true, it will necessarily appear implausible, since one way of stating part of the hypothesis is precisely to assert that we are in a condition which almost nobody recognizes and which perhaps nobody at all can recognize fully. If my hypothesis appeared initially plausible, it would certainly be false. And at least if even to entertain this hypothesis puts me into an antagonistic stance, it is a very different antagonistic stance from that of, for example, modern radicalism. For the modern radical is as confident in the moral expression of his stances and consequently in the assertive uses of the rhetoric of morality as any conservative has ever been. Whatever else he denounces in our culture he is certain that it still possesses the moral resources which he requires in order to denounce it. Everything else may be, in his eyes, in disorder; but the language of moral- ity is in order, just as it is. That he too may be being betrayed by the very language he uses is not a thought available to him. It is the aim of this book to make that thought available to radicals, liberals and conservatives alike.

I cannot however expect to make it palatable; for if it is true, we are all already in a state so disastrous that there are no large remedies for it.

Do not however suppose that the conclusion to be drawn will turn out to be one of despair. *Angst* is an intermittently fashionable emotion and the misreading of some existentialist texts has turned despair itself into a kind of psychological nostrum. But if we are indeed in as bad a state as I take us to be, pessimism too will turn out to be one more cultural luxury that we shall have to dispense with in order to survive in these hard times.

I cannot of course deny, indeed my thesis entails, that the language and the appearances of morality persist even though the integral substance of morality has to a large degree been fragmented and then in part destroyed. Because of this there is no inconsistency in my speaking, as I shall shortly do, of contemporary moral attitudes and arguments. I merely pay to the present the courtesy of using its own vocabulary to speak of it.

2

The Nature
of Moral Disagreement Today
and the Claims of Emotivism

The most striking feature of contemporary moral utterance is that so much of it is used to express disagreements; and the most striking feature of the debates in which these disagreements are expressed is their interminable character. I do not mean by this just that such debates go on and on and on — although they do — but also that they apparently can find no terminus. There seems to be no rational way of securing moral agreement in our culture. Consider three examples of just such contemporary moral debate framed in terms of characteristic and well-known rival moral arguments:

1 (a) A just war is one in which the good to be achieved outweighs the evils involved in waging the war and in which a clear distinction can be made between combatants — whose lives are at stake — and innocent non-combatants. But in a modern war calculation of future escalation is never reliable and no practically applicable distinction between combatants and noncombatants can be made. Therefore no modern war can be a just war and we all now ought to be pacifists.

(b) If you wish for peace, prepare for war. The only way to achieve peace is to deter potential aggressors. Therefore you must build up your armaments and make it clear that going to war on any particular scale is not necessarily ruled out by your policies. An inescapable part of making *this* clear is being prepared both to fight limited wars and to go not only to, but beyond, the nuclear brink on certain types of occasion. Otherwise you will not avoid war *and* you will be defeated.

(c) Wars between the Great Powers are purely destructive; but wars waged to liberate oppressed groups, especially in the Third World, are a necessary and therefore justified means for destroying the exploitative domination which stands between mankind and happiness.

2 (a) Everybody has certain rights over his or her own person, including his or her own body. It follows from the nature of these rights that at the stage when the embryo is essentially part of the mother's body, the

mother has a right to make her own uncoerced decision on whether she will have an abortion or not. Therefore abortion is morally permissible and ought to be allowed by law.

(b) I cannot will that my mother should have had an abortion when she was pregnant with me, except perhaps if it had been certain that the embryo was dead or gravely damaged. But if I cannot will this in my own case, how can I consistently deny to others the right to life that I claim for myself? I would break the so-called Golden Rule unless I denied that a mother has in general a right to an abortion. I am not of course thereby committed to the view that abortion ought to be legally prohibited.

(c) Murder is wrong. Murder is the taking of innocent life. An embryo is an identifiable individual, differing from a newborn infant only in being at an earlier stage on the long road to adult capacities and, if any life is innocent, that of an embryo is. If infanticide is murder, as it is, abortion is murder. So abortion is not only morally wrong, but ought to be legally prohibited.

3 (a) Justice demands that every citizen should enjoy, so far as is possible, an equal opportunity to develop his or her talents and his or her other potentialities. But prerequisites for the provision of such equal opportunity include the provision of equal access to health care and to education. Therefore justice requires the governmental provision of health and educational services, financed out of taxation, and it also requires that no citizen should be able to buy an unfair share of such services. This in turn requires the abolition of private schools and private medical practice.

(b) Everybody has a right to incur such and only such obligations as he or she wishes, to be free to make such and only such contracts as he or she desires and to determine his or her own free choices. Physicians must therefore be free to practice on such terms as they desire and patients must be free to choose among physicians; teachers must be free to teach on such terms as they choose and pupils and parents to go where they wish for education. Freedom thus requires not only the existence of private practice in medicine and private schools in education, but also the abolition of those restraints on private practice which are imposed by licensing and regulation by such bodies as universities, medical schools, the A.M.A. and the state.

These arguments have only to be stated to be recognized as being widely influential in our society. They have of course their articulate expert spokesmen: Herman Kahn and the Pope, Che Guevara and Milton Friedman are among the authors who have produced variant versions of them. But it is their appearance in newspaper editorials and high-school debates, on radio talk shows and letters to congressmen, in bars, barracks and boardrooms, it is their typicality that makes them important examples here. What salient characteristics do these debates and disagreements share?

They are of three kinds. The first is what I shall call, adapting an expression from the philosophy of science, the conceptual incommensurability of the rival arguments in each of the three debates. Every one of the arguments is logically valid or can be easily expanded so as to be made so; the conclusions do indeed follow from the premises. But the rival premises are such that we possess no rational way of weighing the claims of one as against another. For each premise employs some quite different normative or evaluative concept from the others, so that the claims made upon us are of quite different kinds. In the first argument, for example, premises which invoke justice and innocence are at odds with premises which invoke success and survival; in the second, premises which invoke rights are at odds with those which invoke universalizability; in the third it is the claim of equality that is matched against that of liberty. It is precisely because there is in our society no established way of deciding between these claims that moral argument appears to be necessarily interminable. From our rival conclusions we can argue back to our rival premises; but when we do arrive at our premises argument ceases and the invocation of one premise against another becomes a matter of pure assertion and counter-assertion. Hence perhaps the slightly shrill tone of so much moral debate.

But that shrillness may have an additional source. For it is not only in arguments with others that we are reduced so quickly to assertion and counter-assertion; it is also in the arguments that we have within ourselves. For whenever an agent enters the forum of public debate he has already presumably, explicitly or implicitly, settled the matter in question in his own mind. Yet if we possess no unassailable criteria, no set of compelling reasons by means of which we may convince our opponents, it follows that in the process of making up our own minds we can have made no appeal to such criteria or such reasons. If I lack any good reasons to invoke against you, it must seem that I lack any good reasons. Hence it seems that underlying my own position there must be some non-rational decision to adopt that position. Corresponding to the interminability of public argument there is at least the appearance of a disquieting private arbitrariness. It is small wonder if we become defensive and therefore shrill.

A second, equally important, but contrasting, characteristic of these arguments is that they do none the less purport to be *impersonal* rational arguments and as such are usually presented in a mode appropriate to that impersonality. What is that mode? Consider two different ways in which I may provide backing for an injunction to someone else to perform some specific action. In the first type of case I say, 'Do so-and-so'. The person addressed replies, 'Why should I do so-and-so?' I reply, 'Because I wish it.' Here I have given the person addressed no reason to do what I command or request unless he or she independently possesses some particular reason for paying regard to my wishes. If I am your superior officer—in the police, say, or the army—or otherwise have power or authority over you, or if you love me or fear me or want something from me, then by saying 'Because I wish it' I have indeed given *you* a reason, although not perhaps a sufficient reason, for doing what it is that I enjoin. Notice that in this type of case whether my utterance gives you a reason or not depends on certain characteristics possessed at the time of hearing or otherwise learning of the utterance by you. What reason-giving force the injunction has depends in this way on the personal context of the utterance.

Contrast with this the type of case in which the answer to the question 'Why should I do so-and-so?' (after someone has said 'Do so-and-so') is not 'Because I wish it', but some such utterance as 'Because it would give pleasure to a number of people' or 'Because it is your duty'. In this type of case the reason given for action either is or is not a good reason for performing the action in question independently of who utters it or even of whether it is uttered at all. Moreover the appeal is to a type of consideration which is independent of the relationship between speaker and hearer. Its use presupposes the existence of *impersonal* criteria—the existence, independently of the preferences or attitudes of speaker and hearer, of standards of justice or generosity or duty. The particular link between the context of utterance and the force of the reason-giving which always holds in the case of expressions of personal preferences or desire is severed in the case of moral and other evaluative utterances.

This second characteristic of contemporary moral utterance and argument, when combined with the first, imparts a paradoxical air to contemporary moral disagreement. For if we attended solely to the first characteristic, to the way in which what at first appears to be argument relapses so quickly into unargued disagreement, we might conclude that there is nothing to such contemporary disagreements but a clash of antagonistic wills, each will determined by some set of arbitrary choices of its own. But this second characteristic, the use of expressions whose distinctive function in our language is to embody what purports to be an appeal to objective standards, suggests otherwise. For even if the surface appearance of argument is only a masquerade, the question remains 'Why *this* masquerade?' What is it about rational argument which is so important that it is the nearly universal appearance assumed by those who engage in moral conflict? Does not this suggest that the practice of moral argument

Accounts [handwritten margin note]

in our culture expresses at least an aspiration to be or to become rational in this area of our lives?

A third salient characteristic of contemporary moral debate is intimately related to the first two. It is easy to see that the different conceptually incommensurable premises of the rival arguments deployed in these debates have a wide variety of historical origins. The concept of justice in the first argument has its roots in Aristotle's account of the virtues; the second argument's genealogy runs through Bismarck and Clausewitz to Machiavelli; the concept of liberation in the third argument has shallow roots in Marx, deeper roots in Fichte. In the second debate a concept of rights which has Lockean antecedents is matched against a view of universalizability which is recognizably Kantian and an appeal to the moral law which is Thomist. In the third debate an argument which owes debts to T.H. Green and to Rousseau competes with one which has Adam Smith as a grandfather. This catalogue of great names is suggestive; but it may be misleading in two ways. The citing of individual names may lead us to underestimate the complexity of the history and the ancestry of such arguments; and it may lead us to look for that history and that ancestry only in the writings of philosophers and theorists instead of in those intricate bodies of theory and practice which constitute human cultures, the beliefs of which are articulated by philosophers and theorists only in a partial and selective manner. But the catalogue of names does suggest how wide and heterogeneous the variety of moral sources is from which we have inherited. The surface rhetoric of our culture is apt to speak complacently of moral pluralism in this connection, but the notion of pluralism is too imprecise. For it may equally well apply to an ordered dialogue of intersecting viewpoints and to an unharmonious melange of ill-assorted fragments. The suspicion—and for the moment it can only be a suspicion—that it is the latter with which we have to deal is heightened when we recognize that all those various concepts which inform our moral discourse were originally at home in larger totalities of theory and practice in which they enjoyed a role and function supplied by contexts of which they have now been deprived. Moreover the concepts we employ have in at least some cases changed their character in the past three hundred years; the evaluative expressions we use have changed their meaning. In the transition from the variety of contexts in which they were originally at home to our own contemporary culture 'virtue' and 'justice' and 'piety' and 'duty' and even 'ought' have become other than they once were. How ought we to write the history of such changes?

It is in trying to answer this question that the connection between these features of contemporary moral debate and my initial hypothesis becomes clear. For if I am right in supposing that the language of morality passed from a state of order to a state of disorder, this passage will surely be reflected in—in part indeed will actually consist in—just such changes of meaning. Moreover, if the characteristics of our own moral arguments which I have identified—most notably the fact that we simultaneously and inconsistently treat moral argument as an exercise of our rational powers and as mere expressive assertion—are symptoms of moral disorder, we ought to be able to construct a true historical narrative in which at an earlier stage moral argument is very different in kind. Can we?

One obstacle to our so doing has been the persistently unhistorical treatment of moral philosophy by contemporary philosophers in both the writing about and the teaching of the subject. We all too often still treat the moral philosophers of the past as contributors to a single debate with a relatively unvarying subject-matter, treating Plato and Hume and Mill as contemporaries both of ourselves and of each other. This leads to an abstraction of these writers from the cultural and social milieus in which they lived and thought and so the history of their thought acquires a false independence from the rest of the culture. Kant ceases to be part of the history of Prussia, Hume is no longer a Scotsman. For from the standpoint of moral philosophy as *we* conceive it these characteristics have become irrelevances. Empirical history is one thing, philosophy quite another. But are we right in understanding the division between academic disciplines in the way that we conventionally do? Once again there seems to be a possible relationship between the history of moral discourse and the history of the academic curriculum.

Yet at this point it may rightly be retorted: You keep speaking of possibilities, of-suspicions, of hypotheses. You allow that what you are suggesting will initially seem implausible. You are in this at least right. For all this resort to conjectures about history is unnecessary. The way in which you have stated the problem is misleading. Contemporary moral argument is rationally interminable, because *all* moral, indeed all evaluative, argument is and always must be rationally interminable. Contemporary moral disagreements of a certain kind cannot be resolved, because *no* moral disagreements of that kind in any age, past, present or future, can be resolved. What you present as a contingent feature of our culture, standing in need of some special, perhaps historical explanation, is a necessary feature of all cultures which possess evaluative discourse. This is a challenge which cannot be avoided at an early stage in this argument. Can it be defeated?

One philosophical theory which this challenge specifically invites us to confront is emotivism. Emotivism is the doctrine that all evaluative judgments and more specifically all moral judgments are *nothing but* expressions of preference, expressions of attitude or feeling, insofar as they are moral or evaluative in character. Particular judgments may of course unite moral and factual elements. 'Arson, being destructive of property, is wrong' unites the factual judgment that arson destroys property with the moral judgment that arson is wrong. But the moral element in such a judgment is always to be sharply distinguised from the factual. Factual judgments are true or false; and in the realm of fact there are rational criteria by means of which we may secure agreement as to what is true and what is false. But moral judgments, being expressions of attitude or feeling, are neither true nor false; and agreement in moral judgment is not to be secured by any rational method, for there are none. It is to be secured, if at all, by producing certain non-rational effects on the emotions or attitudes of those who disagree with one. We use moral judgments not only to express our own feelings and attitudes, but also precisely to produce such effects in others.

Emotivism is thus a theory which professes to give an account of *all* value judgments whatsoever. Clearly if it *is* true, *all* moral disagreement *is* rationally interminable; and clearly if that is true then certain of the features of contemporary moral debate to which I drew attention earlier do indeed have nothing to do with what is specifically contemporary. But is it true?

Emotivism has been presented by its most sophisticated protagonists hitherto as a theory about the meaning of the sentences which are used to make moral judgments. C.L. Stevenson, the single most important exponent of the theory, asserted that the sentence 'This is good' means roughly the same as 'I approve of this; do so as well', trying to capture by this equivalence both the function of the moral judgment as expressive of the speaker's attitudes and the function of the moral judgment as designed to influence the hearer's attitudes (Stevenson 1945, ch.2). Other emotivists suggested that to say 'This is good' was to utter a sentence meaning roughly 'Hurrah for this!' But as a theory of the meaning of a certain type of sentence emotivism plainly fails for at least three very different reasons.

The first is that, if the theory is to elucidate the meaning of a certain class of sentences by referring to their function, when uttered, of expressing feelings or attitudes, an essential part of the theory will have to consist in an identification and characterization of the feelings or attitudes in question. On this subject proponents of the emotive theory are in general silent, and perhaps wisely. For all attempts so far to identify the relevant types of feelings or attitudes have found it impossible to avoid an empty circularity. 'Moral judgments express feelings or attitudes,' it is said. 'What kind of feelings or attitudes?' we ask. 'Feelings or attitudes of approval,' is the reply. 'What kind of approval?' we ask, perhaps remarking that approval is of many kinds. It is in answer to this question that every version of emotivism either remains silent or, by identifying the relevant kind of approval as moral approval—that is, the type of approval expressed by a specifically moral judgment—becomes vacuously circular.

It becomes easy to understand why the theory is vulnerable to this first type of criticism, if we consider two other reasons for rejecting it. One is that emotivism, as a theory of the meaning of a certain type of sentence, is engaged in an impossible task from the beginning, because it is dedicated to characterizing as equivalent in meaning two kinds of expression which, as we have already seen derive their distinctive function in our language in key part from the contrast and difference between them. I have already suggested that there are good reasons for distinguishing between what I called expressions of personal preference and evaluative (including moral) expressions, citing the way in which utterances of the first kind depend upon who utters them to whom for any reason-giving force that they may have, while utterances of the second kind are not similarly dependent for their reason-giving force on the context of utterance. This seems sufficient to show that there is some large difference in meaning between members of the two classes; yet the emotive theory wishes to make them equivalent in meaning. This is not just a mistake; it is a mistake that demands explanation. A sign of where explanation should be sought is found in a third defect of the emotive theory, considered as a theory of meaning.

The emotive theory, as we have seen, purports to be a theory about the meaning of sentences; but the expression of feeling or attitude is characteristically a function not of the meaning of sentences, but of their use on particular occassions. The angry schoolmaster, to use one of Gilbert Ryle's examples, may vent his feelings by shouting at the small boy who has just made an arithmetical mistake, 'Seven times seven equals forty-nine!' But the use of this sentence to express feelings or attitudes has nothing whatsoever to do with its meaning. This suggests that we should not simply rely on these objections to reject the emotive theory, but that we should rather consider whether it ought not to have been proposed as a theory about the use — understood as purpose or function — of members of a certain class of expressions rather than about their meaning—understood as including all that Frege intended by 'sense' and 'reference'.

Clearly the argument so far shows that when someone utters a moral judgment, such as 'This is right' or 'This is good', it does not mean the same as 'I approve of this; do so as well' or 'Hurrah for this!' or any of the other attempts at equivalence suggested by emotive theorists; but even if the

meaning of such sentences were quite other than emotive theorists supposed, it might be plausibly claimed, if the evidence was adequate, that in
using such sentences to *say* whatever they mean, the agent was in fact *doing*
nothing other than expressing his feelings or attitudes and attempting to
influence the feelings and attitudes of others. If the emotive theory thus
interpreted were correct it would follow that the meaning and the use of
moral expressions were, or at the very least had become, radically discrepant with each other. Meaning and use would be at odds in such a way that
meaning would tend to conceal use. We could not safely infer what someone who uttered a moral judgment was doing merely by listening to what
he said. Moreover the agent himself might well be among those for whom
use was concealed by meaning. He might well, precisely because he was
self-conscious about the meaning of the words that he used, be assured that
he was appealing to independent impersonal criteria, when all that he was
in fact doing was expressing his feelings to others in a manipulative way.
How might such a phenomenon come to occur?

   Let us in the light of such considerations disregard emotivism's claim to
universality of scope; and let us instead consider emotivism as a theory
which has been advanced in historically specific conditions. In the eighteenth century Hume embodied emotivist elements in the large and complex fabric of his total moral theory; but it is only in this century that
emotivism has flourished as a theory on its own. And it did so as a
response to a set of theories which flourished, especially in England, between 1903 and 1939. We ought therefore to ask whether emotivism as
a theory may not have been both a response to, and in the very first instance, an account of *not*, as its protagonists indeed supposed, moral
language as such, but moral language in England in the years after 1903
as and when that language was interpreted in accordance with that body
of theory to the refutation of which emotivism was primarily dedicated.
The theory in question borrowed from the early nineteenth century the
name of 'intuitionism' and its immediate progenitor was G.E. Moore.

   'I went up to Cambridge at Michaelmas 1902, and Moore's *Principia
Ethica* came out at the end of my first year . . . it was exciting, exhilarating,
the beginning of a renaissance, the opening of a new heaven on a new
earth.' So wrote John Maynard Keynes (quoted in Rosenbaum 1975, p.
52), and so in their own rhetorical modes Lytton Strachey and Desmond
McCarthy and later Virginia Woolf, who struggled through *Principia
Ethica* page by page in 1908, and a whole network of Cambridge and London friends and acquaintances. What opened the new heaven was Moore's
quiet but apocalyptic proclamation in 1903 that after many centuries he
had at last solved the problems of ethics by being the first philosopher to

attend with sufficient care to the precise nature of the questions which it is the task of ethics to answer. What Moore believed that he had discovered by attending to the precise nature of these questions was threefold.

First that 'good' is the name of a simple indefinable property, a property different from that named by 'pleasant' or 'conducive to evolutionary survival' or any other natural property. Hence Moore speaks of good as a non-natural property. Propositions declaring this or that to be good are what Moore called 'intuitions'; they are incapable of proof or disproof and indeed no evidence or reasoning whatever can be adduced in their favor or disfavor. Although Moore disclaims any use of the word 'intuition' which might suggest the name of a faculty of intuition comparable to our power of vision, he none the less does compare good as a property with yellow as a property in such a way as to make verdicts that a given state of affairs is or is not good comparable to the simplest judgments of normal visual perception.

Secondly, Moore takes it that to call an action right is simply to say that of the available alternative actions it is the one which does or did as a matter of fact produce the most good. Moore is thus a utilitarian; every action is to be evaluated solely by its consequences, as compared with the consequences of alternative possible courses of action. And as with at least some other versions of utilitarianism it follows that no action is ever right or wrong as such. Anything whatsoever may under certain circumstances be permitted.

Thirdly, it turns out to be the case, in the sixth and final chapter of *Principia Ethica*, that 'personal affections and aesthetic enjoyments include *all* the greatest, and *by far* the greatest' goods we can imagine . . . .' This is 'the ultimate and fundamental truth of Moral Philosophy'. The achievement of friendship and the contemplation of what is beautiful in nature or in art become certainly almost the sole and perhaps the sole justifiable ends of all human action.

We ought to notice immediately two crucial facts about Moore's moral theory. The first is that his three central positions are logically independent of each other. There would be no breach in consistency if one were to affirm any one of the three and deny the other two. One can be an intuitionist without being a utilitarian; most English intuitionists came to hold the view that there was a non-natural property of 'right' as well as of 'good' and held that to perceive that a certain type of action was 'right' was to see that one had at least a *prima facie* obligation to perform that type of action, independently of its consequences. Likewise a utilitarian has no necessary commitment to intuitionism. And neither utilitarians nor intuitionists have any necessary commitment to the values of Moore's sixth chapter. The second crucial fact is easy to see retrospectively: the first part of what Moore says is *plainly* false and the second and third parts are at the very least highly contentious. Moore's arguments at times are, it must seem now, *obviously* defective—he tries to show that 'good' is indefinable, for example, by relying on a bad dictionary definition of 'definition'—and a great deal is asserted rather than argued. And yet it is this to us plainly false, badly argued position which Keynes treated as 'the beginning of a renaissance', which Lytton Strachey declared to have 'shattered all writers on ethics from Aristotle and Christ to Herbert Spencer and Mr. Bradley' and which Leonard Woolf described as 'substituting for the religious and philosophical nightmares, delusions, hallucinations in which Jehovah, Christ and St. Paul, Plato, Kant and Hegel had entangled us, the fresh air and pure light of commonsense' (quoted in Gadd 1974).

This is great silliness of course; but it is the great silliness of highly intelligent and perceptive people. It is therefore worth asking if we can discern any clues as to why they accepted Moore's naive and complacent apocalypticism. One suggests itself. It is that the group who were to become Bloomsbury had already accepted the values of Moore's sixth chapter, but could not accept these as merely their own personal preferences. They felt the need to find objective and impersonal justification for rejecting all claims except those of personal intercourse and of the beautiful. What specifically were they rejecting? Not in fact the doctrines of Plato or St. Paul or any other of the great names in Woolf's or Strachey's catalogue of deliverance, but those names as symbols of the culture of the late nineteenth century. Sidgwick and Leslie Stephen are being dismissed along with Spencer and Bradley, and the whole of the past is envisaged as a burden that Moore has just helped them cast off. What was it about the moral culture of the late nineteenth century which made it a burden to be escaped from? That is a question to which an answer ought to be deferred, precisely because it is going to be forced on us more than once in the course of the argument and later on we shall be better equipped to answer it. But we ought to notice how dominant the theme of that rejection is in the lives and writings of the Woolfs, of Lytton Strachey, of Roger Fry. Keynes emphasized the rejection not only of the Benthamite version of utilitarianism and of Christianity, but of all claims on behalf of social action conceived as a worthwhile end. What was left?

The answer is: a highly impoverished view of how 'good' may be used. Keynes gives examples of central topics of discussion among Moore's followers: 'If A was in love with B and believed that B reciprocated his feelings, whereas in fact B did not, but was in love with C, the state of affairs was certainly not as good as it would have been if A had been right, but was it worse or better than it would become if A discovered his mistake?' Or again: 'If A was in love with B under a misapprehension as to B's qualities, was this better or worse than A's not being in love at all?' How were such questions to be answered? By following Moore's prescriptions in precise fashion. Do you or do you not discern the presence or absence of the non-natural property of good in greater or lesser degree? And what if two observers disagree? Then, so the answer went, according to Keynes, either the two were focusing on different subject matters, without recognizing this, or one had perceptions superior to the other. But, of course, as Keynes tells us, what was really happening was something quite other: 'In practice, victory was with those who could speak with the greatest appearance of clear, undoubting conviction and could best use the accents of infallibility' and Keynes goes on to describe the effectiveness of Moore's gasps of incredulity and head-shaking, of Strachey's grim silences and of Lowes Dickinson's shrugs.

There is evident here precisely that gap between the meaning and purport of what was being said and the use to which utterance was being put to which our reinterpretation of emotivism drew attention. An acute observer at the time and Keynes himself retrospectively might well have put matters thus: these people take themselves to be identifying the presence of a non-natural property, which they call 'good'; but there is in fact no such property and they are doing no more and no other than expressing their feelings and attitudes, disguising the expression of preference and whim by an interpretation of their own utterance and behavior which confers upon it an objectivity that it does not in fact possess.

It is, I take it, no accident that the acutest of the modern founders of emotivism, philosophers such as F.P. Ramsey (in the 'Epilogue' to *The Foundation of Mathematics*, 1931), Austin Duncan-Jones and C.L. Stevenson, were pupils of Moore; it is not implausible to suppose that they did in fact confuse moral utterance at Cambridge (and in other places with a similar inheritance) after 1903 with moral utterance as such, and that they therefore presented what was in essentials a correct account of the former as though it were an account of the latter. Moore's followers had behaved as if their disagreements over what is good were being settled by an appeal to an objective and impersonal criterion; but in fact the stronger and psychologically more adroit will was prevailing. It is unsurprising that emotivists sharply distinguished between factual, including perceptual, disagreement and what Stevenson called 'disagreement in attitude'. But if the claims of emotivism, understood as claims about the use of moral utterance at Cambridge after 1903 and its heirs and successors in London and elsewhere rather than about the meaning of moral expressions at all times and places, seem remarkably cogent, it turns out to be for reasons which at first sight seem to undermine emotivism's universal claims and with them emotivism's apparent threat to my original thesis.

What makes emotivism convincing as a thesis about a certain kind of moral utterance at Cambridge after 1903 are certain features specific to that historical episode. Those whose evaluative utterances embodied Moore's interpretations of those utterances could not have been doing what they took themselves to be doing because of the falsity of Moore's thesis. But nothing whatsoever seems to follow about moral utterance in general. Emotivism on this account turns out to be an empirical thesis, or rather a preliminary sketch of an empirical thesis, presumably to be filled out later by psychological and sociological and historical observations, about those who continue to use moral and other evaluative expressions, as if they were governed by objective and impersonal criteria, when all grasp of any such criterion has been lost. We should therefore expect emotivist types of theory to arise in a specific local circumstance as a response to types of theory and practice which share certain key features of Moore's intuitionism. Emotivism thus understood turns out to be, as a cogent theory of use rather than a false theory of meaning, connected with one specific stage in moral development or decline, a stage which our own culture entered early in the present century.

I spoke earlier of emotivism as an account not only of moral utterance at Cambridge after 1903, but also of moral utterance 'in other places with a similar inheritance'. For it at once might be objected to my thesis that emotivism has been after all propounded in a variety of times, places and circumstances, and hence that my stress upon Moore's part in generating emotivism is mistaken. To this I should reply first that I am interested in emotivism only insofar as it has been a plausible and defensible thesis. Carnap's version of emotivism, for example—in which the characterization of moral utterances as expressions of feeling or attitude is a desperate attempt to find *some* status for them after his theory of meaning and his theory of science have expelled them from the realm of the factual and the descriptive—was based on the most meagre attention to their specific character. And secondly I should retort that there is an Oxford history beginning from Prichard's intuitionism to parallel Moore's Cambridge history and indeed that wherever something like emotivism is found to flourish it generally is the successor theory to views analogous to Moore's or Prichard's.

The scheme of moral decline which these remarks presuppose would, as I suggested earlier, be one which required the discrimination of three distinct stages; a first at which evaluative and more especially moral theory and practice embody genuine objective and impersonal standards which provide rational justification for particular policies, actions and judgments and which themselves in turn are susceptible of rational justification; a second stage at which there are unsuccessful attempts to maintain the objectivity and impersonality of moral judgments, but during which the project of providing rational justifications both by means of and for the standards continuously breaks down; and a third stage at which theories of an emotivist kind secure wide implicit acceptance because of a general implicit recognition in practice, though not in explicit theory, that claims to objectivity and impersonality cannot be made good.

Yet the very statement of this scheme is enough to suggest that the *general* claims of emotivism reinterpreted as a theory of use cannot be so easily put on one side. For a presupposition of the scheme of development which I have just sketched is that genuine objective and impersonal moral standards can in some way or other be rationally justified, even if in some cultures at some stages the possibility of such rational justification is no longer available. And this is what emotivism denies. What I have suggested to be the case by and large about our own culture—that in moral argument the apparent assertion of principles functions as a mask for expressions of personal preference—is what emotivism takes to be universally the case. Moreover it does so on grounds which require no general historical and sociological investigation of human cultures. For what emotivism asserts is in central part that there are and can be *no* valid rational justification for any claims that objective and impersonal moral standards exist and hence that there are no such standards. Its claim is of the same order as the claim that it is true of all cultures whatsoever that they lack witches. Purported witches there may be, but real witches there cannot have been, for there are none. So emotivism holds that purported rational justifications there may be, but real rational justifications there cannot have been, for there are none.

Emotivism thus rests upon a claim that every attempt, whether past or present, to provide a rational justification for an objective morality has in fact failed. It is a verdict upon the whole history of moral philosophy and as such obliterates the contrast between the present and the past embodied in my initial hypothesis. What emotivism however did fail to reckon with is the difference that it would make to morality if emotivism were not only true but also widely believed to be true. Stevenson, for example, understood very clearly that saying 'I disapprove of this; do so as well!' does not have the same force as saying 'That is bad!' He noted that a kind of prestige attaches to the latter, which does not attach to the former. What he did not note however—precisely because he viewed emotivism as a theory of meaning—is that the prestige derives from the fact that the use of 'That is bad!' implies an appeal to an objective and impersonal standard in a way

in which 'I disapprove of this; do so as well!' does not. That is, if and insofar as emotivism is true, moral language is seriously misleading and, if
and insofar as emotivism is justifiably believed, presumably the use of traditional and inherited moral language ought to be abandoned. This conclusion none of the emotivists drew; and it is clear that, like Stevenson, they
failed to draw it because they miscontrued their own theory as a theory
of meaning.

   This is also of course why emotivism did not prevail within analytical
moral philosophy. Analytical philosophers had defined the central task of
philosophy as that of deciphering the meaning of key expressions in both
everyday and scientific language; and since emotivism fails precisely as a
theory of the *meaning* of moral expressions, analytical philosophers by and
large rejected emotivism. Yet emotivism did not die and it is important to
note how often in widely different modern philosophical contexts something very like emotivism's attempted reduction of morality to personal
preference continually recurs in the writings of those who do not think of
themselves as emotivists. The unrecognized philosophical power of emotivism is one clue to its cultural power. Within analytical moral philosophy
the resistance to emotivism has arisen from the perception that moral
reasoning does occur, that there can be logical linkages between various
moral judgments of a kind that emotivism itself could not allow for ('therefore' and 'if . . . then . . .' are obviously not used as expressions of feeling).
Yet the most influential account of moral reasoning that emerged in response to this critique of emotivism was one according to which an agent
can only justify a particular judgment by referring to some universal rule
from which it may be logically derived, and can only justify that rule in
turn by deriving it from some more general rule or principle; but on this
view since every chain of reasoning must be finite, such a process of justi-
ficatory reasoning must always terminate with the assertion of some rule
or principle for which no further reason can be given. 'Thus a complete
justification of a decision would consist of a complete account of its effects
together with a complete account of the principles which it observed, and
the effect of observing those principles. . . . If the enquirer still goes on asking "But why should I live like that?" then there is no further answer to
give him, because we have already, *ex hypothesi*, said everything that could
be included in the further answer' (Hare 1952, p. 69).

   The terminus of justification is thus always, on this view, a not further
to be justified choice, a choice unguided by criteria. Each individual implicitly or explicitly has to adopt his or her own first principles on the basis
of such a choice. The utterance of any universal principle is in the end an
expression of the preferences of an individual will and for that will its prin-

ciples have and can have only such authority as it chooses to confer upon them by adopting them. Thus emotivism has not been left very far behind after all.

To this it might well be replied that I am only able to reach this conclusion by omitting to notice the wide variety of positive positions incompatible with emotivism taken within analytical moral philosophy. Such writing has characteristically been preoccupied with attempts to show that the notion of rationality itself supplies morality with a basis and a basis such that we have adequate grounds for rejecting emotivist and subjectivist accounts. Consider, it will be said, the variety of claims advanced not only by Hare, but also by Rawls, Donegan, Gert and Gewirth, to name only a few. About the arguments which are adduced in support of such claims I want to make two points. The first is that none of them in fact succeed. I shall later on—in Chapter 6—use Gewirth's argument as an exemplary case; he is to date the latest of such writers, he is self-consciously and scrupulously aware of the contributions of other analytical moral philosophers to the debate and his arguments therefore provide us with an ideal test case. If they do not succeed, that is strong evidence that the project of which they are a part is not going to succeed. And, as I shall show later, they do not succeed.

Secondly, it is very much to the point that such writers cannot agree among themselves either on what the character of moral rationality is or on the substance of the morality which is to be founded on that rationality. The diversity of contemporary moral debate and its interminability are indeed mirrored in the controversies of analytical moral philosophers. But if those who claim to be able to formulate principles on which rational moral agents ought to agree cannot secure agreement on the formulation of those principles from their colleagues who share their basic philosophical purpose and method, there is once again *prima facie* evidence that their project has failed, even before we have examined their particular contentions and conclusions. Each of them in his criticism offers testimony to the failure of his colleagues' constructions.

I therefore take it that we have no good reason to believe that analytical philosophy can provide any convincing escape from an emotivism the substance of which it so often in fact concedes, once that emotivism is understood as a theory of use rather than meaning. But it is not only analytical moral philosophy of which this is true. It also holds of certain at first sight very different moral philosophies in Germany and France. Nietzsche and Sartre deploy philosophical vocabularies which are in large part alien to the English-speaking philosophical world; and in style and rhetoric as well as in vocabulary each differs from the other as much as from analytical philosophy. Nonetheless when Nietzsche sought to indict the making of would-be objective moral judgments as the mask worn by the will-to-power of those too weak and slavish to assert themselves with archaic and aristocratic grandeur, and when Sartre tried to exhibit the bourgeois rationalist morality of the Third Republic as an exercise in bad faith by those who cannot tolerate the recognition of their own choices as the sole source of moral judgment, both conceded the substance of that for which emotivism contended. Both indeed saw themselves as by their analysis condemning conventional morality, while most English and American emotivists believed themselves to be doing no such thing. Both saw their own task as in part that of founding a new morality, but in the writings of both it is at this point that their rhetoric—very different as each is from the other—becomes cloudy and opaque, and metaphorical assertion replaces argument. The *Übermensch* and the Sartrian Existentialist-cum-Marxist belong in the pages of a philosophical bestiary rather than in serious discussion. Both by contrast are at their philosophically most powerful and cogent in the negative part of their critiques.

The appearance of emotivism in this variety of philosophical guises suggests strongly that it is indeed in terms of a confrontation with emotivism that my own thesis must be defined. For one way of framing my contention that morality is not what it once was is just to say that to a large degree people now think, talk and act *as if* emotivism were true, no matter what their avowed theoretical standpoint may be. Emotivism has become embodied in our culture. But of course in saying this I am not merely contending that morality is not what it once was, but also and more importantly that what once was morality has to some large degree disappeared—and that this marks a degeneration, a grave cultural loss. I am therefore committed to two distinct but related tasks.

The first is that of identifying and describing the lost morality of the past and of evaluating its claims to objectivity and authority; this is a task partly historical and partly philosophical. The second is that of making good my claim about the specific character of the modern age. For I have suggested that we live in a specifically emotivist culture, and if this is so we ought presumably to discover that a wide variety of our concepts and modes of behavior—and not only our explicitly moral debates and judgments—presuppose the truth of emotivism, if not at the level of self-conscious theorizing, at least in everyday practice. But is this so? To this latter issue I turn immediately.

3

Emotivism: Social Content
and Social Context

A moral philosophy—and emotivism is no exception—characteristically presupposes a sociology. For every moral philosophy offers explicitly or implicitly at least a partial conceptual analysis of the relationship of an agent to his or her reasons, motives, intentions and actions, and in so doing generally presupposes some claim that these concepts are embodied or at least can be in the real social world. Even Kant, who sometimes seems to restrict moral agency to the inner realm of the noumenal, implies otherwise in his writings on law, history and politics. Thus it would generally be a decisive refutation of a moral philosophy to show that moral agency on its own account of the matter could never be socially embodied; and it also follows that we have not yet fully understood the claims of any moral philosophy until we have spelled out what its social embodiment would be. Some moral philosophers in the past, perhaps most, have understood this spelling out as itself one part of the task of moral philosophy. So, it scarcely needs to be said, Plato and Aristotle, so indeed also Hume and Adam Smith; but at least since Moore the dominant narrow conception of moral philosophy has ensured that the moral philosophers could ignore this task; as notably do the philosophical proponents of emotivism. We therefore must perform it for them.

What is the key to the social content of emotivism? It is the fact that emotivism entails the obliteration of any genuine distinction between manipulative and non-manipulative social relations. Consider the contrast between, for example, Kantian ethics and emotivism on this point. For Kant—and a parallel point could be made about many earlier moral philosophers—the difference between a human relationship uninformed by morality and one so informed is precisely the difference between one in which each person treats the other primarily as a means to his or her ends and one in which each treats the other as an end. To treat someone else as an end is to offer them what I take to be good reasons for acting in one way rather than another, but to leave it to them to evaluate those reasons. It is to be unwilling to influence another except by reasons which that other he or she judges to be good. It is to appeal to impersonal criteria of the validity of which each rational agent must be his or her own judge. By contrast, to treat someone else as a means is to seek to make him or her an instrument of my purposes by adducing whatever influences or considerations will in fact be effective on this or that occasion. The generalizations of the sociology and psychology of persuasion are what I shall need to guide me, not the standards of a normative rationality.

If emotivism is true, this distinction is illusory. For evaluative utterance can in the end have no point or use but the expression of my own feelings or attitudes and the transformation of the feelings and attitudes of others. I cannot genuinely appeal to impersonal criteria, for there are no impersonal criteria. I may think that I so appeal and others may think that I so appeal, but these thoughts will always be mistakes. The sole reality of distinctively moral discourse is the attempt of one will to align the attitudes, feelings, preference and choices of another with its own. Others are always means, never ends.

What then would the social world *look* like, if seen with emotivist eyes? And what would the social world *be* like, if the truth of emotivism came to be widely presupposed? The general form of the answer to these questions is now clear, but the social detail depends in part on the nature of particular social contexts; it will make a difference in what milieu and in the service of what particular and specific interests the distinction between manipulative and non-manipulative social relationships has been obliterated. William Gass has suggested that it was a principal concern of Henry James to examine the consequences of the obliteration of this distinction in the lives of a particular kind of rich European in *The Portrait of a Lady* (Gass 1971, pp. 181-90), that the novel turns out to be an investigation, in Gass's words, 'of what it means to be a consumer of persons, and of what it means to be a person consumed'. The metaphor of consumption acquires its appropriateness from the milieu; James is concerned with rich aesthetes whose interest is to fend off the kind of boredom that is so characteristic of modern leisure by contriving behavior in others that will be responsive to their wishes, that will feed their sated appetites. Those wishes may or may not be benevolent, but the distinction between characters who entertain themselves by willing the good of others and those who pursue the fulfilment of their desires without a concern for any good but their own—the difference in the novel between Ralph Touchett and Gilbert Osmond—is not as important to James as the distinction between a whole milieu in which the manipulative mode of moral instrumentalism has triumphed and one, such as the New England of *The Europeans*, of which this was not true. James was of course, at least in *The Portrait of a Lady*, concerned with only one restricted and carefully identified social milieu, with a particular kind of rich person at one particular time and place. But that does not at all diminish the importance of his achievement for this enquiry. It will in fact turn out that *The Portrait of a Lady* has a key place within a long tradition of moral commentary, earlier members of which are Diderot's *Le Neveu de Rameau* and Kierkegaard's *Enten-Eller*. The unifying preoccupation of that tradition is the condition of those who see in the social world nothing but a meeting place for individual wills, each with its own set of attitudes and preferences and who understand that world solely as an arena for the achievement of their own satisfaction, who interpret reality as a series of opportunities for their enjoyment and for whom the last enemy is boredom. The younger Rameau, Kierkegaard's 'A' and Ralph Touchett put this aesthetic attitude to work in very different environments, but the attitude is recognizably the same and even the environments have something in common. They are environments in which the problem of enjoyment arises in the context of leisure, in which large sums of money have created some social distance from the necessity of work. Ralph Touchett is rich, 'A' is comfortably off, Rameau is a parasite upon his rich patrons and clients. This is not to say that the realm of what Kierkegaard called the aesthetic is restricted to the rich and to their close neighbors; the rest of us often share the attitudes of the rich in fantasy and aspiration. Nor is it to say that the rich are all Touchetts or Osmonds or 'A's. But it is to suggest that if we are to understand fully the social context of that obliteration of the distinction between manipulative and non-manipulative social relationships which emotivism entails, we ought to consider some other social contexts too.

One which is obviously important is that provided by the life of organizations, of those bureaucratic structures which, whether in the form of private corporations or of government agencies, define the working tasks of so many of our contemporaries. One sharp contrast with the lives of the aesthetic rich secures immediate attention. The rich aesthete with a plethora of means searches restlessly for ends on which he may employ them; but the organization is characteristically engaged in a competitive struggle for scarce resources to put to the service of its predetermined ends. It is therefore a central responsibility of managers to direct and redirect their organizations' available resources, both human and non-human, as effectively as possible toward those ends. Every bureaucratic organization embodies some explicit or implicit definition of costs and benefits from which the criteria of effectiveness are derived. Bureaucratic rationality is the rationality of matching means to ends economically and efficiently.

This familiar—perhaps by now we may be tempted to think overfamil-
iar—thought we owe originally of course to Max Weber. And it at once
becomes relevant that Weber's thought embodies just those dichotomies
which emotivism embodies, and obliterates just those distinctions to which
emotivism has to be blind. Questions of ends are questions of values, and
on values reason is silent; conflict between rival values cannot be rationally
settled. Instead one must simply choose—between parties, classes, nations,
causes, ideals. *Entscheidung* plays the part in Weber's thought that choice
of principles plays in that of Hare or Sarte. 'Values', says Raymond Aron
in his exposition of Weber's view, 'are created by human decisions . . .' and
again he ascribes to Weber the view that 'each man's conscience is ir-
refutable' and that values rest on 'a choice whose justification is purely subjective' (Aron 1967, pp. 206-10 and p. 192). It is not surprising that
Weber's understanding of values was indebted chiefly to Nietzsche and
that Donald G. Macrae in his book on Weber (1974) calls him an existentialist; for while he holds that an agent may be more or less rational in acting consistently with his values, the choice of any one particular evaluative
stance or commitment can be no more rational than that of any other. All
faiths and all evaluations are equally non-rational; all are subjective directions given to sentiment and feeling. Weber is then, in the broader sense
in which I have understood the term, an emotivist and his portrait of a
bureaucratic authority is an emotivist portrait. The consequence of
Weber's emotivism is that in his thought the contrast between power and
authority, although paid lip-service to, is effectively obliterated as a special
instance of the disappearance of the contrast between manipulative and
non-manipulative social relations. Weber of course took himself to be
distinguishing power from authority, precisely because authority serves
ends, serves faiths. But, as Philip Rieff has acutely noted, 'Weber's ends,
the *causes* there to be served, are means of acting; they cannot escape service
to power' (Rieff 1975, p. 22). For on Weber's view no type of authority
can appeal to rational criteria to vindicate itself except that type of bureaucratic authority which appeals precisely to its own *effectiveness*. And what
this appeal reveals is that bureaucratic authority is nothing other than successful power.

Weber's general account of bureaucratic organizations has been sub-
jected to much cogent critcism by sociologists who have analyzed the
specific character of actual bureaucracies. It is therefore relevant to note
that there is one area in which his analysis has been vindicated by experience and in which the accounts of many sociologists who take themselves
to have repudiated Weber's analysis in fact reproduce it. I am referring
precisely to his account of *how managerial authority is justified* in bureau-

cracies. For those modern sociologists who have put in the forefront of their accounts of managerial behavior aspects ignored or underemphasized by Weber's—as, for example, Likert has emphasized the manager's need to influence the motives of his subordinates and March and Simon his need to ensure that those subordinates argue from premises which will produce agreement with his own prior conclusions—have still seen the manager's function as that of controlling behavior and suppressing conflict in such a way as to reinforce rather than to undermine Weber's account of managerial justification. Thus there is a good deal of evidence that actual managers do embody in their behavior this one key part of the Weberian conception of bureaucratic authority, a conception which presupposes the truth of emotivism.

The original of the character of the rich man committed to the aesthetic pursuit of his own enjoyment as drawn by Henry James was to be found in London and Paris in the last century; the original of the character of the manager portrayed by Max Weber was at home in Wilhelmine Germany; but both have by now been domesticated in all the advanced countries and more especially in the United States. The two characters may even on occasion be found in one and the same person who partitions his life between them. Nor are they marginal figures in the social drama of the present age. I intend this dramatic metaphor with some seriousness. There is a type of dramatic tradition—Japanese Noh plays and English medieval morality plays are examples—which possesses a set of stock characters immediately recognizable to the audience. Such characters partially define the possibilities of plot and action. To understand them is to be provided with a means of interpreting the behavior of the actors who play them, just because a similar understanding informs the intentions of the actors themselves; and other actors may define their parts with special reference to these central characters. So it is also with certain kinds of social role specific to certain particular cultures. They furnish recognizable characters and the ability to recognize them is socially crucial because a knowledge of the character provides an interpretation of the actions of those individuals who have assumed the character. It does so precisely because those individuals have used the very same knowledge to guide and to structure their behavior. *Characters* specified thus must not be confused with social roles in general. For they are a very special type of social role which places a certain kind of moral constraint on the personality of those who inhabit them in a way in which many other social roles do not. I choose the word 'character' for them precisely because of the way it links dramatic and moral associations. Many modern occupational roles— that of a dentist or that of a garbage collector, for example—are not *char-*

acters in the way that that of a bureaucratic manager is; many modern
status roles—that of a retired member of the lower middle class, for example—are not *characters* in the way that that of the modern leisured rich
person is. In the case of a *character* role and personality fuse in a more
specific way than in general; in the case of a *character* the possibilities of
action are defined in a more limited way than in general. One of the key
differences between cultures is in the extent to which roles are *characters*;
but what is specific to each culture is in large and central part what is
specific to its stock of *characters*. So the culture of Victorian England was
partially defined by the *characters* of the Public School Headmaster, the
Explorer and the Engineer; and that of Wilhelmine Germany was similarly
defined by such *characters* as those of the Prussian Officer, the Professor
and the Social Democrat.

Characters have one other notable dimension. They are, so to speak, the
moral representatives of their culture and they are so because of the way
in which moral and metaphysical ideas and theories assume through them
an embodied existence in the social world. *Characters* are the masks worn
by moral philosophies. Such theories, such philosophies, do of course enter
into social life in numerous ways: most obviously perhaps as explicit ideas
in books or sermons or conversations, or as symbolic themes in paintings
or plays or dreams. But the distinctive way in which they inform the lives
of *characters* can be illuminated by considering how *characters* merge what
usually is thought to belong to the individual man or woman and what
is usually thought to belong to social roles. Both individuals and roles can,
and do, like *characters*, embody moral beliefs, doctrines and theories, but
each does so in its own way. And the way in which *characters* do so can
only be sketched by contrast with these.

It is by way of their intentions that individuals express bodies of moral
belief in their actions. For all intentions presuppose more or less complex,
more or less coherent, more or less explicit bodies of belief, sometimes of
moral belief. So such small-scale actions as the mailing of a letter or the
handing of a leaflet to a passer-by can embody intentions whose import
derives from some large-scale project of the individual, a project itself intelligible only against the background of some equally large or even larger
scheme of beliefs. In mailing a letter someone may be embarking on a type
of entrepreneurial career whose specification requires belief in both the
viability and the legitimacy of multinational corporations: in handing out
a leaflet someone may be expressing his belief in Lenin's philosophy of
history. But the chain of practical reasoning whose conclusions are expressed in such actions as the mailing of a letter or the distribution of a
leaflet is in this type of case of course the individual's own; and the locus

of that chain of reasoning, the context which makes the taking of each step part of an intelligible sequence, is that particular individual's history of action, belief, experience and interaction.

Contrast the quite different way in which a certain type of social role may embody beliefs so that the ideas, theories and doctrines expressed in and presupposed by the role may at least on some occasions be quite other than the ideas, theories and doctrines believed by the individual who inhabits the role. A Catholic priest in virtue of his role officiates at the mass, performs other rites and ceremonies and takes part in a variety of activities which embody or presuppose, implicitly or explicitly, the beliefs of Catholic Christianity. Yet a particular ordained individual who does all these things may have lost his faith and his own beliefs may be quite other than and at variance with those expressed in the actions presented by his role. The same type of distinction between role and individual can be drawn in many other cases. A trade union official in virtue of his role negotiates with employers' representatives and campaigns among his own membership in a way that generally and characteristically presupposes that trade union goals—higher wages, improvements in working conditions and the maintenance of employment *within* the present economic system—are legitimate goals for the working class and that trade unions are the appropriate instruments for achieving those goals. Yet a particular trade-union official may believe that trade unions are merely instruments for domesticating and corrupting the working class by diverting them from any interest in revolution. The beliefs that he has in his mind and heart are one thing; the beliefs that his role expresses and presupposes are quite another.

There are then many cases where there is a certain distance between role and individual and where consequently a variety of degrees of doubt, compromise, interpretation or cynicism may mediate the relationship of individual to role. With what I have called *characters* it is quite otherwise; and the difference arises from the fact that the requirements of a *character* are imposed from the outside, from the way in which others regard and use *characters* to understand and to evaluate themselves. With other types of social role the role may be adequately specified in terms of the institutions of whose structures it is a part and the relation to those institutions of the individuals who fill the roles. In the case of a *character* this is not enough. A *character* is an object of regard by the members of the culture generally or by some significant segment of them. He furnishes them with a cultural and moral ideal. Hence the demand is that in this type of case role and personality be fused. Social type and psychological type are required to coincide. The *character* morally legitimates a mode of social existence.

It is, I hope, now clear why I picked the examples that I did when I referred to Victorian England and Wilhelmine Germany. The Public School Headmaster in England and the Professor in Germany, to take only two examples, were not just social roles: they provided the moral focus for a whole cluster of attitudes and activities. They were able to discharge this function precisely because they incorporated moral and metaphysical theories and claims. Moreover these theories and claims had a certain degree of complexity and there existed within the community of Public School Headmasters and within the community of Professors public debate as to the significance of their role and function: Thomas Arnold's Rugby was not Edward Thring's Uppingham, Mommsen and Schmöller represented very different academic stances from that of Max Weber. But the articulation of disagreement was always within the context of that deep moral agreement which constituted the *character* that each individual embodied in his own way.

In our own time emotivism is a theory embodied in *characters* who all share the emotivist view of the distinction between rational and non-rational discourse, but who represent the embodiment of that distinction in very different social contexts. Two of these we have already noticed: the Rich Aesthete and the Manager. To these we must now add a third: the Therapist. The manager represents in his *character* the obliteration of the distinction between manipulative and nonmanipulative social relations; the therapist represents the same obliteration in the sphere of personal life. The manager treats ends as given, as outside his scope; his concern is with technique, with effectiveness in transforming raw materials into final products, unskilled labor into skilled labor, investment into profits. The therapist also treats ends as given, as outside his scope; his concern also is with technique, with effectiveness in transforming neurotic symptoms into directed energy, maladjusted individuals into well-adjusted ones. Neither manager nor therapist, in their roles as manager and therapist, do or are able to engage in moral debate. They are seen by themselves, and by those who see them with the same eyes as their own, as uncontested figures, who purport to restrict themselves to the realms in which rational agreement is possible—that is, of course from their point of view to the realm of fact, the realm of means, the realm of measurable effectiveness.

It is of course important that in our culture the concept of the therapeutic has been given application far beyond the sphere of psychological medicine in which it obviously has its legitimate place. In *The Triumph of the Therapeutic* (1966) and also in *To My Fellow Teachers* (1975) Philip Rieff has documented with devastating insight a number of the ways in which truth has been displaced as a value and replaced by psychological effectiveness. The idioms of therapy have invaded all too successfully such spheres as those of education and of religion. The types of theory involved in and invoked to justify such therapeutic modes do of course vary widely; but the mode itself is of far greater social significance than the theories which matter so much to its protagonists.

I have said of *characters* in general that they are those social roles which provide a culture with its moral definitions; it is crucial to stress that I do not mean by this that the moral beliefs expressed by and embodied in the *characters* of a particular culture will secure universal assent within that culture. On the contrary it is partly because they provide focal points for disagreement that they are able to perform their defining task. Hence the morally defining character of the managerial role in our own culture is evidenced almost as much by the variety of contemporary attacks upon managerial and manipulative modes of theory and practice as it is by allegiance to them. Those who persistently attack bureaucracy effectively reinforce the notion that it is in terms of a relationship to bureaucracy that the self has to define itself. Neo-Weberian organization theorists and the heirs of the Frankfurt School unwittingly collaborate as a chorus in the theatre of the present.

I do not want to suggest of course that there is anything peculiar to the present in this type of phenomenon. It is often and perhaps always through conflict that the self receives its social definition. This does not mean however, as some theorists have supposed, that the self is or becomes nothing but the social roles which it inherits. The self, as distinct from its roles, has a history and a social history and that of the contemporary emotivist self is only intelligible as the end product of a long and complex set of developments.

Of the self as presented by emotivism we must immediately note: that it cannot be simply or unconditionally identified with *any* particular moral attitude or point of view (including that of those *characters* which socially embody emotivism) just because of the fact that its judgments are in the end criterionless. The specifically modern self, the self that I have called emotivist, finds no limits set to that on which it may pass judgment for such limits could only derive from rational criteria for evaluation and, as we have seen, the emotivist self lacks any such criteria. Everything may be criticized from whatever standpoint the self has adopted, including the self's choice of standpoint to adopt. It is in this capacity of the self to evade any necessary identification with any particular contingent state of affairs that some modern philosophers, both analytical and existentialist, have seen the essence of moral agency. To be a moral agent is, on this view, precisely to be able to stand back from any and every situation in which one is involved, from any and every characteristic that one may possess, and to pass judgment on it from a purely universal and abstract point of view that is totally detached from all social particularity. Anyone and everyone can thus be a moral agent, since it is in the self and not in social roles or practices that moral agency has to be located. The contrast between this democratization of moral agency and the elitist monopolies of managerial and therapeutic expertise could not be sharper. Any minimally rational agent is to be accounted a moral agent; but managers and therapists enjoy their status in virtue of their membership within hierarchies of imputed skill and knowledge. In the domain of fact there are procedures for eliminating disagreement; in that of morals the ultimacy of disagreement is dignified by the title 'pluralism'.

This democratized self which has no necessary social content and no necessary social identity can then be anything, can assume any role or take any point of view, because it *is* in and for itself nothing. This relationship of the modern self to its acts and its roles has been conceptualized by its acutest and most perceptive theorists in what at first sight appear to be two quite different and incompatible ways. Sartre—I speak now only of the Sartre of the thirties and forties—has depicted the self as entirely distinct from any particular social role which it may happen to assume; Erving Goffman by contrast has liquidated the self into its role-playing, arguing that the self is no more than 'a peg' on which the clothes of the role are hung (Goffman 1959, p. 253). For Sartre the central error is to identify the self with its roles, a mistake which carries the burden of moral bad faith as well as of intellectual confusion; for Goffman the central error is to suppose that there *is* a substantial self over and beyond the complex presentations of role-playing, a mistake committed by those who wish to keep part of the human world 'safe from sociology'. Yet the two apparently contrasting views have much more in common that a first statement would lead one to suspect. In Goffman's anecdotal descriptions of the social world there is still discernible that ghostly 'I', the psychological peg to whom Goffman denies substantial selfhood, flitting evanescently from one solidly role-structured situation to another; and for Sartre the self's self-discovery is characterized as the discovery that the self is 'nothing', is not a substance but a set of perpetually open possibilities. Thus at a deep level a certain agreement underlies Sartre's and Goffman's surface disagreements; and they agree in nothing more than in this, that both see the self as entirely set over against the social world. For Goffman, for whom the social world is everything, the self is therefore nothing at all, it occupies no social space. For Sartre, whatever social space it occupies it does so only accidentally, and therefore he too sees the self as in no way an actuality.

What moral modes are open to the self thus conceived? To answer this question, we must first recall the second key characteristic of the emotivist self, its lack of any ultimate criteria. When I characterize it thus I am referring back to what we have already noticed, that whatever criteria or principles or evaluative allegiances the emotivist self may profess, they are to be construed as expressions of attitudes, preferences and choices which are themselves not governed by criterion, principle or value, since they underlie and are prior to all allegiance to criterion, principle or value. But from this it follows that the emotivist self can have no rational history in its transitions from one state of moral commitment to another. Inner conflicts are for it necessarily *au fond* the confrontation of one contingent arbitrariness by another. It is a self with no given continuities, save those of the body which is its bearer and of the memory which to the best of its ability gathers in its past. And we know from the outcome of the discussions of personal identity by Locke, Berkeley, Butler and Hume that neither of these separately or together are adequate to specify that identity and continuity of which actual selves are so certain.

The self thus conceived, utterly distinct on the one hand from its social embodiments and lacking on the other any rational history of its own, may seem to have a certain abstract and ghostly character. It is therefore worth remarking that a behaviorist account is as much or as little plausible of the self conceived in this manner as of the self conceived in any other. The appearance of an abstract and ghostly quality arises not from any lingering Cartesian dualism, but from the degree of contrast, indeed the degree of loss, that comes into view if we compare the emotivist self with its historical predecessors. For one way of re-envisaging the emotivist self is as having suffered a deprivation, a stripping away of qualities that were once believed to belong to the self. The self is now thought of as lacking any necessary social identity, because the kind of social identity that it once enjoyed is no longer available; the self is now thought of as criterionless, because the kind of *telos* in terms of which it once judged and acted is no longer thought to be credible. What kind of identity and what kind of *telos* were they?

In many pre-modern, traditional societies it is through his or her membership in a variety of social groups that the individual identifies himself or herself and is identified by others. I am brother, cousin and grandson, member of this household, that village, this tribe. These are not characteristics that belong to human beings accidentally, to be stripped away in order to discover 'the real me'. They are part of my substance, defining partially at least and sometimes wholly my obligations and my duties. Individuals inherit a particular space within an interlocking set of social relationships; lacking that space, they are nobody, or at best a stranger or an outcast. To know oneself as such a social person is however not to occupy a static and fixed position. It is to find oneself placed at a certain point on a journey with set goals; to move through life is to make progress—or to fail to make progress—toward a given end. Thus a completed and fulfilled life is an achievement and death is the point at which someone can be judged happy or unhappy. Hence the ancient Greek proverb: 'Call no man happy until he is dead.'

This conception of a whole human life as the primary subject of objective and impersonal evaluation, of a type of evaluation which provides the content for judgment upon the particular actions or projects of a given individual, is something that ceases to be generally available at some point in the progress—if we can call it such—towards and into modernity. It passes to some degree unnoticed, for it is celebrated historically for the most part not as loss, but as self-congratulatory gain, as the emergence of the individual freed on the one hand from the social bonds of those constraining hierarchies which the modern world rejected at its birth and on the other hand from what modernity has taken to be the superstitions of teleology. To say this is of course to move a little too quickly beyond my present argument; but it is to note that the peculiarly modern self, the emotivist self, in acquiring sovereignty in its own realm lost its traditional boundaries provided by a social identity and a view of human life as ordered to a given end.

Nonetheless, as I have already suggested, the emotivist self has its own kind of social definition. It is at home in—it is an integral part of—one distinctive type of social order, that which we in the so-called advanced countries presently inhabit. Its definition is the counterpart to the definition of those *characters* which inhabit and present the dominant social roles. The bifurcation of the contemporary social world into a realm of the organizational in which ends are taken to be given and are not available for rational scrutiny and a realm of the personal in which judgment and debate about values are central factors, but in which no rational social resolution of issues is available, finds its internalization, its inner representation in the relation of the individual self to the roles and *characters* of social life.

This bifurcation is itself an important clue to the central characteristics of modern societies and one which may enable us to avoid being deceived by their own internal political debates. Those debates are often staged in terms of a supposed opposition between individualism and collectivism, each appearing in a variety of doctrinal forms. On the one side there appear the self-defined protagonists of individual liberty, on the other the self-defined protagonists of planning and regulation, of the goods which are available through bureaucratic organization. But in fact what is crucial is that on which the contending parties agree, namely that there are only two alternative modes of social life open to us, one in which the free and arbitrary choices of individuals are sovereign and one in which the bureaucracy is sovereign, precisely so that it may limit the free and arbitrary choices of individuals. Given this deep cultural agreement, it is unsurprising that the politics of modern societies oscillate between a freedom which is nothing but a lack of regulation of individual behavior and forms of collectivist control designed only to limit the anarchy of self-interest. The consequences of a victory by one side or the other are often of the highest immediate importance; but, as Solzhenitzyn has understood so well, both ways of life are in the long run intolerable. Thus the society in which we live is one in which bureaucracy and individualism are partners as well as antagonists. And it is in the cultural climate of this bureaucratic individualism that the emotivist self is naturally at home.

The parallel between my treatment of what I have called the emotivist self and my treatment of emotivist theories of moral judgment—whether Stevensonian, Nietzschean or Sartrian—is now, I hope, clear. In both cases I have argued that we are confronted with what is intelligible only as the end-product of a process of historical change; in both cases I have confronted theoretical positions whose protagonists claim that what I take to be the historically produced characteristics of what is specifically modern are in fact the timelessly necessary characteristics of all and any moral judgment, of all and any selfhood. If my argument is correct we are not, although many of us have become or partly become, what Sartre and Goffman say we are, precisely because we are the last inheritors—so far—of a process of historical transformation.

This transformation of the self and its relationship to its roles from more traditional modes of existence into contemporary emotivist forms could not have occured of course if the forms of moral discourse, the language of morality, had not also been transformed at the same time. Indeed it is wrong to separate the history of the self and its roles from the history of the language which the self specifies and through which the roles are given expression. What we discover is a single history and not two parallel ones. I noted at the outset two central factors of contemporary moral utterance. One was the multifariousness and apparent incommensurability of the concepts invoked. The other was the assertive use of ultimate principles in attempts to close moral debate. To discover where these features of our discourse came from, how and why they are fashioned, is therefore an obvious strategy for my enquiry. To this task I now turn.

4

The Predecessor Culture
and the Enlightenment Project
of Justifying Morality

What I am going to suggest is that the key episodes in the social history which transformed, fragmented and, if my extreme view is correct, largely displaced morality — and so created the possibility of the emotivist self with its characteristic form of relationship and modes of utterance — were episodes in the history of philosophy, that it is only in the light of *that* history that we can understand how the idiosyncrasies of everyday contemporary moral discourse came to be and thus how the emotivist self was able to find a means of expression. Yet how can this be so? In our own culture academic philosophy is a highly marginal and specialized activity. Professors of philosophy do from time to time seek to wear the clothes of relevance and some of the college-educated public are haunted by vague cartoon-like memories of Philosophy 100. But both would find it surprising and the larger public even more surprising if it were suggested, as I am now suggesting, that the roots of some of the problems which now engage the specialized attention of academic philosophers and the roots of some of the problems central to our everyday social and practical lives are one and the same. Surprise would only be succeeded by incredulity if it were further suggested that we cannot understand, let alone solve, one of these sets of problems without understanding the other.

Yet this might become less implausible if the thesis were cast in historical form. For the claim is that both our general culture and our academic philosophy are in central part the offspring of a culture in which philosophy did constitute a central form of social activity, in which its role and function was very unlike that which it has with us. It was, so I shall argue, the failure of that culture to solve its problems, problems at once practical and philosophical, which was *a* and perhaps *the* key factor in determining the form both of our academic philosophical problems and of our practical social problems. What was that culture? One so close to our own that it is not always easy for us to understand its distinctiveness, its difference from our own, and so not easy either to understand its unity and coherence. For this there are also other more accidental reasons.

One such reason why the unity and the coherence of the eighteenth-century culture of Enlightenment sometimes escapes us is that we too often understand it as primarily an episode in *French* cultural history. In fact France is from the standpoint of that culture itself the most backward of the enlightened nations. The French themselves often avowedly looked to English models, but England in turn was overshadowed by the achievements of the Scottish Enlightenment. The greatest figures of all were certainly German: Kant and Mozart. But for intellectual variety as well as intellectual range not even the Germans can outmatch David Hume, Adam Smith, Adam Ferguson, John Millar, Lord Kames and Lord Monboddo.

What the French lacked was threefold: a secularized Protestant background, an educated class which linked the servants of government, the clergy and the lay thinkers in a single reading public, and a newly alive type of university exemplified in Königsberg in the east and in Edinburgh and Glasgow in the west. The French eighteenth-century intellectuals constitute an intelligentsia, a group at once educated and alienated; while the eighteenth-century Scottish, English, Dutch, Danish and Prussian intellectuals are on the contrary at home in the social world, even when they are highly critical of it. The eighteenth-century French intelligentsia have to wait for the nineteenth-century Russians before they find any counterpart elsewhere.

Hence what we are dealing with is a culture that is primarily Northern European. Spaniards, Italians and the Gaelic and Slavonic-speaking peoples do not belong to it. Vico plays no part in its intellectual development. It has of course outposts outside Northern Europe, most notably in New England and Switzerland. It is influential in South Germany, Austria, Hungary and the kingdom of Naples. And most of the eighteenth-century French intelligentsia have the will to belong to it, in spite of the differences in their situation. Indeed at least the first phase of the French revolution can be understood as an attempt to enter by political means this North European culture and so to abolish the gap between French ideas and French social and political life. Certainly Kant recognized the French revolution as a political expression of thought akin to his own.

It was a musical culture and there is perhaps a closer relationship between this fact and the central philosophical problems of the culture than has usually been recognized. For the relationship of our beliefs to sentences that we *only* or *primarily* sing, let alone to the music which accompanies those sentences, is not at all the same as the relationship of our beliefs to the sentences that we primarily say and say in an assertive mode. When the Catholic mass becomes a genre available for concert performance by Protestants, when we listen to the scripture because of what Bach wrote rather than because of what St. Matthew wrote, then sacred texts are being preserved in a form in which the traditional links with belief have been broken, even in some measure for those who still count themselves believers. It is not of course that there is no link with belief; you cannot simply detach the music of Bach or even of Handel from the Christian religion. But a traditional distinction between the religious and the aesthetic has been blurred. And this is as true when the beliefs are new as when they are traditional. Mozart's freemasonry, which is perhaps *the* religion of Enlightenment *par excellence*, stands in as ambiguous a relationship to *The Magic Flute*, as does Handel's *Messiah* to Protestant Christianity.

This is a culture then in which therefore there has been not only the kind of change of belief represented by the secularization of Protestantism but also, even for those who believe, a change in the modes of belief. It is not surprising that key questions arise about the justification of belief, and most of all about the justification of moral belief. We are so accustomed to classifying judgments, arguments and deeds in terms of morality that we forget how relatively new the notion was in the culture of the Enlightenment. Consider one very striking fact: in the culture of the Enlightenment the first language of educated discourse was no longer Latin, but it remained learning's second language. In Latin, as in ancient Greek, there is *no* word correctly translated by our word 'moral'; or rather there is no such word until our word 'moral' is translated back into Latin. Certainly 'moral' is the etymological descendant of 'moralis'. But 'moralis', like its Greek predecessor '*êthikos*' — Cicero invented 'moralis' to translate the Greek word in the *De Fato* — means 'pertaining to character' where a man's character is nothing other than his set dispositions to behave systematically in one way rather than another, to lead one particular kind of life.

The early uses of 'moral' in English translate the Latin and move to its use as a noun where 'the moral' of any literary passage is the practical lesson that it teaches. In these early uses 'moral' contrasts neither with such expressions as 'prudential' or 'self-interested' nor with such expressions as 'legal' or 'religious'. The word to which it is closest in meaning is perhaps simply 'practical'. Its subsequent history is one in which it is at first perhaps most usually part of the expression 'moral virtue' and then becomes a predicate in its own right with a continual tendency to narrow its meaning. It is in the sixteenth and seventeenth centuries that it recognizably takes on its modern meaning and becomes available for use in the contexts which I have just noted. It is in the late seventeenth century that it is used for the first time in its most restricted sense of all, that in which it has to do primarily with sexual behavior. How could it come about that 'being immoral' could be equated even as a special idiom with 'being sexually lax'? The answer to this question must be delayed. For the history of the word 'moral' cannot be told adequately apart from an account of the attempts to provide a rational justification for morality in that historical period—from say 1630 to 1850—when it acquired a sense at once general and specific. In that period 'morality' became the name for that particular sphere in which rules of conduct which are neither theological nor legal nor aesthetic are allowed a cultural space of their own. It is only in the later seventeenth century and the eighteenth century, when this distinguishing of the moral from the theological, the legal and the aesthetic has become a received doctrine that the project of an independent rational justification of morality becomes not merely the concern of individual thinkers, but central to Northern European culture.

A central thesis of this book is that the breakdown of this project provided the historical background against which the predicaments of our own culture can become intelligible. To justify this thesis it is necessary to recount in some detail the history of that project and its breakdown; and the most illuminating way to recount that history is to recount it backwards, beginning from that point at which for the first time the distinctively modern standpoint appears in something like fully-fledged form. What I earlier picked out as the distinctively modern standpoint was of course that which envisages moral debate in terms of a confrontation between incompatible and incommensurable moral premises and moral commitment as the expression of a criterionless choice between such premises, a type of choice for which no rational justification can be given. This element of arbitrariness in our moral culture was presented as a philosophical discovery—indeed as a discovery of a disconcerting, even shocking, kind—long before it became a commonplace of everyday discourse. Indeed that discovery was first presented precisely with the intention of shocking the participants in everyday moral discourse in a book which is at once the outcome and the epitaph of the Enlightenment's systematic attempt to discover a rational justification for morality. The book is Kierkegaard's *Enten-Eller* and, if we do not usually read it in terms of this historical perspective, that is because over-familiarity with its thesis has dulled our sense of its astonishing novelty in the time and place of its writing, the Northern European culture of Copenhagen in 1842.

Enten-Eller has three central features to which we ought to attend. The first is the connection between its mode of presentation and its central thesis. It is a book in which Kierkegaard wears a number of masks and by their very number invents a new literary genre. Kierkegaard was not the first author to divide up the self, to allocate it among a series of masks, each of which acts out the masquerade of an independent self, and so to create a new literary genre in which the author is present as himself more directly and intimately than in any form of traditional drama and yet by his partitioning of his self denies his own presence. Diderot in *Le Neveu de Rameau* was the first master of this new, peculiarly modern genre. But we can see a partial ancestor of both Diderot and Kierkegaard in that argument between the sceptical self and the Christian self which Pascal had intended to conduct in the *Pensées*, an argument of which we possess only the dismembered fragments.

Kierkegaard's professed intention in designing the pseudonymous form of *Enten-Eller* was to present the reader with an ultimate choice, himself not able to commend one alternative rather than another because never appearing as himself. 'A' commends the aesthetic way of life; 'B' commends the ethical way of life; Victor Eremita edits and annotates the papers of both. [The choice between the ethical and the aesthetic is not the choice between good and evil, it is the choice whether or not to choose in terms of good and evil.] At the heart of the aesthetic way of life, as Kierkegaard characterizes it, is the attempt to lose the self in the immediacy of present experience. The paradigm of aesthetic expression is the romantic lover who is immersed in his own passion. By contrast the paradigm of the ethical is marriage, a state of commitment and obligation through time, in which the present is bound by the past and to the future. Each of the two ways of life is informed by different concepts, incompatible attitudes, rival premises.

Suppose that someone confronts the choice between them having as yet embraced neither. He can be offered no *reason* for preferring one to the other. For if a given reason offers support for the ethical way of life—to live in that way will serve the demands of duty *or* to live in that way will be to accept moral perfection as a goal and so give a certain kind of meaning to one's actions—the person who has not yet embraced either the ethical or the aesthetic still has to choose whether or not to treat this reason as having any force. If it already has force for him, he has already chosen the ethical; which *ex hypothesi* he has not. And so it is also with reasons supportive of the aesthetic. The man who has not yet chosen has still to choose whether to treat them as having force. He still has to choose his first principles, and just because they are *first* principles, prior to any others in the chain of reasoning, no more ultimate reasons can be adduced to support them.

Kierkegaard thus presents himself as not endorsing either position. For he is neither 'A' nor 'B'. And if we take him to be presenting the position that there are no rational grounds for choice between either position , that the either/or choice is ultimate, he denies that too, for he is not Victor Eremita any more that he is 'A' or 'B'. Yet at the same time he is everywhere, and perhaps we detect his presence most of all in the belief that he puts into the mouth of 'B' that anyone who faces the choice between the aesthetic and the ethical will in fact choose the ethical; for the energy, the passion, of serious choice will, so to speak, carry the person who chooses into the ethical. (Here, I believe, Kierkegaard asserts—if it is Kierkegaard asserting—what is false: the aesthetic *can* be chosen seriously, although the burden of choosing it can be as passion-ridden as that of choosing the ethical. I think especially of those young men of my father's generation who watched their own earlier ethical principles die along with the deaths of their friends in the trenches in the mass murder of Ypres and the Somme; and who returned determined that nothing was ever going to matter to them again and invented the aesthetic triviality of the nineteen-twenties.)

My account of Kierkegaard's relationship to *Enten-Eller* is of course crucially different from that given by Kierkegaard himself later on, when he came to interpret his own writings retrospectively in terms of a single unchanging vocation; and the best Kierkegaard scholars of our own time such as Louis Mackey and Gregor Malantschuk, have in this respect at least endorsed Kierkegaard's self-portrait. Yet if we take all the evidence that we have of Kierkegaard's attitudes in and up to the end of 1842—and perhaps the text and the pseudonyms of *Enten-Eller* are the best evidence of all—it seems to me that their position is difficult to sustain. A little later in *Philosophiske Smuler* in 1845 Kierkegaard invokes this crucial new idea of radical and ultimate choice to explain how one becomes a Christian and by that time his characterization of the ethical has changed radically too. That had become already abundantly clear even in 1843 in *Frygt og Baeven*. But in 1842 he still stands in the most ambiguous of relationships to his new idea—simultaneously being its author and disowning its authorship. For this idea is not merely at odds with Hegel's philosophy, which already in *Enten-Eller* is one of Kierkegaard's chief targets. This idea destroys the whole tradition of a rational moral culture—*if* it itself cannot be rationally defeated.

The second feature of *Enten-Eller* to which we must now turn concerns the deep internal inconsistency—partially concealed by the book's form—between its concept of radical choice and its concept of the ethical. The ethical is presented as that realm in which principles have authority over us independently of our attitudes, preferences and feelings. How I feel at any given moment is irrelevant to the question of how I must live. This

is why marriage is the paradigm of the ethical. Bertrand Russell has described how one day in 1902 while riding a bicycle he suddenly realized
that he was no longer in love with his first wife—and from this realization
there followed in time the break-up of that marriage. Kierkegaard would
have said, and surely rightly, that any attitude whose absence can be
discovered in a sudden flash while riding a bicycle is only an aesthetic reaction and that such experience has to be irrelevant to the commitment
which genuine marriage involves, to the authority of the moral precepts
which define marriage. But now whence does the ethical derive this kind
of authority?

   To answer this question consider what kind of authority any principle
has which it is open to us to *choose* to regard as authoritative or not. I may
choose for example to observe a regime of asceticism and fasting and I
may do this for reasons of health, let us say, or religion. What authority
such principles possess derives from the reasons for my choice. Insofar as
they are good reasons, the principles have corresponding authority; insofar
as they are not, the principles are to that same extent deprived of authority.
It would follow that a principle for the choice of which no reasons could
be given would be a principle devoid of authority. I might indeed adopt
such a principle from whim or caprice or from some arbitrary purpose—I
just happen to like acting in that way—but if I then chose to abandon
the principle whenever it suited me, I would be entirely free to do so. Such
a principle—and it may even be stretching language to call it a principle—
would seem clearly to belong to Kierkegaard's aesthetic realm.

   But now the doctrine of *Enten-Eller* is plainly to the effect that the principles which depict the ethical way of life are to be adopted *for no reason*,
but for a choice that lies beyond reasons, just because it is the choice of
what is to count for us as a reason. Yet the ethical is to have authority
over us. But how can that which we adopt for one reason have any authority over us? The contradiction in Kierkegaard's doctrine is plain. To this
someone might reply that we characteristically appeal to authority when
we have no reasons; we may appeal to the authority of the custodians
of the Christian revelation, for example, at the very point where reason
breaks down. So that the notion of authority and the notion of reason are
not, as my argument suggests, intimately connected, but are in fact mutually exclusive. Yet this concept of authority as excluding reason is, as I have
already noticed, itself a peculiarly, even if not exclusively, modern concept,
fashioned in a culture to which the notion of authority is alien and repug-
nant, so that appeals to authority appear irrational. But the traditional
authority of the ethical, in the culture which Kierkegaard inherited, was
not of this arbitrary kind. And it is this traditional concept of authority

which must be embodied in the ethical if it is to be as Kierkegaard describes it. (It is not surprising that just as it was Kierkegaard who first discovered the concept of radical choice, so it is in Kierkegaard's writings that the links between reason and authority are broken too.)

I have argued then that there is a deep incoherence in *Enten-Eller*; if the ethical has some basis, it cannot be provided by the notion of radical choice. Before I turn to ask why Kierkegaard should have arrived at this incoherent position, however, let me notice a third feature of *Enten-Eller*. It is the conservative and traditional character of Kierkegaard's account of the ethical. In our own culture the influence of the notion of radical choice appears in our dilemmas over *which* ethical principles to choose. We are almost intolerably conscious of rival moral alternatives. But Kierkegaard combines the notion of radical choice with an unquestioning conception of *the* ethical. Promise-keeping, truth-telling and benevolence embodied in universalizable moral principles are understood in a very simple way; the ethical man has no great problems of interpretation once he has made his initial choice. To notice this is to notice that Kierkegaard is providing a new practical and philosophical underpinning for an older and inherited way of life. It is perhaps this combination of novelty and tradition which accounts for the incoherence at the heart of Kierkegaard's position. It is certainly, so I shall argue, just this deeply incoherent combination of the novel and the inherited which is the logical outcome of the Enlightenment's project to provide a rational foundation for and justification of morality.

To understand why this is so it is necessary to turn back from Kierkegaard to Kant. Because of Kierkegaard's own ceaseless polemics against Hegel, it is all too easy not to notice Kierkegaard's positive debts to Kant. But it is in fact Kant who in almost every area sets the philosophical scene for Kierkegaard. It is Kant's treatment of the proofs of the existence of God and his view of what constitutes rational religion that provide a crucial part of the background for Kierkegaard's account of Christianity; and it is equally Kant's moral philosophy which is the essential background for Kierkegaard's treatment of the ethical. It is not difficult to recognize in Kierkegaard's account of the aesthetic way of life a literary genius's version of Kant's account of inclination—whatever else Kant may be thought, and it is difficult to exaggerate his achievement, he was as clearly *not* a literary genius as any philosopher in history. Yet it is in Kant's honest and unpretentious German that Kierkegaard's elegant but not always transparent Danish finds its paternity.

Central to Kant's moral philosophy are two deceptively simple theses: if the rules of morality are rational, they must be the same for all rational beings, in just the way that the rules of arithmetic are; and if the rules of morality are *binding* on all rational beings, then the contingent ability of such beings to carry them out must be unimportant—what is important is their will to carry them out. The project of discovering a rational justification of morality therefore simply *is* the project of discovering a rational test which will discriminate those maxims which are a genuine expression of the moral law when they determine the will from those maxims which are not such an expression. Kant is not of course himself in any doubt as to *which* maxims are in fact the expression of the moral law; virtuous plain men and women did not have to wait for philosophy to tell them in what a good will consisted and Kant never doubted for a moment that the maxims which he had learnt from his own virtuous parents were those which had to be vindicated by a rational test. Thus the content of Kant's morality was conservative in just the way that the content of Kierkegaard's was, and this is scarcely surprising. Although Kant's Lutheran childhood in Königsberg was a hundred years before Kierkegaard's Lutheran childhood in Copenhagen the same inherited morality marked both men.

Kant then possesses on the one hand a stock of maxims and on the other a conception of what a rational test for a maxim must be. What is this conception and whence is it derived? We can best approach an answer to these questions by considering why Kant rejects two conceptions of such a test which had been widely influential in the European traditions. On the one hand Kant rejects the view that the test of a proposed maxim is whether obedience to it would in the end lead to the happiness of a rational being. Kant has no doubt that all men do indeed desire happiness; and he has no doubt that the highest good conceivable is that of the individual's moral perfection crowned by the happiness which it merits. But he nonetheless believes that our *conception* of happiness is too vague and shifting to provide a reliable moral guide. Moreover any precept designed to secure our happiness would be an expression of a rule holding only conditionally; it would instruct to do such-and-such, if and insofar as doing such-and-such would in fact lead to happiness as a result. Whereas Kant takes it to be the case that all genuine expressions of the moral law have an unconditional categorical character. They do not enjoin us hypothetically; they simply enjoin us.

Morality then can find no basis in our desires; but it can find no basis either in our religious beliefs. For the second traditional view which Kant repudiates is that according to which the test of a given maxim or precept is whether it is commanded by God. On Kant's view it can never follow from the fact that God commands us to do such-and-such that we ought to do such-and-such. In order for us to reach such a conclusion justifiably we would also have to know that we always ought to do what God commands. But this last we could not know unless we ourselves possessed a standard of moral judgment independent of God's commandments by means of which we could judge God's deeds and words and so find the latter morally worthy of obedience. But clearly if we possess such a standard, the commandments of God will be redundant.

We can already notice certain large and obvious features of Kant's thought which declare it to be the immediate ancestor of Kierkegaard's. The sphere in which happiness is to be pursued is sharply distinguished from the sphere of morality and both in turn as sharply from that of divine morality and commandment. Moreover the precepts of morality are not only the same precepts as those which were later to constitute the ethical for Kierkegaard; but they are to inspire the same kind of respect. Yet where Kierkegaard had seen the basis of the ethical in choice, Kant sees it in reason.

Practical reason, according to Kant, employs no criterion external to itself. It appeals to no content derived from experience; hence Kant's independent arguments against the use of happiness or the invocation of God's revealed will merely reinforce a position already entailed by the Kantian view of reason's function and powers. It is of the essence of reason that it lays down principles which are universal, categorical and internally consistent. Hence a rational morality will lay down principles which both can and ought to be held by *all* men, independent of circumstances and conditions, and which could consistently be obeyed by every rational agent on every occasion. The test for a proposed maxim is then easily framed: can we or can we not consistently will that everyone should always act on it?

How are we to decide whether this attempt to formulate a decisive test for the maxims of morality is successful or not? Kant himself tries to show that such maxims as 'Always tell the truth', 'Always keep promises', 'Be benevolent to those in need' and 'Do not commit suicide' pass his test, while such maxims as 'Only keep promises when it is convenient to you' fail. In fact however, even to approach a semblance of showing this, he has to use notoriously bad arguments, the climax of which is his assertion that any man who wills the maxim 'To kill myself when the prospects of pain outweigh those of happiness' is inconsistent because such willing 'contradicts' an impulse to life implanted in all of us. This is as if someone were to assert that any man who wills the maxim 'Always to keep my hair cut short' is inconsistent because such willing 'contradicts' an impulse to the growth of hair implanted in all of us. But it is not just that Kant's own arguments involve large mistakes. It is very easy to see that many immoral and trivial non-moral maxims are vindicated by Kant's test quite as convincingly—in some cases more convincingly—than the moral maxims which Kant aspires to uphold. So 'Keep all your promises throughout your entire life except one', 'Persecute all those who hold false religious beliefs' and 'Always eat mussels on Mondays in March' will all pass Kant's test, for all can be consistently universalized.

To this one rejoinder may be that if this follows from what Kant said, it cannot be what Kant meant. Certainly and obviously it was not what Kant envisaged, for he himself believed that his test of consistent universalizability had a defining moral content which would have excluded such universal and trivial maxims. Kant believed this because he believed that his formulations of the categorical imperative in terms of universalizability were equivalent to a quite different formulation: 'Always act so as to treat humanity, whether in your own person or in that of others, as an end, and not as a means.'

This formulation clearly does have a moral content, although one that is not very precise, if it is not supplemented by a good deal of further elucidation. What Kant means by treating someone as an end rather than as a means seems to be as follows—as I noticed earlier in using Kant's moral philosophy to highlight a contrast with emotivism. I may propose a course of action to someone either by offering him reasons for so acting or by trying to influence him in non-rational ways. If I do the former I treat him as a rational will, worthy of the same respect as is due to myself, for in offering him reasons I offer him an impersonal consideration for him to evaluate. What makes a reason a good reason has nothing to do with who utters it on a given occasion; and until an agent has decided for himself whether a reason is a good reason or not, he has no reason to act. By contrast an attempt at non-rational suasion embodies an attempt to make the agent a mere instrument of *my* will, without any regard for *his* rationality. Thus what Kant enjoins is what a long line of moral philosophers have followed the Plato of the *Gorgias* in enjoining. But Kant gives us no good reason for holding this position. I can without any inconsistency whatsoever flout it; 'Let everyone except me be treated as a means' may be immoral, but it is not inconsistent and there is not even any inconsistency in willing a universe of egotists all of whom live by this maxim. It might be inconvenient for each if everyone lived by this maxim, but it would not be impossible and to invoke considerations of convenience would in any case be to introduce just that prudential reference to happiness which Kant aspires to eliminate from all considerations of morality.

The attempt to found what Kant takes to be the maxims of morality on what Kant takes to be reason therefore fails just as surely as Kierkegaard's attempt to discover a foundation for them in an act of choice failed; and the two failures are closely related. Kierkegaard and Kant agree in their conception of morality, but Kierkegaard inherits that conception together with an understanding that the project of giving a rational vindication of morality has failed. Kant's failure provided Kierkegaard with his starting-point: the act of choice had to be called in to do the work that reason could not do. And yet if we understand Kierkegaardian choice as a surrogate for Kantian reason, we must also in turn understand that Kant too was responding to an earlier philosophical episode, that Kant's appeal to reason was the historical heir and successor of Diderot's and Hume's appeals to desire and to the passions. Kant's project was an historical response to their failure just as Kierkegaard's was to his. Wherein did that earlier failure lie?

We need to note first of all that Diderot and Hume very largely share the view taken by Kierkegaard and Kant of the content of morality; and this is all the more surprising because, unlike Kierkegaard and Kant, they liked to think of themselves as philosophical radicals. Yet, whatever their radical gestures, both Hume and Diderot were by and large and for the most part moral conservatives. Hume is prepared to repeal the traditional Christian prohibition of suicide, but his views of both promising and property are as uncompromising as Kant's; Diderot professes to believe that basic human nature is both revealed in and served by what he portrays as the promiscuous sexuality of the Polynesians, but he is very clear that Paris is not Polynesia, and in *Le Neveu de Rameau* the *moi*, the *philosophe*, with whom the older Diderot so clearly identifies himself, is a conventional *bourgeois* moralist with as staid a view of marriage, of promises, of truth-telling and of conscientiousness as any adherent of Kantian duty or the Kierkegaardian ethical. And this was not merely Diderot's theory; in the upbringing of his own daughter his practice was precisely that of the *bon bourgeois* of his dialogue. In the persona of the *philosophe* the view which he propounds is that if in modern France we all pursue our desires with an enlightened eye to the long-run we shall see that the conservative moral rules are by and large the rules which the appeal to their basis in desire and passion will vindicate. To this the younger Rameau has three replies.

First, why should we have any regard for the long-run if the prospect of immediacy is sufficiently enticing? Secondly, does the *philosophe's* view not entail that even in the long-run we ought to obey the moral rules only when and insofar as they serve our desires? And thirdly is not this indeed the way of the world, that each individual, each class, consults his or its desires and to satisfy them preys on each other? Where the *philosophe* sees principle, the family, a well-ordered natural and social world, Rameau sees these as sophisticated disguises for self-love, seduction and predatory enterprise.

The challenge that Rameau presents to the *philosophe* cannot of course be met within the terms of Diderot's own thought. For what divides them is the question of precisely which of our desires are to be acknowledged as legitimate guides to action, and which on the other hand are to be inhibited, frustrated or re-educated; and clearly this qustion cannot be answered by trying to use our desires themselves as some sort of criterion. Just because all of us have, actually or potentially, numerous desires, many of them conflicting and mutually incompatible, we have to decide between the rival claims of rival desires. We have to decide in what direction to educate our desires, how to order a variety of impulses, felt needs, emotions and purposes. Hence those rules which enable us to decide between the claims of, and so to order, our desires—including the rules of morality—cannot themselves be derived from or justified by reference to the desires among which they have to arbitrate.

Diderot himself elsewhere—in the *Supplement to Bougainville's Voyage*—tried to distinguish between those desires which are natural to man—the desires obeyed by the imaginary Polynesians of his narrative—and those artificially formed and corrupted desires which civilization breeds in us. But in the very act of making this distinction he undermines his own attempt to find a basis for morality in human physiological nature. For he himself is forced to find grounds for discriminating between desires; in the *Supplement* he is able to avoid facing the implications of his own thesis, but in *Le Neveu de Rameau* he forces himself to recognize that there are rival and incompatible desires and rival and incompatible orderings of desire.

Yet Diderot's failure is not of course merely his own. The same difficulties that prevent Diderot from vindicating morality cannot be evaded by a philosophically more sophisticated account such as that given by Hume; and Hume makes as strong a case for his position as could conceivably be made. Like Diderot, he understands particular moral judgments as expressions of feeling, of the passions, for it is the passions and not reason which move us to action. But he also, like Diderot, recognizes that in judging morally we invoke general rules and he aspires to explain these by showing their utility in helping us to attain those ends which the passions set before us. Underlying this view is an implicit, unacknowledged view of the state of the passions in a normal and what we might call, but for Hume's view of reason, reasonable man. Both in his *History* and in the *Enquiry* the passions of 'enthusiasts' and more particularly of the seventeenth-century Levellers on the one hand and of Catholic asceticism on the other are treated as deviant, absurd and—in the case of the Levellers—criminal. The normal passions are those of a complacent heir of the revolution of 1688. Hence Hume is already covertly using some normative standard—in fact a highly conservative normative standard—to discriminate among desires and feelings and by so doing lays himself open to just the charge which Diderot in the person of the younger Rameau brought against himself in the person of the *philosophe*. But this is not all.

In the *Treatise* Hume posed the question why, if such rules as those of justice and of promise-keeping were to be kept because and only because they served our long-term interests, we should not be justified in breaking them whenever they did not serve our interests *and* the breach would have no further ill consequences. In the course of formulating this question he denies explicitly that any innate spring of altruism or sympathy for others could supply the defects of an argument from interest and utility. But in the *Enquiry* he feels compelled to invoke just such a spring. Whence this change? It is clear that Hume's invocation of sympathy is an invention intended to bridge the gap between any set of reasons which could support unconditional adherence to general and unconditional rules and any set of reasons for action or judgment which could derive from our particular, fluctuating, circumstance-governed desires, emotions and interests. Later on Adam Smith was to invoke sympathy for precisely the same purpose. But the gap of course is logically unbridgable, and 'sympathy' as used by Hume and Smith is the name of a philosophical fiction.

What I have not given due weight to so far is the power of Hume's negative arguments. What drives Hume to the conclusion that morality must be understood in terms of, explained and justified by reference to, the place of the passions and desires in human life is his initial assumption that *either* morality is the work of reason *or* it is the work of the passions and his own apparently conclusive arguments that it cannot be the work of reason. Hence he is compelled to the conclusion that morality is a work of the passions quite independently of and prior to his adducing of *any* positive arguments for that position. The influence of negative arguments is equally clear in both Kant and Kierkegaard. Just as Hume seeks to found morality on the passions because his arguments have excluded the possibility of founding it on reason, so Kant founds it on reason because *his* arguments have excluded the possibility of founding it on the passions, and Kierkegaard on criterionless fundamental choice because of what he takes to be the compelling nature of the considerations which exclude both reason and the passions.

Thus the vindication of each position was made to rest in crucial part upon the failure of the other two, and the sum total of the effective criticism of each position by the others turned out to be the failure of all. The project of providing a rational vindication of morality had decisively failed; and from henceforward the morality of our predecessor culture — and subsequently of our own — lacked any public, shared rationale or justification. In a world of secular rationality religion could no longer provide such a shared background and foundation for moral discourse and action; and the failure of philosophy to provide what religion could no longer furnish was an important cause of philosophy losing its central cultural role and becoming a marginal, narrowly academic subject.

Why was the significance of that failure not appreciated in the period in which it occurred? This is a question which needs to be pursued much more fully at a later stage in the argument. For the moment I need only remark that the general literate public was the victim of a cultural history which blinded it to its own true nature; and that moral philosophers began to pursue their debates in much greater isolation from that public than previously. Indeed to the present day Kierkegaard, Kant and Hume do not lack ingenious, academic disciples in the debate between whom the continuing power only of the negative arguments of each tradition against the other is the most significant feature. But before we can understand either the significance of the failure to provide a shared, public rational justification for morality or the explanation of why that significance was not appreciated either at the time or since, we shall have to arrive at a much less superficial understanding of why the project failed and what the character of that failure was.

5

Why the Enlightenment Project
of Justifying Morality
Had to Fail

So far I have presented the failure of the project of justifying morality merely as the failure of a succession of particular arguments; and if that were all that there was to the matter, it might appear that the trouble was merely that Kierkegaard, Kant, Diderot, Hume, Smith and their other contemporaries were not adroit enough in constructing arguments, so that an appropriate strategy would be to wait until some more powerful mind applied itself to the problems. And just this has been the strategy of the academic philosophical world, even though many professional philosophers might be a little embarrassed to admit it. But suppose in fact, what is eminently plausible, that the failure of the eighteenth and nineteenth-century project was of quite another kind. Suppose that the arguments of Kierkegaard, Kant, Diderot, Hume, Smith and the like fail because of certain shared characteristics deriving from their highly specific shared historical background. Suppose that we cannot understand them as contributors to a timeless debate about morality, but only as the inheritors of a very specific and particular scheme of moral beliefs, a scheme whose internal incoherence ensured the failure of the common philosophical project from the outset.

Consider certain beliefs shared by all the contributors to the project. All of them, as I noted earlier, agree to a surprising degree on the content and character of the precepts which constitute genuine morality. Marriage and the family are *au fond* as unquestioned by Diderot's rationalist *philosophe* as they are by Kierkegaard's Judge Wilhelm; promise-keeping and justice are as inviolable for Hume as they are for Kant. Whence did they inherit these shared beliefs? Obviously from their shared Christian past compared with which the divergences between Kant's and Kierkegaard's Lutheran, Hume's Presbyterian and Diderot's Jansenist-influenced Catholic background are relatively unimportant.

At the same time as they agree largely on the character of morality, they agree also upon what a rational justification of morality would have to be.

Its key premises would characterize some feature or features of human nature; and the rules of morality would then be explained and justified as being those rules which a being possessing just such a human nature could be expected to accept. For Diderot and Hume the relevant features of human nature are characteristics of the passions; for Kant the relevant feature of human nature is the universal and categorical character of certain rules of reason. (Kant of course denies that morality is 'based on human nature', but what he means by 'human nature' is merely the physiological non-rational side of man.) Kierkegaard no longer attempts to *justify* morality at all; but his account has precisely the same structure as that which is shared by the accounts of Kant, Hume and Diderot, except that where they appeal to characteristics of the passions or of reason, he invokes what he takes to be characteristics of fundamental decision-making.

Thus all these writers share in the project of constructing valid arguments which will move from premises concerning human nature as they understand it to be to conclusions about the authority of moral rules and precepts. I want to argue that any project of this form was bound to fail, because of an ineradicable discrepancy between their shared conception of moral rules and precepts on the one hand and what was shared — despite much larger divergences — in their conception of human nature on the other. Both conceptions have a history and their relationship can only be made intelligible in the light of that history.

Consider first the general form of the moral scheme which was the historical ancestor of both conceptions, the moral scheme which in a variety of diverse forms and with numerous rivals came for long periods to dominate the European Middle Ages from the twelfth century onwards, a scheme which included both classical and theistic elements. Its basic structure is that which Aristotle analyzed in the *Nicomachean Ethics*. Within that teleological scheme there is a fundamental contrast between man-as-he-happens-to-be and man-as-he-could-be-if-he-realized-his-essential-nature. Ethics is the science which is to enable men to understand how they make the transition from the former state to the latter. Ethics therefore in this view presupposes some account of potentiality and act, some account of the essence of man as a rational animal and above all some account of the human *telos*. The precepts which enjoin the various virtues and prohibit the vices which are their counterparts instruct us how to move from potentiality to act, how to realize our true nature and to reach our true end. To defy them will be to be frustrated and incomplete, to fail to achieve that good of rational happiness which it is peculiarly ours as a species to pursue. The desires and emotions which we possess are to be put in order and educated by the use of such precepts and by the cultivation of those habits of action which the study of ethics prescribes; reason instructs us both as to what our true end is and as to how to reach it. We thus have a threefold scheme in which human-nature-as-it-happens-to-be (human nature in its untutored state) is initially discrepant and discordant with the precepts of ethics and needs to be transformed by the instruction of practical reason and experience into human-nature-as-it-could-be-if-it-realized-its-*telos*. Each of the three elements of the scheme – the conception of untutored human nature, the conception of the precepts of rational ethics and the conception of human-nature-as-it-could-be-if-it-realized-its-*telos* – requires reference to the other two if its status and function are to be intelligible.

This scheme is complicated and added to, but not essentially altered, when it is placed within a framework of theistic beliefs, whether Christian, as with Aquinas, or Jewish with Maimonides, or Islamic with Ibn Roschd. The precepts of ethics now have to be understood not only as teleological injunctions, but also as expressions of a divinely ordained law. The table of virtues and vices has to be amended and added to and a concept of sin is added to the Aritotelian concept of error. The law of God requires a new kind of respect and awe. The true end of man can no longer be completely achieved in this world, but only in another. Yet the threefold structure of untutored human-nature-as-it-happens-to-be, human-nature-as-it-could-be-if-it-realized-its-*telos* and the precepts of rational ethics as the means for the transition from one to the other remains central to the theistic understanding of evaluative thought and judgment.

Thus moral utterance has throughout the period in which the theistic version of classical morality predominates both a twofold point and purpose and a double standard. To say what someone ought to do is at one and the same time to say what course of action will in these circumstances as a matter of fact lead toward a man's true end and to say what the law, ordained by God and comprehended by reason, enjoins. Moral sentences are thus used within this framework to make claims which are true or false. Most medieval proponents of this scheme did of course believe that it was itself part of God's revelation, but also a discovery of reason and rationally defensible. This large area of agreement does not however survive when Protestantism and Jansenist Catholicism – and their immediate late medieval predecessors – appear on the scene. For they embody a new conception of reason. (My argument is at this and other points both deeply indebted to and rather different from that of Anscombe 1958.)

Reason can supply, so these new theologies assert, *no* genuine comprehension of man's true end; that power of reason was destroyed by the fall of man. 'Si Adam integer stetisset', on Calvin's view, reason might have played the part that Aristotle assigned to it. But now reason is powerless to correct our passions (it is not unimportant that Hume's views are those of one who was brought up a Calvinist). Nonetheless the contrast between man-as-he-happens-to-be and man-as-he-could-be-if-he-realized-his-*telos* remains and the divine moral law is still a schoolmaster to remove us from the former state to the latter, even if only grace enables us to respond to and obey its precepts. The Jansenist Pascal stands at a peculiarly important point in the development of this history. For it is Pascal who recognizes that the Protestant-cum-Jansenist conception of reason is in important respects at one with the conception of reason at home in the most innovative seventeenth-century philosophy and science. Reason does not comprehend essences or transitions from potentiality to act; these concepts belong to the despised conceptual scheme of scholasticism. Hence anti-Aristotelian science sets strict boundaries to the powers of reason. Reason is calculative; it can assess truths of fact and mathematical relations but nothing more. In the realm of practice therefore it can speak only of means. About ends it must be silent. Reason cannot even, as Descartes believed, refute scepticism; and hence a central achievement of reason according to Pascal, is to recognize that our beliefs are ultimately founded on nature, custom and habit.

Pascal's striking anticipations of Hume—and since we know that Hume was familiar with Pascal's writings, it is perhaps plausible to believe that here there is a direct influence—point to the way in which this concept of reason retained its power. Even Kant retains its negative characteristics; reason for him, as much as for Hume, discerns no essential natures and no teleological features in the objective universe available for study by physics. Thus their disagreements on human nature coexist with striking and important agreements and what is true of them is true also of Diderot, of Smith and of Kierkegaard. All reject any teleological view of human nature, any view of man as having an essence which defines his true end. But to understand this is to understand why their project of finding a basis for morality had to fail.

The moral scheme which forms the historical background to their thought had, as we have seen, a structure which required three elements: untutored human nature, man-as-he-could-be-if-he-realized-his-*telos* and the moral precepts which enable him to pass from one state to the other. But the joint effect of the secular rejection of both Protestant and Catholic theology and the scientific and philosophical rejection of Aristotelianism was to eliminate any notion of man-as-he-could-be-if-he-realized-his-*telos*. Since the whole point of ethics—both as a theoretical and a practical discipline—is to enable man to pass from his present state to his true end, the elimination of any notion of essential human nature and with it the abandonment of any notion of a *telos* leaves behind a moral scheme composed of two remaining elements whose relationship becomes quite unclear. There is on the one hand a certain content for morality: a set of injunctions deprived of their teleological context. There is on the other hand a certain view of untutored-human-nature-as-it-is. Since the moral injunctions were originally at home in a scheme in which their purpose was to correct, improve and educate that human nature, they are clearly not going to be such as could be deduced from true statements about human nature or justified in some other way by appealing to its characteristics. The injunctions of morality, thus understood, are likely to be ones that human nature, thus understood, has strong tendencies to disobey. Hence the eighteenth-century moral philosophers engaged in what was an inevitably unsuccessful project; for they did indeed attempt to find a rational basis for their moral beliefs in a particular understanding of human nature, while inheriting a set of moral injunctions on the one hand and a conception of human nature on the other which had been expressly designed to be discrepant with each other. This discrepancy was not removed by their revised beliefs about human nature. They inherited incoherent fragments of a once coherent scheme of thought and action and, since they did not recognize their own peculiar historical and cultural situation, they could not recognize the impossible and quixotic character of their self-appointed task.

Yet perhaps 'could not recognize' is too strong; for we can rank order eighteenth-century moral philosophers in respect of how far they approached to such recognition. If we do so, we discover that the Scotsmen Hume and Smith are the least self-questioning, presumably because they are already comfortable and complacent within the epistemological scheme of British empiricism. Hume indeed had had something very like a nervous breakdown before he could come to terms with that scheme; but no hint of that breakdown remains in his writings on morality. No trace of discomfort appears either in those writings which Diderot published in his own lifetime; yet in *Le Neveu de Rameau*, one of the manuscripts which at his death fell into the hands of Catherine the Great, and which had to be smuggled out of Russia to be published in 1803, we find a critique of the whole project of eighteenth-century moral philosophy more trenchant and insightful than that of any external critic of the Enlightenment.

If Diderot is far closer to recognition of the breakdown of the project than Hume, Kant is closer than either. He does indeed look for a foundation of morality in the universalizable prescriptions of that reason which manifests itself both in arithmetic and in morality; and in spite of his strictures against founding morality on human nature, his analysis of the nature of human reason is the basis for his own rational account of morality. Yet in the second book of the second *Critique* he does acknowledge that without a teleological framework the whole project of morality becomes unintelligible. This teleological framework is presented as a 'presupposition of pure practical reason'. Its appearance in Kant's moral philosophy seemed to his nineteenth-century readers, such as Heine and later the Neo-Kantians, an arbitrary and unjustifiable concession to positions which he had already rejected. Yet, if my thesis is correct, Kant was right; morality did in the eighteenth century, as a matter of historical fact, presuppose something very like the teleological scheme of God, freedom and happiness as the final crown of virtue which Kant propounds. Detach morality from that framework and you will no longer have morality; or, at the very least, you will have radically transformed its character.

This change of character, resulting from the disappearance of any connection between the precepts of morality and the facts of human nature already appears in the writings of the eighteenth-century moral philosophers themselves. For although each of the writers we have been concerned with attempted in his positive arguments to base morality on human nature, each in his negative arguments moved toward a more and more unrestricted version of the claim that no valid argument can move from entirely factual premises to any moral or evaluative conclusion—to a principle, that is, which once it is accepted, constitutes an epitaph to their entire project. Hume still expresses this claim in the form of a doubt rather than of a positive assertion. He remarks that in 'every system of morality, which I have hitherto met with' authors make a transition from statements about God or human nature to moral judgments: 'instead of the usual copulations of propositions, *is*, and *is not*, I met with no proposition that is not connected with an *ought*, or an *ought not*' (*Treatise* III. i. 1). And he then goes on to demand 'that a reason should be given, for what seems altogether inconceivable, how this new relation can be a deduction from others, which are entirely different from it'. The same general principle, no longer expressed as a question, but as an assertion, appears in Kant's insistence that the injunctions of the moral law cannot be derived from any set of statements about human happiness or about the will of God and then yet again in Kierkegaard's account of the ethical. What is the significance of this general claim?

Some later moral philosophers have gone so far as to describe the thesis that from a set of factual premises no moral conclusion validly follows as 'a truth of logic', understanding it as derivable from a more general principle which some medieval logicians formulated as the claim that in a valid argument nothing can appear in the conclusion which was not already in the premises. And, such philosophers have suggested, in an argument in which any attempt is made to derive a moral or evaluative conclusion from factual premises something which is not in the premises, namely the moral or evaluative element, will appear in the conclusion. Hence any such argument must fail. Yet in fact the alleged unrestrictedly general logical principle on which everything is being made to depend is bogus—and the scholastic tag applies only to Aristotelian syllogisms. There *are* several types of valid argument in which some element may appear in a conclusion which is not present in the premises. A.N. Prior's counter-example to this alleged principle illustrates its breakdown adequately; from the premise 'He is a sea-captain', the conclusion may be validly inferred that 'He ought to do whatever a sea-captain ought to do'. This counter-example not only shows that there is no general principle of the type alleged; but it itself shows what is at least a grammatical truth—an 'is' premise *can* on occasion entail an 'ought' conclusion.

Adherents of the 'no "ought" from "is" view' could however easily meet part of the difficulty raised by Prior's example by reformulating their own position. What they intended to claim they might and would presumably say, is that no conclusion with substantial evaluative and moral content— and the conclusion in Prior's example certainly does lack any such content—can be derived from factual premises. Yet the problem would remain for them as to why now anyone would accept their claim. For they have conceded that it cannot be derived from any unrestrictedly general logical principle. Yet their claim may still have substance, but a substance that derives from a particular, and in the eighteenth century new, conception of moral rules and judgments. It may, that is, assert a principle whose validity derives not from some general logical principle, but from the meaning of the key terms employed. Suppose that during the seventeenth and eighteenth centuries the meaning and implications of the key terms used in moral utterance had changed their character; it could then turn out to be the case that what had once been valid inferences from or to some particular moral premise or conclusion would no longer be valid inferences from or to what *seemed* to be the same factual premise or moral conclusion. For what in some sense were the same expressions, the same sentences would now bear a different meaning. But do we in fact have any evidence for such a change of meaning? To answer this question it is helpful to consider another type of counter-example to the 'No "ought" conclusions from "is" premises' thesis. From such factual premises as 'This watch is grossly inaccurate and irregular in time-keeping' and 'This watch is too heavy to carry about comfortably', the evaluative conclusion validly follows that

'This is a bad watch'. From such factual premises as 'He gets a better yield for this crop per acre than any farmer in the district', 'He has the most effective programme of soil renewal yet known' and 'His dairy herd wins all the first prizes at the agricultural shows', the evaluative conclusion validly follows that 'He is a good farmer'.

Both of these arguments are valid because of the special character of the concepts of a watch and of a farmer. Such concepts are functional concepts; that is to say, we define both 'watch' and 'farmer' in terms of the purpose or function which a watch or a farmer are characteristically expected to serve. It follows that the concept of a watch cannot be defined independently of the concept of a good watch nor the concept of a farmer independently of that of a good farmer; and that the criterion of something's being a watch and the criterion of something's being a good watch—and so also for 'farmer' and for all other functional concepts—are not independent of each other. Now clearly both sets of criteria—as is evidenced by the examples given in the last paragraph—are factual. Hence any argument which moves from premises which assert that the appropriate criteria are satisfied to a conclusion which asserts that 'That is a good such-and-such', where 'such-and-such' picks out an item specified by a functional concept, will be a valid argument which moves from factual premises to an evaluative conclusion. Thus we may safely assert that, if some amended version of the 'No "ought" conclusion from "is" premises' principle is to hold good, it must exclude arguments involving functional concepts from its scope. But this suggests strongly that those who have insisted that *all* moral arguments fall within the scope of such a principle may have been doing so, because they took it for granted that *no* moral arguments involve functional concepts. Yet moral arguments within the classical, Aristotelian tradition—whether in its Greek or its medieval versions—involve at least one central functional concept, the concept of *man* understood as having an essential nature and an essential purpose or function; and it is when and only when the classical tradition in its integrity has been substantially rejected that moral arguments change their character so that they fall within the scope of some version of the 'No "ought" conclusion from "is" premises' principle. That is to say, 'man' stands to 'good man' as 'watch' stands to 'good watch' or 'farmer' to 'good farmer' within the classical tradition. Aristotle takes it as a starting-point for ethical enquiry that the relationship of 'man' to 'living well' is analogous to that of 'harpist' to 'playing the harp well' (*Nicomachean Ethics*, 1095a 16). But the use of 'man' as a functional concept is far older than Aristotle and it does not initially derive from Aristotle's metaphysical biology. It is rooted in the forms of social life to which the theorists of the classical tradition give expression. For according to that tradition to be a man is to fill a set of roles each of which has its own point and purpose: member of a family, citizen, soldier, philosopher, servant of God. It is only when man is thought of as an individual prior to and apart from all roles that 'man' ceases to be a functional concept.

For this to be so other key moral terms must also have partially at least changed their meaning. The entailment relations between certain types of sentence must have changed. Thus it is not just that moral conclusions cannot be justified in the way that they once were; but the loss of the possibility of such justification signals a correlative change in the meaning of moral idioms. So the 'No "ought" conclusion from "is" premises' principle becomes an inescapable truth for philosophers whose culture possesses only the impoverished moral vocabulary which results from the episodes I have recounted. That it was taken to be a timeless logical truth was a sign of a deep lack of historical consciousness which then informed and even now infects too much of moral philosophy. For its initial proclamation was itself a crucial historical event. It signals both a final break with the classical tradition and the decisive breakdown of the eighteenth-century project of justifying morality in the context of the inherited, but already incoherent, fragments left behind from tradition.

But it is not only that moral concepts and arguments at this point in history radically change their character so that they become recognizably the immediate ancestors of the unsettlable, interminable arguments of our own culture. It is also the case that moral *judgments* change their import and meaning. Within the Aristotelian tradition to call x good (where x may be among other things a person or an animal or a policy or a state of affairs) is to say that it is the kind of x which someone would choose who wanted an x for the purpose for which x's are characteristically wanted. To call a watch good is to say that it is the kind of watch which someone would choose who wanted a watch to keep time accurately (rather than, say, to throw at the cat). The presupposition of this use of 'good' is that every type of item which it is appropriate to call good or bad—including persons and actions—has, as a matter of fact, some given specific purpose or function. To call something good therefore is also to make a factual statement. To call a particular action just or right is to say that it is what a good man would do in such a situation; hence this type of statement too is factual. Within this tradition moral and evaluative statements can be called true or false in precisely the way in which all other factual statements can be so called. But once the notion of essential human purposes or functions disappears from morality, it begins to appear implausible to treat moral judgments as factual statements.

Moreover the secularization of morality by the Enlightenment had put in question the status of moral judgments as ostensible reports of divine law. Even Kant, who still understands moral judgments as expressions of a universal law, even if it be a law which each rational agent utters to himself, does not treat moral judgments as reports of what the law requires or commands, but as themselves imperatives. And imperatives are not susceptible of truth or falsity.

Up to the present in everyday discourse the habit of speaking of moral judgments as true or false persists; but the question of what it is in virtue of which a particular moral judgment is true or false has come to lack any clear answer. That this should be so is perfectly intelligible if the historical hypothesis which I have sketched is true: that moral judgments are linguistic survivals from the practices of classical theism which have lost the context provided by these practices. In that context moral judgments were at once hypothetical and categorical in form. They were hypothetical insofar as they expressed a judgment as to what conduct would be teleologically appropriate for a human being: 'You ought to do so-and-so, if and since your *telos* is such-and-such' or perhaps 'You ought to do so-and-so, if you do not want your essential desires to be frustrated'. They were categorical insofar as they reported the contents of the universal law commanded by God: 'You ought to do so-and-so: that is what God's law enjoins.' But take away from them that in virtue of which they were hypothetical *and* that in virtue of which they were categorical and what are they? Moral judgments lose any clear status and the sentences which express them in a parallel way lose any undebatable meaning. Such sentences become available as forms of expression for an emotivist self which lacking the guidance of the context in which they were originally at home has lost its linguistic as well as its practical way in the world.

Yet to put matters in this way is to anticipate in an unjustified way. For I am apparently taking it for granted that these changes are indeed to be characterized in terms of such concepts as those of survival, loss of context and consequent loss of clarity; whereas, as I noted earlier, many of those who lived through this change in our predecessor culture saw it as a deliverance both from the burdens of traditional theism and the confusions of teleological modes of thought. What I have described in terms of a loss of traditional structure and content was seen by the most articulate of their philosophical spokesmen as the achievement by the self of its proper autonomy. The self had been liberated from all those outmoded forms of social organization which had imprisoned it simultaneously within a belief in a theistic and teleological world order and within those hierarchical structures which attempted to legitimate themselves as part of such a world order.

Yet whether we view this decisive moment of change as loss or liberation, as a transition to autonomy or to *anomie*, two features of it need to be emphasized. The first is the social and political consequences of the change. Abstract changes in moral concepts are always embodied in real, particular events. There is a history yet to be written in which the Medici princes, Henry VIII and Thomas Cromwell, Frederick the Great and Napoleon, Walpole and Wilberforce, Jefferson and Robespierre are understood as expressing in their actions, often partially and in a variety of different ways, the very same conceptual changes which at the level of philosophical theory are articulated by Machiavelli and Hobbes, by Diderot and Condorcet, by Hume and Adam Smith and Kant. There ought not to be two histories, one of political and moral action and one of political and moral theorizing, because there were not two pasts, one populated only by actions, the other only by theories. Every action is the bearer and expression of more or less theory-laden beliefs and concepts; every piece of theorizing and every expression of belief is a political and moral action.

Thus the transition into modernity was a transition both in theory and in practice and a single transition at that. It is because the habits of mind engendered by our modern academic curriculum separate out the history of political and social change (studied under one set of rubrics in history departments by one set of scholars) from the history of philosophy (studied under quite a different set of rubrics in philosophy departments by quite another set of scholars) that ideas are endowed with a falsely independent life of their own on the one hand and political and social action is presented as peculiarly mindless on the other. This academic dualism is of course itself the expression of an idea at home almost everywhere in the modern world; so much so indeed, that Marxism, the most influential adversary theory of modern culture, presents what is just one more version of this same dualism in the distinction between basis and ideological superstructure.

Yet we also need to remember that if the self decisively separates itself from inherited modes both of thought and practice in the course of a single and unified history, it does so in a variety of ways and with a complexity that it would be crippling to ignore. When the distinctively modern self was invented, its invention required not only a largely new social setting, but one defined by a variety of not always coherent beliefs and concepts. What was then invented was the *individual* and to the question of what that invention amounted to and its part in creating our own emotivist culture we must now turn.

6

Some Consequences of the Failure
of the Enlightenment Project

The problems of modern moral theory emerge clearly as the product of the failure of the Enlightenment project. On the one hand the individual moral agent, freed from hierarchy and teleology, conceives of himself and is conceived of by moral philosophers as sovereign in his moral authority. On the other hand the inherited, if partially transformed rules of morality have to be found some new status, deprived as they have been of their older teleological character and their even more ancient categorical character as expressions of an ultimately divine law. If such rules cannot be found a new status which will make appeal to them rational, appeal to them will indeed appear as a mere instrument of individual desire and will. Hence there is a pressure to vindicate them either by devising some new teleology or by finding some new catagorical status for them. The first project is what lends its importance to utilitarianism; the second to all those attempts to follow Kant in presenting the authority of the appeal to moral rules as grounded in the nature of practical reason. Both attempts, so I shall argue, failed and fail; but in the course of the attempt to make them succeed social as well as intellectual transformations were accomplished.

Bentham's original formulations suggest a shrewd perception of the nature and scale of the problems confronting him. His innovative psychology provided a view of human nature in the light of which the problem of assigning a new status to moral rules can be clearly stated; and Bentham did not flinch from the notion that he *was* assigning a new status to moral rules and giving a new meaning to key moral concepts. Traditional morality was on his view pervaded by superstition; it was not until we understood that the only motives for human action are attraction to pleasure and aversion to pain that we can state the principles of an enlightened morality, for which the prospect of the maximum pleasure and absence of pain provides a *telos*. 'Pleasure' Bentham took to be the name of a type of sensation, just as 'pain' is; and sensations of both types vary only in number, intensity and duration. It is worth taking note of this false view of pleasure if only because Bentham's immediate utilitarian successors were so apt to see this as the major source of the difficulties that arise for utilitarianism. They therefore did not always attend adequately to the way in which he makes the transition from his psychological thesis that mankind has two and only two motives to his moral thesis that out of the alternative actions or policies between which we have to choose at any given moment we ought always to perform that action or implement that policy which will produce as its consequences the greatest happiness—that is, the greatest possible quantity of pleasure with the smallest possible quantity of pain—of the greatest number. It is of course on Bentham's view the enlightened, educated mind and it alone which will recognize that the pursuit of my happiness as dictated by my pleasure-seeking, pain-avoiding psychology and the pursuit of the greatest happiness of the greatest number do in point of fact coincide. But it is the aim of the social reformer to reconstruct the social order so that even the unenlightened pursuit of happiness will produce the greatest possible happiness for the greatest possible number; from this aim spring Bentham's numerous proposed legal and penal reforms. Note that the social reformer could not himself find a motive for setting himself to those particular tasks rather than others, were it not the case that an enlightened regard for one's own happiness here and now even in as unreformed a legal and social order as late-eighteenth- and early-nineteenth-century England will lead inexorably to the pursuit of the greatest happiness. This is an empirical claim. Is it true?

It took a nervous breakdown by John Stuart Mill, at once the first Benthamite child and clearly the most distinguished mind and character ever to embrace Benthamism, to make it clear to Mill himself at least that it is not. Mill concluded that it was Bentham's concept of happiness that needed reforming, but what he had actually succeeded in putting in question was the derivation of the morality from the psychology. Yet this derivation provided the whole of the rational grounding for Bentham's project of a new naturalistic teleology. It is not surprising that as this failure was recognized within Benthamism, its teleological content became more and more meagre.

John Stuart Mill was right of course in his contention that the Benthamite conception of happiness stood in need of enlargement; in *Utilitarianism* he attempted to make a key distinction between 'higher' and 'lower' pleasures and in *On Liberty* and elsewhere he connects increase in human happiness with the extension of human creative powers. But the effect of these emendations is to suggest—what is correct, but what no Benthamite no matter how far reformed could concede—that the notion of human happiness is *not* a unitary, simple notion and cannot provide us with a criterion for making our key choices. If someone suggests to us, in the spirit of Bentham and Mill, that we should guide our own choices by the prospects of our own future pleasure or happiness, the appropriate retort is to enquire: 'But which pleasure, which happiness ought to guide me?' For there are too many different kinds of enjoyable activity, too many different modes in which happiness is achieved. And pleasure or happiness are not states of mind for the production of which these activities and modes are merely alternative means. The pleasure-of-drinking-Guinness is not the pleasure-of-swimming-at-Crane's-Beach, and the swimming and the drinking are not two different means for providing the same end-state. The happiness which belongs peculiarly to the way of life of the cloister is not the same happiness as that which belongs peculiarly to the military life. For different pleasures and different happinesses are to a large degree incommensurable: there are no scales of quality or quantity on which to weigh them. Consequently appeal to the criteria of pleasure will not tell me whether to drink or swim and appeal to those of happiness cannot decide for me between the life of a monk and that of a soldier.

To have understood the polymorphous character of pleasure and happiness is of course to have rendered those concepts useless for utilitarian purposes; if the prospect of his or her own future pleasure or happiness cannot for the reasons which I have suggested provide criteria for solving the problems of action in the case of each individual, it follows that the notion of the greatest happiness of the greatest number is a notion without any clear content at all. It is indeed a pseudo-concept available for a variety of ideological uses, but no more than that. Hence when we encounter its use in practical life, it is always necessary to ask what actual project or purpose is being concealed by its use. To say this is not of course to deny that many of its uses have been in the service of socially beneficial ideals. Chadwick's radical reforms in the provision of public health measures, Mill's own support for the extension of the suffrage and for an end to the subjugation of women and a number of other nineteenth-century ideals and causes all invoked the standard of utility to some good purpose. But the use of a conceptual fiction in a good cause does not make it any less of a fiction. We shall have to notice the presence of some other fictions in modern moral discourse later in the argument; but before we do so it is necessary to consider one more feature of nineteenth-century utilitarianism.

It was a mark of the moral seriousness and strenuousness of the great nineteenth-century utilitarians that they felt a continuing obligation to scrutinize and rescrutinize their own positions, so that they might, if at all possible, not be deceived. The culminating achievement of that scrutiny was the moral philosophy of Sidgwick. And it is with Sidgwick that the failure to restore a teleological framework for ethics finally comes to be accepted. He recognized both that the moral injunctions of utilitarianism could not be derived from any psychological foundations and that the precepts which enjoin us to pursue the general happiness are logically independent of and cannot be derived from any precepts enjoining the pursuit of our own happiness. Our basic moral beliefs have two characteristics, Sidgwick found himself forced to conclude not entirely happily; they do not form any kind of unity, they are irreducibly heterogeneous; and their acceptance is and must be unargued. At the foundation of moral thinking lie beliefs in statements for the truth of which no further reason can be given. To such statements Sidgwick, borrowing the word from Whewell, gives the name *intuitions*. Sidgwick's disappointment with the outcome of his own enquiry is evident in his announcement that where he had looked for Cosmos, he had in fact found only Chaos.

It was of course from Sidgwick's final positions that Moore was presently to borrow without acknowledgment, presenting his borrowings with his own penumbra of bad argument in *Principia Ethica*. The important differences between *Principia Ethica* and Sidgwick's later writings are ones of tone rather than of substance. What Sidgwick portrays as failure Moore takes to be an enlightening and liberating discovery. And Moore's readers, for whom, as I noticed earlier, the enlightenment and the liberation were paramount, saw themselves as rescued thereby from Sidgwick and any other utilitarianism as decisively as from Christianity. What they did not see of course was that they had also been deprived of any ground for claims to objectivity and that they had begun in their own lives and judgments to provide the evidence to which emotivism was soon to appeal so cogently.

The history of utilitarianism thus links historically the eighteenth-century project of justifying morality and the twentieth century's decline into emotivism. But the philosophical failure of utilitarianism and its consequences at the level of thought and theory are of course only one part of the relevant history. For utilitarianism appeared in a variety of social embodiments and left its mark upon a variety of social roles and institutions. And these remained as an inheritance long after utilitarianism had lost the philosophical importance which John Stuart Mill's exposition had conferred upon it. But although this social inheritance is far from unimportant to my central thesis, I shall delay remarking upon it until I have considered the failure of a second philosophical attempt to give an account of how the autonomy of the moral agent might be consistently combined with a view of moral rules as having an independent and objective authority.

Utilitarianism advanced its most successful claims in the nineteenth century. Thereafter intuitionism followed by emotivism held sway in British philosophy, while in the United States pragmatism provided the same kind of *praeparatio evangelica* for emotivism that intuitionism provided in Britain. But for reasons that we have already noticed emotivism always seemed implausible to analytical philosophers primarily concerned with questions of *meaning* largely because it is evident that moral reasoning *does* take place, that moral conclusions can often be validly derived from sets of premises. Such analytical philosophers revived the Kantian project of demonstrating that the authority and objectivity of moral rules is precisely that authority and objectivity which belongs to the exercise of reason. Hence their central project was, indeed is, that of showing that any rational agent is logically committed to the rules of morality in virtue of his or her rationality.

I have already suggested that the variety of attempts to carry through this project and their mutual incompatibility casts doubt on their success. But it is clearly necessary to understand not only *that* the project fails, but *why* it fails, and to do this it is necessary to examine one such attempt in a little detail. The example which I have chosen is that made by Alan Gewirth in *Reason and Morality* (1978). I choose Gewirth's book because it is not only one of the most recent of such attempts, but also because it deals carefully and scrupulously with objections and criticisms that have been made of earlier writers. Moreover Gewirth adopts what is at once a clear and a strict view of what reason is: in order to be admitted as a principle of practical reason, a principle must be analytic; and in order for a conclusion to follow from premises of practical reason, it must be demonstrably entailed by those premises. There is none of the looseness and vagueness about what constitutes 'a good reason' which had weakened some earlier analytic attempts to exhibit morality as rational.

The key sentence of Gewirth's book is: 'Since the agent regards as necessary goods the freedom and well-being that constitute the generic features of his successful action, he logically must also hold that he has rights to these generic features and he implicitly makes a corresponding rights-claim' (p.63). Gewirth's argument may be spelled out as follows. Every rational agent has to recognize a certain measure of freedom and well-being as prerequisites for his exercise of rational agency. Therefore each rational agent must will, if he is to will at all, that he possess that measure of these goods. This is what Gewirth means when he writes in the sentence quoted of 'necessary goods'. And there is clearly no reason to quarrel with Gewirth's argument so far. It turns out to be the next step that is at once crucial and questionable.

Gewirth argues that anyone who holds that the prerequisites for his exercise of rational agency are necessary goods is logically committed to holding also that he has a right to these goods. But quite clearly the introduction of the concept of a right needs justification both because it is at this point a concept quite new to Gewith's argument *and* because of the special character of the concept of a right.)

It is first of all clear that the claim that I have a right to do or have something is a quite different type of claim from the claim that I need or want or will be benefited by something. From the first—if it is the only relevant consideration—it follows that others ought not to interfere with my attempts to do or have whatever it is, whether it is for my own good or not. From the second it does not. And it makes no difference what kind of good or benefit is at issue.

Another way of understanding what has gone wrong with Gewirth's argument is to understand why this step is so essential to his argument. It is of course true that if I claim a right in virtue of my possession of certain characteristics, then I am logically committed to holding that anyone else with the same characteristics also possesses this right. But it is just this property of necessary universalizability that does not belong to claims about either the possession of or the need or desire for a good, even a universally necessary good.

One reason why claims about goods necessary for rational agency are so different from claims to the possession of rights is that the latter in fact presuppose, as the former do not, the existence of a socially established set of rules. Such sets of rules only come into existence at particular historical periods under particular social circumstances. They are in no way universal features of the human condition. Gewirth readily acknowledges that expressions such as 'a right' in English and cognate terms in English and other languages only appeared at a relatively late point in the history of the language toward the close of the middle ages. But he argues that the existence of such expressions is not a necessary condition for the embodiment of the concept of a right in forms of human behavior; and in this at least he is clearly right. But the objection that Gewirth has to meet is precisely that those forms of human behavior which presuppose notions of some ground to entitlement, such as the notion of a right, always have a highly specific and socially local character, and that the existence of particular types of social institution or practice is a necessary condition for the notion of a claim to the possession of a right being an intelligible type of human performance. (As a matter of historical fact such types of social institution or practice have not existed universally in human societies.) Lacking any such social form, the making of a claim to a right would be like presenting a check for payment in a social order that lacked the institution of money. Thus Gewirth has illicitly smuggled into his argument a conception which does not in any way belong, as it must do if his case is to succeed, to the minimal characterization of a rational agent.

I take it then that both the utilitarianism of the middle and late nineteenth century and the analytical moral philosophy of the middle and late twentieth century are alike unsuccessful attempts to rescue the autonomous moral agent from the predicament in which the failure of the Enlightenment project of providing him with a secular, rational justification for his moral allegiances had left him. I have already characterized that predicament as one in which the price paid for liberation from what appeared to be the external authority of traditional morality was the loss of any authoritative content from the would-be moral utterances of the newly autonomous agent. Each moral agent now spoke unconstrained by the externalities of divine law, natural teleology or hierarchical authority; but why should anyone else now listen to him? It was and is to this question that both utilitarianism and analytical moral philosophy must be understood as attempting to give cogent answers; and if my argument is correct, it is precisely this question which both fail to answer cogently. Nonetheless almost everyone, philosopher and non-philosopher alike, continues to speak and write as if one of these projects had succeeded. And hence derives one of the features of contemporary moral discourse which I noticed at the outset, the gap between the *meaning* of moral expressions and the ways in which they are put to *use*. For the *meaning* is and remains such as would have been warranted only if at least one of the philosophical projects had been successful; but the use, the emotivist use, is precisely what one would expect if the philosophical projects had all failed.

Contemporary moral experience as a consequence has a paradoxical character. For each of us is taught to see himself or herself as an autonomous moral agent; but each of us also becomes engaged by modes of practice, aesthetic or bureaucratic, which involve us in manipulative relationships with others. Seeking to protect the autonomy that we have learned to prize, we aspire ourselves *not* to be manipulated by others; seeking to incarnate our own principles and stand-point in the world of practice, we find no way open to us to do so except by directing towards others those very manipulative modes of relationship which each of us aspires to resist in our own case. The incoherence of our attitudes and our experience arises from the incoherent conceptual scheme which we have inherited.

Once we have understood this it is possible to understand also the key place that three other concepts have in the distinctively modern moral scheme, that of *rights*, that of *protest*, and that of *unmasking*. By 'rights' I do not mean those rights conferred by positive law or custom on specified classes of person; I mean those rights which are alleged to belong to human beings as such and which are cited as a reason for holding that people ought not to be interfered with in their pursuit of life, liberty and happiness. They are the rights which were spoken of in the eighteenth century as natural rights or as the rights of man. Charactistically in that century they were defined negatively, precisely as rights *not* to be interfered with. But sometimes in that century and much more often in our own positive rights—rights to due process, to education or to employment are examples—are added to the list. The expression 'human rights' is now commoner than either of the eighteenth-century expressions. But whether negative or positive and however named they are supposed to attach equally to all individuals, whatever their sex, race, religion, talents or deserts, and to provide a ground for a variety of particular moral stances.

It would of course be a little odd that there should be such rights attaching to human beings simply *qua* human beings in light of the fact, which I alluded to in my discussion of Gewirth's argument, that there is no expression in any ancient or medieval language correctly translated by our expression 'a right' until near the close of the middle ages: the concept lacks any means of expression in Hebrew, Greek, Latin or Arabic, classical or medieval, before about 1400, let alone in Old English, or in Japanese even as late as the mid-nineteenth century. From this it does not of course follow that there are no natural or human rights; it only follows that no one could have known that there were. And this at least raises certain questions. But we do not need to be distracted into answering them, for the truth is plain: there are no such rights, and belief in them is one with belief in witches and in unicorns.

The best reason for asserting so bluntly that there are no such rights is indeed of precisely the same type as the best reason which we possess for asserting that there are no witches and the best reason which we possess for asserting that there are no unicorns: every attempt to give good reasons for believing that there *are* such rights has failed. The eighteenth-century philosophical defenders of natural rights sometimes suggest that the assertions which state that men possess them are self-evident truths; but we know that there are no self-evident truths. Twentieth-century moral philosophers have sometimes appealed to their and our intuitions; but one of the things that we ought to have learned from the history of moral philosophy is that the introduction of the word 'intuition' by a moral philosopher is always a signal that something has gone badly wrong with an argument. In the United Nations declaration on human rights of 1949 what has since become the normal UN practice of not giving good reasons for *any* assertions whatsoever is followed with great rigor. And the latest defender of such rights, Ronald Dworkin (*Taking Rights Seriously*, 1976) concedes that the existence of such rights cannot be demonstrated, but remarks on this point simply that it does not follow from the fact that a statement cannot be demonstrated that it is not true (p.81). Which is true, but could equally be used to defend claims about unicorns and witches.

Natural or human rights then are fictions—just as is utility—but fictions with highly specific properties. In order to identify them it is worth noticing briefly once more the other moral fiction which emerges from the eighteenth century's attempts to reconstruct morality, the concept of utility. When Bentham first turned 'utility' into a quasi-technical term, he did so, as I have already noticed, in a way that was designed to make plausible the notion of summing individual prospects of pleasure and pain. But, as John Stuart Mill and other utilitarians expanded their notion of the variety of aims which human beings pursue and value, the notion of its being possible to sum all those experiences and activities which give satisfaction became increasingly implausible for reasons which I suggested earlier. The objects of natural and educated human desire are irreducibly heterogeneous and the notion of summing them either for individuals or for some population has no clear sense. But if utility is thus not a clear concept, then to use it as if it is, to employ it as if it could provide us with a rational criterion, is indeed to resort to a fiction.

A central characteristic of moral fictions which comes clearly into view when we juxtapose the concept of utility to that of rights is now identifiable: they purport to provide us with an objective and impersonal criterion, but they do not. And for this reason alone there would have to be a gap between their purported meaning and the uses to which they are actually put. Moreover we can now understand a little better how the phenomenon of incommensurable premises in modern moral debate arises. The concept of rights was generated to serve one set of purposes as part of the social invention of the autonomous moral agent; the concept of utility was devised for quite another set of purposes. And both were elaborated in a situation in which substitute artifacts for the concepts of an older and more traditional morality were required, substitutes that had to have a radically innovative character if they were to give even an appearance of performing their new social functions. Hence when claims invoking rights are matched against claims appealing to utility or when either or both are matched against claims based on some traditional concept of justice, it is not surprising that there is no rational way of deciding which type of claim is to be given priority or how one is to be weighed against the other. Moral incommensurability is itself the product of a particular historical conjunction.

This provides us with an insight important for understanding the politics of modern societies. For what I described earlier as the culture of bureaucratic individualism results in their characteristic overt political debates being between an individualism which makes its claims in terms of rights and forms of bureaucratic organization which make their claims in terms of utility. But if the concept of rights and that of utility are a matching pair of incommensurable fictions, it will be the case that the moral idiom employed can at best provide a semblance of rationality for the modern political process, but not its reality. The mock rationality of the debate conceals the arbitrariness of the will and power at work in its resolution.

It is easy also to understand why *protest* becomes a distinctive moral feature of the modern age and why *indignation* is a predominant modern emotion. 'To protest' and its Latin predecessors and French cognates are originally as often or more often positive as negative; to protest was once to bear witness *to* something and only as a consequence of that allegiance to bear witness *against* something else.

But protest is now almost entirely that negative phenomenon which characteristically occurs as a reaction to the alleged invasion of someone's *rights* in the name of someone else's *utility*. The self-assertive shrillness of protest arises because the facts of incommensurability ensure that protestors can never win an *argument*; the indignant self-righteousness of protest arises because the facts of incommensurability ensure equally that the protestors can never lose an argument either. Hence the *utterance* of protest is characteristically addressed to those who already *share* the protestors' premises. The effects of incommensurability ensure that protestors rarely have anyone else to talk to but themselves. This is not to say that protest cannot be effective; it is to say that it cannot be *rationally* effective and that its dominant modes of expression give evidence of a certain perhaps unconscious awareness of this.

The claim that the major protagonists of the distinctively modern moral causes of the modern world—I am not here speaking at all of those who seek to uphold older traditions which have somehow or other survived into some sort of coexistence with modernity—offer a rhetoric which serves to conceal behind the masks of morality what are in fact the preferences of arbitrary will and desire is not of course an original claim. For each of the contending protagonists of modernity, while for obvious reasons unwilling to concede that the claim is true in their own case, is prepared to make it about those against whom they contend. So the Evangelicals of the Clapham Sect saw in the morality of the Enlightenment a rational and rationalizing disguise for selfishness and sin; so in turn the emancipated grandchildren of the Evangelicals and their Victorian successors saw Evangelical piety as mere hypocrisy; so later Bloomsbury, liberated by G.E. Moore, saw the whole semi-official cultural paraphernalia of the Victorian age as a pompous charade concealing the arrogant self-will not only of fathers and clergymen, but also of Arnold, Ruskin and Spencer; and so in precisely the same way D.H. Lawrence 'saw through' Bloomsbury. When emotivism was finally proclaimed as an entirely *general* thesis about the nature of moral utterance, it did no more than generalize what each party of cultural revolt in the modern world had already said about its particular moral predecessors. *Unmasking* the unacknowledged motives of arbitrary will and desire which sustain the moral masks of modernity is itself one of the most characteristically modern of activities.

It was Freud's achievement to discover that unmasking arbitrariness in others may always be a defence against uncovering it in ourselves. At the beginning of the twentieth century, autobiographies like Samuel Butler's clearly evoked an intense response from all those who felt the oppressive weight of assertive paternal self-will behind the cultural forms in which they had been educated. And this oppressive weight was surely due to the extent to which educated men and woman had internalized what they aspired to reject. Hence the importance of Lytton Strachey's mockery of the Victorians as part of the liberation of Bloomsbury and hence also the exaggerated rhetoric of Strachey's reaction to Moore's ethics. But even more important was Freud's presentation of the inherited conscience as superego, as an irrational part of ourselves whose commands we need, for the sake of our psychic health, to be freed from. Freud of course took himself to have made a discovery about morality as such and not just about what morality had become in late nineteenth-century and early twentieth-century Europe. But this mistake must not be allowed to detract from what he did achieve.

It is worth at this point recalling the thread of my central argument. I began from the way in which contemporary moral debate is interminable and I tried to explain that interminability as a consequence of the truth of an amended version of the emotivist theory of moral judgment, originally advanced by C.L. Stevenson and others. But I treated that theory not only as a philosophical analysis, but also as a sociological hypothesis. (I am unhappy about this way of putting the matter; it is not clear to me, for reasons which I gave in Chapter 3, how *any* adequate philosophical analysis in this area could escape being also a sociological hypothesis, and *vice versa*. There seems something deeply mistaken in the notion enforced by the conventional curriculum that there are two distinct subjects or disciplines—moral philosophy, a set of conceptual enquiries, on the one hand and the sociology of morals, a set of empirical hypotheses and findings, on the other. Quine's death-blow to any substantial version of the analytic-synthetic distinction casts doubt in any case on this kind of contrast between the conceptual and the empirical.)

My argument was thus to the effect that emotivism informs a great deal of contemporary moral utterance and practice and more specifically that the central *characters* of modern society—in the special sense which I assigned to the word 'character'—embody such emotivist modes in their behavior. These characters, it will be recalled, are the aesthete, the therapist and the manager, the bureaucratic expert. The historical discussion of those developments which made the victories of emotivism possible has now revealed something else about these specifically modern characters, namely the extent to which they trade and cannot escape trading in moral fictions. But how far does the range of moral fiction extend beyond those of rights and utility? And who is going to be deceived by them?

The aesthete is the character least likely to be their victim. Those insolent scoundrels of the philosophical imagination, Diderot's Rameau and Kierkegaard's 'A', who lounge so insolently at the entrance to the modern world, specialize in seeing through illusory and fictitious claims. If they are deceived, it is only by their own cynicism. When aesthetic deception occurs in the modern world, it is rather because of the reluctance of the aesthete to admit that that is what he is. So great can the burden of enjoying oneself become, so clearly can the emptiness and boredom of pleasure appear as a threat, that the aesthete sometimes has to resort to even more elaborate devices than were available to the younger Rameau or to 'A'. He may even become an addicted reader of Kierkegaard and make of that despair which Kierkegaard saw as the aesthete's fate a new form of self-indulgence. And if over-indulgence in despair seems to be injuring his capacities for enjoyment, he will take himself to the therapist, just as he would for over-indulgence in alcohol, and make of his therapy one more aesthetic experience.

The therapist by contrast is not only the most liable of the three typical characters of modernity to be deceived, but is also the most liable to be seen to be deceived, and not only by moral fictions. Devastating hostile critiques of the standard therapeutic theories of our culture are easily available; indeed each school of therapists is all too anxious to make clear the theoretical defects of each rival school. Thus the problem is not why the claims of psychoanalytic or behavioral therapies are not exposed as ill-founded; it is rather why, since they have been so adequately undermined, the practices of therapy continue for the most part as though nothing had happened. And this problem, like that of the aesthete, is not only or merely a problem of moral fictions.

Of course both aesthete and therapist are doubtless as liable as anyone else to trade in such fictions; but they have no fictions which are peculiarly their own, which belong to the very definition of their role. With the manager, that dominant figure of the contemporary scene, it is quite otherwise. For beside rights and utility, among the central moral fictions of the age we have to place the peculiarly managerial fiction embodied in the claim to possess systematic effectiveness in controlling certain aspects of social reality. And this thesis may at first sight seem surprising for two quite different kinds of reason: we are not accustomed to doubt the effectiveness of managers in achieving what they set out to achieve and we are equally unaccustomed to think of effectiveness as a distinctively *moral* concept, to be classed with such concepts as those of rights or of utility. Managers themselves and most writers about management conceive of themselves as morally neutral characters whose skills enable them to devise the most efficient means of achieving whatever end is proposed. Whether a given manager is effective or not is on the dominant view a quite different question from that of the morality of the ends which his effectiveness serves or fails to serve. Nonetheless there are strong grounds for rejecting the claim that effectiveness is a morally neutral value. For the whole concept of effectiveness is, as I noticed earlier, inseparable from a mode of human existence in which the contrivance of means is in central part the manipulation of human beings into compliant patterns of behavior; and it is by appeal to his own effectiveness in this respect that the manager claims authority within the manipulative mode.

Thus effectiveness is a defining and definitive element of a way of life which competes for our allegiance with other alternative contemporary ways of life; and if we are to evaluate the claims of the bureaucratic, managerial mode to a place of authority in *our* lives, an assessment of the bureaucratic managerial claim to effectiveness will be an essential task. The concept of effectiveness as it is embodied in the utterences and practices of managerial roles and character is of course an extremely general concept; it is bound up with equally general notions of social control exercised downwards in corporations, government agencies, trade unions and a variety of other bodies. Egon Bittner some years ago identified a crucial gap between this generalized conception and any actual criteria which are precise enough to be usable in particular situations. 'While Weber is quite clear,' he noted, 'in stating that the sole justification of bureaucracy is its efficiency, he provides us with no clear-cut guide on how this standard of judgment is to be used. Indeed, the inventory of features of bureaucracy contains not one single item that is not arguable relative to its efficiency function. Long-range goals cannot be used definitely for calculating it because the impact of contingent factors multiplies with time and makes it increasingly difficult to assign a determinate value to the efficiency of a stably controlled segment of action. On the other hand, the use of short-term goals in judging efficiency may be in conflict with the ideal of economy itself. Not only do short-term goals change with time and compete with one another in indeterminate ways, but short-term results are of notoriously deceptive value because they can be easily manipulated to show whatever one wishes them to show' (Bittner 1965, p.247).

It is the gap between the generalized notion of effectiveness and the actual behavior that is open to managers which suggests that the social uses of the notion are other than they purport to be. That the notion is used to sustain and extend the authority and power of managers is not of course in question; but its use in connection with those tasks derives from the belief that managerial authority and power are justified because managers possess an ability to put skills and knowledge to work in the service of achieving certain ends. But what if effectiveness is part of a masquerade of social control rather than a reality? What if effectiveness were a quality widely imputed to managers and bureaucrats both by themselves and others, but in fact a quality which rarely exists apart from this imputation?

The word that I shall borrow to name this alleged quality of effectiveness is 'expertise'. I am not of course questioning the existence of genuine experts in many areas: the biochemistry of insulin, historical scholarship, the study of antique furniture. It is specifically and only managerial and bureaucratic expertise that I am going to put in question. And the conclusion to which I shall finally move is that such expertise does indeed turn out to be one more moral fiction, because the kind of knowledge which would be required to sustain it does not exist. But what would it be like if social control were indeed a masquerade? Consider the following possibility: that what we are oppressed by is not power, but impotence; that one key reason why the presidents of large corporations do not, as some radical critics believe, control the United States is that they do not even succeed in controlling their own corporations; that all too often, when imputed organizational skill and power are deployed and the desired effect follows, all that we have witnessed is the same kind of sequence as that to be observed when a clergyman is fortunate enough to pray for rain just before the unpredicted end of a drought; that the levers of power—one of managerial experitse's own key metaphors—produce effects unsystematically and too often only coincidentally related to the effects of which their users boast.

Were all this to be the case, it would of course be socially and politically important to disguise the fact, and deploying the concept of managerial effectiveness as both managers and writers about management do deploy it would be an essential part of any such disguise. Fortunately I do not need to establish as part of the present argument precisely what it is that is being disguised in order to show that the concept of managerial effectiveness functions as a moral fiction; all that I need to show is that its use presupposes knowledge claims which cannot be made good, and further that the difference between the uses to which it is put and the meaning of the assertions which embody it is precisely similar to that identified by the emotive theory in the case of other modern moral concepts.

The mention of emotivism is very much to the point; for the thesis which I am presenting about belief in managerial effectiveness parallels to some degree the thesis advanced by certain emotivist moral philosophers – Carnap and Ayer – about belief in God. Carnap and Ayer both extended the emotive theory beyond the realm of moral judgment and argued that metaphysical assertions more generally and religious assertions more particularly, while they purport to give information about a transcendent reality, actually do no more than express the feelings and attitudes of those who utter them. They disguise certain psychological realities with religious utterances. Carnap and Ayer thus open up the possibility of providing a sociological explanation for the prevalence of these illusions, although they themselves do not aspire to furnish one.

I am suggesting that 'managerial effectiveness' functions much as Carnap and Ayer supposed 'God' to function. It is the name of a fictitious, but believed-in reality, appeal to which disguises certain other realities; its effective use is expressive. And just as Carnap and Ayer reached their conclusion principally by considering what they claimed was the lack of the appropriate kind of rational justification for belief in God, so the core of my argument is the contention that interpretations of managerial effectiveness in the same way lack the appropriate kind of rational justification.

If I am right in this, the characterization of the contemporary moral scene will have been taken one stage further than my previous arguments took it. Not only will we be justified in concluding that an emotivist account is both true of, and embodied in, a very great deal of our moral utterance and practice *and* that much of that utterance and practice is a trading in moral fictions (such as those of *utility* and of *rights*), but we shall also have to conclude that another moral fiction – and perhaps the most culturally powerful of them all – is embodied in the claims to effectiveness and hence to authority made by that central character of the modern social drama, the bureaucratic manager. To a disturbing extent our morality will be disclosed as a theatre of illusions.

The claim that the manager makes to effectiveness rests of course on the further claim to possess a stock of knowledge by means of which orgainizations and social structures can be molded. Such knowledge would have to include a set of factual law-like generalizations which would enable the manager to predict that, if an event or state of affairs of a certain type were to occur or to be brought about, some other event or state of affairs of some specific kind would result. For only such law-like generalizations could yield those particular casual explanations and predictions by means of which the manager could mold, influence and control the social environment.

There are thus two parts to the manager's claims to justified authority. One concerns the existence of a domain of morally neutral fact about which the manager is to be expert. The other concerns the law-like generalizations and their applications to particular cases derived from the study of this domain. Both claims mirror claims made by the natural sciences; and it is not surprising that expressions such as 'management science' should be coined. The manager's claim to moral neutrality, which is itself an important part of the way the manager presents himself and functions in the social and moral world, is thus parallel to the claims to moral neutrality made by many physical scientists. What it amounts to can best be understood by beginning from a consideration of how the relevant notion of 'fact' first became socially available and was put to use by the seventeenth- and eighteenth-century intellectual ancestors of the bureaucratic manager. It will turn out to be the case that this history is related in an important way to the history which I have already recounted of how the concept of the autonomous moral subject emerged in moral philosophy. That emergence involved a rejection of all those Aristotelian and quasi-Aristotelian views of the world in which a teleological perspective provided a context in which evaluative claims functioned as a particular kind of factual claim. And with that rejection the concepts both of value and of fact acquired a new character.

It is thus not a timeless truth that moral or otherwise evaluative conclusions cannot be entailed by factual premises; but it is true that the meaning assigned to moral and indeed to other key evaluative expressions so changed during the late seventeenth and the eighteenth centuries that what are by then commonly allowed to be factual premises cannot entail what are by then commonly taken to be evaluative or moral conclusions. The historical enactment of this apparent division between fact and value was not however merely a matter of the way in which value and morality came to be reconceived; it was also reinforced by a changed and changing conception of fact, a conception whose examination has to precede any assessment of the modern manager's claim to possession of the kind of knowledge which would justify his authority.

7

'Fact', Explanation and Expertise

'Fact' is in modern culture a folk-concept with an aristocratic ancestry. When Lord Chancellor Bacon as part of the propaganda for his astonishing and idiosyncratic amalgam of past Platonism and future empiricism enjoined his followers to abjure speculation and collect facts, he was immediately understood by such as John Aubrey to have identified facts as collectors' items, to be gathered in with the same kind of enthusiasm that at other times has informed the collection of Spode china or the numbers of railway engines. The other early members of the Royal Society recognized very clearly that, whatever Aubrey was doing, it was not natural science as the rest of them understood it; but they did not recognize that on the whole it was he rather than they who was being faithful to the letter of Bacon's inductivism. Aubrey's error was of course not only to suppose that the natural scientist is a kind of magpie; it was also to suppose that the observer can confront a fact face-to-face without any theoretical interpretation interposing itself.

That this was an error, although a pertinacious and long-lived one, is now largely agreed upon by philosophers of science. The twentieth-century observer looks into the night sky and sees stars and planets; some earlier observers saw instead chinks in a sphere through which the light beyond could be observed. What each observer takes himself or herself to perceive is identified and has to be identified by theory-laden concepts. Perceivers without concepts, as Kant almost said, are blind. Empiricist philosophers have contended that common to the modern and the medieval observer is that which each really sees or saw, prior to all theory and interpretation, namely many small light patches against a dark surface; and it is at the very least clear that what both saw *can* be so described. But if all our experience were to be characterized exclusively in terms of this bare sensory type of description—a type of description which it is certainly useful for a variety of special purposes to resort to from time to time—we would be confronted with not only an uninterpreted, but an uninterpretable world, with not merely a world not yet comprehended by theory but with a world that never could be comprehended by theory. A world of textures, shapes, smells, sensations, sounds and nothing more invites no questions and gives no grounds for furnishing any answers.

The empiricist concept of experience was a cultural invention of the late seventeenth and eighteenth centuries. It is at first sight paradoxical that it should have arisen in the same culture in which natural science arose. For it was invented as a panacea for the epistemological crises of the seventeenth century; it was intended as a device to close the gap between *seems* and *is*, between appearance and reality. It was to close this gap by making every experiencing subject a closed realm; there is to be nothing beyond my experience for me to compare my experience with, so that the contrast between *seems to me* and *is in fact* can never be formulated. This requires an even more radical kind of privacy for experience than is possessed by such genuinely private objects as after-images. For after-images can be misdescribed; subjects in psychological experiments concerning them have to learn to report them accurately. The distinction between *seems* and *is* does indeed apply to real private objects such as these, but not to the invented private objects of empiricism even though it is in terms of real private objects (after-images, hallucinations, dreams) that some empiricists try to explain their invented notion. It is scarely surprising that empiricists had to press old words into new forms of service—'idea', 'impression' and even 'experience' itself. By 'experience' was originally meant the act of putting something to the test or trial—a meaning that was later reserved to 'experiment' and later still involvement in some form of activity, as when we speak of 'five years experience as a carpenter'. The empiricist concept of experience was unknown for most of human history. It is understandable then that empiricism's linguistic history is one of continuous innovation and invention, culminating in the barbarous neologism 'sense-datum'.

By contrast the natural scientific concepts of observation and experiment were intended to enlarge the distance between *seems* and *is*. The lenses of the telescope and the microscope are given priority over the lenses of the eye; in the measurement of temperature the effect of heat on spirits of alcohol or mercury is given priority over the effect of heat on sunburnt skin or parched throats. Natural science teaches us to attend to some experiences rather than to others and only to those when they have been cast into the proper form for scientific attention. It redraws the lines between *seems* and *is*; it creates new forms of distinction between both appearance and reality and illusion and reality. The meaning of 'experiment' and the meaning of 'experience' diverge more sharply than they had done for the seventeenth century.

There are of course other crucial divergences. The empiricist concept was intended to discriminate the basic elements from which our knowledge is constructed and on which it is founded; beliefs and theories are to be vindicated or not, depending on the verdict of the basic elements of experience. But the observations of the natural scientist are never in this sense basic. We do indeed bring hypotheses to the test of observation; but our observations in turn can always be put to the question. The belief that Jupiter has seven moons is put to the test of observation through a telescope; but the observation itself has to be vindicated by the theories of geometrical optics. Theory is required to support observation, just as much as observation theory.

There is indeed therefore something extraordinary in the coexistence of empiricism and natural science in the same culture, for they represent radically different and incompatible ways of approaching the world. But in the eighteenth century both could be incorporated and expressed within one and the same world-view. It follows that that world-view is at its best radically incoherent; that keen and cold-eyed observer Laurence Sterne drew the conclusion that philosophy—albeit unwittingly—had at last represented the world as a series of jokes and out of these jokes he made *Tristram Shandy*. What obscured the incoherence of their own world-view for those about whom Sterne joked was in part the extent of their agreement on what was to be denied and excluded from their view of the world. What they agreed in denying and excluding was in large part all those aspects of the classical view of the world which were Aristotelian. From the seventeenth century onwards it was a commonplace that whereas the scholastics had allowed themselves to be deceived about the character of the facts of the natural and social world by interposing an Aristotelian interpretation between themselves and experienced reality, we moderns— that is, we seventeenth-century and eighteenth-century moderns—had stripped away interpretation and theory and confronted fact and experience just as they are. It was precisely in virtue of this that those moderns proclaimed and named themselves the Enlightenment, and understood the medieval past by contrast as the Dark Ages. What Aristotle obscured, they see. This conceit of course was, as such conceits always are, the sign of an unacknowledged and unrecognized transition from one stance of theoretical interpretation to another. The Enlightenment is consequently the period *par excellence* in which most intellectuals lack self-knowledge. What were the most important components in this seventeenth- and eighteenth-century transition in which the blind acclaim their own vision?

For the middle ages mechanisms were efficient causes in a world to be comprehended ultimately in terms of final causes. Every species has a natural end, and to explain the movements of and changes in an individual is to explain how that individual moves toward the end appropriate to members of that particular species. The ends to which men as members of such a species move are conceived by them as goods, and their movement towards or away from various goods are to be explained with reference to the virtues and vices which they have learned or failed to learn and the forms of practical reasoning which they employ. Aristotle's *Ethics* and *Politics* (together of course with the *De Anima*) are as much treatises concerned with how human action is to be explained and understood as with what acts are to be done. Indeed within the Aristotelian framework the one task cannot be discharged without discharging the other. The modern contrast between the sphere of morality on the one hand and the sphere of the human sciences on the other is quite alien to Aristotelianism because, as we have already seen, the modern fact-value distinction is also alien to it.

When in the seventeenth and eighteenth centuries the Aristotelian understanding of nature was repudiated, at the same time as Aristotle's influence had been expelled from both Protestant and Jansenist theology, the Aristotelian account of action was also rejected. 'Man' ceases, except within theology – and not always there – to be what I called earlier a functional concept. The explanation of action is increasingly held to be a matter of laying bare the physiological and physical mechanisms which underlie action; and, when Kant recognizes that there is a deep incompatibility between any account of action which recognizes the role of moral imperatives in governing action and any such mechanical type of explanation, he is compelled to the conclusion that actions obeying and embodying moral imperatives must be from the standpoint of science inexplicable and unintelligible. After Kant the question of the relationship between such notions as those of intention, purpose, reason for action and the like on the one hand and the concepts which specify the notion of mechanical explanation on the other becomes part of the permanent repertoire of philosophy. The former notions are however now treated as detached from notions of good or virtue; those concepts have been handed over to the separate subdiscipline of ethics. Thus the disjunctions and divorces of the eighteenth century perpetuate and reinforce themselves in contemporary curricular divisions.

But what is it to try to understand human action in mechanical terms, in terms that is of antecedent conditions understood as efficient causes? In the seventeenth and eighteenth century understanding of the matter – and in many subsequent versions – at the core of the notion of mechanical explanation is a conception of invariences specified by law-like generalizations. To cite a cause is to cite a necessary condition *or* a sufficient condition *or* a necessary and sufficient condition as the antecedent of whatever behavior is to be explained. So every mechanical causal sequence exemplifies some universal generalization and that generalization has a precisely specifiable scope. Newton's laws of motion which purport to be universal in scope provide the paradigm case of such a set of generalizations. Being universal they extend beyond what has actually been observed in the present or the past to what has escaped observation and to what has not yet been observed. If we know such a generalization to be true, we know not only that, for example, the hitherto observed planets do all obey Kepler's Second Law, but that if there were to be some planet other than those hitherto observed, it would also obey that law. If we know the truth of a statement expressing a genuine law, that is, we also know the truth of a set of well-defined counterfactual conditionals.

This ideal of mechanical explanation was transferred from physics to the understanding of human behavior by a number of English and French thinkers in the seventeenth and eighteenth centuries who differed a good deal among themselves over the details of their enterprise. And it was only somewhat later that the precise requirements that such an enterprise would have to meet could be spelled out. One such requirement, and a very important one, was identified only in our own time by W.V. Quine (1960, ch. 6).

Quine argued that if there is to be a science of human behavior whose key expressions characterize that behavior in terms precise enough to provide us with genuine laws, those expressions must be formulated in a vocabulary which omits all reference to intentions, purposes, and reasons for action. Just as physics, to become a genuine mechanical science, had to purify its descriptive vocabulary, so must the human sciences. What is it about intentions, purposes and reasons that makes them thus unmentionable? It is the fact that all these expressions refer to or presuppose reference to the beliefs of the agents in question. The discourse which we use to speak about beliefs has two great disadvantages from the point of view of what Quine takes to be a science. First sentences of the form 'X believes that p' (or for that matter, 'X enjoys its being the case that p' or 'X fears that p') have an internal complexity which is not truth-functional, which is to say that they cannot be mapped on to the predicate calculus; and in this they differ in a crucial respect from the sentences used to express the laws of physics. Secondly, the concept of a state or belief or enjoyment or fear involves too many contestable and doubtful cases to furnish the kind of evidence we need to confirm or disconfirm claims to have discovered a *law*.

Quine's conclusion is that therefore any genuine science of human behavior must eliminate such intentional expressions; but it is perhaps necessary to do to Quine what Marx did to Hegel, that is, to stand his argument on its head. For it follows from Quine's position that *if* it proved impossible to eliminate references to such items as beliefs and enjoyments and fears from our understanding of human behavior, that understanding could not take the form which Quine considers the form of human science, namely embodiment in law-like generalizations. An Aristotelian account of what is involved in understanding human behavior involves an in-eliminable reference to such items; and hence it is not surprising that any attempt to understand human behavior in terms of mechanical explanation must conflict with Aristotelianism.

The notion of 'fact' with respect to human beings is thus transformed in the transition from the Aristotelian to the mechanist view. On the former view human action, because it is to be explained teleologically, not only can, but must be, characterized with reference to the hierarchy of goods which provide the ends of human action. On the latter view human action not only can, but must be, characterized without any reference to such goods. On the former view the facts about human action include the facts about what is valuable to human beings (and *not* just the facts about what they think to be valuable); on the latter view there are no facts about what is valuable. 'Fact' becomes value-free, 'is' becomes a stranger to 'ought' and explanation, as well as evaluation, changes its character as a result of this divorce between 'is' and 'ought'.

Another implication of this transition was noted somewhat earlier, by Marx in the third of his *Theses on Feuerbach*. It is clear that the Enlighten-ment's mechanistic account of human action included both a thesis about the predictability of human behavior and a thesis about the appropriate ways to manipulate human behavior. As an observer, if I know the rele-vant laws governing the behavior of others, I can whenever I observe that the antecedent conditions have been fulfilled predict the outcome. As an agent, if I know these laws, I can whenever I can contrive the fulfilment of the same antecedent conditions produce the outcome. What Marx un-derstood was that such an agent is forced to regard his own actions quite differently from the behavior of those whom he is manipulating. For the behavior of the manipulated is being contrived in accordance with *his* in-tentions, reasons and purposes; intentions, reasons and purposes which he is treating, at least while he is engaged in such manipulation, as exempt from the laws which govern the behavior of the manipulated. To them he stands at least for the moment as the chemist does to the samples of po-tassium chloride and sodium nitrate with which he experiments; but in the chemical changes which the chemist or the technologist of human behavior brings about the chemist or the technologist must see exemplified not only the laws which govern such changes but the imprinting of his own will on nature or society. And that imprinting he will treat, as Marx saw, as the expression of his own rational autonomy and not the mere outcome of antecedent conditions. Of course the question remains open whether in the case of the agent who claims to be applying the science of human behavior we are genuinely observing the application of a real technology or rather instead the deceptive and self-deceptive histrionic mimicry of such a technology. Which it is depends upon whether we believe that the mechanistic programme for social science has or has not in fact been substantially achieved. And in the eighteenth century at least the notion of a mechanistic science of man remained programme and prophecy. But prophecies in this area may be translated *not* into real achievement, but into a social performance which disguises itself as such achievement. And this—as the argument which I develop in the next chapter will show—is what in fact happened.

The history of how intellectual prophecy became social performance is of course a complex one. It begins quite independently of the development of the concept of manipulative expertise with the story of how the modern state acquired its civil servants, a story that is not the same for Prussia as for France, and England differs yet again from both, and the United States from all three. But as the functions of modern states become more and more the same, their civil services come to be more and more the same too; and while their various political masters come and go, civil servants maintain the administrative continuity of government and thus confer on the government much of its character.

The civil servant has as his nineteenth-century counterpart and opposite the social reformer: Saint Simonians, Comtians, utilitarians, English ameliorists such as Charles Booth, the early Fabian socialists. *Their* characteristic lament is: if only government could learn to be scientific! And the long-term response of government is to claim that it has indeed become scientific in just the sense that the reformers required. Government insists more and more that its civil servants themselves have the kind of education that will qualify them as experts. It more and more recruits those who claim to be experts into its civil service. And it characteristically recruits too the heirs of the nineteenth-century reformers. Government itself becomes a hierarchy of bureaucratic managers, and the major justification advanced for the intervention of government in society is the contention that government has resources of competence which most citizens do not possess.

Private corporations similarly justify *their* activities by referring to their possession of similar resources of competence. Expertise becomes a commodity for which rival state agencies and rival private corporations compete. Civil servants and managers alike justify themselves and their claims to authority, power and money by invoking their own competence as scientific managers of social change. Thus there emerges an ideology which finds its classical form of expression in a pre-existing sociological theory, Weber's theory of bureaucracy. Weber's account of bureaucracy notoriously has many flaws. But in his insistence that the rationality of adjusting means to ends in the most economical and efficient way is the central task of the bureaucrat and that therefore the appropriate mode of justification of his activity by the bureaucrat lies in the appeal to his (or later her) ability to deploy a body of scientific and above all social scientific knowledge, organized in terms of and understood as comprising a set of universal lawlike generalizations, Weber provided the key to much of the modern age.

I argued in Chapter 3 that modern theories of bureaucracy or of administration which differ widely from Weber's at many other points tend on this issue of managerial justification to agree with him and that this consensus suggests strongly that what the books written by modern organization theorists describe is genuinely a part of modern managerial practice. So we can now see in bare skeletal outline a progress first from the Enlightenment's ideal for a social science to the aspirations of social reformers, next from the aspirations of social reformers to the ideals of practice and justification of civil servants and managers, then from the practices of management to the theoretical codification of these practices and of the norms governing them by sociologists and organization theorists and finally from the employment of the textbooks written by those theorists in schools of management and business schools to the theoretically informed managerial practice of the contemporary technocratic expert. If this history were to be written out in all its concrete detail, it would of course not be the same in each advanced country. The sequences would not be quite the same, the role of the Grandes Écoles is not precisely the same as either that of the London School of Economics or of the Harvard Business School, and the German civil servant's intellectual and institutional ancestry is notably different from that of some of his other European counterparts. But in every case the rise of managerial expertise would have to be the same central theme, and such expertise, as we have already seen, has two sides to it: there is the aspiration to value neutrality and the claim to manipulative power. Both of these, we can now perceive, derive from the history of the way in which the realm of fact and the realm of value were distinguished by the philosophers of the seventeenth and eighteenth centuries. Twentieth-century social life turns out in key part to be the concrete and dramatic re-enactment of eighteenth-century philosophy. And the legitimation of the characteristic institutional forms of twentieth-century social life depends upon a belief that some of the central claims of that earlier philosophy have been vindicated. But is this true? Do we now possess that set of law-like generalizations governing social behavior of the possession of which Diderot and Condorcet dreamed? Are our bureaucratic rulers thereby justified or not? It has not been sufficiently remarked that how we ought to answer the question of the moral and political legitimacy of the characteristically dominant institutions of modernity turns on how we decide an issue in the philosophy of the social sciences.

8

The Character
of Generalizations in Social Science
and their Lack of Predictive Power

What managerial expertise requires for its vindication is a justified conception of social science as providing a stock of law-like generalizations with strong predictive power. It might therefore seem at first sight that the claims of managerial expertise can be easily sustained. For just this conception of social science has dominated the philosophy of social science for two hundred years. According to this conventional account—from the Enlightenment through Comte and Mill to Hempel—the aim of the social sciences is to explain specifically social phenomena by supplying law-like generalizations which do not differ in their logical form from those applicable to natural phenomena in general, precisely the kind of law-like generalizations to which the managerial expert would have to appeal. This account however seems to entail—what is certainly not the case—that the social sciences are almost or perhaps completely devoid of achievement. For the salient fact about those sciences is the absence of the discovery of any law-like generalizations whatsoever.

It is of course true that the claim is occasionally made that at last a true law governing human behavior has been discovered; the only problem is that the alleged laws—the Phillips curve in economics for instance or G.C. Homan's 'If the interactions between the members of a group are frequent in the external system, sentiments of liking will grow up between them, and these sentiments will in turn lead to further interaction, over and above the interactions of the external system'—all turn out to be false and as Stanislav Andreski has trenchantly pointed out in the case of Homan's formulation so unquestionably false that no one but a professional social scientist dominated by the conventional philosophy of science would ever have been tempted to believe them. Given then that conventional philosophy of social science has asserted that the task of the social scientist is the production of law-like generalizations, and given further that social science does not produce generalizations of this kind, one might have expected a hostile and dismissive attitude on the part of many social scientists to the conventional philosophy of social science. Yet this has certainly not occurred, and I have identified one good reason for not being too surprised at this.

It is of course that if social science does not present its findings in the form of law-like generalizations, the grounds for employing social scientists as expert advisors to government or to private corporations become unclear and the very notion of managerial expertise is imperilled. For the central function of the social scientist as expert advisor or manager is to predict the outcomes of alternative policies, and if his predictions do not derive from a knowledge of law-like generalizations, the status of the social scientist as predictor becomes endangered — as, so it turns out, it ought to be; for the record of social scientists as predictors is very bad indeed, insofar as the record can be pieced together. No economist predicted 'stagflation' before it occurred, the writings of monetary theorists have signally failed to predict the rates of inflation correctly (Levy 1975) and D.J.C. Smyth and J.C.K. Ash have shown that the forecasts produced on the basis of the most sophisticated economic theory for OECD since 1967 have produced less successful predictions than would have been arrived at by using the commonsense, or as they say, naive methods of forecasting rates of growth by taking the average rate of growth for the last ten years as a guide or rates of inflation by assuming that the next six months will resemble the last six months (Smyth and Ash 1975). One could go on multiplying examples of the predictive ineptitude of economists, and with demography the situation has been even worse, but this would be grossly unfair; for economists and demographers have at least gone on record with their predictions in systematic fashion. But most sociologists and political scientists keep no systematic records of their predictions and those futurologists who scatter predictions lavishly around rarely, if ever, advert to their predictive failures afterward. Indeed in the notorious article by Karl Deutsch, John Platt and Dieter Senghors (*Science*, March 1971) where sixty-two alleged major social science achievements are listed it is impressive that in not a single case is the predictive power of the theories listed assessed in statistical terms — a wise precaution, given the authors' point of view.

That the social sciences are predictively weak *and* that they do not discover law-like generalizations may clearly turn out to be two symptoms of the same condition. But what is that condition? Ought we simply to conclude that predictive weakness reinforces the conclusion implied by the conjunction of the conventional philosophy of social science and the facts about what social scientists do and do not achieve; namely, that the social sciences have substantially failed at their task? Or ought we perhaps instead to question both the conventional philosophy of social science *and* the claim to expertise by social scientists who seek to hire themselves out to government and corporations? What I am suggesting is that the true achievements of the social sciences are being concealed from us—and from many social scientists themselves—by systematic misinterpretation. Consider for example four highly interesting generalizations that have been advanced by modern social scientists.

The first is James C. Davies's famous thesis (1962) which generalizes—to revolutions as a class—Tocqueville's observation that the French revolution occurred when a period of rising and to some degree gratified expectations was followed by a period of set-back when expectations continued to rise and were sharply disappointed. The second is Oscar Newman's generalization that the crime rate rises in high-rise buildings with the height of the building up to a height of thirteen floors, but at more than thirteen floors levels off (Newman 1973, p. 25). The third is Egon Bittner's discovery of the differences between the understanding of the import of law embodied in police work and the understanding of that same import embodied in the practice of courts and of lawyers (Bittner 1970). The fourth is the contention advanced by Rosalind and Ivo Feierabend (1966) that the most and least modernized societies are the most stable and least violent, whereas those at midpoint in the approach to modernity are most liable to instability and political violence.

All four of these generalizations rest on distinguished research; all are buttressed by an impressive set of confirming instances. But they share three notable characteristics. First of all, they all coexist in their disciplines with recognized counter-examples, and the recognition of these counter-examples—if not by the authors of the generalizations themselves, at least by colleagues at work in the same areas—does not seem to affect the standing of the generalizations in anything like the way in which it would affect the standing of generalizations in physics or chemistry. Some critics from outside the social scientific disciplines—the historian Walter Laqueur, for example (1972)—have treated these counter-examples as affording reasons for dismissing both such generalizations and the disciplines that are so lax as to allow generalizations and counter-examples to coexist. So Laqueur has cited the Russian revolution of 1917 and the Chinese of 1949 as examples *refuting* Davis's generalization and the patterns of political violence in Latin America as *refuting* the Feierabends' claim. For the moment all I want to note is that social scientists themselves characteristically and for the most part do in fact adopt just such a tolerant attitude to counter-examples, an attitude very different from that of either natural scientists themselves or of Popperian philosophers of science and to leave open the question of whether their attitude might not after all be justified.

A second characteristic, closely linked to the first, of all four generalizations is that they lack not only universal quantifiers but also scope
modifiers. That is, they are not only not genuinely of the form 'For all x
and some y if x has property ϕ, then y has property ψ', but we cannot
say of them in any precise way under what conditions they hold. Of the
gas law equations relating pressure, temperature and volume we know not
only that they hold of all gases; but the original formulation whereby they
were held to hold under all conditions has since been revised to modify
their scope. We now know that they hold for all gases under all conditions
except those *of very low temperature and very high pressure* (where we can
say exactly what we mean by 'very high' and 'very low'). None of our four
social scientific generalizations is presented with such clauses attached.

Thirdly, these generalizations do not entail any well-defined set of
counterfactual conditionals in the way that the law-like generalizations of
physics and chemistry do. We do not know how to apply them systematically beyond the limits of observation to unobserved or hypothetical instances. Thus they are not laws, whatever else they may be. What then
is their status? To respond to this question is not going to be easy, because
we do not possess any philosophical account of them which respects them
for what they are, rather than treating them as failed attempts at the formulation of laws. Some social scientists, it is true, have seen no problem
here. Confronted with the kind of consideration which I have adduced
they have thought it appropriate to reply: 'What the social sciences discover are probabilistic generalizations; and where a generalization is only
probabilistic of course there can be cases which would be counter-examples
if the generalization was non-probabilistic and universal.' But this reply
misses the point completely. For if the type of generalization which I have
cited is to be a generalization at all, it must be something more than a mere
list of instances. The probabilistic generalizations of natural science—those,
say, of statistical mechanics—are indeed more than this precisely because
they are as law-like as any non-probabilistic generalizations. They possess
universal quantifiers—quantification is over sets, not over individuals—they
entail well-defined sets of counter-factual conditionals and they are refuted
by counter-examples in precisely the same way and to the same degree that
other law-like generalizations are. Hence we throw no light on the status
of the characteristic generalizations of the social sciences by calling them
probabilistic; for they are as different from the generalizations of statistical
mechanics as they are from the generalizations of Newtonian mechanics
or of the gas law equations.

We therefore have to start out afresh and in so doing to consider
whether the social sciences may not have looked in the wrong place for

their philosophical ancestry as well as for their logical structure. It is because modern social scientists have seen themselves as the successors of Comte and Mill and Buckle, of Helvétuis and Diderot and Condorcet, that they have presented their writings as attempted answers to the questions of their eighteenth- and nineteenth-century masters. But let us suppose once again that the eighteenth and nineteenth centuries, brilliant and creative as they were, were in fact centuries not as we and they take them to be of Enlightenment, but of a peculiar kind of darkness in which men so dazzled themselves that they could no longer see and ask whether the social sciences might not have an alternative ancestry.

The name which I wish to invoke is that of Machiavelli, for Machiavelli takes a very different view of the relationship between explanation and prediction from that taken by the Enlightenment. The thinkers of the Enlightenment were infant Hempelians. To explain is on their view to invoke a law-like generalization retrospectively; to predict is to invoke a similar generalization prospectively. For this tradition the diminution of predictive failure is the mark of progress in science; and those social scientists who have espoused it must face the fact that if they are right at some point an unpredicted war or revolution will become as disgraceful for a political scientist, an unpredicted change in the rate in inflation as disgraceful for an economist, as would an unpredicted eclipse for an astronomer. That this has not occurred yet has itself to be explained within this tradition and explanations have not been lacking: the human sciences are still young sciences, it is said—but clearly falsely. They are in fact as old as the natural sciences. Or it is said that the natural sciences attract the most able individuals in modern culture and the social sciences only those not able enough to do natural science—this was the claim of H.T. Buckle in the nineteenth century and there is some evidence that it is still partly true. A 1960 study of the I.Q.s of those completing Ph.D. requirements in various disciplines showed that natural scientists *are* significantly more intelligent than social scientists (although chemists drag down the natural science averages and economists raise the social science average). But the same reasons that make me reluctant to judge deprived minority children by their I.Q. scores make me equally reluctant to judge my colleagues by them—or myself. Yet perhaps explanations are not needed, for perhaps the failure that the dominant tradition tries to explain is like King Charles II's dead fish. Charles II once invited the members of the Royal Society to explain to him why a dead fish weighs more than the same fish alive; a number of subtle explanations were offered to him. He then pointed out that it does not.

Wherein does Machiavelli differ from the Enlightenment tradition? Above all in his concept of *Fortuna*. Machiavelli certainly believed as passionately as any thinker of the Enlightenment that our investigations should issue in generalizations which may furnish maxims for enlightened practice. But he also believed that no matter how good a stock of generalizations one amassed and no matter how well one reformulated them, the factor of *Fortuna* was ineliminable from human life. Machiavelli also believed that we might be able to contrive a quantitative measure of *Fortuna*'s influence in human affairs; but this belief for the moment I shall set on one side. What I want to emphasize is Machiavelli's belief that, given the best possible stock of generalizations, we may on the day be defeated by an unpredicted and unpredictable counter-example—and yet still see no way to improve upon our generalizations and still have no reason to abandon them or even to reformulate them. We can by improvements in our knowledge limit the sovereignty of *Fortuna*, bitch-goddess of unpredictability; we cannot dethrone her. If Machiavelli was right, the logical condition of the four generalizations which we inspected would be that which we could expect to hold for the most successful generalizations of the social sciences; it would in no way be a mark of failure. But was he right?

I want to argue that there are four sources of systematic unpredictability in human affairs. The first derives from the nature of radical conceptual innovation. Sir Karl Popper suggested the following example. Some time in the Old Stone Age you and I are discussing the future and I predict that within the next ten years someone will invent the wheel. 'Wheel?' you ask. 'What is that?' I then describe the wheel to you, finding words, doubtless with difficulty, for the very first time to say what a rim, spokes, a hub and perhaps an axle will be. Then I pause, aghast. 'But no one can be *going to* invent the wheel, for I have just invented it.' In other words, the invention of the wheel cannot be predicted. For a necessary part of predicting an invention is to say what a wheel is; and to say what a wheel is just *is* to invent it. It is easy to see how this example can be generalized. Any invention, any discovery, which consists essentially in the elaboration of a radically new concept cannot be predicted, for a necessary part of the prediction is the present elaboration of the very concept whose discovery or invention was to take place only in the future. The notion of the prediction of radical conceptual innovation is itself conceptually incoherent.

Why do I say 'radically new' rather than just 'new'? Consider the following objection to this thesis. Many inventions and discoveries have in fact been predicted and these predictions have involved new concepts. Jules Verne predicted lighter-than-air flying machines and so long before him did the anonymous author of the myth of Icarus. Whoever may have been the first predictor of human flight, it may be thought that he or she certainly provides a counter-example to my thesis. In the face of this rejoinder two points must be made.

The first is that for anyone familiar with the concepts of a bird or even a pterodactyl and a machine the concept of a flying machine involves no radical innovation; it is merely an additive construction from the existing stock of concepts—new, if you like, but not radically new. By saying this I hope that I make the point of saying 'radically new' or 'radically innovative' clear and that I also make it clear that what was alleged to be a counter-example is not in fact one. The second point is that although Jules Verne may be said to have predicted the invention of aeroplanes or submarines, this is in the same sense of the word as those in which Mother Shipton too may be said to have predicted the invention of aeroplanes in the early sixteenth century. But my present thesis is concerned not with mere foretelling but with rationally grounded prediction, and it is the systematic limitations on such prediction with which I am concerned.

What is important about the systematic unpredictability of radical conceptual innovation is of course the consequent unpredictability of the future of science. Physicists are able to tell us a good deal about the future of nature in such areas as thermodynamics; but they are able to tell us nothing about the future of physics insofar as that future involves radical conceptual innovation. Yet it is the future of physics which we need to know about if we are to know about the future of our own physics-based society.

The conclusion that we cannot predict the future of physics is also supported by another argument, independent of Popper's. Suppose that someone were to improve computing hardware and software, so that it became possible to write a program which would enable a computer to predict, on the basis of information about the present state of mathematics, the past history of mathematics and the talents and energies of present day mathematicians, which well-formed formulas in a given branch of mathematics—algebraic topology, say, or number theory—for which at the present we possess neither a proof nor a proof of their negation would receive such a proof within ten years. (We are not requiring that the computer identify all such well-formed formulas, but only some of them.) Such a program would have to embody a decision procedure whereby a sub-set of well-formed formulas, provable but not yet proven, were discriminated from the set of well-formed formulas. But Church has provided us with the strongest reasons for believing that for any calculus rich enough to express arithmetic, let alone algebraic topology or number theory, there can be no such decision procedure. Hence it is a truth of logic that no such computer program will ever be written and more generally therefore it is a truth of logic that the future of mathematics is unpredictable. But if the future of mathematics is unpredictable, so is a great deal else.

Consider just one example. It follows from the preceding argument that before Turing proved the theorem which underlies a good deal of modern computing science in the nineteen-thirties, its proof could not have been rationally predicted (unless we count Babbage as a precursor of Turing— but this would not affect the conceptual point). From this it follows that such subsequent scientific and technological work on computing machines as depends on the possession of that proof could not have been predicted either; but it is just that work which has shaped so many of our lives.

It is of course worth noting that Popper's argument holds of *any* area in which radical conceptual innovation takes place and not just natural science. What made the discoveries of quantum mechanics or special relativity unpredictable before they occurred also made unpredictable for precisely the same reasons the invention of the genre of tragedy at Athens in the late sixth century B.C. or the first preaching of Luther's distinctive doctrine of justification *fide sola* or the first elaboration of Kant's theory of knowledge. The striking implications for social life in general are clear.

It is also clear that nothing in these arguments entails that discovery or radical innovation are *inexplicable*. Particular discoveries or innovations may always be explained after the event—although it is not entirely clear what such an explanation would be and whether there are any. Explanations of the incidence of discovery and innovation in particular periods are however not only possible, but for some types of discovery well-established on the basis of work which goes back to Francis Galton (see de Solla Price 1963). And this coexistence of unpredictability and explicability holds not just for the first type of systematic unpredictability, but for three others.

The second type of systematic unpredictability to which I now turn is that which derives from the way in which the unpredictability of certain of his own future actions by each agent individually generates another element of unpredictability as such in the social world. It is at first sight a trivial truth that when I have not yet made up my mind which of two or more alternative and mutually exclusive courses of action to take I cannot predict which I shall take. Decisions contemplated but not yet made by me entail unpredictability of me by me in the relevant areas. But this truth seems trivial precisely because what I cannot predict of myself others may well be able to predict about me. My own future from my point of view may be representable only as a set of ramifying alternatives with each node in the branching system representing a point of as yet unmade decision-making. But from the point of view of an adequately informed observer provided both with the relevant data about me and the relevant stock of generalizations concerning people of my type, my future, so it seems, may be representable as an entirely determinable set of stages. Yet a difficulty at once arises. For this observer who is able to predict what I cannot is of course unable to predict his own future in just the way that I am unable to predict mine; and one of the features which he will be unable to predict, since it depends in substantial part upon decisions as yet unmade by him, is how far his actions will impact upon and change the decisions made by others—both what alternatives they will choose and what sets of alternatives will be offered to them for choice. Now among those others is me. It follows that insofar as the observer cannot predict the impact of his future actions on my future decision-making, he cannot predict my future actions any more than he can his own; and this clearly holds for all agents and all observers. The unpredictability of my future by me does indeed generate an inportant degree of unpredictability as such.

Someone of course might challenge one premise of my argument, what I described as the apparently trivial truth that where my future actions depend on the outcome of decisions as yet unmade by me I cannot predict those actions. Consider a possible counter-example. I am a chess-player and so is my identical twin. I know from experience that in end-games, given the same situation on the board, we always make the same moves. I am puzzling over whether to move my knight or my bishop in an end-game situation when someone says to me, 'Yesterday your brother was in the same situation.' I can now predict that I will make the same move that my brother made. So surely here is a case of my being able to predict a future action of mine which depends upon an as yet unmade decision. But what is crucial is that I can only predict my action under the description 'the same move as that which my brother made yesterday' but not under either of the descriptions 'move the knight' or 'move the bishop'. What this counter-example leads to therefore is a reformulation of the premise: I cannot predict my own future actions so far as these depend upon decisions as yet unmade by me—under the descriptions which characterize the alternatives defining the decision. And the premise thus reworded yields the corresponding conclusion about unpredictability as such.

Another way of putting the same point would be to note that omniscience excludes the making of decisions. If God knows everything that will occur, he confronts no as yet unmade decision. He has a single will (*Summa Contra Gentiles*, cap. LXXIX, *Quod Deus Vult Etiam Ea Quae Nondum Sunt*). It is precisely insofar as we differ from God that unpredictability invades our lives. This way of putting the point has one particular merit: it suggests precisely what project those who seek to eliminate unpredictability from the social world or to deny it may in fact be engaging in.

A third source of systematic unpredictability arises from the game-theoretic character of social life. To some theorists in political science the formal structures of game theory have served to provide a possible basis for explanatory and predictive theory incorporating law-like generalizations. Take the formal structure of an *n*-person game, identify the relevant interests of the players in some empirical situation and we shall at the very least be able to predict what alliances and coalitions a fully rational player will enter into and, at a perhaps Utopian most, the pressures upon and the subsequent behavior of not fully rational players. This recipe and its criticism have inspired some notable work (especially that of William H. Riker). But the large hope that it embodied in its original optimistic form seems to be illusory. Consider three types of obstacle to the transfer of the formal structures of game theory to the interpretation of actual social and political situations.

The first concerns the indefinite reflexivity of game-theoretic situations. I am trying to predict what move you will make; in order to predict this I must predict what you will predict as to what move I will make; and in order to predict this I must predict what you will predict about what I will predict about what you will predict . . . and so on. At each stage each of us will simultaneously be trying to render himself or herself unpredictable by the other; and each of us will also be relying on the knowledge that the other will be trying to make himself or herself unpredictable in forming his or her own predictions. Here the formal structures of the situation can never be an adequate guide. A knowledge of them may be necessary, but even a knowledge of them backed by a knowledge of each player's interest cannot tell us what the simultaneous attempt to render others predictable and oneself unpredictable will produce.

This first type of obstacle may not by itself be insuperable. The chances that it will be are however heightened by the existence of a second type of obstacle. Game-theoretic situations are characteristically situations of imperfect knowledge, and this is no accident. For it is a major interest of each actor to maximize the imperfection of the information of certain other actors at the same time as he improves his own. Moreover a condition of success at misinforming other actors is likely to be the successful production of false impressions in external observers too. This leads to an interesting inversion of Collingwood's odd thesis that we can only hope to understand the actions of the victorious and the successful, while those of the defeated must remain opaque to us. But if I am right the conditions of success include the ability to deceive successfully and hence it is the defeated whom we are more likely to be able to understand and it is those who are going to be defeated whose behavior we are more likely to be able to predict.

Once again this second type of obstacle need not be insuperable, even in conjunction with the first. But there is yet a third type of obstacle to prediction in game-theoretic situations. Consider the following familiar type of situation. The management of a major industry are negotiating the terms of the next long-term contract with the labor union leadership. Representatives of the government are present, not only in an arbitrating and mediating role, but because the government has a particular interest in the industry—its products are crucial for defence, say, or it is an industry which powerfully affects the rest of the economy. At first sight it ought to be easy to map this situation in game-theoretic terms: three collective players each with a distinctive interest. But now let us introduce some of those features that so often make social reality so messy and untidy in contrast with the neat examples in the text-books.

Some of the union leadership are approaching the time when they are going to retire from their posts in the union. If they cannot obtain relatively highly paid jobs with either the employers or the government, they may have to return to the shop floor. The employers are not only concerned with government in its present public interest capacity; they have a longer-term concern with obtaining a different type of government contract. One of the representatives of government is considering running for elected office in a district where the labor vote is crucial. That is to say, in any given social situation it is frequently the case that many different transactions are taking place at one and the same time between members of the same group. Not one game is being played, but several, and, if the game metaphor may be stretched further, the problem about real life is that moving one's knight to QB3 may always be replied to with a lob across the net.

Even when we can identify with some certainty what game is being played, there is another problem. In real life situations, unlike both games and the examples in books about game-theory, we often do not start with a determinate set of players and pieces or a determinate area in which the game is to take place. There is—or perhaps used to be—on the market a cardboard and plastic version of the battle of Gettysburg which reproduces with great accuracy the terrain, the chronology and the units involved in that battle. It had this peculiarity, that a moderately good player taking the Confederate side can win. Yet clearly no player of war games is likely to be as intelligent at generalship as Lee was, and he lost. Why? The answer of course is that the player knows from the outset what Lee did not—what the time scale of the preliminary stages of the battle must be, precisely what units are going to get involved, what the limits to the terrain are on which the battle is to be fought. And all this entails that the game does *not* reproduce Lee's situation. For Lee did not and could not know that it was the *Battle of Gettysburg*—an episode on which a determinate shape was conferred only retrospectively by its outcome—which was about to be fought. Failure to realize this affects the predictive power of many computer simulations which seek to transfer analyses of past determinate situations to the prediction of future indeterminate ones. Consider one example from the Vietnam war.

Using Lewis F. Richardson's analysis (1960) of the Anglo-German naval race in the years before 1914 Jeffrey S. Milstein and William Charles Mitchell (1968) constructed a simulation of the Vietnam War which embodied some of Richardson's generalizations. Their predictions failed in two ways. First they relied on official U.S. figures for their statistics about such matters as Vietcong killing of civilians or numbers of Vietcong defectors. Perhaps in 1968 they could not have known what we know now about the systematic falsification of numbers by the American military in Vietnam. But had they been sensitive in any way to that need of players to maximize the imperfection of information of which I wrote earlier they would not have treated the confirming instances of their predictions so confidently. What is striking however is their response to their second source of failure, one which they do note themselves: their predictions were radically upset by the Tet offensive. The response of Milstein and Mitchell is to speculate as to how future studies might be extended so that the factors which led to the Tet offensive might be included. What they ignore is the necessarily open and indeterminate character of all situations as complex as the Vietnam war. There is at the outset no determinate, enumerable set of factors, the totality of which comprise the situation. To suppose otherwise is to confuse a retrospective standpoint with a prospective one. To say this is not at all the same as saying that all computer simulation is valueless; but what simulation cannot evade are the systematic sources of unpredictability.

I turn now to the fourth such source: pure contingency. J.B. Bury once followed Pascal in suggesting that the cause of the foundation of the Roman Empire was the length of Cleopatra's nose: had her features not been perfectly proportioned, Mark Antony would not have been entranced; had he not been entranced he would not have allied himself with Egypt against Octavian; had he not made that alliance, the battle of Actium would not have been fought—and so on. One does not need to accept

Bury's argument to see that trivial contingencies can powerfully influence the outcome of great events: the molehill which killed William III or Napoleon's cold at Waterloo which led him to delegate command to Ney, who in turn had four horses shot from under him that day, which led to faults in judgment, most notably in sending in the *Garde Impériale* two hours too late. There is no way in which all such contingencies as moles and bacteria provide can be allowed for in battle plans.

We have then four independent but often related sources of systematic unpredictability in human life. It is important to emphasize that not only does unpredictability not entail inexplicability, but that its presence is compatible with the truth of determinism in a strong version. Suppose we are able at some future date – and I see no reason why this should not be so – to build and to program computers which are able to simulate wide ranges of human behavior. They are mobile; they acquire, exchange and reflect upon information; they have competitive as well as cooperative goals; they make decisions between alternative courses of action. It is important to recognize that such computers would simultaneously be completely specified mechanical and electronic systems of a determinate kind and yet would be liable to all four types of unpredictability. All of them would be unable to predict radical conceptual innovation or future proofs in mathematics, for precisely the same reasons that we are unable to. All of them would be unable to predict the outcome of their own as yet unmade decisions. Each of them would be involved in its relations to other computers in the same types of game-theoretic tangle which entrap us. And all of them would be vulnerable to external contingencies – power failures, for example. Yet each particular movement of and in each computer would be wholly explicable in mechanical or electronic terms.

It follows that the description of their behavior at the level of activity – in terms of decisions, relationships, goals and the like – would be very different in its logical and conceptual structures from the description of behavior at the level of electrical impulses. It would be difficult to give the notion of reducing the one mode of description to the other any clear sense; and if this is true of these imaginary, but possible computers, it seems likely to be true of us too. (It does indeed seem likely that we *are* these computers.)

It is at this point that someone may want to query the status of the whole argument so far. It may be suggested that there is an internal incoherence in my contentions. For on the one hand I have asserted that we cannot predict radical conceptual innovation, while on the other I have asserted that there are systematic and permanently unpredictable elements in human life. But surely the first of these assertions entails that I cannot know that tomorrow or next year some genius will not produce an innovative theory which will enable us to predict what will turn out to have been merely so far unpredictable, but not unpredictable as such. On my own terms, it may be argued, it must remain unpredictable by me whether the future will not turn out to be fully predictable after all. Or the point may be put in another way: it may be asked, have you shown that certain matters are necessarily and in principle unpredictable or merely that as a matter of contingent fact they are unpredictable?

Now certainly I have not claimed that the prediction of the human future is *logically impossible* in three of the four areas which I have picked out. And in the case of the argument which uses as a premise a corollary to Church's theorem I have selected a premise in an area of some logical controversy — even though I believe it to be entirely soundly based. Am I then vulnerable to the charge that what is today unpredictable may tomorrow become predictable? I think not. In *philosophy* there are in fact very few and perhaps no valid logical impossibility or *reductio ad absurdum* proofs. The reason for this is that to produce such a proof we need to be able to map the relevant parts of our discourse on to a formal calculus in such a way as to enable us to move from given formula 'q' to a consequence of the form '$p.\sim p$' and thence as a further consequence to '$\sim q$'. But the kind of clarity that is required to formalize our discourse in this way is characteristically precisely what eludes us in areas where philosophical problems arise. Hence what are treated as *reductio ad absurdum* proofs are often arguments of quite another kind.

Wittgenstein, for example, has sometimes been interpreted as trying to offer a proof of the logical impossibility of a private language, conjoining an analysis of the notion of language as essentially teachable and public and an account of the notion of inner states as essentially private in order to show that a contradiction is involved in speaking of a private language. But such an interpretation misconstrues Wittgenstein who, I take it, was saying to us something like this: on the best account of language that I can give and the best account of inner mental states that I can give, I can make nothing of the notion of a private language, I cannot render it adequately intelligible.

Just this is my own response to the suggestion that perhaps some genuis might render what is now unpredictable predictable. I have offered no proof to bar the way to this; I do not even view the introduction of Church's thesis into the argument as contributing to any such proof. It is just that, given the type of consideration which I have been able to adduce,

I can make nothing of the proposal. I cannot render it adequately intelligible either to assent to it or dissent from it.

Given then that there are these unpredictable elements in social life, it is crucial to notice their intimate relationship to the predictable elements. What are the predictable elements? They are of at least four kinds. The first arises from the necessity of scheduling and coordinating our social actions. In every culture most people most of the time structure their activities in terms of some notion of a normal day. They get up at roughly the same time each day, dress and wash or fail to wash, eat meals at set times, go to work and return from work at set times and so on. Those who prepare the food have to be able to expect those who eat to appear in particular times and particular places; the secretary who picks up the telephone in one office has to be able to expect the secretary in another office to answer it; the bus and train must meet the travellers at prearranged points. We all have a great deal of tacit, unspelled-out knowledge of the predictable expectations of others as well as a large stock of explicitly-stored information. Thomas Schelling in a famous experiment told a group of a hundred subjects that they had the task of meeting an unknown person in Manhattan on a given date. The only other fact they knew about the unknown person was that he knew everything that they knew. What they had to supply was the time and place for the encounter. More than eighty of them selected the spot under the large clock in the Concourse of Grand Central Station at twelve noon; and precisely because over eighty per cent gave this answer it is the right answer. What Schelling's experiment suggests is that we all know more about what other people's expectations about our expectations are—and vice versa—than we usually recognize.

A second source of systematic predictability in human behavior arises from statistical regularities. We know that we all tend to catch more colds in winter, that the suicide rate rises sharply around Christmas, that multiplying the number of qualified scientists at work on a well-defined problem increases the probability that it will be solved sooner rather than later, that Irishmen are more likely than Danes to be mentally ill, that the best indicator of how a man will vote in Britain is how his best friend votes, that your wife or husband is more likely to murder you than a criminal stranger, and that everything in Texas tends to be bigger including the homicide rates. What is interesting about this knowledge is its relative independence of causal knowledge.

No one knows the causes of some of these phenomena and about others many of us actually have false causal beliefs. Just as unpredictability does not entail inexplicability, so predictability does not entail explicability.

Knowledge of statistical regularities plays as important a part in our elaboration and carrying out of plans and projects as does knowledge of scheduling and coordinated expectations. Lacking either we would not be able to make rational choices between alternative plans in terms of their chances of success and failure. This is also true of the two other sources of predictability in social life. The first of these is the knowledge of the causal regularities of nature: snowstorms, earthquakes, plague bacilli, height, malnutrition and the properties of protein all place constraints on human possibility. The second is the knowledge of causal regularities in social life. Although the status of the generalizations which express such knowledge is in fact the object of my enquiry, that there are such generalizations and that they do have some predictive power is after all quite clear. An example to add to the fourth that I gave earlier would be the generalization that in societies such as Britain and Germany in the nineteenth and twentieth centuries by and large one's place in the class structure determined one's educational opportunities. Here I am talking about genuine causal knowledge and not mere knowledge of statistical regularity.

We now are at last in a position to approach the question of the relationship of predictability to unpredictability in social life with a view to casting some positive light on the status of the generalizations of the social sciences. It is at once clear that many of the central features of human life derive from the particular and peculiar ways in which predictability and unpredictability interlock. It is the degree of predictability which our social structures possess which enables us to plan and engage in long-term projects; and the ability to plan and to engage in long-term projects is a necessary condition of being able to find life meaningful. A life lived from moment to moment, from episode to episode, unconnected by threads of large-scale intention, would lack the basis for many characteristically human institutions: marriage, war, the remembrance of the lives of the dead, the carrying on of families, cities and services through generations and so on. But the pervasive unpredictability in human life also renders all our plans and projects permanently vulnerable and fragile.

Vulnerability and fragility have other sources too of course, among them the character of the material environment and our ignorance. But the thinkers of the Enlightenment and their nineteenth- and twentieth-century heirs saw these as the sole or at any rate the main sources of vulnerability and fragility. The Marxists added economic competitiveness and ideological blindness. All of them wrote as though fragility and vulnerability could be overcome in some progressive future. And it is now possible to identify the link between this belief and their philosophy of science. The latter with its view of explanation and prediction played a central role in sustaining the former. But with us the argument now has to move in the other direction.

Each of us, individually and as a member of particular social groups, seeks to embody his own plans and projects in the natural and social world. A condition of achieving this is to render as much of our natural and social environment as possible predictable and the importance of both natural and social science in our lives derives at least in part—although only in part—from their contribution to this project. At the same time each of us, individually and as a member of particular social groups, aspires to preserve his independence, his freedom, his creativity, and that inner reflection which plays so great a part in freedom and creativity, from invasion by others. We wish to disclose of ourselves no more than we think right and nobody wishes to disclose all of himself—except perhaps under the influence of some psycho-analytic illusion. We need to remain to some degree *opaque and unpredictable*, particularly when threatened by the predictive practices of others. The satisfaction of this need to at least some degree supplies another necessary condition for human life being meaningful in the ways that it is and can be. It is necessary, if life is to be meaningful, for us to be able to engage in long-term projects, and this requires predictability; it is necessary, if life is to be meaningful, for us to be in possession of ourselves and not merely to be the creations of other people's projects, intentions and desires, and this requires unpredictability. We are thus involved in a world in which we are simultaneously trying to render the rest of society predictable and ourselves unpredictable, to devise generalizations which will capture the behavior of others and to cast our own behavior into forms which will elude the generalizations which others frame. If these are general features of social life, what will be the characteristics of the best possible available stock of generalizations about social life?

It seems probable that they will have three important characteristics. They will be based on a good deal of research, but their inductively-founded character will appear in their failure to approach law-likeness. No matter how well-framed they are the best of them may have to coexist with counter-examples, since the constant creation of counter-examples is a feature of human life. And we shall never be able to say of the best of them precisely what their scope is. It follows of course that they will not entail well-defined sets of counterfactual conditionals. They will be prefaced not by universal quantifiers but by some such phrase as 'Characteristically and for the most part . . .'.

But just these, as I pointed out earlier, turned out to be the characteristics of the generalizations which actual empirical social scientists claim with good reason to have discovered. In other words the logical form of these generalizations—or the lack of it—turns out to be rooted in the form—or lack of it—of human life. We should not be surprised or disappointed that the generalizations and maxims of the best social science share certain characteristics of their predecessors—the proverbs of folk societies, the generalizations of jurists, the maxims of Machiavelli. And it is indeed to Machiavelli that we can now return.

What the argument shows is that *Fortuna* is ineliminable. But this does not mean that we cannot say some more about her in at least two respects. The first concerns the possibility of a measure of *Fortuna*. One of the problems created by the conventional philosophy of science is that it suggests to scientists in general and social scientists in particular that they should treat predictive error merely as a form of failure, except when some crucial question of falsification arises. If instead we kept careful records of error, and made of error itself a topic for research, my guess is that we should discover that predictive error is not randomly distributed. To learn whether this is so or not would be a first step to doing more than I have done in this chapter; that is, to talking about the specific parts played by *Fortuna* in different areas of human life rather than merely about the general role of *Fortuna* in all human life.

The second aspect of *Fortuna* which requires comment concerns its permanence. I earlier disclaimed the status of proof for my arguments; how then can I have grounds for believing in the permanence of *Fortuna*? My reasons are partly empirical. For suppose that someone were to accept the argument so far and to agree in the identification of the four systematic sources of unpredictability, but was then to propose that we try to eliminate or at least to limit as far as possible the part that these sources of unpredictability play in social life. He proposes to prevent as far as possible the occurrence of situations in which conceptual innovation, or the unforeseen consequences of unmade decisions, or the game-theoretic character of human life or pure contingency can disrupt the predictions already made, the regularities already identified. Could such a man achieve his goal? Could he render a now-unpredictable social world wholly or largely predictable?

Clearly his first step would have to be the creation of an organization to provide an instrument for his project and equally clearly his first task would have to be to render the activity of his own organization wholly or largely predictable. For if he were unable to achieve this, he could scarcely achieve his larger goal. But he would also have to render his organization efficient and effective, capable of dealing with its highly original task and of surviving in the very environment which it is committed to changing. Unfortunately these two characteristics, total or near total predictability on the one hand and organizational effectiveness on the other, turn out on the basis of the best empirical studies we have to be incompatible. Defining the conditions of effectiveness in an environment that requires innovative adaptation Tom Burns has listed such characteristics as 'continual redefinition of individual task', 'communication which consists of information and advice rather than instructions and decisions', 'knowledge may be located anywhere in the network' and so on (Burns 1963 and Burns and Stalker 1968). One can safely generalize what Burns and Stalker say about the need to allow for individual initiative, a flexible response to changes in knowledge, the multiplication of centres of problem-solving and decision-making as adding up to the thesis that an effective organization has to be able to tolerate a high degree of unpredictability within itself. Other studies confirm this. Attempts to monitor what every subordinate is doing all the time tend to be counter-productive; attempts to make the activity of others predictable necessarily routinize, suppress intelligence and flexibility and turn the energies of subordinates to frustrating the projects of at least some of their superiors (Kaufman 1973, and see also Burns and Stalker on the effects of attempts to subvert and circumvent managerial hierarchies).

Since organizational success and organizational predictability exclude one another, the project of creating a wholly or largely predictable organization committed to creating a wholly or largely predictable society is doomed and doomed by the facts about social life. Totalitarianism of a certain kind, as imagined by Aldous Huxley or George Orwell, is therefore impossible. What the totalitarian project will always produce will be a kind of rigidity and inefficiency which may contribute in the long run to its defeat. We need to remember however the voices from Auschwitz and Gulag Archipelago which tell us just how long that long run is.

There is then nothing paradoxical in offering a prediction, vulnerable in the way that all social predictions are, about the permanent unpredictability of human life. Underlying that prediction is a vindication of the practice and of the findings of empirical social science and a rebuttal of what has been the dominant ideology of much social science as well as of the conventional philosophy of social science.

But that rebuttal entails also a large rejection of the claims of what I called bureaucratic managerial expertise. And with this rejection one part of my argument at least has been completed. The expert's claim to status and reward is fatally undermined when we recognize that he possesses no sound stock of law-like generalizations and when we realize how weak the predictive power available to him is. The concept of managerial effectiveness is after all one more contemporary moral fiction and perhaps the most important of them all. The dominance of the manipulative mode in our culture is not and cannot be accompanied by very much actual success in manipulation. I do not of course mean that the activities of purported experts do not have effects and that we do not suffer from those effects and suffer gravely. But the notion of social control embodied in the notion of expertise is indeed a masquerade. Our social order is in a very literal sense out of our, and indeed anyone's, control. No one is or could be in charge.

Belief in managerial expertise *is* then, on the view that I have taken, very like what belief in God was thought to be by Carnap and Ayer. It is one more illusion and a peculiarly modern one, the illusion of a power not ourselves that claims to make for righteousness. Hence the manager as *character* is other than he at first sight seems to be: the social world of everyday hard-headed practical pragmatic no-nonsense realism which is the environment of management is one which depends for its sustained existence on the systematic perpetuation of misunderstanding and of belief in fictions. The fetishism of commodities has been supplemented by another just as important fetishism, that of bureaucratic skills. For it follows from my whole argument that the realm of managerial expertise is one in which what purport to be objectively-grounded claims function in fact as expressions of arbitrary, but disguised, will and preference. Keynes's description of how Moore's disciples advanced their private preferences under the cover of identifying the presence or absence of a non-rational property of goodness, a property which was in fact a fiction, deserves a contemporary sequel in the form of an equally elegant and telling description of how in the social world of corporations and governments private preferences are advanced under the cover of identifying the presence or absence of the findings of experts. And just as the Keynesian description suggested why emotivism is so convincing a thesis, so would such a modern sequel. The effects of eighteenth-century prophecy have been to produce *not* scientifically managed social control, but a skillful dramatic imitation of such control. It is histrionic success which gives power and authority in our culture. The most effective bureaucrat is the best actor.

To this many managers and many bureaucrats will reply: you are attacking a straw man of your own construction. We make no large claims, Weberian or otherwise. We are as keenly aware of the limitations of social scientific generalizations as you are. We perform a modest function with a modest and unpretentious competence. But we do have specialized knowledge, we are entitled in our own limited fields to be called experts.

Nothing in my argument impugns these modest claims; but it is not claims of this kind which achieve power and authority either within or for bureaucratic corporations, whether public or private. For claims of this modest kind could never legitimate the possession or the uses of power either within or by bureaucratic corporations in anything like the way or on anything like the scale on which that power is wielded. So the modest and unpretentious claims embodied in this reply to my argument may themselves be highly misleading, as much to those who utter them as to anyone else. For they seem to function not as a rebuttal of my argument that a metaphysical belief in managerial expertise has been institutionalized in our corporations, but as an excuse for continuing to participate in the charades which are consequently enacted. The histrionic talents of the player with small walking-on parts are as necessary to the bureaucratic drama as the contributions of the great managerial character actors.

9

Nietzsche or Aristotle?

The contemporary vision of the world, so I have suggested, is predominantly, although not perhaps always in detail, Weberian. At once there will be protests. Most liberals will argue that there is no such thing as 'the' contemporary vision of the world; there are a multiplicity of visions deriving from that irreducible plurality of values of which Sir Isaiah Berlin is at once the most systematic and the most cogent defender. Many socialists will argue that the dominant contemporary world view is a Marxist one, that Weber is *vieux jeu*, his claims fatally undermined by his critics from the Left. To the former I will reply that belief in an irreducible plurality of values is itself an insistent and central Weberian theme. And to the latter I will say that as Marxists organize and move toward power they always do and have become Weberians in substance, even if they remain Marxists in rhetoric; for in our culture we know of no organized movement towards power which is not bureaucratic and managerial in mode and we know of no justifications for authority which are not Weberian in form. And if this is true of Marxism when it is on the road to power, how much more so is it the case when it arrives. All power tends to coopt and absolute power coopts absolutely.

Yet if my argument is correct this Weberian vision of the world cannot be rationally sustained; it disguises and conceals rather than illuminates and it depends for its power on its success at disguise and concealment. And at this point a second set of protests will be heard. Why throughout my account has there been no place for the word 'ideology'? Why have I said so much about masks and concealments and so little—almost nothing—about what is masked and concealed? The short answer to the latter question is that I have no general answer to give; but I am not pleading simple ignorance. When Marx changed the meaning of the word 'ideology' and set it on its modern course, he sometimes did so with reference to certain easily understood examples. The French revolutionaries of 1789, for example, on Marx's view of them conceived of themselves as possessing the same modes of moral and political existence as did ancient republicans; by doing so they disguised from themselves their social roles as spokesmen for the bourgeoisie. The English revolutionaries of 1649 similarly conceived of themselves in the guise of Old Testament servants of God; and by doing so similarly disguised *their* social role. But on the occasions when Marx's particular examples were generalized into a theory—either by Marx himself or by others—quite different types of issue were raised. For the generality of the theory derived precisely from its attempted embodiment of the theory in a set of law-like generalizations which link the material conditions and class structures of societies as kinds of cause to ideologically informed beliefs as kinds of effect. This is the import of Marx's and Engel's early formulations in *The German Ideology* as it is of Engel's later ones in *Anti-Dühring*. Thus the theory of ideology became one more example of the type of would-be social science which, so I have already argued, *both* misrepresents the form of the actual discoveries of social scientists *and* itself functions as a disguised expression of arbitrary preference. In fact the *theory* of ideology turns out itself to be one more example of the very phenomenon which its proponents aspired to understand. Hence while we still have much to learn from the history of the *Eighteenth Brumaire*, the general Marxist *theory* of ideology and its many heirs are themselves only one more set of symptoms disguised as a diagnosis.

Yet of course part of the conception of ideology of which Marx is the ancestral begetter—and which has been put to a range of illuminating uses by thinkers as diverse as Karl Mannheim and Lucien Goldmann—does indeed underlie my central thesis about morality. If moral utterance is put to uses at the service of arbitrary will, it is someone's arbitrary will; and the question of *whose* will it is is obviously of both moral and political importance. But to answer that question is not my task here. What I need to show to accomplish my present task is only how morality has become available for a certain type of use and that it is so used.

What we need therefore to supplement the kind of account of specifically modern moral discourse and practice that I have given are a series of historical accounts which will show how moral countenance can now be given to far too many causes, how the form of moral utterance provides a possible mask for almost any face. For morality *has* become *generally available* in a quite new way. It was indeed Nietzsche's perception of this vulgarized facility of modern moral utterance which partly informed his disgust with it. And this perception is one of the features of Nietzsche's moral philosophy which makes it one of the two genuine theoretical alternatives confronting anyone trying to analyze the moral condition of our culture, *if* my argument so far is substantially correct. Why is this so? An adequate answer to that question requires me first to say something more about my own thesis and secondly to say something about Nietzsche's insights.

A key part of my thesis has been that modern moral utterance and practice can only be understood as a series of fragmented survivals from an older past and that the insoluble problems which they have generated for modern moral theorists will remain insoluble until this is well understood. If the deontological character of moral judgments is the ghost of conceptions of divine law which are quite alien to the metaphysics of modernity and if the teleological character is similarly the ghost of conceptions of human nature and activity which are equally not at home in the modern world, we should expect the problems of understanding and of assigning an intelligible status to moral judgments both continually to arise and as continually to prove inhospitable to philosophical solutions. What we need here is not only philosophical acuteness but also the kind of vision which anthropologists at their best bring to the observation of other cultures, enabling them to identify survivals and unintelligibilities unperceived by those who inhabit those cultures. One way to educate our own vision might be to enquire if the predicaments of our cultural and moral state may not resemble those of social orders which we have hitherto thought of as very different from ourselves. The specific example which I have in mind is that of certain Pacific island kingdoms at the end of the eighteenth and the beginning of the nineteenth century.

In the journal of his third voyage Captain Cook records the first discovery by English speakers of the Polynesian word *taboo* (in a variety of forms). The English seamen had been astonished at what they took to be the lax sexual habits of the Polynesians and were even more astonished to discover the sharp contrast with the rigorous prohibition placed on such conduct as that of men and women eating together. When they enquired why men and women were prohibited from eating together, they were told that the practice was *taboo*. But when they enquired further what *taboo* meant, they could get little further information. Clearly *taboo* did not simply mean *prohibited*; for to say that something—person or practice or theory—is *taboo* is to give some particular sort of reason for its prohibition. But what sort of reason? It has not only been Cook's seamen who have had trouble with that question; from Frazer and Tylor to Franz Steiner and Mary Douglas the anthropologists have had to struggle with it. From that struggle two keys to the problem emerge. The first is the significance of the fact that Cook's seamen were unable to get any intelligible reply to their queries from their native informants. What this *suggests* is—and any hypothesis is to some degree speculative—that the native informants themselves did not really understand the word they were using, and this suggestion is reinforced by the ease with which Kamehameha II abolished the taboos in Hawaii forty years later in 1819 and the lack of social consequence when he did.

But could the Polynesians come to be using a word which they themselves did not really understand? It is here that Steiner and Douglas are illuminating. For what they both suggest is that taboo rules often and perhaps characteristically have a history which falls into two stages. In the first stage they are embedded in a context which confers intelligibility upon them. So Mary Douglas has argued that the taboo rules of Deuteronomy presuppose a cosmology and a taxonomy of a certain kind. Deprive the taboo rules of their original context and they at once are apt to appear as a set of arbitrary prohibitions, as indeed they characteristically do appear when the initial context is lost, when those background beliefs in the light of which the taboo rules had originally been understood have not only been abandoned but forgotten.

In such a situation the rules have been deprived of any status that can secure their authority and, if they do not acquire some new status quickly, both their interpretation and their justification become debatable. When the resources of a culture are too meagre to carry through the task of reinterpretation, the task of justification becomes impossible. Hence perhaps the relatively easy, although to some contemporary observers astonishing, victory of Kamehameha II over the taboos (and the creation thereby of a moral vacuum in which the banalities of the New England Protestant missionaries were received all too quickly). But had the Polynesian culture enjoyed the blessings of analytical philosophy it is all too clear that the question of the meaning of taboo could have been resolved in a number of ways. *Taboo*, it would have been said by one party, is clearly the name of a non-natural property; and precisely the same reasoning which led Moore to see *good* as the name of such a property and Prichard and Ross to see *obligatory* and *right* as the names of such properties would have been available to show that *taboo* is the name of such a property. Another party would doubtless have argued that 'This is *taboo*' means roughly the same as 'I disapprove of this; do so as well'; and precisely the same reasoning which led Stevenson and Ayer to see 'good' as having primarily an emotive use would have been available to support the emotive theory of *taboo*. A third party would presumably have arisen which would have argued that the grammatical form of 'This is taboo' disguises a universalizable imperative prescription.

The pointlessness of this imaginary debate arises from a shared presupposition of the contending parties, namely that the set of rules whose status and justification they are investigating provides an adequately demarcated subject matter for investigation, provides the material for an autonomous field of study. We from our standpoint in the real world know that this is not the case, that there is no way to understand the character of the taboo rules, except as a survival from some previous more elaborate cultural background. We know also and as a consequence that any theory which makes the taboo rules of the late eighteenth century in Polynesia intelligible just as they are without reference to their history is necessarily a false theory; the only true theory can be one which exhibits their unintelligibility as they stand at that point in time. Moreover the only adequate true story will be one which will *both* enable us to distinguish between what it is for a set of taboo rules and practices to be in good order and what it is for a set of such rules and practices to have been fragmented and thrown into disorder *and* enable us to understand the historical transitions by which the latter state emerged from the former. Only the writing of a certain kind of history will supply what we need.

And now the question inexorably arises to reinforce my own earlier argument: why should we think about real analytical moral philosophers such as Moore, Ross, Prichard, Stevenson, Hare and the rest in any different way from that in which we were thinking just now about their imaginary Polynesian counterparts? Why should we think about our modern uses of *good, right* and *obligatory* in any different way from that in which we think about late eighteenth-century Polynesian uses of *taboo?* And why should we not think of Nietzsche as the Kamehameha II of the European tradition?

For it was Nietzsche's historic achievement to understand more clearly than any other philosopher—certainly more clearly than his counterparts in Anglo-Saxon emotivism and continental existentialism—not only that what purported to be appeals to objectivity were in fact expressions of subjective will, but also the nature of the problems that this posed for moral philosophy. It is true that Nietzsche, as I shall later argue, illegitimately generalized from the condition of moral judgment in his own day to the nature of morality as such; and I have already said justifiably harsh words about Nietzsche's construction of that at once absurd and dangerous fantasy, the *Übermensch*. But it is worth noting how even that construction began from a genuine insight.

In a famous passage in *The Gay Science* (section 335) Nietzsche jeers at the notion of basing morality on inner moral sentiments, on conscience, on the one hand, or on the Kantian categorical imperative, on universalizability, on the other. In five swift, witty and cogent paragraphs he disposes of both what I have called the Enlightenment project to discover rational foundations for an objective morality and of the confidence of the everyday moral agent in post-Enlightenment culture that his moral practice and utterance are in good order. But Nietzsche then goes on to confront the problem that this act of destruction has created. The underlying structure of his argument is as follows: if there is nothing to morality but expressions of will, my morality can only be what my will creates. There can be no place for such fictions as natural rights, utility, the greatest happiness of the greatest number. I myself must now bring into existence 'new tables of what is good'. 'We, however, *want to become those we are* — human beings who are new, unique, incomparable, who give themselves laws, who create themselves' (p. 266). The rational and rationally justified autonomous moral subject of the eighteenth century is a fiction, an illusion; so, Nietzsche resolves, let will replace reason and let us make ourselves into autonomous moral subjects by some gigantic and heroic act of the will, an act of the will that by its quality may remind us of that archaic aristocratic self-assertiveness which preceded what Nietzsche took to be the disaster of slave-morality and which by its effectiveness may be the prophetic precursor of a new era. The problem then is how to construct in an entirely original way, how to invent a new table of what is good and a law, a problem which arises for each individual. This problem would constitute the core of a Nietzschean moral philosophy. For it is in his relentlessly serious pursuit of the problem, not in his frivolous solutions that Nietzsche's greatness lies, the greatness that makes him *the* moral philosopher *if* the only alternatives to Nietzsche's moral philosophy turn out to be those formulated by the philosophers of the Enlightenment and their successors.

In another way too Nietzsche is *the* moral philosopher of the present age. For I have already argued that the present age is in its presentation of itself to itself dominantly Weberian; and I have also noticed that Nietzsche's central thesis was presupposed by Weber's central categories of thought. Hence Nietzsche's prophetic irrationalism — irrationalism because Nietzsche's problems remain unsolved and his solutions defy reason — remains immanent in the Weberian managerial forms of our culture. Whenever those immersed in the bureaucratic culture of the age try to think their way through to the moral foundations of what they are and what they do, they will discover suppressed Nietzschean premises. And consequently it is possible to predict with confidence that in the apparently quite unlikely contexts of bureaucratically managed modern societies there will periodically emerge social movements informed by just that kind of prophetic irrationalism of which Nietzsche's thought is the ancestor. Indeed just because and insofar as contemporary Marxism is Weberian in substance we can expect prophetic irrationalisms of the Left as well as of the Right. So it was with much student radicalism of the sixties. (For theoretical versions of this Left Nietzscheanism see both the papers by Kathryn Pyne Parsons and Tracy Strong in Solomon 1973, and Miller 1979).

So Weber and Nietzsche together provide us with the key theoretical articulations of the contemporary social order; but what they delineate so clearly are the large-scale and dominant features of the modern social land-scape. Just because they are so very effective in this regard, they may be of little help in deciphering the small-scale counterparts of those features in the mundane transactions of everyday life. Fortunately, as I noticed earlier, we already have a sociology of everyday life which is the precise counterpart of the thought of Weber and Nietzsche, the sociology of in-teraction elaborated by Erving Goffman.

The central contrast embodied in Goffman's sociology is precisely the same as that embodied in emotivism. It is the contrast between the pur-ported meaning and point of our utterances and the use to which they are actually being put, between the surface presentations of behavior and the strategies used to achieve those presentations. The unit of analysis in Goffman's accounts is always the individual role-player striving to effect his will within a role-structured situation. The goal of the Goffmanesque role-player is effectiveness and success in Goffman's social universe is noth-ing but what passes for success. There is nothing else for it to be. For Goffman's world is empty of objective standards of achievement; it is so defined that there is no cultural or social space from which appeal to such standards could be made. Standards are established though and in inter-action itself; and moral standards seem to have the function only of sus-taining types of interaction that may always be menaced by over-expansive individuals. 'During any conversation, standards are established as to how much the individual is to allow himself to be carried away by the talk, how thoroughly he is to permit himself to be caught up in it. He will be obliged to prevent himself from becoming so swollen with feelings and a readiness to act that he threatens the bounds regarding affect that have been established for him in the interaction. . . . When the individual does become over-involved in the topic of conversation, and gives others the im-pression that he does not have a necessary measure of self-control over his feelings and actions . . . then the others are likely to be drawn from involve-ment in the talk to an involvement in the talker. What is one man's over-eagerness will become another man's alienation . . . a readiness to become over-involved is a form of tyranny practiced by children, *prima donnas*, and lords of all kinds, who momentarily put their own feelings above the moral rules that ought to have made society safe for interaction' (*Interaction Ritual* 1972, pp. 122-3).

Because success is whatever passes for success, it is in the regard of others that I prosper or fail to prosper; hence the importance of presenta-tion as a—perhaps *the* central—theme. Goffman's social world is one of which a thesis that Aristotle in the *Nicomachean Ethics* considers only to reject is true: the good for man, consists in the possession of honor, honor being precisely whatever embodies and expresses the regard of others. Aristotle's reason for rejecting this thesis is to the point. We honor others, he says, in virtue of something that they are or have done to merit the honor; honor cannot therefore be at best more than secondary good. That in virtue of which honor is assigned must be more important. But in Goffman's social world imputations of merit are themselves part of the contrived social reality whose function is to aid or to contain some striving, role-playing will. Goffman's is a sociology which by intention deflates the pretensions of appearance to be anything more than appearance. It is a sociology which it would be tempting to call cynical—in the modern, not the ancient sense—but for the fact that, if Goffman's portrait of human life is a true likeness, there can be no such thing as a cynical disregard for objective merit, since there is no such thing as objective merit for the cynic to disregard.

It is important to notice that the concept of honor in the society for which Aristotle was the spokesman—and in many subsequent societies as different as that of the Icelandic sagas and of the Bedouin of the Western desert—just because honor and worth were connected in the way which Aristotle remarks, was—in spite of the resemblance—a very different concept from anything that we find in Goffman's pages and from *almost* anything that we find in modern societies. In many pre-modern societies a man's honor is what is due to him and to his kin and his household by reason of their having their *due* place in the social order. To dishonor someone is to fail to acknowledge what is thus due. Hence the concept of an insult becomes a socially crucial one and in many such societies a certain kind of insult merits death. Peter Berger and his co-authors (1973) have pointed out the significance of the fact that in modern societies we have neither legal nor quasi-legal recourse if we are insulted. Insults have been displaced to the margins of our cultural life where they are expressive of private emotions rather than public conflicts. And unsurprisingly this is the only place left for them in Goffman's writings.

The comparison of Goffman's books—I am thinking more particularly of *The Presentation of Self in Everyday Life, Encounters, Interaction Ritual* and *Strategic Interaction*—with the *Nicomachean Ethics* is very much to the point. At an earlier point in the argument I stressed the close relationship between moral philosophy and sociology; and just as Aristotle's *Ethics* and *Politics* are as much contributions to the latter as to the former, so Goffman's books presuppose a moral philosophy. They do so in part because they are a perceptive account of forms of behavior within a particular society which itself incorporates a moral theory in its characteristic modes of action and practice; and in part because of the philosophical commitments presupposed by Goffman's own theoretical stances. So Goffman's sociology, since it claims to show us not just what human nature can become under certain highly specific conditions, but what human nature must be and therefore always has been, clearly makes the implicit claim that Aristotle's moral philosophy is false. This is not a question that Goffman himself raises or needs to raise. But it is both raised and brilliantly dealt with by Goffman's great predecessor and anticipator, Nietzsche, in *The Genealogy of Morals* and elsewhere. Nietzsche rarely refers explicitly to Aristotle except on aesthetic questions. He *does* borrow the name and notion of 'the great-souled man' from the *Ethics*, although it becomes in the context of his theory something quite other than it was in Aristotle's. But his interpretation of the history of morality makes it quite clear that the Aristotelian account of ethics and politics would have to rank for Nietzsche with all those degenerate disguises of the will to power which follow from the false turning taken by Socrates.

Yet it is not of course just that Nietzsche's moral philosophy is false if Aristotle's is true and *vice versa*. In a much stronger sense Nietzsche's moral philosophy is matched specifically against Aristotle's by virtue of the historical role which each plays. For, as I argued earlier, it was because a moral tradition of which Aristotle's thought was the intellectual core was repudiated during the transitions of the fifteenth to seventeenth centuries that the Enlightenment project of discovering new rational secular foundations for morality had to be undertaken. And it was because that project failed, because the views advanced by its most intellectually powerful protagonists, and more especially by Kant, could not be sustained in the face of rational criticism that Nietzsche and all his existentialist and emotivist successors were able to mount their apparently successful critique of all previous morality. Hence the defensibility of the Nietzschean position turns *in the end* on the answer to the question: was it right in the first place to reject Aristotle? For if Aristotle's position in ethics and politics—or something very like it—could be sustained, the whole Nietzschean enterprise would be pointless. This is because the power of Nietzsche's position depends upon the truth of one central thesis: that all rational vindications of morality manifestly fail and that *therefore* belief in the tenets of morality needs to be explained in terms of a set of rationalizations which conceal the fundamentally non-rational phenomena of the will. My own argument obliges me to agree with Nietzsche that the philosophers of the Enlightenment never succeeded in providing grounds for doubting his central thesis; his epigrams are even deadlier than his extended arguments. But, if my earlier argument is correct, that failure itself was nothing other than an historical sequel to the rejection of the Aristotelian tradition. And thus the key question does indeed become: can Aristotle's ethics, or something very like it, after all be vindicated?

It is an understatement to call this a large and complex question. For the issues which divide Aristotle and Nietzsche are of a number of very different kinds. At the level of philosophical theory there are questions in politics and in philosophical psychology as well as in moral theory; and what confront each other are not in any case merely two theories, but the theoretical specification of two different ways of life. The role of Aristotelianism in my argument is not entirely due to its historical importance. In the ancient and medieval worlds it was always in conflict with other standpoints, and the various ways of life of which it took itself to be the best theoretical interpreter had other sophisticated theoretical protagonists. It is true that no doctrine vindicated itself in so wide a variety of contexts as did Aristotelianism: Greek, Islamic, Jewish and Christian; and that when modernity made its assaults on an older world its most perceptive exponents understood that it was Aristotelianism that had to be overthrown. But all these historical truths, crucial as they are, are unimportant compared with the fact that Aristotelianism is *philosophically* the most powerful of pre-modern modes of moral thought. If a premodern view of morals and politics is to be vindicated against modernity, it will be in *something like* Aristotelian terms or not at all.

What then the conjunction of philosophical and historical argument reveals is that *either* one must follow through the aspirations and the collapse of the different versions of the Enlightenment project until there remains only the Nietzschean diagnosis and the Nietzschean problematic *or* one must hold that the Enlightenment project was not only mistaken, but should never have been commenced in the first place. There is no third alternative and more particularly there is no alternative provided by those thinkers at the heart of the contemporary conventional curriculum in moral philosophy, Hume, Kant and Mill. It is no wonder that the teaching of ethics is so often destructive and skeptical in its effects upon the minds of those taught.

But *which* ought we to choose? And *how* ought we to choose? It is yet another of Nietzsche's merits that he joins to his critique of Enlightenment moralities a sense of their failure to address adequately, let alone to answer the question: what sort of person am I to become? This is in a way an inescapable question in that an answer to it is given *in practice* in each human life. But for characteristically modern moralities it is a question to be approached only by indirection. The primary question from their standpoint has concerned rules: what rules ought we to follow? And why ought we to obey them? And that this has been the primary question is unsurprising when we recall the consequences of the expulsion of Aristotelian teleology from the moral world. Ronald Dworkin has recently argued that the central doctrine of modern liberalism is the thesis that questions about the *good life for man* or the ends of human life are to be regarded from the public standpoint as systematically unsettlable. On these individuals are free to agree or to disagree. The rules of morality and law hence are not to be derived from or justified in terms of some more fundamental conception of the good for man. In arguing thus Dworkin has, I believe, identified a stance characteristic not just of liberalism, but of modernity. Rules become the primary concept of the moral life. Qualities of character then generally come to be prized only because they will lead us to follow the right set of rules. 'The virtues are sentiments, that is, related families of dispositions and propensities regulated by a higher-order desire, in this case a desire to act from the corresponding moral principles', asserts John Rawls, one of the latest moral philosophers of modernity (1971, p. 192) and elsewhere he defines 'the fundamental moral virtues' as 'strong and normally effective desires to act on the basic principles of right ' (p. 436).

Hence on the modern view the justification of the virtues depends upon some prior justification of rules and principles; and if the latter become radically problematic, as they have, so also must the former. Suppose however that in articulating the problems of morality the ordering of evaluative concepts has been misconceived by the spokesmen of modernity and more particularly of liberalism; suppose that we need to attend to *virtues* in the first place in order to understand the function and authority of rules; we ought then to begin the enquiry in the quite different way from that in which it is begun by Hume or Diderot or Kant or Mill. On this interestingly Nietzsche and Aristotle agree.

Moreover it is clear that if we are to make a new start to the enquiry in order to put Aristotelianism to the question all over again, it will be necessary to consider Aristotle's own moral philosophy not merely as it is expressed in key texts in his own writings, but as an attempt to inherit and to sum up a good deal that had gone before and in turn as a source of stimulus to much later thought. It will be necessary, that is, to write a short history of conceptions of the virtues in which Aristotle provides a central point of focus, but which yield the resources of a whole tradition of acting, thinking and discourse of which Aristotle's is only a part, a tradition of which I spoke earlier as 'the classical tradition' and whose view of man I called 'the classical view of man'. To this task I now turn, and its starting-point provides by what is perhaps too fortunate to be coincidence an initial test case for deciding the issue between Nietzsche and Aristotle. For Nietsche saw himself as the last inheritor of the message of those Homeric aristocrats whose deeds and virtues provided the poets from whom we inescapably begin with a subject matter. It is therefore in a strict sense poetic justice to Nietzsche to begin our consideration of that classical tradition in which Aristotle is to emerge as the central figure with a consideration of the nature of the virtues in the kind of heroic society which is portrayed in the *Iliad*.

10

The Virtues in Heroic Societies

In all those cultures, Greek, medieval or Renaissance, where moral thinking and action is structured according to some version of the scheme that
I have called classical, the chief means of moral education is the telling of
stories. Where Christianity or Judaism or Islam have prevailed, biblical
stories are as important as any other; and each culture of course has stories
that are peculiarly its own; but every one of these cultures, Greek or Christian, also possesses a stock of stories which derive from and tell about its
own vanished heroic age. In sixth-century Athens the formal recitation of
the Homeric poems was established as a public ceremony; the poems
themselves were substantially composed no later than the seventh-century,
but they speak of a very much earlier time even than that. In thirteenth-
century Christian Iceland men wrote sagas about the events of the hundred
years after A.D. 930, the period immediately before and immediately after
the first coming of Christianity, when the old religion of the Norsemen
still flourished. In the twelfth century in the monastery of Clonmacnoise
Irish monks wrote down in the *Lebor na hUidre* stories of Ulster heroes,
some of whose language enables scholars to date them back to the eighth
century, but whose plots are situated centuries before that in an era when
Ireland was still pagan. Exactly the same kind of scholarly controversy has
flourished in each case over the question of how far, if at all, the Homeric
poems or the Sagas or the stories of the Ulster cycle, such as the *Taín Bó
Cuailnge*, provide us with reliable historical evidence about the societies
which they portray. Happily I need not involve myself with the detail of
those arguments. What matters for my own argument is a relatively in-
disputable historical fact, namely that such narratives did provide the
historical memory, adequate or inadequate, of the societies in which they
were finally written down. More than that they provided a moral background to contemporary debate in classical societies, an account of a now-
transcended or partly-transcended moral order whose beliefs and concepts
were still partially influential, but which also provided an illuminating contrast to the present. The understanding of heroic society—whether it ever
existed or not—is thus a necessary part of the understanding of classical
society and of its successors. What are its key features?

M.I. Finley has written of Homeric society: 'The basic values of society were given, predetermined and so were a man's place in the society and the privileges and duties that followed from his status' (Finley 1954, p. 134). What Finley says of Homeric society is equally true of other forms of heroic society in Iceland or in Ireland. Every individual has a given role and status within a well-defined and highly determinate system of roles and statuses. The key structures are those of kinship and of the household. In such a society a man knows who he is by knowing his role in these structures; and in knowing this he knows also what he owes and what is owed to him by the occupant of every other role and status. In Greek (*dein*) and in Anglo-Saxon (*ahte*) alike, there is originally no clear distinction between 'ought' and 'owe'; in Icelandic the word 'skyldr' ties together 'ought' and 'is kin to'.

But it is not just that there is for each status a prescribed set of duties and privileges. There is also a clear understanding of what actions are required to perform these and what actions fall short of what is required. For what are required are actions. A man in heroic society is what he does. Hermann Fränkel wrote of Homeric man that 'a man and his actions become identical, and he makes himself completely and adequately comprehended in them; he has no hidden depths. . . . In [the epics] factual report of what men do and say, everything that men are, is expressed, because they are no more than what they do and say and suffer' (Fränkel 1975, p. 79). To judge a man therefore is to judge his actions. By performing actions of a particular kind in a particular situation a man gives warrant for judgment upon his virtues and vices; for the virtues just are those qualities which sustain a free man in his role and which manifest themselves in those actions which his role requires. And what Fränkel says and suggests about Homeric man holds also of man in other heroic portrayals.

The word *aretê*, which later comes to be translated as 'virtue', is in the Homeric poems used for excellence of any kind; a fast runner displays the *aretê* of his feet (*Iliad* 20. 411) and a son excels his father in every kind of *aretê*—as athlete, as soldier and in mind (*Iliad* 15. 642). This concept of virtue or excellence is more alien to us than we are apt at first to recognize. It is not difficult for us to recognize the central place that strength will have in such a conception of human excellence or the way in which courage will be one of the central virtues, perhaps the central virtue. What is alien to our conception of virtue is the intimate connection in heroic society between the concept of courage and its allied virtues on the one hand and the concepts of friendship, fate and death on the other.

Courage is important, not simply as a quality of individuals, but as the quality necessary to sustain a household and a community. *Kûdos*, glory, belongs to the individual who excels in battle or in contest as a mark of recognition by his household and his community. Other qualities linked to courage also merit public recognition because of the part they play in sustaining the public order. In the Homeric poems cunning is such a quality because cunning may have its achievements where courage is lacking or courage fails. In the Icelandic sagas a wry sense of humor is closely bound up with courage. In the saga account of the battle of Clontarf in 1014, where Brian Boru defeated a Viking army, one of the norsemen, Thorstein, did not flee when the rest of his army broke and ran, but remained where he was, tying his shoestring. An Irish leader, Kerthialfad, asked him why he was not running. 'I couldn't get home tonight,' said Thorstein. 'I live in Iceland.' Because of the joke, Kerthialfad spared his life.

To be courageous is to be someone on whom reliance can be placed. Hence courage is an important ingredient in friendship. The bonds of friendship in heroic societies are modelled on those of kinship. Sometimes friendship is formally vowed, so that by the vow the duties of brothers are mutually incurred. Who my friends are and who my enemies, is as clearly defined as who my kinsmen are. The other ingredient of friendship is fidelity. My friend's courage assures me of his power to aid me and my household; my friend's fidelity assures me of his will. My household's fidelity is the basic guarantee of its unity. So in women, who constitute the crucial relationships within the household, fidelity is the key virtue. Andromache and Hector, Penelope and Odysseus are friends (*philos*) as much as are Achilles and Patroclus.

What I hope this account makes clear already is the way in which any adequate account of the virtues in heroic society would be impossible which divorced them from their context in its social structure, just as no adequate account of the social structure of heroic society would be possible which did not include an account of the heroic virtues. But to put it in this way is to understate the crucial point: morality and social structure are in fact one and the same in heroic society. There is only one set of social bonds. Morality as something distinct does not yet exist. Evaluative questions *are* questions of social fact. It is for this reason that Homer speaks always of *knowledge* of what to do and how to judge. Nor are such questions difficult to answer, except in exceptional cases. For the given rules which assign men their place in the social order and with it their identity also prescribe what they owe and what is owed to them and how they are to be treated and regarded if they fail and how they are to treat and regard others if those others fail.

Without such a place in the social order, a man would not only be incapable of receiving recognition and response from others; not only would others not know, but he would not himself know who he was. It is precisely because of this that heroic societies commonly have a well-defined status to which any stranger who arrives in the society from outside can be assigned. In Greek the word for 'alien' and the word for 'guest' are the same word. A stranger has to be received with hospitality, limited but well-defined. When Odysseus encounters the Cyclopes the question as to whether they possess *themis* (the Homeric concept of *themis* is the concept of customary law shared by all civilized peoples) is to be answered by discovering how they treat strangers. In fact they eat them—that is, for them strangers have no recognized human identity.

We might thus expect to find in heroic societies an emphasis upon the contrast between the expectations of the man who not only possesses courage and its allied virtues, but who also has kinsmen and friends on the one hand and the man lacking all these on the other. Yet one central theme of heroic societies is also that death waits for both alike. Life is fragile, men are vulnerable and it is of the essence of the human situation that they are such. For in heroic societies life is the standard of value. If someone kills you, my friend or brother, I owe you their death and when I have paid my debt to you their friend or brother owes them my death. The more extended my system of kinsmen and friends, the more liabilities I shall incur of a kind that may end in my death.

Moreover there are powers in the world which no one can control. Human life is invaded by passions which appear sometimes as impersonal forces, sometimes as gods. Achilles' wrath disrupts Achilles as well as his relationship to the other Greeks. These forces and the rules of kinship and friendship together constitute patterns of an ineluctable kind. Neither willing nor cunning will enable anyone to evade them. Fate is a social reality and the descrying of fate an important social role. It is no accident that the prophet or the seer flourishes equally in Homeric Greece, in saga Iceland and in pagan Ireland.

The man therefore who does what he ought moves steadily towards his fate and his death. It is defeat and not victory that lies at the end. To understand this is itself a virtue; indeed it is a necessary part of courage to understand this. But what is involved in such understanding? What would have been understood if the connections between courage, friendship, fidelity, the household, fate and death had been grasped? Surely that human life has a determinate form, the form of a certain kind of story. It is not just that poems and sagas narrate what happens to men and women, but that in their narrative form poems and sagas capture a form that was already present in the lives which they relate.

'What is character but the determination of incident?' wrote Henry James. 'What is incident but the illustration of character?' But in heroic society character of the relevant kind can only be exhibited in a succession of incidents and the succesion itself must exemplify certain patterns. Where heroic society agrees with James is that character and incident cannot be characterized independently of each other. So to understand courage as a virtue is not just to understand how it may be exhibited in character, but also what place it can have in a certain kind of enacted story. For courage in heroic society is a capacity not just to face particular harms and dangers but to face a particular kind of pattern of harms and dangers, a pattern in which individual lives find their place and which such lives in turn exemplify.

What epic and saga then portray is a society which already embodies the form of epic or saga. Its poetry articulates its form in individual and social life. To say this is still to leave open the question of whether there ever were such societies; but it does suggest that if there were such societies they could only be adequately understood through their poetry. Yet epic and saga are certainly not simple mirror images of the society they profess to portray. For it is quite clear that the poet or the saga writer claims for himself a kind of understanding which is denied to the characters about whom he writes. The poet does not suffer from the limitations which define the essential condition of his characters. Consider especially the *Iliad*.

As I said earlier of heroic society in general, the heroes in the *Iliad* do not find it difficult to know what they owe one another; they feel *aidôs*—a proper sense of shame—when confronted with the possibility of wrong-doing, and if that is not sufficient, other people are always at hand to drive home the accepted view. Honor is conferred by one's peers and without honor a man is without worth. There is indeed in the vocabulary available to Homer's characters no way for them to view their own culture and society as if from the outside. The evaluative expressions which they employ are mutually interdefined and each has to be explained in terms of the others.

Let me use a dangerous, but illuminating analogy. The rules which govern both action and evaluative judgment in the *Iliad* resemble the rules and the precepts of a game such as chess. It is a question of fact whether a man is a good chess player, whether he is good at devising end-game strategies, whether a move is the right move to make in a particular situation. The game of chess presupposes, indeed is partially constituted by, agreement on how to play chess. Within the vocabulary of chess it makes no sense to say 'That was the one and only move which would achieve checkmate, but was it the right move to make?' And therefore someone

After Virtue

who said this and understood what he was saying would have to be employing some notion of 'right' which receives its definition from outside chess, as someone might ask this whose purpose in playing chess was to amuse a small child rather than to win.

One reason why the analogy is dangerous is that we do play games such as chess for a variety of purposes. But there is nothing to be made of the question: for what purpose do the characters in the *Iliad* observe the rules that they observe and honor the precepts which they honor? It is rather the case that it is only within their framework of rules and precepts that they are able to frame purposes at all; and just because of this the analogy breaks down in another way, too. All questions of choice arise within the framework; the framework itself therefore cannot be chosen.

There is thus the sharpest of contrasts between the emotivist self of modernity and the self of the heroic age. The self of the heroic age lacks precisely that characteristic which we have already seen that some modern moral philosophers take to be an essential characteristic of human self-hood: the capacity to detach oneself from any particular standpoint or point of view, to step backwards, as it were, and view and judge that standpoint or point of view from the outside. In heroic society there is no 'outside' except that of the stranger. A man who tried to withdraw himself from his given position in heroic society would be engaged in the enterprise of trying to make himself disappear.

Identity in heroic society involves particularity and accountability. I am answerable for doing or failing to do what anyone who occupies my role owes to others and this accountability terminates only with death. I have until my death to do what I have to do. Moreover this accountability is particular. It is to, for and with specific individuals that I must do what I ought, and it is to these same and other individuals, members of the same local community, that I am accountable. The heroic self does not itself aspire to universality even although in retrospect we may recognize universal worth in the achievements of that self.

The exercise of the heroic virtues thus requires both a particular kind of human being and a particular kind of social structure. Just because this is so, an inspection of the heroic virtues may at first sight appear irrelevant to any general enquiry into moral theory and practice. If the heroic virtues require for their exercise the presence of a kind of social structure which is now irrevocably lost—as they do—what relevance can they possess for us? Nobody now can be a Hector or a Gisli. The answer is that perhaps what we have to learn from heroic societies is twofold: first that all morality is always to some degree tied to the socially local and particular and that the aspirations of the morality of modernity to a universality freed from all particularity is an illusion; and secondly that there is no way to possess the virtues except as part of a tradition in which we inherit them and our understanding of them from a series of predecessors in which series heroic societies hold first place. If this is so, the contrast between the freedom of choice of values of which modernity prides itself and the absence of such choice in heroic cultures would look very different. For freedom of choice of values would from the standpoint of a tradition ultimately rooted in heroic societies appear more like the freedom of ghosts—of those whose human substance approached vanishing point—than of men.

It is the certitude which this absence of choice provides that at one level makes the task of the commentator upon the *Iliad* so relatively easy. What is an *aretê* and what is not is easily determined; there is no disagreement within the *Iliad* on such matters. But when the lexicographer has completed his list, a more difficult question does arise. I have already noted that physical strength, courage and intelligence are among the excellences. In the *Odyssey* Penelope speaks of her *aretai* where we should speak of her attractions. But, more puzzlingly to us, in the *Odyssey* prosperity too is spoken of as an excellence. The unity of the notion of an *aretê* resides, as we have already seen, in the concept of that which enables a man to discharge his role; and it is easy to see that prosperity—and happiness—have also a different part in the Homeric poems. When Sarpedon remembers his orchards and his cornfields back in Lycia during the agonies of battle by the ships, he reflects that it is because he and Glaucus are foremost among the warriors that they are held to deserve such good things. Prosperity is thus a by-product of achievement in war and from this springs the paradox: those who pursue that course which entitles them to the happiness that is represented by orchards and cornfields, by life with Andromache or Penelope, pursue a course whose characteristic end is death.

Death in Homer is an unmixed evil; the ultimate evil is death followed by desecration of the body. The latter is an evil suffered by the kin and the household of the dead man as well as by the corpse. Conversely it is through the performance of burial rites that the family and the community can restore their integrity after the death of what was part of themselves. Thus funeral rites and funeral games are key episodes in the moral scheme, and grief, understood as the ability to mourn, is a key human emotion.

As Simone Weil saw so clearly, the condition of slavery in the *Iliad* is very close to the condition of death. The slave is someone who may be killed at any minute; he is outside the heroic community. The suppliant too, who has been forced to beg for what he must have, has put himself at the mercy of another and so renders himself a potential corpse or slave. Hence the role of the suppliant is to be assumed only under the most ex-

treme of necessities. It is only when the desecration of Hector's body is
to be followed by the deprivation of burial rites that Priam, being a king,
is compelled to become a suppliant.

To be a suppliant, to be a slave, to be slain on the battlefield is to have
been defeated; and defeat is the moral horizon of the Homeric hero, that
beyond which nothing is to be seen, nothing lies. But defeat is not the
Homeric poet's moral horizon, and it is precisely by reason of this difference that the Homer of the *Iliad* transcends the limitations of the society
which he portrays. For what Homer puts in question, as his characters do
not, is what it is to win and what it is to lose. Here once more the analogy
with later conceptions of a game and of winning and losing in the context
of games is dangerous but unavoidable. For our games, like our wars, are
descendants of the Homeric *agón* and yet are as different as they are in
key part because the concepts of winning and losing have so different a
place in our culture.

What the poet of the *Iliad* sees and his characters do not is that winning
too may be a form of losing. The poet is not a theorist; he offers no general
formulas. His own knowledge is indeed at a more general and abstract level
than that even of his most insightful characters. For Achilles in his moment
of reconciliation with Priam has no way of representing to himself what
Homer is able in his account of Achilles and Priam to represent to others.
Thus the *Iliad* puts in question what neither Achilles nor Hector can put
in question; the poem lay claim to a form of understanding which it denies
to those whose actions it describes.

What I have said of the *Iliad* is certainly not true of all heroic poetry;
but it is true of some of the Icelandic sagas. Indeed in a late saga such as
Njáls Saga the saga writer is at pains to distinguish those characters who
are able to transcend the values of the saga world from those who are not.
In *Gísla Saga Súrsonnar* what the saga writer understands, as the characters
do not, is the complementary truth to that of the *Iliad*: losing may on occasion be a form of winning. When Gisli after his years of outlawry finally
dies fighting back to back with his wife and sister-in-law, the three of them
killing or fatally wounding eight of the fifteen men who had hoped to earn
the price on Gisli's head, it is not Gisli who loses.

Thus this type of heroic poetry represents a form of society about
whose moral structure two central claims are made. The first is that that
structure embodies a conceptual scheme which has three central interrelated elements: a conception of what is required by the social role which
each individual inhabits; a conception of excellences or virtues as those
qualities which enable an individual to do what his or her role requires;
and a conception of the human condition as fragile and vulnerable to

destiny and to death, such that to be virtuous is not to avoid vulnerability and death, but rather to accord them their due. None of these three elements can be made fully intelligible without reference to the other two; but the relationship between them is not merely conceptual. It is rather that all three elements can find their interrelated places only within a larger unitary framework, deprived of which we could not understand their significance for each other. This framework is the narrative form of epic or saga, a form embodied in the moral life of individuals and in the collective social structure. Heroic social structure *is* enacted epic narrative.

The characters in the epic have, as I noticed earlier, no means of viewing the human and natural world except that provided by the conceptions which inform their world-view. But just for that reason they have no doubt that reality is as they represent it to themselves. They present us with a view of the world for which they claim truth. The implicit epistemology of the heroic world is a thoroughgoing realism.

It is indeed partly because the literature of heroic societies makes *this* claim that it so difficult to recognize Nietzsche's later self-serving portrait of their aristocratic inhabitants. The poets of the *Iliad* and the saga writers were implicitly claiming an objectivity for their own standpoint of a kind quite incompatible with a Nietzschean perspectivism. But if the poets and the saga writers fail to be proto-Nietzscheans, what about the characters whom they portray? Here again it is clear that Nietzsche had to mythologize the distant past in order to sustain his vision. What Nietzsche portrays is aristocratic *self*-assertion; what Homer and the sagas show are forms of assertion proper to and required by a certain *role*. The self becomes what it is in heroic societies only through its role; it is a social creation, not an individual one. Hence when Nietzsche projects back on to the archaic past his own nineteenth-century individualism, he reveals that what looked like an historical enquiry was actually an inventive literary construction. Nietzsche replaces the fictions of the Enlightenment individualism, of which he is so contemptuous, with a set of individualist fictions of his own. From this it does not follow that one could not be an undeceived Nietzschean; and the whole importance of being a Nietzschean does after all lie in the triumph of being finally undeceived, being, as Nietzsche put it, truthful at last. It is simply, one might be tempted to conclude, that any would-be true Nietzschean will after all have to go further than Nietzsche. But is this indeed all?

The contemporary Nietzschean by his rejection of his immediate cultural environment—as Nietzsche himself rejected Wilhelmine Germany—and by his discovery that that in the past which Nietzsche praised was fiction rather than fact is condemned to an existence which aspires to transcend all relationship to the past. But is such transcendence possible? We are, whether we acknowledge it or not, what the past has made us and we cannot eradicate from ourselves, even in America, those parts of ourselves which are formed by our relationship to each formative stage in our history. If this is so, then even heroic society is still inescapably a part of us all, and we are narrating a history that is peculiarly *our own history* when we recount its past in the formation of our moral culture.

Any attempt to write this history will necessarily encounter Marx's claim that the reason why Greek epic poetry has the power over us which it still retains derives from the fact that the Greeks stand to civilized modernity as the child to the adult. That is one way of conceiving the relationship of the past to the present. Whether it is a way in which justice can be done to the relationship between ourselves and the *Iliad* is a question which could only be answered if we had enquired into the intervening stages of social and moral order which at once separate us from and connect us to the world in which the *Iliad* was rooted. Those intervening stages will put to the question two central beliefs of the heroic age. They will force us to ask in the context of forms of complexity quite alien to heroic society whether it can remain true that a human life as a whole can be envisaged as a victory or a defeat and what winning and losing really consist in and amount to. And they will press upon us the question as to whether the narrative forms of the heroic age are not mere childlike storytelling, so that moral discourse while it may use fables and parables as aids to the halting moral imagination ought in its serious adult moments to abandon the narrative mode for a more discursive style and genre.

11

The Virtues at Athens

Heroic societies, as they are represented by the Homeric poems or the Icelandic or Irish sagas may or may not have existed; but the belief that they had existed was crucial to those classical and Christian societies which understood themselves as having emerged from the conflicts of heroic society and which defined their own standpoint partially in terms of that emergence. No fifth-century Athenian could behave just as Agamemnon or Achilles behaved. No thirteenth-century Icelander could have behaved quite like the men of the tenth century. The monks at Clonmacnoise were very different from Conchobor or Cúchulainn. Yet the heroic literature provided a central part of the moral scriptures of those later societies; and it is from the difficulties involved in relating those scriptures to actual practice that many of the key moral characteristics of the later societies arise.

In many of Plato's earlier dialogues Socrates interrogates one or more Athenians as to the nature of some virtue—courage in the *Lachês*, piety in the *Euthyphro*, justice in *Republic I*—in such a way as to convict the other of inconsistency. The casual modern reader might easily suppose at first that Plato is contrasting Socrates' rigor with the carelessness of the ordinary Athenian; but as the pattern recurs again and again, another interpretation suggests itself, namely that Plato is pointing to a general state of incoherence in the use of evaluative language in Athenian culture. When Plato in the *Republic* produces his own coherent well-integrated account of the virtues, part of his strategy is to expel the Homeric inheritance from the city-state. One starting point for an enquiry into the virtues in classical society would be to establish a connection between some of the basic incoherences in classical society and the Homeric background. But the task turns out to have been already accomplished, most notably perhaps by Sophocles in the *Philoctêtês*.

Odysseus has been sent on a mission with Neoptolemus, the son of Achilles, to secure Philoctetes' magical bow to aid in the taking of Troy. Odysseus behaves in the play according to precisely the same canons which govern his behavior in the *Odyssey*. He does good to his friends, harm to his foes (thus satisfying one of the definitions of justice which Plato rejects at the beginning of the *Republic*). If he cannot get the aid of the bow by

open means, his cunning will devise deceitful means. In the *Odyssey* that
cunning is treated unambiguously as a virtue; and it is of course for his exercise of the virtues that a hero received honor. But Neoptolemus sees
Odysseus' stratagem to deceive Philoctetes as dishonorable. Philoctetes had
been grossly wronged by the Greeks who had left him to suffer for nine
long years on Lemnos; Philoctetes has nevertheless received Neoptolemus
and Odysseus with trust. Even though he now refuses to come to the aid
of the Greeks at Troy, it is wrong to deceive him. Sophocles uses Odysseus
and Neoptolemus to confront us with two incompatible conceptions of
honorable conduct, two rival standards for behavior. It is crucial to the
structure of the tragedy that Sophocles offers us no resolution of this conflict; the action is interrupted, rather than completed by the intervention
of the semi-divine Heracles, which rescues the characters from their
impasse.

The intervention of a god in Greek tragedy—or at the very least an appeal to a god to intervene—often signals the disclosure of an incoherence
in moral standards and vocabulary. Consider the *Oresteia*. The archaic and
heroic rules of vendetta both enjoin and forbid Orestes to kill Clytem-
nestra. The intervention of Athena and the resolution of the issue between
her and Apollo establish a conception of justice which shifts the center of
authority in moral questions from the family and the household to the
polis. In the *Antigone* the demands of the family and the demands of the
polis appear precisely as rival and incompatible demands. Thus the first
massive fact that we have to reckon with is the difference that it makes
to the conception of the virtues when the primary moral community is no
longer the kinship group, but the city-state, and not merely the city-state
in general, but the Athenian democracy in particular.

Yet it is far too simple to see the difference between the Homeric view
and the classical view of the virtues as residing in a transition from one set
of social forms to another, and this for at least two very different reasons.
The first is that, as the *Antigone* alone is sufficient to suggest, the forms
and claims of kinship, although not the same in fifth-century Athens as
they had been in earlier centuries, survive in substantial form. The
aristocratic household preserves a good deal of Homer in life as well as in
poetry. But the Homeric values no longer define the moral horizon, just
as the household or kinship group are now part of a larger and very different unit. There are no more kings, even though many of the virtues of
kingship are still held to be virtues.

A second reason for not seeing the difference in the conception of the
virtues simply in terms of changed social contexts is that the conception
of a virtue has now become strikingly detached from that of any *particular*

social role. Neoptolemus confronts Philoctetes in Sophocles' play in a way very different from that in which his father confronted Agamemmon in the *Iliad*. In Homer the question of honor is the question of what is due to a king; in Sophocles the question of honor has become the question of what is due to a man.

Nonetheless it seems no accident that the question of what is due to a man is raised in an Athenian—and not in a Theban or a Corinthian, let alone a barbarian—context. To characterize a good man is in crucial part to characterize the relationship in which such a man stands to others and both poets and philosophers for the most part do not distinguish in their account of these relationships what is universal and human from what is local and Athenian. The claim is often explicit; Athens is praised because she *par excellence* exhibits human life as it ought to be. Yet in these very acts of praise Athenian particularity is distinguished from Homeric particularity. For Homeric man there could be no standard external to those embodied in the structures of his own community to which appeal could be made; for Athenian man, the matter is more complex. His understanding of the virtues does provide him with standards by which he can question the life of his own community and enquire whether this or that practice or policy is just. Nonetheless he also recognizes that he possesses his understanding of the virtues only because his membership in the community provides him with such understanding. The city is a guardian, a parent, a teacher, even though what is learnt from the city may lead to a questioning of this or that feature of its life. Thus the question of the relationship between *being a good citizen* and *being a good man* becomes central and knowledge of the variety of possible human practices, barbarian as well as Greek, provided the factual background to the asking of that question.

Of course all the evidence is that the overwhelming majority of all Greeks, whether Athenian or not, took it for granted that the way of life of their own city was unquestionably the best way of life for man, if it even occurred to them to raise the question at all; and it was equally taken for granted that what Greeks shared was clearly superior to any barbarian way of life. But what then did Greeks share? And what did Athenians share?

A.W.H. Adkins has usefully contrasted the cooperative with the competitive virtues. The competitive he sees as Homeric in their ancestry; the cooperative represent the social world of the Athenian democracy. But at this point complexity enters, for moral disagreement in the fifth and fourth centuries does not only arise because one set of virtues is counterposed to another. It is also and perhaps more importantly because rival conceptions of one and the same virtue coexist that conflict is engendered. The nature of *dikaiosunê*—which we have come to translate as 'justice'—is the subject of just such disagreement. Moreover *dikaiosunê*, disagreement over which may be a source of social conflict, is one of the virtues which Adkins sees as cooperative rather than competitive. But *dikaiosunê*, although the word itself does not appear in Homer, has Homeric overtones. *Dikê* and *dikaios* which do appear in Homer are its ancestors, and already in Homer the competitive virtues presuppose the acceptance of the cooperative. It is because *dikê* has been outraged that Achilles falls out with Agamemnon and it is because *dikê* has been outraged that Athena aids Odysseus against the suitors. What then is the virtue which becomes *dikaiosunê*?

'*Dikê* means basically the order of the universe,' wrote Hugh Lloyd-Jones (1971, p.161); and the *dikaios* is the man who respects and does not violate that order. At once the difficulty in translating *dikaios* by 'just' is clear; for someone in our own culture may use the word 'just' without any reference to or belief in a moral order in the universe. But even in the fifth century the nature of the relationship between *dikaiosunê* and some cosmic order is not clear in the way that it was in the Homeric poems. There the order in which kings reign, admittedly imperfectly, is part of the larger order in which gods, and especially Zeus, reign, admittedly imperfectly. To be *dikaios* in Homer is *not to transgress that order*; thus in Homer the virtue of the *dikaios* is to do what the accepted order requires; and in this his virtue is like every other Homeric virtue. But by the latter part of the fifth century it is possible to ask if it is or is not *dikaiosunê* to do what the established order requires; and it is possible to disagree radically as to what it would be to act in accordance with *dikê*, to be *dikaios*. So in *Philoctêtês* both Neoptolemus and Odysseus claim *dikaiosunê* for their side of the argument (1245-51) and within the same few lines they disagree also about what it is to be *sophos* (wise) and to be *aischros* (disgraceful).

There are then a received set of virtue-words in fifth-century Greek and in that sense a received set of virtues: friendship, courage, self-restraint, wisdom, justice—and not only these. But as to what each of these requires and as to why each is counted as a virtue there is extended disagreement. So that those who unreflectively rely on ordinary usage, on what they have been taught, will all too easily find themselves trapped in inconsistency in just the way that Socrates' partners in dialogue so often are. I have of course oversimplified both the causes and the effects of that inconsistency. Even if heroic society did exist in, say, ninth-century Greece, the transition from that society to the fifth century was far more complex and many-layered than I have indicated. The conceptions of the virtues in the sixth century, in the early fifth century and in the later fifth century all differ in important respects and each earlier period leaves its mark on each of its successors. The effect of this is evident as much in modern scholarly disputes as in ancient moral disagreements. Dodds, Adkins, Lloyd-Jones — and the list could be extended into a very long one — all present largely coherent pictures of the Greek moral outlook; each coherent view differs from each of the others and all seem to be largely right. What none allow for adequately is the possibility that the Greek moral vocabulary and outlook is a good deal more incoherent than we find it easy to recognize, and one reason is obvious. Too many of the sources are texts in which a deliberate reorganization and redefinition of the moral vocabulary is taking place, texts in which words are being assigned a clear meaning which they earlier did not possess. Philosophers, poets, historians may all be apt to betray us in this way, and we have very few sources which do not come to us through one or the other of these.

We therefore have to be wary of speaking too easily of 'the Greek view of the virtues' not just because we often say 'Greek' where we should say 'Athenian' but also because there were a number of Athenian views. For my present purposes I need to consider at least four: those of the sophists, of Plato, of Aristotle and of the tragedians, especially Sophocles. But it is important in each case to remember that we are dealing with a response to incoherence, a response in each case informed by a different purpose. Yet before I consider these four, let me underline at least one thing that they all do share. All do take it for granted that the milieu in which the virtues are to be exercised and in terms of which they are to be defined is the *polis*. In the *Philoctêtês* it is essential to the action that Philoctetes by being left on a desert island for ten years has not been merely exiled from the company of mankind, but also from the status of a human being: 'You left me friendless, solitary, without a city, a corpse among the living.' This is not mere rhetoric. For us the notion that friendship, company and a city-state are essential components of humanity is alien; and between us and this concept lies a great historical divide. For example, the word for solitary, *erêmos*, is the ancestor of our word 'hermit'; and for Christianity the life of a hermit could be among the most important types of human life. And the concept of friendship has itself undergone continuous later transformations. But in Sophocles' world — where so much is contestable — that friendship, companionship and citizenship are essential aspects of humanity is not contestable. And in this at least Sophocles is at one with the rest of the Athenian world.

The common Athenian assumption then is that the virtues have their place within the social context of the city-state. To be a good man will on every Greek view be at least closely allied to being a good citizen. What are the virtues which make the good man and the good citizen and what are the corresponding vices? When Isocrates praised Pericles he described him as excelling all other citizens in being *sôphrôn* and *dikaios* and *sophos*. Orators and comic poets generally denounce meanness and lack of generosity. It is a Greek commonplace that the free man tells the truth fearlessly and takes responsibility for his actions. Some writers praise simplicity of character and straightforwardness. Lack of sensitivity and lack of pity are often condemned; so is boorishness. Courage is always praised. But, if these are some of the most important virtues, what is it that makes them virtues?

There is a danger that we shall be misled in trying to answer this question *either* if we attend only to those qualities which we too take to be virtuous *or*, as I have already suggested, if we ignore the extent to which Greeks disagree with one another. So I begin by doing two things: one is to note that humility, thrift and conscientiousness could appear in *no* Greek list of the virtues; the other is to stress once more the alternative interpretations of one and the same virtue which were possible. Consider not only honor and justice, but the virtue whose name is *sôphrosunê*. In origin it is an aristocratic virtue. It is the virtue of the man who could but does not abuse his power. One part of such restraint is the ability to control one's passions and when the word is applied to women – and *sôphrosunê* is for the Greeks *the* womanly virtue – that ability and only that is commonly what is being praised. But very clearly this is not what Isocrates was primarily praising in Pericles.

Indeed Isocrates' praise of Pericles as *sôphrôn* must be recognized as compatible with the acknowledgment of those qualities which, in Thucydides' version, Pericles himself ascribed to the Athenians: incessant activity in the pursuit of their own interests, a drive to do more and to push further. Thus *sôphrosunê* on this view does not necessarily imply restraint so far as one's goals are concerned; it is rather restraint in the manner of realizing these goals that is being praised, the quality of knowing how far to go on a particular occasion and when to pause or temporarily draw back. So that *sôphrosunê* can now be at home with the *polupragmosunê* of the Athenian democracy as well as with the aristocratic ideals of restraint and of *hêsuchia*, leisure. Yet the ideals of *polupragmosunê* and of *hêsuchia* are certainly themselves sharply opposed. So that *sôphrosunê* has now found a place not just in two different, but in two incompatible moral schemes. In what ways are *polupragmosunê* and *hêsuchia* opposed?

Hêsuchia appears in Pindar (*Pythian Odes* 8.1) as the name of a goddess; she represents that peacefulness of spirit to which the victor in a contest in entitled when he is at rest afterwards. Respect for her is bound up with the notion that we strive in order to be at rest, rather than in order to struggle ceaselessly from goal to goal, from desire to desire. *Poluprag-mosunê*, by contrast, is not merely a matter of being busy about many things, but a quality in which pride comes to be taken. The Athenian milieu in which it is at home is one in which *pleonexia* also comes naturally enough to be at home. *Pleonexia* is sometimes translated so as to make it appear that the vice which it picks out is simply that of wanting more than one's share. This how J.S. Mill translated it and to follow Mill is to diminish the gap between the ancient world and modern individualism, for we have no problem—how could anyone have a problem?—with the thought that it is wrong to take more than one's share. But in fact the vice picked out is that of acquisitiveness as such, a quality that modern individualism both in its economic activity and in the *character* of the consuming aesthete does not perceive to be a vice at all. Nietzsche translated *pleonexia* with insight as well as precision: *haben und mehrwollhaben*, because in the modern world, as we shall later see, the notion that the wish to have more *simpliciter*, acquisitiveness as such, might be a vice, was increasingly lost sight of. Hence presumably Mill's misunderstanding, for in fact *pleonexia* is the name of just that vice.

For those possessed by *pleonexia* the *agôn*, the contest, becomes something quite other than it was in the games or for Pindar. It becomes an instrument of the individual will in grasping after success in satisfying its desires. Of course in any society where contests are central to activity, the victor will achieve the prizes of success and will at least appear to be and will probably in fact be nearer than others to satisfying his desires. But the achievement and the excellence recognized by himself, by the community and by such people as the poet whose task it is to praise that achievement and that excellence are what is valued primarily; it is because they are valued that prizes and satisfactions attach to them; *not* vice versa.

Consider now the place of the *agôn*, the contest, in classical Greek society. The Homeric epics are narratives which recount a series of contests. In the *Iliad* the character of these contests is gradually transformed until it is acknowledged in the confrontation between Achilles and Priam that to win is also to lose and that in the face of death winning and losing no longer divide. This is the first great enunciation of moral truth in Greek culture and later we shall have to consider its status as *truth*. For the moment we need only note that it was in the context of the *agôn* that that truth had to be discovered.

The *agôn* of course changes its character. First in the Olympic games the actual wars between city-states were suspended by a truce every four years from 776 B.C. onward and every Greek community, no matter how widely scattered, aspired to send representatives. Wrestling, running, horse-racing and the discus were celebrated by the praise of poetry and sculpture. Around this center there grew up other practices: Olympia, originally and always a shrine of Zeus, became an archive where records were kept and treaties preserved. The implicit definition of a Greek, as contrasted with a barbarian, becomes—a member of a community entitled to attend the Olympic games. But the *agôn* is a central institution not only in uniting all Greeks from their different city-states. It is also central within each city-state, a context in which once again the form of the *agôn* changes. Among the contests into which it is transformed are the debates in the assemblies and law courts of Greek democracy, the conflicts at the heart of tragedy, a piece of symbolic (and very serious) buffoonery in the plot-line of comedy, and finally the dialogue form of philosophical argument. In understanding each of these as a manifestation of the *agôn*, we ought to recognize that the categories *political, dramatic, philosophical* were much more intimately related in the Athenian world than in our own. Politics and philosophy were shaped by dramatic form, the preoccupations of drama were philosophical and political, philosophy had to make its claims in the arena of the political and the dramatic. At Athens the audience for each was potentially largely and actually to some degree one and the same; and the audience itself was a collective actor. The producer of drama was a holder of political office; the philosopher risked comic portrayal and political punishment. The Athenians had not insulated, as we have by a set of institutional devices, the pursuit of political ends from dramatic representation or the asking of philosophical questions from either. Hence we lack, as they did not, *any* public, generally shared communal mode either for representing politcal conflict or for puttting our politics to the philosophical question. It will be important later to notice more precisely how these possibilities were closed to us. But for the moment enough has been said to return to the central question.

We have noticed in turn that different and rival lists of virtues, different and rival attitudes toward the virtues and different and rival definitions of individual virtues are at home in fifth-century Athens and that nonetheless the city-state and the *agôn* provide the shared contexts in which the virtues are to be exercised. Just because these rivalries and inconsistencies are symptoms of conflict it is scarcely surprising that rival and competing philosophical accounts of the virtues appear, making overt and explicit the underlying conflicts. Of these perhaps the simplest and most radical is that of a certain type of sophist.

A.W.H. Adkins has noticed the resemblance between Thrasymachus as portrayed by Plato and the cruder versions of the Homeric hero. 'Scratch Thrasymachus and you find Agamemnon.' Agamemnon is the prototype of the Homeric hero who has never learnt the truth that the *Iliad* was written to teach; he wants only to win and to have the fruits of victory for himself. Everyone else is to be used or overcome: Iphigeneia, Briseis, Achilles. So the sophist of whom Plato's Thrasymachus is the type makes success the only goal of action and makes the acquisition of power to do and to get whatever one wants the entire content of success. A virtue is then naturally enough defined as a quality which will ensure success. But success for the sophists, as for other Greeks, must be success in some particular city. Hence the ethics of success comes to be combined with a certain kind of relativism.

To be successful is to be successful in a particular city; but in different cities there may be different conceptions of the virtues. What is taken to be just in democratic Athens may be different from what is taken to be just in aristocratic Thebes or in military Sparta. The sophistic conclusion is that in each particular city the virtues are what they are taken to be in that city. There is no such thing as justice-as-such, but only justice-as-understood-in-Athens and justice-as-understood-at-Thebes and justice-as-understood-at-Sparta. This relativism, when combined with the view that a virtue is a quality which leads to individual success, involves its adherents in a number of related difficulties.

Part of the original impulse behind the sophistic view seems to have been the wish to provide a consistent and coherent redefinition of the central evaluative expressions in fifth-century Greek as a basis for educating the young, particularly the aristocratic young, for political success. But the achievement of a certain degree of consistency by elevating competitive conceptions and definitions of the virtues above the cooperative ones turns out to have generated inconsistency at other points. By accepting the evaluative vocabulary of his own particular city the sophist will sometimes find himself using expressions which themselves embody a non-relativistic standpoint inconsistent with the relativism which led him to use that vocabulary. And the sophist who has redefined expressions such as 'just', 'virtue' and 'good' so that they refer to qualities which are conducive to individual success, but who also wishes to employ the conventional vocabulary in order to achieve that success, may well find himself in one situation praising justice, because by 'justice' nothing more is to be meant that 'what is to the interest of the stronger' and in another praising injustice over justice because it is the practice of injustice (as conventionally understood) which is in fact to the interest of the stronger.

There is of course nothing in this type of sophistic tradition which makes it *necessary* for someone who holds it to be trapped in this kind of inconsistency—and so become the victim of his opponents in debate—but inconsistency could only be escaped by a more radical redefinition of the virtues than many sophists were prepared to embark upon.

So in Plato's *Gorgias* Gorgias himself and his pupil Polus are successively defeated in argument by Socrates as a result of this kind of inconsistency, whereas Callicles cannot be so defeated. For Callicles is prepared to carry through a systematic statement of his standpoint whatever the deductive consequences and whatever the degree of the breach with ordinary moral usage. That standpoint is one which glorifies the man who uses his intelligence to dominate and who uses his domination to satisfy his desires without limit. Socrates is able to raise difficulties for this view, but none of them is conclusive in the way his objections to Gorgias and Polus had been.

Thus Callicles does seem to succeed in providing one way of resolving the incoherences of the oridinary Greek mind. Are there good reasons why we should not accept that resolution? Some later writers—Stoic in the ancient world, Kantian in the modern—have supposed that the only possible answer to Callicles lies in arguing for the severance of all connection between what is good (or, as modern writers would say, *morally* good) and human desires. They take it that *if* what we ought to do is also what satisfies our desires, then Callicles must be in the right. Plato of course does not attack Callicles from this standpoint; indeed it is doubtful if any fifth- or fourth-century Greek could have done so in a systematic way. For Plato—and in this at least both Plato and Callicles agree with ordinary Greek usage as well as with each other—accepts the view that the concepts of virtue and goodness on the one hand and those of happiness, success and the fulfilment of desire on the other are indissolubly linked. He cannot therefore challenge Callicles' view that what is good will lead to happiness and the satisfaction of desire; instead he has to challenge Callicles' conceptions of happiness and of the satisfaction of desire. It is the need to sustain this latter challenge that leads straight to the psychology of the *Phaedo* and of the *Republic*; and the psychology of those dialogues provides the basis for a rival conception of and an accompanying list of the virtues.

If for Callicles the satisfaction of desire is to be found in domination over a *polis*, in the life of a tyrant, for Plato rational desire could be genuinely satisfied in no *polis* that actually existed in the physical world, but only in an ideal state with an ideal constitution. Thus the good to which rational desire aspires and the actual life of the city-state have to be sharply distinguished. What is politically attainable is unsatisfying; what is satisfying is attainable only by philosophy and not by politics. The former lesson Plato finally learnt in Sicily and doubtless he felt that he ought to have learnt it once and for all from the death of Socrates. Nonetheless the concept of virtue remains a political concept; for Plato's account of the virtuous man in inseparable from his account of the virtuous citizen. Indeed this is an understatement, there is no way to be excellent as a man which does not involve excellence as a citizen and *vice versa*. But the excellent citizen will not be at home in any actual city, in Athens or Thebes or even in Sparta. In none of these places are those who rule the city themselves ruled by reason. What does reason enjoin?

That each part of the soul shall perform its specific function. The exercise of each specific function is a particular virtue. So the bodily appetites are to accept the restraint imposed by reason; the virtue thus exhibited is *sôphrosunê*. That high-spirited virtue which responds to the challenge of danger, when it responds as reason bids it, exhibits itself as courage, *andreia*. Reason itself, when it has been disciplined by mathematical and dialectical enquiry, so that it is able to discern what justice itself is, what beauty itself is and above all the other forms what the Form of the Good is, exhibits its own specific virtue of *sophia*, wisdom. These three virtues can only be exhibited when a fourth, the virtue of *dikaiosunê*, is also exhibited; for *dikaiosunê*—which, on Plato's account, is very different from any of our modern conceptions of justice, although 'justice' is the translation used by almost all of Plato's translators—is precisely the virtue of allocating each part of the soul its particular function and no other.

Plato's account and redefinition of the virtues is thus derived from a complex theory, a theory without which we will be unable to grasp what a virtue is. He both rejects and tries to explain what his theory must envisage as the ordinary Greek's inadequate linguistic usage and corrupted practice. When certain of the sophists translate the variety and the inconsistencies of ordinary use into a would-be consistent relativism, Plato rejects not only the relativism and the inconsistency, but also the variety.

I emphasized earlier that Plato's theory links the virtues to the political practice of an ideal rather than actual state; it is important also to emphasize that Plato claims for his theory an ability to explain the conflicts and disharmonies of actual states as well as the harmony and disharmony of actual personalities. In both the political and the personal realm conflict and virtue are mutually incompatible and exclusive. This is perhaps one source of Plato's view that dramatic art is an enemy of virtue. Certainly there are other sources for Plato's view: his metaphysics leads him to treat all *mimêsis*, all representation, as a movement away from genuine reality into illusion and his view of the didactic effect of art makes him disapprove of the content of much epic and dramatic poetry. But he is also deeply committed to the view that both within the city and within the person virtue cannot be in conflict with virtue. There cannot be rival goods at war with each other. Yet it is just what Plato takes to be impossible which makes tragic drama possible.

Tragic drama had very early explored the conflicts that could arise within a post-Homeric framework. Aeschylus relied on the contradictory imperatives of kinship loyalties and the equally contradictory imperatives of the theology that sustained kinship. But it is Sophocles who systematically explores rival allegiances to incompatible goods, especially in the *Antigone* and the *Philoctêtês*, in a way that raises a key and a complex set of questions about the virtues. It seems to be clear that there can be rival conceptions of the virtues, rival accounts of what a virtue is. And it seems to be equally clear that there can be disputes over whether a particular quality is to be accounted a virtue or a vice. But it might of course be argued that in all such disagreements at least one party to the argument is simply mistaken and that we can rationally settle all such disputes and arrive at a single rationally justifiable account of and list of the virtues. Suppose indeed for the moment that this were so. Could it then be the case that in certain circumstances at least the possession of one virtue might exclude the possession of some other? Could one virtue be temporarily at least at war with another? And both qualities genuinely be accounted virtues? Can the exercise of the virtue of doing what is required of a sister (Antigone) or a friend (Odysseus) be at odds with the exercise of the virtues of justice (Creon) or of compassion and truthfulness (Neoptolemus)? We inherit two systematic sets of answers to such questions.

The ancestor of one of these sets of answers is Plato, for whom as we have seen the virtues are not merely compatible with each other, but the presence of each requires the presence of all. This strong thesis concerning the unity of the virtues is reiterated both by Aristotle and by Aquinas, even though they differ from Plato—and from each other—in a number of important ways. The presupposition which all three share is that there exists a cosmic order which dictates the place of each virtue in a total harmonious scheme of human life. Truth in the moral sphere consists in the conformity of moral judgment to the order of this scheme.

There is a sharply contrasting modern tradition which holds that the variety and heterogeneity of human goods is such that their pursuit cannot be reconciled in any single moral order and that consequently any social order which *either* attempts such a reconciliation *or* which enforces the hegemony of one set of goods over all other is bound to turn into a straitjacket and very probably a totalitarian straitjacket for the human condition. This is a view which Sir Isaiah Berlin has urged upon us strenuously, and its ancestry, as we noted earlier, is in Weber's writings. I take it that this view entails a heterogeneity of the virtues as well as of goods in general and that choice between rival claims in respect of the virtues has the same central place in the moral life for such theorists that choice between goods in general does. And where judgments express choices of this kind, we cannot characterize them as either true or false.

The interest of Sophocles lies in his presentation of a view equally difficult for a Platonist or a Weberian to accept. There are indeed crucial conflicts in which different virtues appear as making rival and incompatible claims upon us. But our situation is tragic in that we have to recognize the authority of both claims. There *is* an objective moral order, but our perceptions of it are such that we cannot bring rival moral truths into complete harmony with each other and yet the acknowledgment of the moral order and of moral truth makes the kind of choice which a Weber or a Berlin urges upon us out of the question. For to choose does not exempt me from the authority of the claim which I chose to go against.

In the conflicts of Sophoclean tragedy therefore the attempt at resolution unsurprisingly invokes an appeal to and a verdict by some god. But the divine verdict always ends rather than resolves the conflict. It leaves unbridged the gap between the acknowledgment of authority, of a cosmic order and of the claims to truth involved in the recognition of the virtues on the one hand and our particular perceptions and judgments in particular situations on the other. It is worth recalling that this aspect of the Sophoclean view is only part of his account of the virtues, an account which has two other central characteristics which I have already noted.

The first is that the moral protagonist stands in a relationship to his community and his social roles which is neither the same as that of the epic hero nor again the same as that of modern individualism. For like the epic hero the Sophoclean protagonist would be nothing without his or her place in the social order, in the family, the city, the army at Troy. He or she is what society takes him to be. But he or she is not *only* what society takes him or her to be; he or she both belongs to a place in the social order and transcends it. And he or she does so precisely by encountering and acknowledging the kind of conflict which I have just identified.

Secondly the life of the Sophoclean protagonist has its own specific narrative form just as that of the epic hero had. I am not here making the trivial and obvious point that Sophoclean protagonists are characters in plays; I am rather ascribing to Sophocles a belief analogous to that which Anne Righter (1962) has ascribed to Shakespeare: that he portrayed human life in dramatic narratives because he took it that human life already had the form of dramatic narrative and indeed the form of one specific type of dramatic narrative. Hence I take it also that the difference between the heroic account of the virtues and the Sophoclean amounts precisely to a difference over what narrative form captures best the central characteristics of human life and agency. And this suggests an hypothesis: that generally to adopt a stance on the virtues will be to adopt a stance on the narrative character of human life. Why this might be so is easy to understand.

If a human life is understood as a progress through harms and dangers, moral and physical, which someone may encounter and overcome in better and worse ways and with a greater or lesser measure of success, the virtues will find their place as those qualities the possession and exercise of which generally tend to success in this enterprise and the vices likewise as qualities which likewise tend to failure. Each human life will then embody a story whose shape and form will depend upon what is counted as a harm and danger and upon how success and failure, progress and its opposite, are understood and evaluated. To answer these questions will also explicitly and implicitly be to answer the question as to what the virtues and vices are. The answer to this linked set of questions given by the poets of heroic society is not the same as that given by Sophocles; but the link is the same in both, and it reveals how belief in the virtues being of a certain kind and belief in human life exhibiting a certain narrative order are internally connected.

The nature of this connection is reinforced by a further consideration. A little earlier I contrasted the Sophoclean view of the virtues with that taken by Plato on the one hand and Weberian individualists on the other. And in each of these cases the account of the virtues is closely linked to attitudes to the narrative form of human life. Plato has to expel the dramatic poets from the *Republic* because in part of the rivalry between their view and his. (It has been justly remarked that the *Republic* itself, like some of its predecessor dialogues, is a dramatic poem; but the dramatic form is not that of tragedy, is not Sophoclean.) And for the Weberian individualist life of itself has in this sense no form, save that which we choose to project on to it in our aesthetic imaginings. But such points must for the present be put on one side. Instead it is necessary to amplify the Sophoclean view in two ways.

The first is to emphasize once more that what is at stake in Sophoclean dramatic encounter is not simply the fate of individuals. When Antigone and Creon contend, the life of the clan and the life of the city are weighed against each other. When Odysseus and Philoctetes confront each other, it is the outcome for the Greek community which is in the balance. It is the individual in his or her role, representing his or her community, who is as in epic the dramatic character. Hence in some important sense the community too is a dramatic character which enacts the narrative of *its* history.

Secondly and correlatively the Sophoclean self differs from the emotivist self as much as does the heroic self, although in more complex ways. The Sophoclean self transcends the limitations of social roles and is able to put those roles in question, but it remains accountable to the point of death and accountable precisely for the way in which it handles itself in those conflicts which make the heroic point of view no longer possible. Thus the presupposition of the Sophoclean self's existence is that it can indeed win or lose, save itself or go to moral destruction, that there is an order which requires from us the pursuit of certain ends, an order relationship to which provides our judgments with the property of truth or falsity. But is there such an order? We can no longer delay turning away from poetry to philosophy, from Sophocles to Aristotle.

12

Aristotle's Account of the Virtues

Any attempt to treat Aristotle's account of the virtues from the standpoint which I have adopted presents me with an initial problem. On the one hand he is *the* protagonist against whom I have matched the voices of liberal modernity; so that I am clearly committed to giving his own highly specific account of the virtues a central place. On the other hand I have already made it clear that I want to regard him not just as an individual theorist, but as the representative of a long tradition, as someone who articulates what a number of predecessors and successors also articulate with varying degrees of success. And to treat Aristotle as part of a tradition, even as its greatest representative, is a very unAristotelian thing to do.

Aristotle of course recognized that he had predecessors. Indeed he tried to write the history of previous philosophy is such a way that it culminated with his own thought. But he envisaged the relationship of that thought to those precedessors in terms of the replacement of *their* errors or at least partial truths by *his* comprehensively true account. From the standpoint of truth, on Aristotle's own view, once his work had been done, theirs could be discarded without loss. But to think in this way is to exclude the notion of a tradition of thought, at least as I intend it. For it is central to the conception of such a tradition that the past is never something merely to be discarded, but rather that the present is intelligible only as a commentary upon and response to the past in which the past, if necessary and if possible, is corrected and transcended, yet corrected and transcended in a way that leaves the present open to being in turn corrected and transcended by some yet more adequate future point of view. Thus the notion of a tradition embodies a very unAristotelian theory of knowledge according to which each particular theory or set of moral or scientific beliefs is intelligible and justifiable – insofar as it is justifiable – only as a member of an historical series. It is scarcely necessary to say that in such a series the later is not necessarily superior to the earlier; a tradition may cease to progress or may degenerate. But when a tradition is in good order, when progress *is* taking place, there is always a certain cumulative element to a tradition. Not everything in the present is equally liable to be overthrown in the future, and some elements of present theory or belief may be such that it is difficult to envisage their being abandoned without the tradition as a whole being discarded. So it is for example in our present-day scientific tradition with the account of the relationship between cells and molecules in contemporary biochemistry; and so it is with Aristotle's account of some central virtues within the classical tradition.

Aristotle's importance therefore can only be specified in terms of a kind of tradition whose existence he himself did not and could not have acknowledged. And just as the absence of any sense of the specifically historical—in our sense—in Aristotle, as in other Greek thinkers, debars Aristotle from recognizing his own thought as part of a tradition, it also severely limits what he can say about narrative. Hence the task of integrating what Aristotle had to say about the virtues with the kind of thesis about the relationship between virtues and forms of narratives which I have suggested is present in epic and tragic writers has to wait—a very long wait—for successors to Aristotle whose biblical culture has educated them to think historically. Some questions central to the classical tradition can receive no answer from Aristotle himself. Nonetheless it is Aristotle whose account of the virtues decisively constitutes the classical tradition as a tradition of moral thought, firmly establishing a good deal that his poetic predecessors had only been able to assert or suggest and making the classical tradition a rational tradition, without surrendering to Plato's pessimism about the social world. Yet we ought also to note at the outset that we possess Aristotle's thought in a form which itself makes scholarly and sometimes unsettlable debate over the content of that thought unavoidable. Moreover, it has recently been argued (Kenny 1978) that it is in the *Eudemian Ethics* and not, as almost every scholar has believed, in the *Nicomachean Ethics* that Aristotle's mature positions are to be found. The debate over this contention will continue (Irwin 1980), but happily I need not enter into it. For the tradition within which I am placing Aristotle was one which made the *Nicomachean Ethics* the canonical text for Aristotle's account of the virtues.

The *Nicomachean Ethics*—dedicated to Aristotle's son Nicomachus, says Porphyry; edited by him, say others—is the most brilliant set of lecture notes ever written; and just because they are lecture notes, with all the disadvantages of occasional compression or repetition or inaccurate cross-referencing, we can almost hear in them from time to time the tone of Aristotle's spoken voice. It is magisterial and it is unique; but it is also a voice that seeks to be more than merely Aristotle's own. 'What do *we* say on such and such a topic?' is a question that he continuously asks, not 'What do *I* say?' Who is this 'we' in whose name he writes? Aristotle takes himself not to be inventing an account of the virtues, but to be articulating an account that is implicit in the thought, utterance and action of an educated Athenian. He seeks to be the rational voice of the best citizens of the best city-state; for he holds that the city-state is the unique political form in which alone the virtues of human life can be genuinely and fully exhibited. Thus a philosophical theory of the virtues is a theory whose subject-matter is that pre-philosophical theory already implicit in and pre-supposed by the best contemporary practice of the virtues. This of course does not entail that practice, and the pre-philosophical theory implicit in practice are normative for philosophy necessarily has a sociological, or as Aristotle would have said, political starting-point.

Every activity, every enquiry, every practice aims at some good; for by 'the good' or 'a good' we mean that at which human beings characteristi-cally aim. It is important that Aristotle's initial arguments in the *Ethics* pre-suppose that what G.E. Moore was to call the 'naturalistic fallacy' is not a fallacy at all and that statements about what is good—and what is just or courageous or excellent in other ways—just are a kind of factual state-ment. Human beings, like the members of all other species, have a specific nature; and that nature is such that they have certain aims and goals, such that they move by nature towards a specific *telos*. The good is defined in terms of their specific characteristics. Hence Aristotle's ethics, expounded as he expounds it, presupposes his metaphysical biology. Aristotle thus sets himself the task of giving an account of the good which is at once local and particular—located in and partially defined by the characteristics of the *polis*—and yet also cosmic and universal. The tension between these poles is felt throughout the argument of the *Ethics*.

What then does the good for man turn out to be? Aristotle has cogent arguments against identifying that good with money, with honor or with pleasure. He gives to it the name of *eudaimonia*—as so often there is a dif-ficulty in translation: blessedness, happiness, prosperity. It is the state of being well and doing well in being well, of a man's being well-favored himself and in relation to the divine. But when Aristotle first gives this name to the good for man, he leaves the question of the content of *eudaimonia* largely open.

The virtues are precisely those qualities the possession of which will enable an individual to achieve *eudaimonia* and the lack of which will frustrate his movement toward that *telos*. But although it would not be in-correct to describe the exercise of virtues as a means to the end of achieving the good for man, that description is ambiguous. Aristotle does not in his writings explicitly distinguish between two different types of means-end relationship. When we speak of any happening or state or activity as a means to some other, we may on the one hand mean that the world is as a matter of contingent fact so ordered that if you are able to bring about a happening or state or activity of the first kind, an event or state or activity of the second kind will ensue. The means and the end can each be adequately characterized without reference to the other; and a number of quite different means may be employed to achieve one and the same end. But the exercise of the virtues is not in this sense *a* means to the end of the good for man. For what constitutes the good for man is a complete human life lived at its best, and the exercise of the virtues is a necessary and central part of such a life, not a mere preparatory exercise to secure such a life. We thus cannot characterize the good for man adequately without already having made reference to the virtues. And within an Aristotelian framework the suggestion therefore that there might be some means to achieve the good for man without the exercise of the virtues makes no sense.

The immediate outcome of the exercise of a virtue is a choice which issues in right action: 'It is the correctness of the end of the purposive choice of which virtue is the cause' (1228a1, Kenny's translation, Kenny 1978) wrote Aristotle in the *Eudemian Ethics*. It does not of course follow that in the absence of the relevant virtue a right action may not be done. To understand why, consider Aristotle's answer to the question: what would someone be like who lacked to some large degree an adequate training in the virtues of character? In part this would depend on his natural traits and talents; some individuals have an inherited natural disposition to do on occasion what a particular virtue requires. But this happy gift of fortune is not to be confused with the possession of the corresponding virtue; for just because it is not informed by systematic training and by principle even such fortunate individuals will be the prey of their own emotions and desires. This victimization by one's own emotions and desires would be of more than one kind. On the one hand one would lack any means of ordering one's emotions and desires, of deciding rationally which to cultivate and encourage, which to inhibit and reduce; on the other hand on particular occasions one would lack those dispositions which enable a desire for something other than what is actually one's good to be held in check. Virtues are dispositions not only to act in particular ways, but also to feel in particular ways. To act virtuously is not, as Kant was later to think, to act against inclination; it is to act from inclination formed by the cultivation of the virtues. Moral education is an 'éducation sentimentale'.

The educated moral agent must of course know what he is doing when he judges or acts virtuously. Thus he does what is virtuous *because* it is virtuous. It is this fact that distinguishes the exercise of the virtues from the exercise of certain qualities which are not virtues, but rather simulacra of virtues. The well-trained soldier, for instance, may do what courage would have demanded in a particular situation, but not because he is courageous but because he is well-trained or perhaps—to go beyond Aristotle's example by remembering Frederick the Great's maxim—because he is more frightened of his own officers than he is of the enemy. The genuinely virtuous agent however acts on the basis of a true and rational judgment.

An Aristotelian theory of the virtues does therefore presuppose a crucial distinction between what any particular individual at any particular time takes to be good for him and what is really good for him as a man. It is for the sake of achieving this latter good that we practice the virtues and we do so by making choices about means to achieve that end, means in both senses characterized earlier. Such choices demand judgment and the exercise of the virtues requires therefore a capacity to judge and to do the right thing in the right place at the right time in the right way. The exercise of such judgment is not a routinizable application of rules. Hence perhaps the most obvious and astonishing absence from Aristotle's thought for any modern reader: there is relatively little mention of rules anywhere in the *Ethics*. Moreover Aristotle takes that part of morality which is obedience to rules to be obedience to laws enacted by the city-state—if and when the city-state enacts as it ought. Such law prescribes and prohibits certain types of action absolutely and such actions are among those which a virtuous man would do or refrain from doing. Hence it is a crucial part of Aristotle's view that certain types of action are absolutely prohibited or enjoined irrespective of circumstances or consequences. Aristotle's view is teleological, but it is not consequentialist. Moreover the examples Aristotle gives of what is absolutely prohibited resemble the precepts of what is at first sight a completely different kind of moral system, that of the Jewish law. What he says about the law is very brief, although he does insist that there are natural and universal as well as conventional and local rules of justice. It seems likely that he means to insist that natural and universal justice absolutely prohibits certain types of act; but that which penalties are assigned to which offence may vary from city to city. Nonetheless what he says on this topic is so brief as to be cryptic. It therefore seems worth asking in a more general way—rather than imputing to Aristotle views that would go too far beyond what is in the text—how it might be that views such as Aristotle's on the place of the virtues in human life should require some reference to the absolute prohibitions of natural justice. And in asking this question it is worth remembering Aristotle's insistence that the virtues find their place not just in the life of the individual, but in the life of the city and that the individual is indeed intelligible only as a *politikon zôon*.

This last remark suggests that one way to elucidate the relationship between virtues on the one hand and a morality of laws on the other is to consider what would be involved in any age in founding a community to achieve a common project, to bring about some good recognized as their shared good by all those engaging in the project. As modern examples of such a project we might consider the founding and carrying forward of a school, a hospital or an art gallery; in the ancient world the characteristic examples would have been those of a religious cult or of an expedition or of a city. Those who participated in such a project would need to develop two quite different types of evaluative practice. On the one hand they would need to value—to praise as excellences—those qualities of mind and character which would contribute to the realization of their common good or goods. That is, they would need to recognize a certain set of qualities as virtues and the corresponding set of defects as vices. They would also need however to identify certain types of action as the doing or the production of harm of such an order that they destroy the bonds of community in such a way as to render the doing or achieving of good impossible in some respect at least for some time. Examples of such offences would characteristically be the taking of innocent life, theft and perjury and betrayal. The table of the virtues promulgated in such a community would teach its citizens what kinds of actions would gain them merit and honor; the table of legal offences would teach them what kinds of actions would be regarded not simply as bad, but as intolerable.

The response to such offences would have to be that of taking the person who committed them to have thereby excluded himself or herself from the community. A violation of the bonds of community by the offender has to be recognized for what it is by the community, if the community is not itself to fail. Hence the offender in one crucial sense has excluded him or herself, has by his or her own action invited punishment. Whether the exclusion were permanent—by way of execution or irrevocable exile— or temporary—by way of imprisonment or exile for a term—would depend upon the gravity of the particular offence. A broad measure of agreement on a scale of gravity of offences would be partially constitutive of such a community as would a similar broad measure of agreement on the nature and importances of the various virtues.

The need for *both* these types of practice arises from the fact that an individual member of such a community could fail in his role as a member of that community in two quite different ways. He could on the one hand simply fail to be good enough; that is he could be deficient in the virtues to such an extent as to render his contribution to the achievement of the community's common good negligible. But someone could fail in this way without committing any of the particular offences specified in the com-

munity's laws; indeed it might be precisely because of his vices that someone abstained from committing offences. Cowardice can be someone's reason for not committing murder; vanity and boastfulness can on occasion
lead someone to tell the truth.

Conversely to fail the community by committing an offence against the
law is *not* simply to fail by not being good enough. It is to fail in a quite
different way. Indeed although someone who possesses the virtues to a
high degree will be far less apt than others to commit grave offences, a
brave and modest man may on occasion commit murder and his offence
is no less and no more than the offence of a coward or a braggart. To do
positive wrong is not the same as to be defective in doing or being good.
Nonetheless the two kinds of failure are intimately related. For both injure the community to some degree and make its shared project less likely
to be successful. An offence against the laws destroys those relationships
which make common pursuit of the good possible; defective character,
while it may also render someone more liable to commit offences, makes
one unable to contribute to the achievement of that good without which
the community's common life has no point. Both are bad because deprivations of good, but deprivations of very different kinds. So that an account
of the virtues while an essential part of an account of the moral life of such
a community could never be complete by itself. And Aristotle, as we have
seen, recognizes that his account of the virtues has to be supplemented by
some account, even if a brief one, of those types of action which are absolutely prohibited.

There is however another crucial link between the virtues and law, for
knowing how to apply the law is itself possible only for someone who
possesses the virtue of justice. To be just is to give each person what each
deserves; and the social presuppositions of the flourishing of the virtue of
justice in a community are therefore twofold: that there are rational
criteria of desert and that there is socially established agreement as to what
those criteria are. A great part of the assignation of goods and penalties
in accordance with desert is of course rule-governed. Both the distribution
of public office within the city and the retribution accorded to criminal
acts are to be specified by the laws of the city. (Notice how on an Aristotelian view law and morality are not two separate realms, as they are
for modernity.) But, partly because laws are general, particular cases will
always arise in which it is unclear how the law is to be applied and unclear
what justice demands. Thus there are bound to be occasions on which no
formula is available in advance; it is on such occasions that we have to
act *kata ton orthon logon* ('according to right reason', *Nicomachean Ethics*
1138b25), a phrase misleadingly translated by W.D. Ross 'in accordance

with the right rule'. (This misreading by someone who is usually a meticulous translator of Aristotle is perhaps not unimportant; for it reflects the large and un-Aristotelian preoccupation with rules of modern moral philosophers.) What Aristotle seems to mean here can be usefully illustrated by a contemporary example. There is at the time at which I am writing a lawsuit in progress between the Wampanoag Indian tribe and the town of Mashpee, Massachusetts. The Wampanoag Indians claim that their tribal lands in the township were illegally and unconstitutionally appropriated and they are suing for their return. (The case has since been decided *against* the Wampanoag by a jury verdict notable only for its incoherence.) The claim has been quite some time coming to court and the hearings themselves will not be over soon. The party who loses in the lower court will almost certainly appeal and the process of appeal is extended. During this long period property values in Mashpee have fallen drastically and it is for the moment almost impossible to sell certain types of property at all. This creates hardship generally for homeowners and more especially for certain classes of homeowners, for example, retired people who had legitimately expected to be able to sell their property and move elsewhere, relying on the proceeds of the sale to reestablish their lives, perhaps nearer their children. What in this type of situation does justice demand? We ought to note that two rule-specified concepts of justice recently advanced by contemporary moral philosophers can give us no help at all. John Rawls argues that 'social and economic inequalities are to be arranged so that they are to the greatest benefit of the least advantaged . . .' (p. 302) and Robert Nozick asserts that 'the holdings of a person are just if he is entitled to them by the principles of justice in acquisition and transfer . . .' (p. 153). But the problem in Mashpee concerns a period of time in which we do not as yet know *either* who has a just title by acquisition and transfer, for precisely that is to be decided by the current legal case *or* which is the least advantaged group in Mashpee, for that will be determined as a consequence of the outcome of the case. If it goes one way, the Wampanoag will turn out to be the richest group in Mashpee, but if the other, they will remain the poorest. Nonetheless a just solution has been devised by the tribal claimants (a solution to which after an apparent initial agreement the Selectmen of Mashpee refused their assent): this is, that all properties of one acre or less on which a dwelling house stands shall be exempted from the suit. It would be difficult to represent this as in any way the application of a rule; indeed it had to be devised because no application of the rules could afford small homeowners justice. The solution is the result of rough and ready reasoning involving such considerations as the proportion of the land claimed which comprises such properties and the number of people affected if the size of property exempted were fixed at one acre rather than more or less. To judge *kata ton orthon logon* is indeed to judge of more or less and Aristotle tries to use the notion of a mean between the more or the less to give a general characterization of the virtues: courage lies between rashness and timidity, justice between doing injustice and suffering injustice, liberality between prodigality and meanness. For each virtue therefore there are two corresponding vices. And what it is to fall into a vice cannot be adequately specified independently of circumstances: the very same action which would in one situation be liberality could in another be prodigality and in a third meanness. Hence judgment has an indispensable role in the life of the virtuous man which it does not and could not have in, for example, the life of the merely law-abiding or rule-abiding man.

A central virtue therefore is *phronêsis*. *Phronêsis* like *sôphrosunê* is originally an aristocratic term of praise. It characterizes someone who knows what is due to him, who takes pride in claiming his due. It comes to mean more generally someone who knows how to exercise judgment in particular cases. *Phronêsis* is an intellectual virtue; but it is that intellectual virtue without which none of the virtues of character can be exercised. Aristotle's distinction between these two kinds of virtue is initially made in terms of a contrast between the ways in which they are acquired; intellectual virtues are acquired through teaching, the virtues of character from habitual exercise. We become just or courageous by performing just or courageous acts; we become theoretically or practically wise as a result of systematic instruction. Nonetheless these two kinds of moral education are intimately related. As we transform our initial naturally given dispositions into virtues of character, we do so by gradually coming to exercise those dispositions *kata ton orthon logon*. The exercise of intelligence is what makes the crucial difference between a natural disposition of a certain kind and the corresponding virtue. Conversely the exercise of practical intelligence requires the presence of the virtues of character; otherwise it degenerates into or remains from the outset merely a certain cunning capacity for linking means to any end rather than to those ends which are genuine goods for man.

According to Aristotle then excellence of character and intelligence cannot be separated. Here Aristotle expresses a view characteristically at odds with that dominant in the modern world. The modern view is expressed at one level in such banalities as 'Be good, sweet maid, and let who will be clever' and at another in such profundities as Kant's distinction between the good will, the possession of which alone is both necessary and sufficient for moral worth, and what he took to be a quite distinct natural gift, that of knowing how to apply general rules to particular cases, a gift the lack of which is called stupidity. So for Kant one can be both good and stupid; but for Aristotle stupidity of a certain kind precludes goodness. Moreover genuine practical intelligence in turn requires knowledge of the good, indeed itself requires goodness of a kind in its possessor: '. . . it is clear that a man cannot have practical intelligence unless he is good' (1144a37).

I noticed earlier that modern social practice and theory follows Kant rather than Aristotle at this point—not surprisingly. Hence those characters so essential to the dramatic scripts of modernity, the expert who matches means to ends in an evaluatively neutral way and the moral agent who is anyone and everyone not actually mentally defective, have no genuine counterpart in Aristotle's scheme or indeed within the classical tradition at all. It is indeed difficult to envisage the exaltation of bureaucratic expertise in any culture in which the connection between practical intelligence and the moral virtues is firmly established.

This connection between practical intelligence and the virtues of character is invoked by Aristotle in the course of his argument that one cannot possess any of the virtues of character in a developed form without possessing all the others. It is difficult to suppose that he seriously means 'all'—it seems obvious that someone can be genuinely brave without being socially agreeable, yet agreeableness is counted by Aristotle among the virtues, as of course is courage—but that is what he says (*Nicomachean Ethics*, 1145a). Nonetheless it is easy to understand why Aristotle held that the *central* virtues are intimately related to each other. The just man does not fall into the vice of *pleonexia* which is one of the two vices corresponding to the virtue of justice. But in order to avoid *pleonexia* it is clear that one must possess *sôphrosunê*. The brave man does not fall into the vices of rashness and cowardice; but 'the rash man seems to be a braggart' and boastfulness is one of the vices relative to the virtue of truthfulness about oneself.

This interrelationship of the virtues explains why they do not provide us with a number of distinct criteria by which to judge the goodness of a particular individual, but rather with one complex measure. The application of that measure in a community whose shared aim is the realization of the human good presupposes of course a wide range of agreement in that community on goods and virtues, and it this agreement which makes possible the kind of bond between citizens which, on Aristotle's view, constitutes a *polis*. That bond is the bond of friendship and friendship is itself a virtue. The type of friendship which Aristotle has in mind is that which embodies a shared recognition of and pursuit of a good. It is this sharing which is essential and primary to the constitution of any form of community, whether that of a household or that of a city. 'Law-givers,' says

Aristotle, 'seem to make friendship a more important aim than justice' (1155a24); and the reason is clear. Justice is the virtue of rewarding desert and of repairing failures in rewarding desert within an already constituted community; friendship is required for that initial constitution.

How can we reconcile this view of Aristotle's with his assertion that one cannot have many friends of this kind? Estimates of the population of Athens in the fifth and fourth centuries vary widely, but the number of adult male citizens clearly ran into some tens of thousands. How can a population of such a size be informed by a shared vision of the good? How can friendship be the bond between them? The answer surely is by being composed of a network of small groups of friends, in Aristotle's sense of that word. We are to think then of friendship as being the sharing of all in the common project of creating and sustaining the life of the city, a sharing incorporated in the immediacy of an individual's particular friendships.

This notion of the political community as a common project is alien to the modern liberal individualist world. This is how we sometimes at least think of schools, hospitals or philanthropic organizations; but we have no conception of such a form of community concerned, as Aristotle says the *polis* is concerned, with the whole of life, not with this or that good, but with man's good as such. It is no wonder that friendship has been relegated to private life and thereby weakened in comparison to what it once was.

Friendship of course, on Aristotle's view, involves affection. But that affection arises within a relationship defined in terms of a common allegiance to and a common pursuit of goods. The affection is secondary, which is not in the least to say unimportant. In a modern perspective affection is often the central issue; our friends are said to be those whom we *like*, perhaps whom we like very much. 'Friendship' has become for the most part the name of a type of emotional state rather than of a type of social and political relationship. E.M. Forster once remarked that if it came to a choice between betraying his country and betraying his friend, he hoped that he would have the courage to betray his country. In an Aristotelian perspective anyone who can formulate such a contrast has no country, has no *polis*; he is a citizen of nowhere, an internal exile wherever he lives. Indeed from an Aristotelian point of view a modern liberal political society can appear only as a collection of citizens of nowhere who have banded together for their common protection. They possess at best that inferior form of friendship which is founded on mutual advantage. That they lack the bond of friendship is of course bound up with the self-avowed moral pluralism of such liberal societies. They have abandoned the moral unity of Aristotelianism, whether in its ancient or medieval forms.

A spokesman for the modern liberal view has of course at first sight an easy rejoinder to Aristotelianism. Aristotle, he might argue with a good deal of cogency, simply offers too simple and too unified a view of the complexities of human good. If we look at the realities of Athenian society, let alone of Greek society as a whole or the rest of the ancient world, what we in fact find is a recognition of a diversity of values, of conflicts between goods, of the virtues not forming a simple, coherent, hierarchical unity. Aristotle's portrait is at best an idealization and his tendency is always, so it might be said, to exaggerate moral coherence and unity. So, for example, on the unity of the virtues what he has to argue about the detailed variety in interrelationships between different virtues and vices does not seem to warrant anything like his own strong conclusion about the unity and inseparability of all the virtues in the character of the good man.

With this last particular charge it is perhaps, as I have already suggested, difficult to disagree. But it is worth asking why Aristotle should in this particular case have insisted on what seems to be, even from his own point of view, an unnecessarily strong conclusion. Aristotle's belief in the unity of the virtues is one of the few parts of his moral philosophy which he inherits directly from Plato. As with Plato, the belief is one aspect of an hostility to and denial of conflict either within the life of the individual good man or in that of the good city. Both Plato and Aristotle treat conflict as an evil and Aristotle treats it as an eliminable evil. The virtues are all in harmony with each other and the harmony of individual character is reproduced in the harmony of the state. Civil war is the worst of evils. For Aristotle, as for Plato, the good life for man is itself single and unitary, compounded of a hierarchy of goods.

It follows that conflict is simply the result either of flaws of character in individuals or of unintelligent political arrangements. This has consequences not only for Aristotle's politics, but also for his poetics and even his theory of knowledge. In all three the *agôn* has been displaced from its Homeric centrality. Just as conflict is not central to a city's life, but is reduced to a threat to that life, so tragedy as understood by Aristotle cannot come near the Homeric insight that tragic conflict is the essential human condition — the tragic hero on Aristotle's view fails because of his own flaw, not because the human situation is sometimes irremediably tragic — and dialectic is no longer the road to truth, but for the most part only a semi-formal procedure ancillary to enquiry. Where Socrates argued dialectically with particular individuals and Plato wrote dialogues, Aristotle therefore produces expository lectures and treatises. There is naturally enough a corresponding striking contrast between the Aristotelian standpoint on theology and either that of Aeschylus or of Sophocles; for Aristotle that particular appeal to the divine which in both Aeschylus and Sophocles signals the recognition of tragic impasse can have made no realistic sense. The impersonal unchanging divinity of which Aristotle speaks, the metaphysical contemplation of which furnishes man with his specific and ultimate *telos*, can itself take no interest in the merely human, let alone in the dilemmatic; it is nothing other than thought timelessly thinking itself and conscious of nothing but itself.

Since such contemplation is the ultimate human *telos*, the essential final and completing ingredient in the life of the man who is *eudaimôn*, there is a certain tension between Aristotle's view of man as essentially political and his view of man as essentially metaphysical. To become *eudaimôn* material prerequisites and social prerequisites are necessary. The household and the city-state make the metaphysical human project possible; but the goods which they provide are, although necessary, and although themselves part of that whole human life, subordinate from the metaphysical standpoint. Nonetheless in many passages where Aristotle discusses individual virtues, the notion that their possession and practice is in the end subordinate to metaphysical contemplation would seem oddly out of place. (For an excellent discussion of the issues, see Ackrill 1974 and Clark 1979). Consider for example once again Aristotle's discussion of friendship.

Aristotle, probably responding to Plato's discussion of friendship in the *Lysis*, distinguishes three kinds of friendship: that which derives from mutual utility, that which derives from mutual pleasure and that which derives from a shared concern for goods which are the goods of both and therefore exclusively of neither. It is, as I have already had occasion to emphasize, the third which is genuine friendship and which provides the paradigm for the relationship between husband and wife in the household as well as for that between citizen and citizen in the *polis*. Thus the good man's final achieved self-sufficiency in his contemplation of timeless reason does not entail that the good man does not need friends, just as it does not entail that he does not need a certain level of material prosperity. Correspondingly a city founded on justice and friendship can only be the best kind of city if it enables its citizens to enjoy the life of metaphysical contemplation.

Within this metaphysical and social structure what is the place of liberty? It is crucial to the structure of Aristotle's extended argument that the virtues are unavailable to slaves or to barbarians and so therefore is the good for man. What is a barbarian? Not merely a non-Greek (whose language sounds to Hellenic ears like 'ba, ba, ba') but someone who lacks a *polis* and thereby shows—on Aristotle's view—that he is incapable of political relationships. What are political relationships? The relationships of free men to each other, that is the relationships between those members of a community who both rule and are ruled over. The free self is simultaneously political subject and political sovereign. Thus to be involved in political relationships entails freedom from any position that is mere subjection. Freedom is the presupposition of the exercise of the virtues and the achievement of the good.

With this part of Aristotle's conclusion we need not quarrel. What is likely to affront us—and rightly—is Aristotle's writing off of non-Greeks, barbarians and slaves, as not merely not possessing political relationships, but as incapable of them. With this we may couple his view that only the affluent and those of high status can achieve certain key virtues, those of munificence and of magnanimity; craftsmen and tradesmen constitute an inferior class, even if they are not slaves. Hence the peculiar excellences of the exercise of craft skill and manual labor are invisible from the standpoint of Aristotle's catalogue of the virtues.

This blindness of Aristotle's was not of course private to Aristotle; it was part of the general, although not universal, blindness of his culture. It is intimately connected with another form of limitation. Aristotle writes as if barbarians and Greeks both had fixed natures and in so viewing them he brings home to us once again the ahistorical character of his understanding of human nature. Individuals as members of a species have a *telos*, but there is no history of the *polis* or of Greece or of mankind moving towards a *telos*. History indeed is not a reputable form of enquiry—less philosophical than poetry because it aspires genuinely to deal with individuals, whereas even poetry, on Aristotle's view, deals with types. Aristotle was well aware that the kind of knowledge which he takes to be genuinely scientific, to constitute *epistêmê*—knowledge of essential natures grasped through universal necessary truths, logically derivable from certain first principles—cannot characteristically be had of human affairs at all. He knew that the appropriate generalizations are ones which hold only *epi to polu* ('for the most part') and what he says about *them* agrees with what I asserted earlier about the generalizations of the modern social scientist. But in spite of this recognition he apparently felt no need to pursue the question of their character further. This is presumably the source of the paradox that Aristotle who saw the forms of social life of the city-state as normative for essential human nature was himself a servant of that Macedonian royal power which destroyed the city-state as a free society. Aristotle did not understand the transience of the *polis* because he had little or no understanding of historicity in general. Thus a whole range of questions cannot arise for him including those which concern the ways in which men might pass from being slaves or barbarians to being citizens of a *polis*. Some men just *are* slaves 'by nature', on Aristotle's view.

Yet it remains true that these limitations in Aristotle's account of the virtues do not necessarily injure his general scheme for understanding the place of the virtues in human life, let alone deform his multitude of more particular insights. Two of these deserve particular emphasis in any account of the virtues. The first concerns the place of enjoyment in human life. Aristotle's characterization of enjoyment as supervening upon successful activity enables us to understand *both* why it is plausible to treat enjoyment—or pleasure or happiness—as the *telos* of human life *and* why nonetheless this would be a mistake. The enjoyment which Aristotle identifies is that which characteristically accompanies the achievement of excellence in activity. Such activity may be of very different kinds: the writing or translation of poetry, the playing of games, the carrying through of some complex social project. And what counts as excellence will always be relative to the standards of performance for people like us so far. Hence generally to seek to excel is to aim at doing that which will be enjoyable, and it is natural to conclude that we seek to do that which will give us pleasure and so that enjoyment or pleasure or happiness is the *telos* of our activity. But it is important to note that the very same Aristotelian considerations which lead us towards this conclusion debar us from accepting any view which treats enjoyment or pleasure or happiness as a criterion for guiding our actions. Just because enjoyment of a highly specific kind—I emphasized both the specific and the heterogeneous character of enjoyment earlier when I was discussing Benthamite utilitarianism—supervenes upon each different type of successfully achieved activity, the enjoyment of itself provides us with no good reason for embarking upon one type of activity rather than another.

Moreover what *I* particularly enjoy will of course depend upon what sort of person I am, and what sort of person I am is of course a matter of my virtues and vices. After the expulsion of Aristotelianism from our culture there was a period in the eighteenth century when it was a commonplace to suggest—on tombstones as well as in philosophical works—that the virtues are nothing but those qualities which we happen to find generally pleasant or useful. The oddity of this suggestion lies in the fact that what we find generally pleasant or useful will depend on what virtues are generally possessed and cultivated in our community. Hence the virtues cannot be defined or identified in terms of the pleasant or useful. To this it may be replied that surely there are qualities which are useful or pleasant to human beings *qua* members of a particular biological species with a particular kind of environment. The standard of utility or pleasure is set by man *qua* animal, man prior to and without any particular culture. But man without culture is a myth. Our biological nature certainly places constraints on all cultural possibility; but man who has nothing but a biological nature is a creature of whom we know nothing. It is only man with practical intelligence—and that, as we have seen, is intelligence informed by virtues—whom we actively meet in history. And it is on the nature of practical reasoning that Aristotle provides another discussion which is crucially relevant to the character of the virtues.

Aristotle's account of practical reasoning is in essentials surely right. It has a number of key features. The first is that Aristotle takes the conclusion to a practical syllogism to be a particular kind of action. The notion that an argument can terminate in an action of course offends Humean and post-Humean philosophical prejudices, according to which only statements (or, in some particularly barbarous versions, sentences) can have truth-values and enter into those relationships of consistency and inconsistency which partially define deductive argument. But statements themselves only possess these characteristics in virtue of their capacity to express beliefs; and actions can of course express beliefs as certainly, although not always as clearly and unambiguously, as utterances can. It is because and only because of this that we can be puzzled by the inconsistency between a given agent's actions and his statements. We should be puzzled for example by someone of whom we knew three things: first that he wanted to keep healthy, secondly that he had sincerely asserted *both* that to get cold and wet could be bad for his health *and* that the only way to keep warm and dry in winter was to wear his overcoat, and thirdly that he habitually in winter went out without his overcoat. For his action appears to express a belief inconsistent with his other expressed beliefs. Were anyone systematically inconsistent in this way, he or she would soon become unintelligible to those around them. We should not know how to respond to them, for we could no longer hope to identify either what they were doing or what they meant by what they said or both. Thus Aristotle's account of the practical syllogism can be construed as providing a statement of necessary conditions for intelligible human action and as doing so in a way that must hold for any recognizably human culture.

Practical reasoning then has, on Aristotle's view, four essential elements. There are first of all the wants and goals of the agent, presupposed by but not expressed in, his reasoning. Without these there would be no context for the reasoning, and the major and minor premises could not adequately determine what kind of thing the agent is to do. The second element is the major premise, an assertion to the effect that doing or having or seeking such-and-such is the type of thing that is good for or needed by a so-and-so (where the agent uttering the syllogism falls under the latter description). The third element is the minor premise wherein the agent, relying on a perceptual judgment, asserts that this is an instance or occasion of the requisite kind. The conclusion, as I already said, is the action.

This account returns us to the question of the relationship between practical intelligence and the virtues. For the judgments which provide the agent's practical reasoning with premises will include judgments as to what it is good for someone like him to do and to be; and an agent's capacity to make and to act upon such judgments will depend upon what intellectual and moral virtues and vices compose his or her character. The precise nature of this connection could only be elucidated by a fuller account of practical reasoning than Aristotle gives us; his account is notably elliptical and in need of paraphrase and interpretation. But he says quite enough to show us how, from an Aristotelian standpoint, reason cannot be the servant of the passions. For the education of the passions into conformity with pursuit of what theoretical reasoning identifies as the *telos* and practical reasoning as the right action to do in each particular time and place is what ethics is about.

We have in the course of this account identified a number of points at which Aristotle's account of the virtues can be seriously put in question. Some of these concern parts of Aristotle's theory which not only have to be rejected, but whose rejection need not carry any large implications for our attitudes to his overall theory. So it is, I have suggested, with Aristotle's indefensible defence of slavery. But in at least three areas questions arise which, unless they can be answered satisfactorily, endanger the whole Aristotelian structure. The first of these concerns the way in which Aristotle's teleology presupposes his metaphysical biology. If we reject that biology, as we must, is there any way in which that teleology can be preserved?

Some modern moral philosophers who are deeply sympathetic to Aristotle's account of the virtues have seen no problem here. It has been argued that all we need to provide in order to justify an account of the virtues and vices is some very general account of what human flourishing and well-being consists in. The virtues can then be adequately characterized as those qualities necessary to promote such flourishing and well-being, because, whatever our disagreements in detail on *that* subject, we ought to be able to agree rationally on what is a virtue and what a vice. This view ignores the place in our cultural history of deep conflicts over what human flourishing and well-being do consist in and the way in which rival and incompatible beliefs on that topic beget rival and incompatible tables of the virtues. Aristotle and Nietzsche, Hume and the New Testament are names which represent polar oppositions on these matters. Hence any adequate teleological account must provide us with some clear and defensible account of the *telos*; and any adequate generally Aristotelian account must supply a teleological account which can replace Aristotle's metaphysical biology.

A second area of questioning concerns the relationship of ethics to the structure of the *polis*. If a good deal of the detail of Aristotle's account of the virtues presupposes the now-long-vanished context of the social relationships of the ancient city-state, how can Aristotelianism be formulated so as to be a moral presence in a world in which there are no city-states? Or to put matters in another way: is it possible to be an Aristotelian and yet to view the city-state in an historical perspective as only one—even if a very important one—in a series of social and political forms in and through which the kind of self which can exemplify the virtues can be found and educated and in which that self can find its arena?

Thirdly there are the questions posed by Aristotle's inheritance of Plato's belief in the unity and harmony of both the individual soul and the city-state and Aristotle's consequent perception of conflict as something to be avoided or managed. The problem which I am raising is best stated initially in terms of a confrontation between Aristotle and Sophocles. For Aristotle, as I have already suggested, the tragic form of narrative is enacted when and only when we have a hero with a flaw, a flaw in practical intelligence which springs from inadequate possession or exercise of some virtue. In a world in which everyone is good enough therefore there would be no tragic hero to be portrayed. Aristotle clearly derives this view partly from his moral psychology, but partly from his own reading of tragic drama and especially of *Oedipus Rex*. Yet, if my earlier account of Sophocles is correct, Aristotle's moral psychology has led him to misread Sophocles. For the conflicts of tragedy certainly may *in part* take the form that they do because of the flaws in Antigone and Creon, Odysseus and Philoctetes; but what constitutes those individuals' *tragic* opposition and conflict is the conflict of good with good embodied in their encounter prior to and independent of *any* individual characteristics; and to this aspect of tragedy Aristotle in the *Poetics* is and has to be blind. The absence of this view of the centrality of opposition and conflict in human life conceals from Aristotle also one important source of human learning about and one important milieu of human practice of the virtues.

The great Australian philosopher John Anderson urged us 'not to ask of a social institution: "What end or purpose does it serve?" but rather, "Of what conflicts is it the scene?" ' (Passmore 1962, p. xxii). If Aristotle had asked this question both of the *polis* and of the individual agent, he would have had an additional resource for understanding the teleological character of both the virtues and the social forms which provide them with a context. For it was Anderson's insight—a Sophoclean insight—that it is through conflict and sometimes only through conflict that we learn what our ends and purposes are.

13

Medieval Aspects and Occasions

We therefore turn to later writers in the Aristotelian tradition with a set of already formulated questions. But before we pose these questions to certain medieval writers, it is important to make two initial remarks. The first is to underline the fact that the tradition of thinking about the virtues which I am trying to delineate is not to be confused with that narrower tradition of Aristotelianism which consists simply in commentary upon and exegesis of Aristotle's texts. When I first spoke of the tradition with which I am concerned in Chapter 5, I used the equally misleading expression, 'classical morality', equally misleading since 'classical' is too wide, just as 'Aristotelian' is too narrow. But although the tradition is not easy to name, it is not too difficult to recognize. After Aristotle, it always uses the *Nicomachean Ethics* and the *Politics* as key texts, when it can, but it never surrenders itself wholly to Aristotle. For it is a tradition which always sets itself in a relationship of dialogue with Aristotle, rather than in any relationship of simple assent.

When eighteen or nineteen hundred years after Aristotle the modern world came systematically to repudiate the classical view of human nature—and with it in the end a great deal that had been central to morality—it did repudiate it very precisely as Aristotelianism. 'That buffoon who has misled the church' said Luther of Aristotle, setting the tone; and when Hobbes explained the Reformation he saw it as partly due to 'the fayling of Vertue in the Pastors', but partly 'from bringing of the Philosophy, and doctrine of Aristotle into Religion' (*Leviathan*, 1, 12). In fact of course—and this is the second initial remark that needs to be made—the medieval world encountered Aristotle relatively late and even Aquinas encountered him only in translation; and when it did encounter him, what he provided was at best a partial solution to a medieval problem which had already been stated time and again. That problem was how to educate and civilize human nature in a culture in which human life was in danger of being torn apart by the conflict of too many ideals, too many ways of life.

Of all the mythological ways of thinking which have disguised the middle ages for us none is more misleading than that which portrays a unified and monolithic Christian culture and this not just because the medieval achievement was also Jewish and Islamic. Medieval culture, insofar as it was a unity at all, was a fragile and complex balance of a variety of disparate and conflicting elements. To understand the place of the theory and practice of the virtues within it, it is necessary to recognize a number of different and conflicting strands in medieval culture, each of which imposed its own strains and tensions on the whole.

The first is that which derives from the fact that in a multiplicity of ways medieval society had only just made its own transition out of what I earlier called heroic society. Germans, Anglo-Saxons, Norwegians, Icelanders, Irishmen and Welshmen all had a pre-Christian past to remember, and many of their social forms and much of their poetry and story embodied those pasts. Often both forms and stories were Christianized so that the pagan warrior-king could emerge as the Christian knight, remarkably unchanged. Often Christian and pagan elements coexisted in varying degrees of compromise and tension, much as Homeric values coexisted with those of the city-state in the fifth century. In one part of Europe it was the Icelandic sagas which came to play much the same role as that of the Homeric poems, in another it was the *Taín Bó Cuailnge* and the tales of the Fianna, in a third the already Christianized Arthurian cycle. So the memory of heroic society is present in the tradition which I am identifying twice over: once as the background to fifth- and fourth-century Athenian society and once again in the background to the high middle ages. It is this double presence which makes the moral standpoint of heroic society a necessary starting-point for moral reflection within the tradition with which we are concerned. So the medieval order cannot reject the heroic table of the virtues. Loyalty to family and to friends, the courage required to sustain the household or a military expedition and a piety which accepts the moral limits and impositions of the cosmic order are central virtues, partially defined in terms of institutions such as the code of revenge in the sagas.

In early medieval Germanic law, for example, murder is a crime only when it is the secret killing of an unidentified person. When a known person kills another known person, not the criminal law but revenge by a kinsman is regarded as the appropriate response. And this distincition between two classes of killing seems to survive in England as late as the reign of Edward I. Nor is this merely a point about law, as contrasted with morals. The moralization of mediaval society lies precisely in creating general categories of right and wrong and general modes of understanding right and wrong—and out of them a code of law—which could replace the particular bonds and fractures of an older paganism. Viewed retrospectively, trial by ordeal seems to many modern writers superstitious; but when trial by ordeal was first introduced, its function too was precisely to place in a public and cosmic context in a quite new way the wrongs of private and local life.

When therefore in the twelfth century the question of the relationship of pagan to Christian virtues is explicitly posed by theologians and philosophers, it is much more than a theoretical question. It was indeed the rediscovery of classical texts, and of a strange assortment of classical texts—Macrobius, Cicero, Virgil—which first occasioned the theoretical problem. But the paganism with which scholars such as John of Salisbury and Peter Abelard or William of Conches wrestled was partly within themselves and their own society, even if in a form quite other than that of the ancient world. Moreover the solutions which they propounded had to be translated into a curriculum not only for the schools of cathedral chapters or of regular canons, but also in turn for universities. Some of them even became the schoolmasters of the powerful: Thomas Becket studied at Paris while Abelard was teaching and William of Conches was the tutor of England's Henry II. It may have been William of Conches who wrote the *Moralium Dogma Philosophorum*, a textbook which owed most to Cicero's *De Officiis*, but a great deal to other classical writers.

This acceptance of the classical tradition, even in so partially and fragmentarily recovered a form, was a course completely at variance with one type of Christian teaching, influential to varying degrees throughout the middle ages, which dismissed all pagan teaching as the devil's work and sought to find in the Bible an all-sufficient guide. Luther indeed was the heir of *this* medieval tradition. But its negative dismissals left the problem of the shape of a Christian life in the twelfth-century world, or in any other specific social world, insoluble. That problem is one of translating the Bible's message into a particular and detailed set of discriminations among contemporary alternatives and for that task one needs types of concepts and types of enquiry not made available by the Bible itself. There are of course times and places when what the contemporary secular world offers merits only complete rejection, the kind of rejection with which Jewish and Christian communities under the Roman Empire had to confront the demand that they worship the Emperor. These are the moments of martyrdom. But for long periods of Christian history this total either/or is not the choice with which the world confronts the church; it is not how to die as a martyr but how to relate to the forms of daily life that the Christian has to learn. For the writers of the twelfth century this question is posed in terms of the virtues. How is the practice of the four cardinal virtues of justice, prudence, temperance and courage to be related to that of the theological virtues—faith, hope and charity? As early as 1300 this classification of the virtues is found in vernacular as well as in Latin writers.

In Abelard's *Ethics*, written about 1138, the key distinction which is put to the service of answering this question is that between a vice and a sin. What Abelard took to be Aristotle's definition of a virtue, transmitted to him by Boethius, is put to use to provide a corresponding definition of a vice. Elsewhere, in Abelard's *Dialogue Between a Philosopher, a Jew and a Christian*, the Philosopher, who is the voice of the ancient world, lists and defines the cardinal virtues in Cicero's, not Aristotle's, terms. Abelard's accusation against the philosopher is not only or even principally one of positive error; what he stresses are the errors of omission in the pagan moral view, the incompleteness of the pagan account of the virtues, even in its best representatives. This incompleteness is ascribed to the inadequacy both of the Philosopher's conception of the supreme good and of the Philosopher's beliefs about the relationship of the human will to good and evil. But it is the latter that Abelard wishes to stress.

What Christianity requires is a conception not merely of defects of character, or vices, but of breaches of divine law, of sins. An individual's character may at any given time be a compound of virtues and vices, and these dispositions will preempt the will to move in one direction or another. But it is always open to the will to assent to or dissent from these promptings. Even the possession of a vice does not necessitate the performance of any particular wrong action. Everything turns on the character of the interior act of will. Character therefore, the arena of the virtues and vices, simply becomes one more circumstance, external to will. The true arena of morality is that of the will and of the will alone.

This interiorization of the moral life with its stress on will and law looks back not only to certain New Testament texts, but also to Stoicism. It is worth considering its Stoic ancestry in order to bring out the tension between any morality of the virtues and a certain type of morality of law.

On the Stoic view, unlike the Aristotelian, *arete* is essentially a singular expression and its possession by an individual an all or nothing matter; either someone possesses that perfection which *arete* (*virtus* and *honestas* are both used as Latin translations) requires or he does not. With virtue one has moral worth; without it one is morally worthless. There are no intermediate degrees. Since virtue requires right judgment, the good man is, on the Stoic view, also the wise man. But he is not necessarily successful or effective in his actions. To do what is right need not necessarily produce pleasure or happiness, bodily health or worldly or indeed any other success. None of these however are genuine goods; they are goods only conditionally upon their ministering to right action by an agent with a rightly formed will. Only such a will is unconditionally good. Hence Stoicism abandoned any notion of a *telos*.

The standard to which a rightly acting will must conform is that of the law which is embodied in nature itself, of the cosmic order. Virtue is thus conformity to cosmic law both in internal disposition and in external act. That law is one and the same for all rational beings; it has nothing to do with local particularity or circumstance. The good man is a citizen of the universe; his relation to all other collectivities, to city, kingdom or empire is secondary and accidental. Stoicism thus invites us to stand *against* the world of physical and political circumstance at the very same time that it requires us to act in conformity with nature. There are symptoms of paradox here and they are are not misleading.

For on the one hand virtue finds purpose and point outside itself; to live well is to the live the divine life, to live well is to serve not one's private purposes, but the cosmic order. Yet in each individual case to do what is right is to act without any eye to my further purpose at all, it is simply to do whatever is right for its own sake. The plurality of the virtues and their teleological ordering in the good life – as both Plato and Aristotle and beyond them Sophocles and Homer had understood them – disappear; a simple monism of virtue takes its place. It is unsurprising that the Stoics and Aristotle's later followers were never able to live in argumentative peace with each other.

Stoicism is not of course only an episode in Greek and Roman culture; it sets a pattern for all those later European moralities that invoke the notion of law as central in such a way as to displace conceptions of the virtues. This is a type of opposition which, given my discussion in the previous chapter of the relationship between that part of morality which consists in the negative prohibiting rules of the law and that part which concerns the positive goods toward which virtues move us, ought to appear surprising; although subsequent moral history has made us so familiar with it that we are in fact unlikely to be surprised. In discussing Aristotle's brief remarks on natural justice, I suggested that a community which envisages its life as directed toward a shared good which provides that community with its common tasks will need to articulate its moral life in terms *both* of the virtues *and* of law. This suggestion is perhaps a clue to what happened in Stoicism; for given the disappearance of such a form of community, just such a disappearance as was involved in the replacement of the city-state as the form of political life by first the Macedonian kingdom and later the Roman *imperium*, any intelligible relationship between the virtues and law would disappear. There would be no genuine shared common good; the only goods would be the goods of individuals. And the pursuit of *any* private good, being often and necessarily in these circumstances liable to clash with the good of others, would appear to be at odds with the requirements of the moral law. Hence if I adhere to the law, I will have to suppress the private self. The point of the law cannot be the achievement of some good beyond the law; for there now appears to be no such good.

If I am right then, Stoicism is a response to one particular type of social and moral development, a type of development which strikingly anticipates some aspects of modernity. Hence we should expect, and we do in fact find, recurrences of Stoicism.

Indeed whenever the virtues begin to lose their central place, Stoic patterns of thought and action at once reappear. Stoicism remains one of the permanent moral possibilities within the cultures of the West. That it did not provide the only or even the most important model for those moralists who later were to make the concept of a moral law into the whole of or almost the whole of morality is due to the fact that another, even sterner morality of law, that of Judaism, converted the ancient world. It was of course Judaism in the form of Christianity which thus prevailed. But those such as Nietzsche and the Nazis who have understood Christianity as essentially Judaic have in their hostility perceived a truth which has been disguised from many modern would-be friends of Christianity. For the Torah remains the law uttered by God in the New Testament as in the Old; and on the New Testament view Jesus as Messiah is, as the Council of Trent emphasized in a decree, lawgiver as well as a mediator to whom we owe obedience. 'If,' writes Karl Barth, agreeing in this at least for once with Trent, 'He were not the Judge, He would not be the Saviour' (*K.D.*, IV 1, p. 216).

How then can a morality of implacable law be related to any conception of the virtues? Abelard's retreat into interiority is from the standpoint of his contemporaries a refusal to face the tasks which provided the specific context for their posing of this question. As we have seen, from Abelard's point of view, the external social world was merely a set of contingent and accidental circumstances; but for many of Abelard's contemporaries it is these circumstances which define the moral task. For they do not inhabit a society in which institutional circumstance can almost be taken for granted; the twelfth century is a time when institutions have to be created. It is no accident that John of Salisbury is preoccupied with the question of the character of a statesman. What yet has to be invented in the twelfth century is an institutional order in which the demands of divine law can

more easily be heard and lived out in a secular society outside the
monasteries. The question of the virtues thus becomes inescapable: what
kind of man can do this? What type of education can foster this type of
man?

It is in terms of such questions that the difference between Abelard on
the one hand and, for example, Alan of Lille on the other is perhaps to
be understood. Writing in the 1170s Alan sees the pagan writers not so
much as representing a rival moral scheme as providing resources for
answering political questions. The virtues of which the pagan writers treat
are useful qualities in creating and sustaining an earthly social order; charity can transform them into genuine virtues, the practice of which leads
to man's supernatural and heavenly end. So Alan begins a movement to
synthesize ancient philosophy and the New Testament. His treatment of
Plato's and Cicero's texts anticipates Aquinas' use of parts of Aristotle
which only became available in the latter part of the twelfth and in the
thirteenth century; but unlike Aquinas Alan stresses the political and social
point of the virtues,

What were the political problems whose solution required the practice
of virtues? They are the problems of a society in which the central and
equitable administration of justice, universities and other means of sustaining learning and culture and the kind of civility which peculiarly belongs
to urban life are all still in the process of being created. The institutions
which will sustain them have yet for the most part to be invented. The
cultural space in which they will be able to exist has yet to be located
somewhere between the particularist claims of the intense local rural com-
unity which threatens to absorb everything into custom and local power
and the universal claims of the church. The resources available for this task
are slender: feudal institutions, monastic discipline, the Latin language,
ideas once Roman of order and of law, and the new culture of the twelfth-
century renascence: how is so little culture going to be able to control so
much behavior and invent so many institutions?

Part of the answer is: by generating just the right kinds of tension or
even conflict, creative rather than destructive, on the whole and in the long
run, between secular and sacred, local and national, Latin and vernacular,
rural and urban. It is in the context of such conflicts that moral education
goes on and that the virtues come to be valued and redefined. Three
aspects of this process need to be emphasized by considering in turn the
virtues of loyalty and justice, the military and chivalric virtues and the virtues of purity and patience.

It is easy to recognize the key place that loyalty must have in the hierarchies of a feudal society; it is as easy to understand the need for justice in

a society of motley competing claims and easy oppression. But loyalty to whom? And justice from whom? Consider the conflict between Henry II of England and Archbishop Thomas Becket. Each was a man of energy, hot temper and impetuosity. Each represented a great cause. Although Henry was primarily concerned to increase the royal power, the way in which he did so extended the rule of law in a fundamental sense, replacing feuds, self-help and local custom by a more stable, centralized, equitable and just system of courts and officials than had ever existed before. Becket in turn represented more than the manoeuvrings of ecclesiastical power, however much these preoccupied him. Embedded within the self-assertion of episcopal and papal power was the claim that human law is the shadow cast by divine law, that the institutions of law embody the virtue of justice. Becket represents the appeal to an absolute standard that lies beyond all secular and particular codifications. On this medieval view, as on the ancient, there is no room for the modern liberal distinction between law and morality, and there is no room for this because of what the medieval kingdom shares with the *polis*, as Aristotle conceived it. Both are conceived as communities in which men in company pursue *the* human good and not merely as—what the modern liberal state takes itself to be—providing the arena in which each individual seeks his or her own private good.

It follows that in much of the ancient and medieval worlds, as in many other premodern societies, the individual is identified and constituted in and through certain of his or her roles, those roles which bind the individual to the communities in and through which alone specifically human goods are to be attained; I confront the world as a member of this family, this household, this clan, this tribe, this city, this nation, this kingdom. There is no 'I' apart from these. To this it may be replied: what about my immortal soul? Surely in the eyes of God I am an individual, prior to and apart from my roles. This rejoinder embodies a misconception, which in part arises from a confusion between the Platonic notion of the soul and that of Catholic Christianity. For the Platonist, as later for the Cartesian, the soul, preceding all bodily and social existence, must indeed possess an identity prior to all social roles; but for the Catholic Christian, as earlier for the Aristotelian, the body and the soul are not two linked substances. I am my body and my body is social, born to those parents in this community with a specific social identity. What does make a difference for the Catholic Christian is that I, whatever earthly community I may belong to, am *also* held to be a member of a heavenly, eternal community in which I also have a role, a community represented on earth by the church. Of course I can be expelled from, defect from or otherwise lose my place in any of these forms of community. I can become an exile, a stranger, a wanderer. These too are assigned social roles, recognized within ancient and medieval communities. But it is always as part of an ordered community that I have to seek the human good, and in this sense of community the solitary anchorite or the shepherd on the remote mountainside is as much a member of a community as is a dweller in cities. Hence solitariness is no longer what it was for Philoctetes. The individual carries his communal roles with him as part of the definition of his self, even into his isolation.

Thus when Henry II and Becket confronted each other, each had to recognize in the other not just an individual will, but an individual who was the bearer of an authoritative role. Becket had to recognize what in justice he owed to the king; and when in 1164 the king demanded an obedience which he could not give, Becket had the insight to cast himself in the role of one about to be martyred. Before this the secular power at the very least trembled; no one could be found who had the temerity to deliver the hostile judgment of the royal court to the archbishop. When finally Henry occasioned Becket's death, he could not evade in the end the need to do penance, and I mean by penance something more and other than what was required for his reconciliation to Pope Alexander III. For more than a year before that reconciliation, immediately on hearing of Becket's death, he took to his own room, in sackcloth and ashes and fasting; and two years later he did public penance at Canterbury and was scourged by the monks. Henry's quarrel with Becket took place within a shared framework of detailed agreement on human and divine justice. Henry's quarrel with Becket was only possible because of their deep shared agreement on what constituted winning and losing for antagonists whose past history had brought them to this point and who occupied the position of king and archbishop. So when Becket was forced into a position where he could dramatically assume the role of martyr, he and Henry were not in disagreement as to the criteria, meaning and consequences of martyrdom.

There is thus a crucial difference between this quarrel and that later quarrel between Henry VIII and Thomas More in which what is in dispute is precisely how events are to be interpreted. Henry II and Thomas Becket inhabit a single narrative structure; Henry VIII and Thomas Cromwell on the one hand and Thomas More and Reginald Pole on the other inhabit rival conceptual worlds and tell, as they act and after they act, different and incompatible stories about what they do. In the medieval quarrel agreement in narrative understanding is manifested also in agreement about the virtues and vices; in the Tudor quarrel that framework of medieval agreement has already been lost. And it was that framework which the medieval Aristotelians tried to articulate.

In so doing they had of course to recognize virtues of which Aristotle knew nothing. One of these merits special consideration. It is the theological virtue of charity. Aristotle in considering the nature of friendship had concluded that a good man could not be the friend of a bad man; and since the bond of authentic friendship is a shared allegiance to the good, this is unsurprising. But at the centre of biblical religion is the conception of a love for those who sin. What is it that Aristotle's universe omits which makes the notion of such a love inconceivable within it? In the course of trying to understand the relationship of a morality of virtues to one of law I suggested earlier that the context which needed to be supplied to make that relationship intelligible was that of a form of community constituted by the shared project of achieving a common good and thus needing to recognize both a set of types of quality of character conducive to achieving that good—the virtues—and a set of types of action breaching the relationships necessary to such a form of community—the offences to be prosecuted by the community's law. The appropriate response to the latter was punishment, and this is how human societies do generally respond to such types of action. But in the culture of the Bible, in contrast to that of Aristotle, an alternative response became available, that of forgiveness.

What is the condition of forgiveness? It requires that the offender already accepts as just the verdict of the law upon his action and behaves as one who acknowledges the justice of the appropriate punishment; hence the common root of 'penance' and of 'punishment'. The offender can then be forgiven, if the person offended against so wills. The practice of forgiveness presupposes the practices of justice, but there is this crucial difference. Justice is characteristically administered by a judge, an impersonal authority representing the whole community; but forgiveness can only be extended by the offended party. The virtue exhibited in forgiveness is charity. There is no word in the Greek of Aristotle's age correctly translated 'sin', 'repentance' or 'charity'.

Charity is not of course, from the biblical point of view, just one more virtue to be added to the list. Its inclusion alters the conception of the good for man in a radical way; for the community in which the good is achieved has to be one of reconciliation. It is thus a community with a history of a particular kind. In the discussion of the conception and role of the virtues in heroic societies I emphasized the connection between that conception and role and the way in which human life is understood as embodying a certain type of narrative structure. It is now possible, tentatively, to generalize that thesis. Every particular view of the virtues is linked to some particular notion of the narrative structure or structures of human life. In the high medieval scheme a central genre is the tale of a quest or journey. Man is essentially *in via*. The end which he seeks is something which if gained can redeem all that was wrong with his life up to that point. This notion of man's end is of course not Aristotelian in at least two crucial ways.

First Aristotle takes the *telos* of human life to be *a certain kind of life*; the *telos* is not something to be achieved at some future point, but in the way our whole life is constructed. It is true that the good life which is the *telos* culminates in the contemplation of the divine and that therefore, for Aristotle as for the medievals, the good life moves to a climax. Nonetheless, if such scholars as J.L. Ackrill are correct (pp. 16-18), Aristotle's discussion of the place of contemplation is still situated within an account of the good life as a whole in which a variety of human excellences have to be achieved at the various relevant stages. This is why the notion of a final redemption of an almost entirely unregenerate life has no place in Aristotle's scheme; the story of the thief on the cross is unintelligible in Aristotelian terms. And it is unintelligible precisely because charity is not a virtue for Aristotle. Secondly the notion of human life as a quest or a journey in which a variety of forms of evil are encountered and overcome requires a conception of evil of which there are at most only intimations in Aristotle's writings. To be vicious is, on Aristotle's view, to fail to be virtuous. All badness of character is defect, is deprivation. It is therefore very difficult in Aristotelian terms to distinguish between *failure to be good* on the one hand and *positive evil* on the other, between the character of a Henry II and that of Gilles de Retz, or between that in every one of us which is potentially one or the other. This dimension of evil is one which St. Augustine had had to face in a way that Aristotle did not. Augustine followed the Neoplatonic tradition in understanding all evil as a privation of good; but he sees the evil of human nature in the consent which the will gives to evil, a consent prior to because presupposed in every particular explicit set of choices. Evil is somehow or other such and the human will is somehow or other such that the will can delight in evil. This evil is expressed in defiance of divine law and of human law insofar as it is the mirror of divine law; for to consent to evil is precisely to will to offend against the law.

The narrative therefore in which human life is embodied has a form in which the subject—which may be one or more individual persons, or, for example, the people of Israel, or the citizens of Rome—is set a task in the completion of which lies their peculiar appropriation of the human good; the way towards the completion of that task is barred by a variety of inward and outward evils. The virtues are those qualities which enable the evils to be overcome, the task to be accomplished, the journey to be completed. Thus although the conception of the virtues remains teleological, it is a very different conception from Aristotle's in at least two important ways over and above its Christian and Augustinian understanding of evil.

First Aristotle takes it that the possibility of achieving the human good, *eudaimonia*, can be frustrated by external misfortune. The virtues, he grants, will enable one to a large degree to cope with adversity, but great misfortunes such as Priam's exclude one from *eudaimonia* — as do ugliness, low birth and childlessness. What matters in the medieval perspective is not only the belief that no human being is excluded from the human good by such characteristics, but also the belief that no evil whatsoever that can happen to us need exclude us either, if we do not become its accomplice.

Secondly the medieval vision is historical in a way that Aristotle's could not be. It situates our aiming at the good not just in specific contexts — Aristotle situates that aiming within the *polis* — but in contexts which themselves have a history. To move towards the good is to move in time and that movement may itself involve new understandings of what it is to move towards the good. Modern historians of the middle ages often emphasize the weakness and inadequacy of medieval historiography; and the narratives which the greatest writers use to describe that journey which they take to be man's life are fictional and allegorical. But that is in part because medieval thinkers took the basic historical scheme of the Bible to be one within which they could rest assured. They did indeed lack a conception of history as invoking a continuous discovery and rediscovery of what history is; but they did not thereby lack a conception of human life as historical.

The virtues are then on this kind of medieval view those qualities which enable men to survive evils on their historical journey. I have already emphasized that medieval societies are in general societies of conflict, lawlessness and multiplicity. John Gardner has written of the fifteenth-century circle around John of Gaunt, Edward III of England's fourth son, 'What they desired of their world was law and order, firm and unchallenged monarchy, or, in Dante's phrase, "The one will that resolves the many"; what they saw all around them, and ardently hated, was instability, debased values, endless struggle, a mad commingling of high and low, not Oneness but Manyness — what Chaucer would describe, in his magnificent elaboration of a poem by Boethius, as a cosmic fornication' (Gardner 1977, p. 227). This passage suggests a common ambiguity in the medieval vision of the moral life.

On the one hand that life is informed by an idealized view of the world as an integrated order, in which the temporal mirrors the eternal. Every particular item has its due place in the order of things. This is that intellectual vision of total system which finds its supreme expression in Dante and in Aquinas, but to which a great deal of ordinary medieval thought continuously aspires. Yet even medieval thought, let alone medieval life, finds it difficult to be entirely systematic. There is not only the difficulty of fitting together the feudal with its inheritance from the heroic and the Christian, but there is also the tension between the Bible and Aristotle. Aquinas in his treatise on the virtues treats of them in terms of what had become the conventional scheme of the cardinal virtues (prudence, justice, temperance, courage) and the triad of theological virtues. But what then of, for example, patience? Aquinas quotes the Epistle of St James: 'Patience has its perfect work' (*S. Th.* qu. LXI, art. 3) and considers whether patience should not therefore be listed as a principal virtue. But then Cicero is quoted against St James, and it is argued that all the other virtues are contained within the four cardinal virtues. Yet if this is so Aquinas cannot of course mean by the Latin names of the cardinal virtues entirely what Aristotle meant by their Greek equivalents, since one or more of the cardinal virtues must contain within itself both patience and another biblical virtue which Aquinas explicitly acknowledges, namely humility. Yet in the only place in Aristotle's account of the virtues where anything resembling humility is mentioned, it is as a vice, and patience is not mentioned at all by Aristotle.

Even this does not suggest the range and variety that is to be found in medieval treatments of the virtues. When Giotto represented the virtues and vices at Padua he presented them in pairs, and the pairs by their original and imaginative forms of visual presentation suggest that a new mode of imaging may itself be a form of rethinking; and Berenson argued that in his frescoes of such vices as avarice and injustice Giotto answered the question: what are the significant traits in the appearance of someone exclusively dominated by each of the vices? His visual answers represent a view of the vices that both seems to argue with and to presuppose the Aristotelian scheme. There could not be more striking evidence of the heterogeneity of medieval thought.

Even ideal synthesis is therefore to some degree precarious. In medieval practice bringing the virtues to bear on the conflicts and evils of medieval life produces in different circumstances quite different perspectives on the rank order of the virtues. Patience and purity can become very important indeed. Purity is crucially important because the medieval world is one which recognizes how easily any grasp of the notion of a supreme good may be lost by worldly distraction; patience too is crucial because it is the virtue of endurance in the face of evil. An English fourteenth-century poet who was preoccupied with these themes wrote one poem, *Pearl*, in which a man who in a dream encounters the ghost of his dead daughter finds himself loving her more than he loves God, and another, *Patience*, in which Jonah is at first distressed by God's putting off the destruction of Nineveh because the delay is casting doubt on his, Jonah's, prophecies, but has to learn that it is only because God is patient and slow to anger that this wicked world is allowed to survive at all. The medieval consciousness is one which recognizes its hold upon the conception of the supreme good as always fragile and always threatened. The medieval world then is one in which not only is the scheme of the virtues enlarged beyond an Aristotelian perspective, but above all in which the connection between the distinctively narrative element in human life and the character of the vices comes to the forefront of consciousness and not only in biblical terms.

At this point therefore a crucial question has to be posed. If so much of medieval theory and practice is at odds with certain central theses advanced by Aristotle, in what sense was that theory and practice Aristotelian, if at all? Or to put the same point in another way: does not my account of medieval thinking about the virtues make a strict Aristotelian, such as Aquinas, a highly deviant medieval figure? It does indeed. And it is worth picking out some central features of Aquinas' treatment of the virtues which make of Aquinas an unexpectedly marginal figure to the history which I am writing. This is not to deny Aquinas' crucial role as an interpreter of Aristotle; Aquinas' commentary on the *Nicomachean Ethics* has never been bettered. But at key points Aquinas adopts a mode of treatment of the virtues which is questionable.

There is first of all his overall scheme of classification which I have already remarked. Aquinas presents the table of virtues in terms of what is presented as an exhaustive and consistent classificatory scheme. Such large classificatory schemes ought always to arouse our suspicions. A Linnaeus or a Mendeleev may indeed have grasped by a brilliant intuition an ordering of the empirical materials which is vindicated by a later theory; but where our knowledge is genuinely empirical we have to be careful not to confuse what we have learnt empirically with what is inferred from theory, even from true theory. And a good deal of our knowledge of the virtues is in this way empirical: we learn what kind of quality truthfulness or courage is, what its practice amounts to, what obstacles it creates and what it avoids and so on only in key part by observing its practice in others and in ourselves. And since we have to be educated into the virtues and most of us are incompletely and unevenly educated in them for a good part of our lives, there is necessarily a kind of empirical untidiness in the way that our knowledge of the virtues is ordered, more particularly in respect of how the practice of each relates to the practice of all the others. In the face of these considerations Aquinas' treatment of the classification of the virtues and his consequent treatment of their unity raises questions to which we find in his text no answer.

For on the one hand the theoretical backing for his classificatory scheme has two parts: one is a reiteration of the Aristotelian cosmology and the other is specifically Christian and theological. Yet we have every reason to reject Aristotle's physical and biological science, and the part of Christian theology which concerns man's true end and which is not Aristotelian metaphysics is on Aquinas' own account a matter of faith, not of reason. Consider in this light Aquinas' claim that if we encounter genuine moral conflict, it is always because of some previous wrong action of our own. Clearly this is *one* source of conflict. But will it cover Antigone and Creon, Odysseus and Philoctetes, or even Oedipus? Will it cover Henry II and Thomas Becket? For we have to be clear that if the kind of account of these situations which I have given is even roughly correct, each of these conflicts could as genuinely be *within* a single individual as between individuals.

Aquinas' point of view, like Aristotle's, precludes tragedy that is not the outcome of human flaws, of sin and error. And, unlike Aristotle, this is the outcome of a theology which holds that the world and man were made good and are only flawed as the result of acts of human will. When such a theology is allied to an Aristotelian account of knowledge of the natural world, it requires a *scientia* of both the physical and the moral order, a form of knowledge in which every item can be placed in a deductive hierarchy in which the highest place is taken by a set of first principles the truth of which can be known with certainty. But there is a problem for anyone holding this Aristotelian view of knowledge, a problem which has engaged many commentators. For on Aristotle's own account the generalizations of politics and ethics are not such as would fit into such a deductive account. They hold not necessarily and universally, but only *hôs epi to polu*, generally and for the most part. But if this is true, then we ought not to expect to be able to give, or want to be able to give, the kind of account of the virtues which Aquinas gives us.

What is at stake here is moral as well as epistemological. P.T. Geach, a contemporary follower of Aquinas—on this at least—has presented the problem of the unity of the virtues in the following way (Geach 1977). Suppose it is claimed that someone whose aims and purposes were generally evil, a devoted and intelligent Nazi, for example, possessed the virtue of courage. We ought to reply, says Geach, that either it was not courage that he possessed or that in that kind of case courage is not a virtue. This kind of reply is clearly one that must be made by anyone who holds anything like Aquinas' view of the unity of the virtues. What is wrong with it?

Consider what would be involved, what was in fact involved, in the moral re-education of such a Nazi: there were many vices that he had to unlearn, many virtues about which he had to learn. Humility and charity would be in most ways, if not quite in every way, new to him. But it is crucial that he would not have to unlearn or relearn what he knew about avoiding both cowardice and intemperate rashness in the face of harm and danger. Moreover it was precisely because such a Nazi was not devoid of the virtues that there was a point of moral contact between him and those who had the task of re-educating him, that there was something on which to build. To deny that that kind of Nazi was courageous or that his courage was a virtue obliterates the distinction between what required moral re-education in such a person and what did not. Thus I take it that if any version of moral Aristotelianism were necessarily committed to a strong thesis concerning the unity of the virtues (as not only Aquinas, but Aristotle himself were) there would be a serious defect in that position.

It is therefore important to stress both that Aquinas' version of Aristotle on the virtues is not the only possible version and that Aquinas is an uncharacteristic medieval thinker, even if the greatest of medieval theorists. And my own emphasis on the variety and untidiness of medieval uses of, extensions of and amendments to Aristotle is essential to understanding how medieval thinking was not only part of, but marked a genuine advance in the tradition of moral theory and practice which I am describing. Nonetheless the medieval stage in that tradition was in a strong sense Aristotelian, and not only in its Christian versions. When Maimonides encountered the question as to why God in the Torah had instituted so many holidays, he replied that it was because holidays provide opportunities for the making and growth of friendship and that Aristotle has pointed out that the virtue of friendship is the bond of human community. It is this linking of a biblical historical perspective with an Aristotelian one in the treatment of the virtues which is the unique achievement of the middle ages in Jewish and Islamic terms as well as in Christian.

14

The Nature of the Virtues

One response to the history which I have narrated so far might well be to suggest that even within the relatively coherent tradition of thought which I have sketched there are just too many different and incompatible conceptions of a virtue for there to be any real unity to the concept or indeed to the history. Homer, Sophocles, Aristotle, the New Testament and medieval thinkers differ from each other in too many ways. They offer us different and incompatible lists of the virtues; they give a different rank order of importance to different virtues; and they have different and incompatible theories of the virtues. If we were to consider later Western writers on the virtues, the list of differences and incompatibilities would be enlarged still further; and if we extended our enquiry to Japanese, say, or American Indian cultures, the differences would become greater still. It would be all too easy to conclude that there are a number of rival and alternative conceptions of the virtues, but, even within the tradition which I have been delineating, no single core conception.

The case for such a conclusion could not be better constructed than by beginning from a consideration of the very different lists of items which different authors in different times and places have included in their catalogues of virtues. Some of these catalogues—Homer's, Aristotle's and the New Testament's—I have already noticed at greater or lesser length. Let me at the risk of some repetition recall some of their key features and then introduce for further comparison the catalogues of two later Western writers, Benjamin Franklin and Jane Austen.

The first example is that of Homer. At least some of the items in a Homeric list of the *aretai* would clearly not be counted by most of us nowadays as virtues at all, physical strength being the most obvious example. To this it might be replied that perhaps we ought not to translate the word *aretê* in Homer by our word 'virtue', but instead by our word 'excellence'; and perhaps, if we were so to translate it, the apparently surprising difference between Homer and ourselves would at first sight have been removed. For we could allow without any kind of oddity that the possession of physical strength is the possession of an excellence. But in fact we would not have removed, but instead would merely have relocated, the difference between Homer and ourselves. For we would now seem to be saying that Homer's concept of an *aretê*, an excellence, is one thing and that our concept of a virtue is quite another since a particular quality can be an excellence in Homer's eyes, but not a virtue in ours and *vice versa*.

But of course it is not that Homer's list of virtues differs only from our own; it also notably differs from Aristotle's. And Aristotle's of course also differs from our own. For one thing, as I noticed earlier, some Greek virtue-words are not easily translated into English or rather out of Greek. Moreover consider the importance of friendship as a virtue in Aristotle's list—how different from us! Or the place of *phronêsis*—how different from Homer and from us! The mind receives from Aristotle the kind of tribute which the body receives from Homer. But it is not just the case that the difference between Aristotle and Homer lies in the inclusion of some items and the omission of others in their respective catalogues. It turns out also in the way in which those catalogues are ordered, in which items are ranked as relatively central to human excellence and which marginal.

Moreover the relationship of virtues to the social order has changed. For Homer the paradigm of human excellence is the warrior; for Aristotle it is the Athenian gentleman. Indeed according to Aristotle certain virtues are only available to those of great riches and of high social status; there are virtues which are unavailable to the poor man, even if he is a free man. And those virtues are on Aristotle's view ones central to human life; magnanimity—and once again, any translation of *megalopsuchia* is unsatisfactory—and munificence are not just virtues, but important virtues within the Aristotelian scheme.

At once it is impossible to delay the remark that the most striking contrast with Aristotle's catalogue is to be found neither in Homer's nor in our own, but in the New Testament's. For the New Testament not only praises virtues of which Aristotle knows nothing—faith, hope and love—and says nothing about virtues such as *phronêsis* which are crucial for Aristotle, but it praises at least one quality as a virtue which Aristotle seems to count as one of the vices relative to magnanimity, namely humility. Moreover since the New Testament quite clearly sees the rich as destined for the pains of Hell, it is clear that the key virtues cannot be available to them; yet they *are* available to slaves. And the New Testament of course differs from both Homer and Aristotle not only in the items included in its catalogue, but once again in its rank ordering of the virtues.

Turn now to compare all three lists of virtues considered so far—the Homeric, the Aristotelian, and the New Testament's—with two much later lists, one which can be compiled from Jane Austen's novels and the other which Benjamin Franklin constructed for himself. Two features stand out in Jane Austen's list. The first is the importance that she allots to the virtue which she calls 'constancy', a virtue about which I shall say more in a later chapter. In some ways constancy plays a role in Jane Austen analogous to that of *phronêsis* in Aristotle; it is a virtue the possession of which is a prerequisite for the possession of other virtues. The second is the fact that what Aristotle treats as the virtue of agreeableness (a virtue for which he says there is no name) she treats as only the simulacrum of a genuine virtue—the genuine virtue in question is the one she calls amiability. For the man who practices agreeableness does so from considerations of honor and expediency, according to Aristotle; whereas Jane Austen thought it possible and necessary for the possessor of that virtue to have a certain real affection for people as such. (It matters here that Jane Austen is a Christian.) Remember that Aristotle himself had treated military courage as a simulacrum of true courage. Thus we find here yet another type of disagreement over the virtues; namely, one as to which human qualities are genuine virtues and which mere simulacra.

In Benjamin Franklin's list we find almost all the types of difference from at least one of the catalogues we have considered and one more. Franklin includes virtues which are new to our consideration such as cleanliness, silence and industry; he clearly considers the drive to acquire itself a part of virtue, whereas for most ancient Greeks this is the vice of *pleonexia*; he treats some virtues which earlier ages had considered minor as major; but he also redefines some familiar virtues. In the list of thirteen virtues which Franklin compiled as part of his system of private moral accounting, he elucidates each virtue by citing a maxim obedience to which *is* the virtue in question. In the case of chastity the maxim is 'Rarely use venery but for health or offspring—never to dullness, weakness or the injury of your own or another's peace or reputation'. This is clearly not what earlier writers had meant by 'chastity'.

We have therefore accumulated a startling number of differences and incompatibilities in the five stated and implied accounts of the virtues. So the question which I raised at the outset becomes more urgent. If different writers in different times and places, but all within the history of Western culture, include such different sets and types of items in their lists, what grounds have we for supposing that they do indeed aspire to list items of one and the same kind, that there is any shared concept at all? A second kind of consideration reinforces the presumption of a negative answer to this question. It is not just that each of these five writers lists different and differing kinds of items; it is also that each of these lists embodies, is the expression of a different theory about what a virtue is.

In the Homeric poems a virtue is a quality the manifestation of which enables someone to do exactly what their well-defined social role requires. The primary role is that of the warrior king and that Homer lists those virtues which he does becomes intelligible at once when we recognize that the key virtues therefore must be those which enable a man to excel in combat and in the games. It follows that we cannot identify the Homeric virtues until we have first identified the key social roles in Homeric society and the requirements of each of them. The concept of *what anyone filling such-and-such a role ought to do* is prior to the concept of a virtue; the latter concept has application only via the former.

On Aristotle's account matters are very different. Even though some virtues are available only to certain types of people, nonetheless virtues attach not to men as inhabiting social roles, but to man as such. It is the *telos* of man as a species which determines what human qualities are virtues. We need to remember however that although Aristotle treats the acquisition and exercise of the virtues as means to an end, the relationship of means to end is internal and not external. I call a means internal to a given end when the end cannot be adequately characterized independently of a characterization of the means. So it is with the virtues and the *telos* which is the good life for man on Aristotle's account. The exercise of the virtues is itself a crucial component of the good life for man. This distinction between internal and external means to an end is not drawn by Aristotle himself in the *Nicomachean Ethics*, as I noticed earlier, but it is an essential distinction to be drawn if we are to understand what Aristotle intended. The distinction *is* drawn explicitly by Aquinas in the course of his defence of St. Augustine's definition of a virtue, and it is clear that Aquinas understood that in drawing it he was maintaining an Aristotelian point of view.

The New Testament's account of the virtues, even if it differs as much as it does in content from Aristotle's—Aristotle would certainly not have admired Jesus Christ and he would have been horrified by St Paul—does have the same logical and conceptual structure as Aristotle's account. A virtue is, as with Aristotle, a quality the exercise of which leads to the achievement of the human *telos*. *The* good for man is of course a supernatural and not only a natural good, but supernature redeems and completes nature. Moreover the relationship of virtues as means to the end which is human incorporation in the divine kingdom of the age to come is internal and not external, just as it is in Aristotle. It is of course this parallelism which allows Aquinas to synthesize Aristotle and the New Testament. A key feature of this parallelism is the way in which the concept of *the good life for man* is prior to the concept of a virtue in just the way in which on the Homeric account the concept of a social role was prior. Once again it is the way in which the former concept is applied which determines how the latter is to be applied. In both cases the concept of a virtue is a secondary concept. The intent of Jane Austen's theory of the virtues is of another kind. C.S. Lewis has rightly emphasized how profoundly Christian her moral vision is and Gilbert Ryle has equally rightly emphasized her inheritance from Shaftesbury and from Aristotle. In fact her views combine elements from Homer as well, since she is concerned with social roles in a way that neither the New Testament nor Aristotle are. She is therefore important for the way in which she finds it possible to combine what are at first sight disparate theorectical accounts of the virtues. But for the moment any attempt to assess the significance of Jane Austen's systhesis must be delayed. Instead we must notice the quite different style of theory articulated in Benjamin Franklin's account of the virtues.

Franklin's account, like Aristotle's, is teleological; but unlike Aristotle's, it is utilitarian. According to Franklin in his *Autobiography* the virtues are means to an end, but he envisages the means-ends relationship as external rather than internal. The end to which the cultivation of the virtues ministers is happiness, but happiness understood as success, prosperity in Philadelphia and ultimately in heaven. The virtues are to be useful and Franklin's account continuously stresses utility as a criterion in individual cases: 'Make no expence but to do good to others or yourself; i.e. waste nothing', 'Speak not but what may benefit others or yourself. Avoid trifling conversation' and, as we have already seen, 'Rarely use venery but for health or offspring . . .'. When Franklin was in Paris he was horrified by Parisian architecture: 'Marble, porcelain and gilt are squandered without utility.'

We thus have at least three very different conceptions of a virtue to confront: a virtue is a quality which enables an individual to discharge his or her social role (Homer); a virtue is a quality which enables an individual to move towards the achievement of the specifically human *telos*, whether natural or supernatural (Aristotle, the New Testament and Aquinas); a virtue is a quality which has utility in achieving earthly and heavenly success (Franklin). Are we to take these as three different rival accounts of the same thing? Or are they instead accounts of three different things? Perhaps the moral structures in archaic Greece, in fourth-century Greece, and in eighteenth-century Pennsylvannia were so different from each other that we should treat them as embodying quite different concepts, whose difference is initially disguised from us by the historical accident of an inherited vocabulary which misleads us by linguistic resemblance long after conceptual identity and similarity have failed. Our intitial question has come back to us with redoubled force.

Yet although I have dwelt upon the *prima facie* case for holding that the differences and incompatibilities between different accounts at least suggest that there is no single, central, core conception of the virtues which might make a claim for universal allegiance, I ought also to point out that each of the five moral accounts which I have sketched so summarily does embody just such a claim. It is indeed just this feature of those accounts that makes them of more than sociological or antiquarian interest. Every one of these accounts claims not only theoretical, but also an institutional hegemony. For Odysseus the Cyclopes stand condemned because they lack agriculture, an *agora* and *themis*. For Aristotle the barbarians stand condemned because they lack the *polis* and are therefore incapable of politics. For New Testament Christians there is no salvation outside the apostolic church. And we know that Benjamin Franklin found the virtues more at home in Philadelphia than in Paris and that for Jane Austen the touchstone of the virtues is a certain kind of marriage and indeed a certain kind of naval officer (that is, a certain kind of *English* naval officer).

The question can therefore now be posed directly: are we or are we not able to disentangle from these rival and various claims a unitary core concept of the virtues of which we can give a more compelling account than any of the other accounts so far? I am going to argue that we can in fact discover such a core concept and that it turns out to provide the tradition of which I have written the history with its conceptual unity. It will indeed enable us to distinguish in a clear way those beliefs about the virtues which genuinely belong to the tradition from those which do not. Unsurprisingly perhaps it is a complex concept, different parts of which derive from different stages in the development of the tradition. Thus the concept itself in some sense embodies the history of which it is the outcome.

One of the features of the concept of a virtue which has emerged with some clarity from the argument so far is that it always requires for its application the acceptance for some prior account of certain features of social and moral life in terms of which it has to be defined and explained. So in the Homeric account the concept of a virtue is secondary to that of *a social role*, in Aristotle's account it is secondary to that of *the good life for man* conceived as the *telos* of human action and in Franklin's much later account it is secondary to that of utility. What is it in the account which I am about to give which provides in a similar way the necessary background against which the concept of a virtue has to be made intelligible? It is in answering this question that the complex, historical, multi-layered character of the core concept of virtue becomes clear. For there are no less than three stages in the logical development of the concept which have to be identified in order, if the core conception of a virtue is to be understood, and each of these stages has its own conceptual background. The first stage requires a background account of what I shall call a practice, the second an account of what I have already characterized as the narrative order of a single human life and the third an account a good deal fuller than I have given up to now of what constitutes a moral tradition. Each later stage presupposes the earlier, but not *vice versa*. Each earlier stage is both modified by and reinterpreted in the light of, but also provides an essential constituent of each later stage. The progress in the development of the concept is closely related to, although it does not recapitulate in any straightforward way, the history of the tradition of which it forms the core.

In the Homeric account of the virtues—and in heroic societies more generally—the exercise of a virtue exhibits qualities which are required for sustaining a social role and for exhibiting excellence in some well-marked area of social practice: to excel is to excel at war or in the games, as Achilles does, in sustaining a household, as Penelope does, in giving counsel in the assembly, as Nestor does, in the telling of a tale, as Homer himself does. When Aristotle speaks of excellence in human activity, he sometimes though not always, refers to some well-defined type of human practice: flute-playing, or war, or geometry. I am going to suggest that this notion of a particular type of practice as providing the arena in which the virtues are exhibited and in terms of which they are to receive their primary, if incomplete, definition is crucial to the whole enterprise of identifying a core concept of the virtues. I hasten to add two *caveats* however.

The first is to point out that my argument will not in any way imply that virtues are *only* exercised in the course of what I am calling practices. The second is to warn that I shall be using the word 'practice' in a specially defined way which does not completely agree with current ordinary usage, including my own previous use of that word. What am I going to mean by it?

By a 'practice' I am going to mean any coherent and complex form of socially established cooperative human activity through which goods internal to that form of activity are realized in the course of trying to achieve those standards of excellence which are appropriate to, and partially definitive of, that form of activity, with the result that human powers to achieve excellence, and human conceptions of the ends and goods involved, are systematically extended. Tic-tac-toe is not an example of a practice in this sense, nor is throwing a football with skill; but the game of football is, and so is chess. Bricklaying is not a practice; architecture is. Planting turnips is not a practice; farming is. So are the enquiries of physics, chemistry and biology, and so is the work of the historian, and so are painting and music. In the ancient and medieval worlds the creation and sustaining of human communties—of households, cities, nations—is generally taken to be a practice in the sense in which I have defined it. Thus the range of practices is wide: arts, sciences, games, politics in the Aristotelian sense, the making and sustaining of family life, all fall under the concept. But the question of the precise range of practices is not at this stage of the first importance. Instead let me explain some of the key terms involved in my definition, beginning with the notion of goods internal to a practice.

Consider the example of a highly intelligent seven-year-old child whom I wish to teach to play chess, although the child has no particular desire to learn the game. The child does however have a very strong desire for candy and little chance of obtaining it. I therefore tell the child that if the child will play chess with me once a week I will give the child 50 cents worth of candy; moreover I tell the child that I will always play in such a way that it will be difficult, but not impossible, for the child to win and that, if the child wins, the child will receive an extra 50 cents worth of candy. Thus motivated the child plays and plays to win. Notice however that, so long as it is the candy alone which provides the child with a good reason for playing chess, the child has no reason not to cheat and every reason to cheat, provided he or she can do so successfully. But, so we may hope, there will come a time when the child will find in those goods specific to chess, in the achievement of a certain highly particular kind of analytical skill, strategic imagination and competitive intensity, a new set of reasons, reasons now not just for winning on a particular occasion, but for trying to excel in whatever way the game of chess demands. Now if the child cheats, he or she will be defeating not me, but himself or herself.

There are thus two kinds of good possibly to be gained by playing chess. On the one hand there are those goods externally and contingently attached to chess-playing and to other practices by the accidents of social circumstance—in the case of the imaginary child candy, in the case of real adults such goods as prestige, status and money. There are always alternative ways for achieving such goods, and their achievement is never to be had *only* by engaging in some particular kind of practice. On the other hand there are the goods internal to the practice of chess which cannot be had in any way but by playing chess or some other game of that specific kind. We call them internal for two reasons: first, as I have already suggested, because we can only specify them in terms of chess or some other game of that specific kind and by means of examples from such games (otherwise the meagerness of our vocabulary for speaking of such goods forces us into such devices as my own resort to writing of 'a certain highly particular kind of'); and secondly because they can only be identified and recognized by the experience of participating in the practice in question. Those who lack the relevant experience are incompetent thereby as judges of internal goods.

This is clearly the case with all the major examples of practices: consider for example—even if briefly and inadequately—the practice of portrait painting as it developed in Western Europe from the late middle ages to the eighteenth century. The successful portrait painter is able to achieve many goods which are in the sense just defined external to the practice of portrait painting—fame, wealth, social status, even a measure of power and influence at courts upon occasion. But those external goods are not to be confused with the goods which are internal to the practice. The internal goods are those which result from an extended attempt to show how Wittgenstein's dictum 'The human body is the best picture of the human soul' (*Investigations*, p. 178e) might be made to become true by teaching us 'to regard . . . the picture on our wall as the object itself (the men, landscape and so on) depicted there' (p. 205e) in a quite new way. What is misleading about Wittgenstein's dictum as it stands is its neglect of the truth in George Orwell's thesis 'At fifty everyone has the face he deserves'. What painters from Giotto to Rembrandt learnt to show was how the face at any age may be revealed as the face that the subject of a portrait deserves.

Originally in medieval paintings of the saints the face was an icon; the question of a resemblance between the depicted face of Christ or St. Peter and the face that Jesus or Peter actually possessed at some particular age did not even arise. The antithesis to this iconography was the relative naturalism of certain fifteenth-century Flemish and German painting. The heavy eyelids, the coifed hair, the lines around the mouth undeniably represent some particular woman, either actual or envisaged. Resemblance has usurped the iconic relationship. But with Rembrandt there is, so to speak, synthesis: the naturalistic portrait is now rendered as an icon, but an icon of a new and hitherto inconceivable kind. Similarly in a very different kind of sequence mythological faces in a certain kind of seventeenth-century French painting become aristocratic faces in the eighteenth century. Within each of these sequences at least two different kinds of good internal to the painting of human faces and bodies are achieved.

There is first of all the excellence of the products, both the excellence in performance by the painters and that of each portrait itself. This excellence—the very verb 'excel' suggests it—has to be understood historically. The sequences of development find their point and purpose in a progress towards and beyond a variety of types and modes of excellence. There are of course sequences of decline as well as of progress, and progress is rarely to be understood as straightforwardly linear. But it is in participation in the attempts to sustain progress and to respond creatively to problems that the second kind of good internal to the practices of portrait painting is to be found. For what the artist discovers within the pursuit of excellence in portrait painting—and what is true of portrait painting is true of the practice of the fine arts in general—is the good of a certain kind of life. That life may not constitute the whole of life for someone who is a painter by a very long way or it may at least for a period, Gauguin-like, absorb him or her at the expense of almost everything else. But it is the painter's living out of a greater or lesser part of his or her life *as a painter* that is the second kind of good internal to painting. And judgment upon these goods requires at the very least the kind of competence that is only to be acquired either as a painter or as someone willing to learn systematically what the portrait painter has to teach.

A practice involves standards of excellence and obedience to rules as well as the achievement of goods. To enter into a practice is to accept the authority of those standards and the inadequacy of my own performance as judged by them. It is to subject my own attitudes, choices, preferences and tastes to the standards which currently and partially define the practice. Practices of course, as I have just noticed, have a history: games, sciences and arts all have histories. Thus the standards are not themselves immune from criticism, but nonetheless we cannot be initiated into a practice without accepting the authority of the best standards realized so far. If, on starting to listen to music, I do not accept my own incapacity to judge correctly, I will never learn to hear, let alone to appreciate, Bartok's last quartets. If, on starting to play baseball, I do not accept that others know better than I when to throw a fast ball and when not, I will never learn to appreciate good pitching let alone to pitch. In the realm of practices the authority of both goods and standards operates in such a way as to rule out all subjectivist and emotivist analyses of judgment. De gustibus *est* disputandum.

We are now in a position to notice an important difference between what I have called internal and what I have called external goods. It is characteristic of what I have called external goods that when achieved they are always some individual's property and possession. Moreover characteristically they are such that the more someone has of them, the less there is for other people. This is sometimes necessarily the case, as with power and fame, and sometimes the case by reason of contingent circumstance as with money. External goods are therefore characteristically objects of competition in which there must be losers as well as winners. Internal goods are indeed the outcome of competition to excel, but it is characteristic of them that their achievement is a good for the whole community who participate in the practice. So when Turner transformed the seascape in painting or W.G. Grace advanced the art of batting in cricket in a quite new way their achievement enriched the whole relevant community.

But what does all or any of this have to do with the concept of the virtues? It turns out that we are now in a position to formulate a first, even if partial and tentative definition of a virtue: *A virtue is an acquired human quality the possession and exercise of which tends to enable us to achieve those goods which are internal to practices and the lack of which effectively prevents us from achieving any such goods.* Later this definition will need amplification and amendment. But as a first approximation to an adequate definition it already illuminates the place of the virtues in human life. For it is not difficult to show for a whole range of key virtues that without them the goods internal to practices are barred to us, but not just barred to us generally, barred in a very particular way.

It belongs to the concept of a practice as I have outlined it—and as we are all familiar with it already in our actual lives, whether we are painters or physicists or quarterbacks or indeed just lovers of good painting or first-rate experiments or a well-thrown pass—that its goods can only be achieved by subordinating ourselves within the practice in our relationship to other practitioners. We have to learn to recognize what is due to whom; we have to be prepared to take whatever self-endangering risks are demanded along the way; and we have to listen carefully to what we are told about our own inadequacies and to reply with the same carefulness for the facts. In other words we have to accept as necessary components of any practice with internal goods and standards of excellence the virtues of justice, courage and honesty. For not to accept these, to be willing to cheat as our imagined child was willing to cheat in his or her early days at chess, so far bars us from achieving the standards of excellence or the goods internal to the practice that it renders the practice pointless except as a device for achieving external goods.

We can put the same point in another way. Every practice requires a certain kind of relationship between those who participate in it. Now the virtues are those goods by reference to which, whether we like it or not, we define our relationships to those other people with whom we share the kind of purposes and standards which inform practices. Consider an example of how reference to the virtues has to be made in certain kinds of human relationship.

A, B, C, and D are friends in that sense of friendship which Aristotle takes to be primary: they share in the pursuit of certain goods. In my terms they share in a practice. D dies in obscure circumstances, A discovers how D died and tells the truth about it to B while lying to C. C discovers the

lie. What A cannot then intelligibly claim is that he stands in the same relationship of friendship to both B and C. By telling the truth to one and
lying to the other he has partially defined a difference in the relationship.
Of course it is open to A to explain this difference in a number of ways;
perhaps he was trying to spare C pain or perhaps he is simply cheating C.
But some difference in the relationship now exists as a result of the lie. For
their allegiance to each other in the pursuit of common goods has been
put in question.

Just as, so long as we share the standards and purposes characteristic of
practices, we define our relationship to each other, whether we acknowledge it or not, by reference to standards of truthfulness and trust, so we
define them too by reference to standards of justice and of courage. If A,
a professor, gives B and C the grades that their papers deserve, but grades
D because he is attracted by D's blue eyes or is repelled by D's dandruff,
he has defined his relationship to D differently from his relationship to the
other members of the class, whether he wishes it or not. Justice requires
that we treat others in respect of merit or desert according to uniform and
impersonal standards; to depart from the standards of justice in some particular instance defines our relationship with the relevant person as in some
way special or distinctive.

The case with courage is a little different. We hold courage to be a virtue because the care and concern for individuals, communities and causes
which is so crucial to so much in practices requires the existence of such
a virtue. If someone says that he cares for some individual, community or
cause, but is unwilling to risk harm or danger on his, her or its own behalf,
he puts in question the genuineness of his care and concern. Courage, the
capacity to risk harm or danger to oneself, has its role in human life because of this connection with care and concern. This is not to say that a
man cannot genuinely care and also be a coward. It is in part to say that
a man who genuinely cares and has not the capacity for risking harm or
danger has to define himself, both to himself and to others, as a coward.

I take it then that from the standpoint of those types of relationship
without which practices cannot be sustained truthfulness, justice and courage — and perhaps some others — are genuine excellences, are virtues in the
light of which we have to characterize ourselves and others, whatever our
private moral standpoint or our society's particular codes may be. For this
recognition that we cannot escape the definition of our relationships in
terms of such goods is perfectly compatible with the acknowledgment that
different societies have and have had different codes of truthfulness, justice
and courage. Lutheran pietists brought up their children to believe that one
ought to tell the truth to everybody at all times, whatever the circum-

stances or consequences, and Kant was one of their children. Traditional Bantu parents brought up their children not to tell the truth to unknown strangers, since they believed that this could render the family vulnerable to witchcraft. In our culture many of us have been brought up not to tell the truth to elderly great-aunts who invite us to admire their new hats. But each of these codes embodies an acknowledgment of the virtue of truthfulness. So it is also with varying codes of justice and of courage.

Practices then might flourish in societies with very different codes; what they could not do is flourish in societies in which the virtues were not valued, although institutions and technical skills serving unified purposes might well continue to flourish. (I shall have more to say about the contrast between institutions and technical skills mobilized for a unified end, on the one hand, and practices on the other, in a moment.) For the kind of cooperation, the kind of recognition of authority and of achievement, the kind of respect for standards and the kind of risk-taking which are characteristically involved in practices demand for example fairness in judging oneself and others—the kind of fairness absent in my example of the professor, a ruthless truthfulness without which fairness cannot find application—the kind of truthfulness absent in my example of A, B, C, and D— and willingness to trust the judgments of those whose achievement in the practice give them an authority to judge which presupposes fairness and truthfulness in those judgments, and from time to time the taking of self-endangering and even achievement-endangering risks. It is no part of my thesis that great violinists cannot be vicious or great chess-players meanspirited. Where the virtues are required, the vices also may flourish. It is just that the vicious and mean-spirited necessarily rely on the virtues of others for the practices in which they engage to flourish and also deny themselves the experience of achieving those internal goods which may reward even not very good chess-players and violinists.

To situate the virtues any further within practices it is necessary now to clarify a little further the nature of a practice by drawing two important contrasts. The discussion so far I hope makes it clear that a practice, in the sense intended, is never just a set of technical skills, even when directed towards some unified purpose and even if the exercise of those skills can on occasion be valued or enjoyed for their own sake. What is distinctive in a practice is in part the way in which conceptions of the relevant goods and ends which the technical skills serve—and every practice does require the exercise of technical skills—are transformed and enriched by these extensions of human powers and by that regard for its own internal goods which are partially definitive of each particular practice or type of practice. Practices never have a goal or goals fixed for all time—painting has no such goal nor has physics—but the goals themselves are transmuted by the history of the activity. It therefore turns out not to be accidental that every practice has its own history and a history which is more and other than that of the improvement of the relevant technical skills. This historical dimension is crucial in relation to the virtues.

To enter into a practice is to enter into a relationship not only with its contemporary practitioners, but also with those who have preceded us in the practice, particularly those whose achievements extended the reach of the practice to its present point. It is thus the achievement, and *a fortiori* the authority, of a tradition which I then confront and from which I have to learn. And for this learning and the relationship to the past which it embodies the virtues of justice, courage and truthfulness are prerequisite in precisely the same way and for precisely the same reasons as they are in sustaining present relationships within practices.

It is not only of course with sets of technical skills that practices ought to be contrasted. Practices must not be confused with institutions. Chess, physics and medicine are practices; chess clubs, laboratories, universities and hospitals are institutions. Institutions are characteristically and necessarily concerned with what I have called external goods. They are involved in acquiring money and other material goods; they are structured in terms of power and status, and they distribute money, power and status as rewards. Nor could they do otherwise if they are to sustain not only themselves, but also the practices of which they are the bearers. For no practices can survive for any length of time unsustained by institutions. Indeed so intimate is the relationship of practices to institutions—and consequently of the goods external to the goods internal to the practices in question— that institutions and practices characteristically form a single causal order in which the ideals and the creativity of the practice are always vulnerable to the acquisitiveness of the institution, in which the cooperative care for common goods of the practice is always vulnerable to the competitiveness of the institution. In this context the essential function of the virtues is clear. Without them, without justice, courage and truthfulness, practices could not resist the corrupting power of institutions.

Yet if institutions do have corrupting power, the making and sustaining of forms of human community—and therefore of institutions—itself has all the characteristics of a practice, and moreover of a practice which stands in a peculiarly close relationship to the exercise of the virtues in two important ways. The exercise of the virtues is itself apt to require a highly determinate attitude to social and political issues; and it is always within some particular community with its own specific institutional forms that we learn or fail to learn to exercise the virtues. There is of course a crucial difference between the way in which the relationship between moral character and political community is envisaged from the standpoint of liberal individualist modernity and the way in which that relationship was envisaged from the standpoint of the type of ancient and medieval tradition of the virtues which I have sketched. For liberal individualism a community is simply an arena in which individuals each pursue their own self-chosen conception of the good life, and political institutions exist to provide that degree of order which makes such self-determined activity possible. Government and law are, or ought to be, neutral between rival concept' ıs of the good life for man, and hence, although it is the task of government to promote law-abidingness, it is on the liberal view no part of the legitimate function of government to inculcate any one moral outlook.

By contrast, on the particular ancient and medieval view which I have sketched political community not only requires the exercise of the virtues for its own sustenance, but it is one of the tasks of parental authority to make children grow up so as to be virtuous adults. The classical statement of this analogy is by Socrates in the *Crito*. It does not of course follow from an acceptance of the Socratic view of political community and political authority that we ought to assign to the modern state the moral function which Socrates assigned to the city and its laws. Indeed the power of the liberal individualist standpoint partly derives from the evident fact that the modern state is indeed totally unfitted to act as moral educator of any community. But the history of how the modern state emerged is of course itself a moral history. If my account of the complex relationship of virtues to practices and to institutions is correct, it follows that we shall be unable to write a true history of practices and institutions unless that history is also one of the virtues and vices. For the ability of a practice to retain its integrity will depend on the way in which the virtues can be and are exercised in sustaining the institutional forms which are the social bearers of the practice. The integrity of a practice causally requires the exercise of the virtues by at least some of the individuals who embody it in their activities; and conversely the corruption of institutions is always in part at least an effect of the vices.

The virtues are of course themselves in turn fostered by certain types of social institution and endangered by others. Thomas Jefferson thought that only in a society of small farmers could the virtues flourish; and Adam Ferguson with a good deal more sophistication saw the institutions of modern commercial society as endangering at least some traditional virtues. It is Ferguson's type of sociology which is the empirical counterpart of the conceptual account of the virtues which I have given, a sociology which aspires to lay bare the empirical, causal connection between virtues, practices and institutions. For this kind of conceptual account has strong empirical implications; it provides an explanatory scheme which can be tested in particular cases. Moreover my thesis has empirical content in another way; it does entail that without the virtues there could be a recognition only of what I have called external goods and not at all of internal goods in the context of practices. And in any society which recognized only external goods competitiveness would be the dominant and even exclusive feature. We have a brilliant portrait of such a society in Hobbes's account of the state of nature; and Professor Turnbull's report of the fate of the Ik suggests that social reality does in the most horrifying way confirm both my thesis and Hobbes's.

Virtues then stand in a different relationship to external and to internal goods. The possession of the virtues—and not only of their semblance and simulacra—is necessary to achieve the latter; yet the possession of the virtues may perfectly well hinder us in achieving external goods. I need to emphasize at this point that external goods genuinely are goods. Not only are they characteristic objects of human desire, whose allocation is what gives point to the virtues of justice and of generosity, but no one can despise them altogether without a certain hypocrisy. Yet notoriously the cultivation of truthfulness, justice and courage will often, the world being what it contingently is, bar us from being rich or famous or powerful. Thus although we may hope that we can not only achieve the standards of excellence and the internal goods of certain practices by possessing the virtues *and* become rich, famous and powerful, the virtues are always a potential stumbling block to this comfortable ambition. We should therefore expect that, if in a particular society the pursuit of external goods were to become dominant, the concept of the virtues might suffer first attrition and then perhaps something near total effacement, although simulacra might abound.

The time has come to ask the question of how far this partial account of a core conception of the virtues—and I need to emphasize that all that I have offered so far is the first stage of such an account—is faithful to the tradition which I delineated. How far, for example, and in what ways is it Aristotelian? It is—happily—not Aristotelian in two ways in which a good deal of the rest of the tradition also dissents from Aristotle. First, although this account of the virtues is teleological, it does not require any allegiance to Aristotle's metaphysical biology. And secondly, just because of the multiplicity of human practices and the consequent multiplicity of goods in the pursuit of which the virtues may be exercised—goods which will often be contingently incompatible and which will therefore make rival claims upon our allegiance—conflict will not spring solely from flaws in individual character. But it was just on these two matters that Aristotle's account of the virtues seemed most vulnerable; hence if it turns out to be the case that this socially teleological account can support Aristotle's general account of the virtues as well as does his own biologically teleological account, these differences from Aristotle himself may well be regarded as strengthening rather than weakening the case for a generally Aristotelian standpoint.

There are at least three ways in which the account that I have given *is* clearly Aristotelian. First it requires for its completion a cogent elaboration of just those distinctions and concepts which Aristotle's account requires: voluntariness, the distinction between the intellectual virtues and the virtues of character, the relationship of both to natural abilities and to the passions and the structure of practical reasoning. On every one of these topics something very like Aristotle's view has to be defended, if my own account is to be plausible.

Secondly my account can accommodate an Aristotelian view of pleasure and enjoyment, whereas it is interestingly irreconcilable with any utilitarian view and more particularly with Franklin's account of the virtues. We can approach these questions by considering how to reply to someone who, having considered my account of the differences between goods internal to and goods external to a practice enquired into which class, if either, does pleasure or enjoyment fall? The answer is, 'Some types of pleasure into one, some into the other.'

Someone who achieves excellence in a practice, who plays chess or football well or who carries through an enquiry in physics or an experimental mode in painting with success, characteristically enjoys his achievement and his activity in achieving. So does someone who, although not breaking the limit of achievement, plays or thinks or acts in a way that leads towards such a breaking of limit. As Aristotle says, the enjoyment of the activity and the enjoyment of achievement are not the ends at which the agent aims, but the enjoyment supervenes upon the successful activity in such a way that the activity achieved and the activity enjoyed are one and the same state. Hence to aim at the one is to aim at the other; and hence also it is easy to confuse the pursuit of excellence with the pursuit of enjoyment *in this specific sense*. This particular confusion is harmless enough; what is not harmless is the confusion of enjoyment *in this specific sense* with other forms of pleasure.

For certain kinds of pleasure are of course external goods along with prestige, status, power and money. Not all pleasure is the enjoyment supervening upon achieved activity; some is the pleasure of psychological or physical states independent of all activity. Such states—for example that produced on a normal palate by the closely successive and thereby blended sensations of Colchester oyster, cayenne pepper and Veuve Cliquot—may be sought as external goods, as external rewards which may be purchased by money or received in virtue of prestige. Hence the pleasures are categorized neatly and appropriately by the classification into internal and external goods.

It is just this classification which can find no place within Franklin's account of the virtues which is framed entirely in terms of external relationships and external goods. Thus although by this stage of the argument it is possible to claim that my account does capture a conception of the virtues which is at the core of the particular ancient and medieval tradition which I have delineated, it is equally clear that there is more than one possible conception of the virtues and that Franklin's standpoint and indeed any utilitarian standpoint is such that to accept it will entail rejecting the tradition and *vice versa*.

One crucial point of incompatibility was noted long ago by D.H. Lawrence. When Franklin asserts, 'Rarely use venery but for health or offspring . . .', Lawrence replies, 'Never *use* venery.' It is of the character of a virtue that in order that it be effective in producing the internal goods which are the rewards of the virtues it should be exercised without regard to consequences. For it turns out to be the case that—and this is in part at least one more empirical factual claim—although the virtues are just those qualities which tend to lead to the achievement of a certain class of goods, nonetheless unless we practice them irrespective of whether in any particular set of contingent circumstances they will produce those goods or not, we cannot possess them at all. We cannot be genuinely courageous or truthful and be so only on occasion. Moreover, as we have seen, cultivation of the virtues always may and often does hinder the achievement of those external goods which are the mark of worldly success. The road to success in Philadelphia and the road to heaven may not coincide after all.

Furthermore we are now able to specify one crucial difficulty for *any* version of utilitarianism—in addition to those which I noticed earlier. Utilitarianism cannot accommodate the distinction between goods internal to and goods external to a practice. Not only is that distinction marked by none of the classical utilitarians—it cannot be found in Bentham's writings nor in those of either of the Mills or of Sidgwick—but internal goods and external goods are not commensurable with each other. Hence the notion of summing goods—and *a fortiori* in the light of what I have said about kinds of pleasure and enjoyment the notion of summing happiness—in terms of one single formula or conception of utility, whether it is Franklin's or Bentham's or Mill's, makes no sense. Nonetheless we ought to note that although *this* distinction is alien to J.S. Mill's thought, it is plausible and in no way patronizing to suppose that something like this is the distinction which he was trying to make in *Utilitarianism* when he distinguished between 'higher' and 'lower' pleasures. At the most we can say 'something like this'; for J.S. Mill's upbringing had given him a limited view of human life and powers, had unfitted him, for example, for appreciating games just because of the way it had fitted him for appreciating philosophy. Nonetheless the notion that the pursuit of excellence in a way that extends human powers is at the heart of human life is instantly recognizable as at home in not only J.S. Mill's political and social thought, but also in his and Mrs. Taylor's life. Were I to choose human exemplars of certain of the virtues as I understand them, there would of course be many names to name, those of St. Benedict and St. Francis of Assisi and St. Theresa *and* those of Frederick Engels and Eleanor Marx and Leon Trotsky among them. But that of John Stuart Mill would have to be there as certainly as any other.

Thirdly my account is Aristotelian in that it links evaluation and explanation in a characteristically Aristotelian way. From an Aristotelian standpoint to identify certain actions as manifesting or failing to manifest a virtue or virtues is never only to evaluate; it is also to take the first step towards explaining why those actions rather than some others were performed. Hence for an Aristotelian quite as much as for a Platonist the fate of a city or an individual can be explained by citing the injustice of a tyrant or the courage of its defenders. Indeed without allusion to the place that justice and injustice, courage and cowardice play in human life very little will be genuinely explicable. It follows that many of the explanatory projects of the modern social sciences, a methodological canon of which is the separation of 'the facts'—this conception of the 'the facts' is the one which I delineated in Chapter 7—from all evaluation, are bound to fail. For the fact that someone was or failed to be courageous or just cannot be recognized as 'a fact' by those who accept that methodological canon. The account of the virtues which I have given is completely at one with Aristotle's on this point. But now the question may be raised: your account may be in many respects Aristotelian, but is it not in some respects false? Consider the following important objection.

I have defined the virtues partly in terms of their place in practices. But surely, it may be suggested, some practices—that is, some coherent human activities which answer to the description of what I have called a practice— are evil. So in discussions by some moral philosophers of this type of account of the virtues it has been suggested that torture and sado-masochistic sexual activities might be examples of practices. But how can a disposition be a virtue if it is the kind of disposition which sustains practices and some practices issue in evil? My answer to this objection falls into two parts.

First I want to allow that there *may* be practices—in the sense in which I understand the concept—which simply *are* evil. I am far from convinced that there are, and I do not in fact believe that either torture or sado-masochistic sexuality answer to the description of a practice which my account of the virtues employs. But I do not want to rest my case on this lack of conviction, especially since it is plain that as a matter of contingent fact many types of practice may on particular occasions be productive of evil. For the range of practices includes the arts, the sciences and certain types of intellectual and athletic game. And it is at once obvious that any of these may under certain conditions be a source of evil: the desire to excel and to win can corrupt, a man may be so engrossed by his painting that he neglects his family, what was initially an honorable resort to war can issue in savage cruelty. But what follows from this?

It certainly is not the case that my account entails *either* that we ought to excuse or condone such evils *or* that whatever flows from a virtue is right. I do have to allow that courage sometimes sustains injustice, that loyalty has been known to strengthen a murderous aggressor and that generosity has sometimes weakened the capacity to do good. But to deny this would be to fly in the face of just those empirical facts which I invoked in criticizing Aquinas' account of the unity of the virtues. That the virtues need initially to be defined and explained with reference to the notion of a practice thus in no way entails approval of all practices in all circumstances. That the virtues—as the objection itself presupposed—*are* defined not in terms of good and right practices, but of practices, does not entail or imply that practices as actually carried through at particular times and places do not stand in need of moral criticism. And the resources for such criticism are not lacking. There is in the first place no inconsistency in appealing to the requirements of a virtue to criticize a practice. Justice may be initially defined as a disposition which in its particular way is necessary to sustain practices; it does not follow that in pursuing the requirements of a practice violations of justice are not to be condemned. Moreover I already pointed out in Chapter 12 that a morality of virtues requires as its counterpart a conception of moral law. Its requirements too have to be met by practices. But, it may be asked, does not all this imply that more needs to be said about the place of practices in some larger moral context? Does not this at least suggest that there is more to the core concept of a virtue than can be spelled out in terms of practices? I have after all emphasized that the scope of any virtue in human life extends beyond the practices in terms of which it is initially defined. What then is the place of the virtues in the larger arenas of human life?

I stressed earlier that any account of the virtues in terms of practices could only be a partial and first account. What is required to complement it? The most notable difference so far between my account and any account that could be called Aristotelian is that although I have in no way restricted the exercise of the virtues to the context of practices, it is in terms of practices that I have located their point and function. Whereas Aristotle locates that point and function in terms of the notion of a type of whole human life which can be called good. And it does seem that the question 'What would a human being lack who lacked the virtues?' must be given a kind of answer which goes beyond anything which I have said so far. For such an individual would not merely fail *in a variety of particular ways* in respect of the kind of excellence which can be achieved through participation in practices and in respect of the kind of human relationship required to sustain such excellence. His own life *viewed as a whole* would perhaps be defective; it would not be the kind of life which someone would describe in trying to answer the question 'What is the best kind of life for this kind of man or woman to live?' And that question cannot be answered without at least raising Aristotle's own question, 'What is the good life for man?' Consider three ways in which human life informed only by the conception of the virtues sketched so far would be defective.

It would be pervaded, first of all, by *too many* conflicts and *too much* arbitrariness. I argued earlier that it is a merit of an account of the virtues in terms of a multiplicity of goods that it allows for the possibility of tragic conflict in a way in which Aristotle's does not. But it may also produce even in the life of someone who is virtuous and disciplined too many occasions when one allegiance points in one direction, another in another. The claims of one practice may be incompatible with another in such a way that one may find oneself oscillating in an arbitrary way, rather than making rational choices. So it seems to have been with T.E. Lawrence. Commitment to sustaining the kind of community in which the virtues can flourish may be incompatible with the devotion which a particular practice — of the arts, for example — requires. So there may be tensions between the claims of family life and those of the arts — the problem that Gauguin solved or failed to solve by fleeing to Polynesia, or between the claims of politics and those of the arts — the problem that Lenin solved or failed to solve by refusing to listen to Beethoven.

If the life of the virtues is continuously fractured by choices in which one allegiance entails the apparently arbitrary renunciation of another, it may seem that the goods internal to practices do after all derive their authority from our individual choices; for when different goods summon in different and in incompatible directions, 'I' have to choose between their rival claims. The modern self with its criterionless choices apparently reappears in the alien context of what was claimed to be an Aristotelian world. This accusation might be rebutted in part by returning to the question of why both goods and virtues do have authority in our lives and repeating what was said earlier in this chapter. But this reply would only be partly successful; the distinctively modern notion of choice would indeed have reappeared, even if with a more limited scope for its exercise than it has usually claimed.

Secondly without an overriding conception of the *telos* of a whole human life, conceived as a unity, our conception of certain individual virtues has to remain partial and incomplete. Consider two examples. Justice, on an Aristotelian view, is defined in terms of giving each person his or her due or desert. To deserve well is to have contributed in some substantial way to the achievement of those goods, the sharing of which and the common pursuit of which provide foundations for human community. But the goods internal to practices, including the goods internal to the practice of making and sustaining forms of community, need to be ordered and evaluated in some way if we are to assess relative desert. Thus any substantive application of an Aristotelian concept of justice requires an understanding of goods and of the good that goes beyond the multiplicity of goods which inform practices. As with justice, so also with patience. Patience is the virtue of waiting attentively without complaint, but not of waiting thus for anything at all. To treat patience as a virtue presupposes some adequate answer to the question: waiting for what? Within the context of practices a partial, although for many purposes adequate, answer can be given: the patience of a craftsman with refractory material, of a teacher with a slow pupil, of a politician in negotiations, are all species of patience. But what if the material is just too refractory, the pupil too slow, the negotiations too frustrating? Ought we always at a certain point just to give up in the interests of the practice itself? The medieval exponents of the virtue of patience claimed that there are certain types of situation in which the virtue of patience requires that I do not ever give up on some person or task, situations in which, as they would have put it, I am required to embody in my attitude to that person or task something of the patient attitude of God towards his creation. But this could only be so if patience served some overriding good, some *telos* which warranted putting other goods in a subordinate place. Thus it turns out that the content of the virtue of patience depends upon how we order various goods in a hierarchy and *a fortiori* on whether we are able rationally so to order these particular goods.

I have suggested so far that unless there is a *telos* which transcends the limited goods of practices by constituting the good of a whole human life, the good of a human life conceived as a unity, it will *both* be the case that a certain subversive arbitrariness will invade the moral life *and* that we shall be unable to specify the context of certain virtues adequately. These two considerations are reinforced by a third: that there is at least one virtue recognized by the tradition which cannot be specified at all except with reference to the wholeness of a human life—the virtue of integrity or constancy. 'Purity of heart,' said Kierkegaard, 'is to will one thing.' This notion of singleness of purpose in a whole life can have no application unless that of a whole life does.

It is clear therefore that my preliminary account of the virtues in terms of practices captures much, but very far from all, of what the Aristotelian tradition taught about the virtues. It is also clear that to give an account that is at once more fully adequate to the tradition and rationally defensible, it is necessary to raise a question to which the Aristotelian tradition presupposed an answer, an answer so widely shared in the pre-modern world that it never had to be formulated explicitly in any detailed way. This question is: is it rationally justifiable to conceive of each human life as a unity, so that we may try to specify each such life as having its good and so that we may understand the virtues as having their function in enabling an individual to make of his or her life one kind of unity rather than another?

15

The Virtues, the Unity of a Human Life
and the Concept of a Tradition

Any contemporary attempt to envisage each human life as a whole, as a unity, whose character provides the virtues with an adequate *telos* encounters two different kinds of obstacle, one social and one philosophical. The social obstacles derive from the way in which modernity partitions each human life into a variety of segments, each with its own norms and modes of behavior. So work is divided from leisure, private life from public, the corporate from the personal. So both childhood and old age have been wrenched away from the rest of human life and made over into distinct realms. And all these separations have been achieved so that it is the distinctiveness of each and not the unity of the life of the individual who passes through those parts in terms of which we are taught to think and to feel.

The philosophical obstacles derive from two distinct tendencies, one chiefly, though not only, domesticated in analytical philosophy and one at home in both sociological theory and in existentialism. The former is the tendency to think atomistically about human action and to analyze complex actions and transactions in terms of simple components. Hence the recurrence in more than one context of the notion of 'a basic action'. That particular actions derive their character as parts of larger wholes is a point of view alien to our dominant ways of thinking and yet one which it is necessary at least to consider if we are to begin to understand how a life may be more than a sequence of individual actions and episodes.

Equally the unity of a human life becomes invisible to us when a sharp separation is made either between the individual and the roles that he or she plays—a separation characteristic not only of Sartre's existentialism, but also of the sociological theory of Ralf Dahrendorf—or between the different role—and quasi-role—enactments of an individual life so that life comes to appear as nothing but a series of unconnected episodes—a liquidation of the self characteristic, as I noticed earlier, of Goffman's sociological theory. I already also suggested in Chapter 3 that both the Sartrian and the Goffmanesque conceptions of selfhood are highly characteristic of the modes of thought and practice of modernity. It is perhaps therefore unsurprising to realize that the self as thus conceived cannot be envisaged as a bearer of the Aristotelian virtues.

For a self separated from its roles in the Sartrian mode loses that arena of social relationships in which the Aristotelian virtues function if they function at all. The patterns of a virtuous life would fall under those condemnations of conventionality which Sartre put into the mouth of Antoine Roquentin in *La Nausée* and which he uttered in his own person in *L'Etre et le néant*. Indeed the self's refusal of the inauthenticity of conventionalized social relationships becomes what integrity is diminished into in Sartre's account.

At the same time the liquidation of the self into a set of demarcated areas of role-playing allows no scope for the exercise of dispositions which could genuinely be accounted virtues in any sense remotely Aristotelian. For a virtue is not a disposition that makes for success only in some one particular type of situation. What are spoken of as the virtues of a good committee man or of a good administrator or of a gambler or a pool hustler are professional skills professionally deployed in those situations where they can be effective, not virtues. Someone who genuinely possesses a virtue can be expected to manifest it in very different types of situation, many of them situations where the practice of a virtue cannot be expected to be effective in the way that we expect a professional skill to be. Hector exhibited one and the same courage in his parting from Andromache and on the battlefield with Achilles; Eleanor Marx exhibited one and the same compassion in her relationship with her father, in her work with trade unionists and in her entanglement with Aveling. And the unity of a virtue in someone's life is intelligible only as a characteristic of a unitary life, a life that can be conceived and evaluated as a whole. Hence just as in the discussion of the changes in and fragmentation of morality which accompanied the rise of modernity in the earlier parts of this book, each stage in the emergence of the characteristically modern views of the moral judgment was accompanied by a corresponding stage in the emergence of the characteristically modern conceptions of selfhood; so now, in defining the particular pre-modern concept of the virtues with which I have been preoccupied, it has become necessary to say something of the concomitant concept of selfhood, a concept of a self whose unity resides in the unity of a narrative which links birth to life to death as narrative beginning to middle to end.

Such a conception of the self is perhaps less unfamiliar than it may appear at first sight. Just because it has played a key part in the cultures which are historically predecessors of our own, it would not be surprising if it turned out to be still an unacknowledged presence in many of our ways of thinking and acting. Hence it is not inappropriate to begin by scrutinizing some of our most taken-for-granted, but clearly correct conceptual insights about human actions and selfhood in order to show how natural it is to think of the self in a narrative mode.

It is a conceptual commonplace, both for philosophers and for ordinary agents, that one and the same segment of human behavior may be correctly characterized in a number of different ways. To the question 'What is he doing?' the answers may with equal truth and appropriateness be 'Digging', 'Gardening', 'Taking exercise', 'Preparing for winter' or 'Pleasing his wife'. Some of these answers will characterize the agent's intentions, other unintended consequences of his actions, and of these unintended consequences some may be such that the agent is aware of them and others not. What is important to notice immediately is that any answer to the questions of how we are to understand or to explain a given segment of behavior will presuppose some prior answer to the question of how these different correct answers to the question 'What is he doing?' are related to each other. For if someone's primary intention is to put the garden in order before the winter and it is only incidentally the case that in so doing he is taking exercise and pleasing his wife, we have one type of behavior to be explained; but if the agent's primary intention is to please his wife by taking exercise, we have quite another type of behavior to be explained and we will have to look in a different direction for understanding and explanation.

In the first place the episode has been situated in an annual cycle of domestic activity, and the behavior embodies an intention which presupposes a particular type of household-cum-garden setting with the peculiar narrative history of that setting in which this segment of behavior now becomes an episode. In the second instance the episode has been situated in the narrative history of a marriage, a very different, even if related, social setting. We cannot, that is to say, characterize behavior independently of intentions, and we cannot characterize intentions independently of the settings which make those intentions intelligible both to agents themselves and to others.

I use the word 'setting' here as a relatively inclusive term. A social setting may be an institution, it may be what I have called a practice, or it may be a milieu of some other human kind. But it is central to the notion of a setting as I am going to understand it that a setting has a history, a history within which the histories of individual agents not only are, but have to be, situated, just because without the setting and its changes through time the history of the individual agent and his changes through time will be unintelligible. Of course one and the same piece of behavior may belong to more than one setting. There are at least two different ways in which this may be so.

In my earlier example the agent's activity may be part of the history both of the cycle of household activity and of his marriage, two histories which have happened to intersect. The household may have its own history stretching back through hundreds of years, as do the histories of some European farms, where the farm has had a life of its own, even though different families have in different periods inhabited it; and the marriage will certainly have its own history, a history which itself presupposes that a particular point has been reached in the history of the institution of marriage. If we are to relate some particular segment of behavior in any precise way to an agent's intentions and thus to the settings which that agent inhabits, we shall have to understand in a precise way how the variety of correct characterizations of the agent's behavior relate to each other first by identifying which characteristics refer us to an intention and which do not and then by classifying further the items in both categories.

Where intentions are concerned, we need to know which intention or intentions were primary, that is to say, of which it is the case that, had the agent intended otherwise, he would not have performed that action. Thus if we know that a man is gardening with the self-avowed purposes of healthful exercise and of pleasing his wife, we do not yet know how to understand what he is doing until we know the answer to such questions as whether he would continue gardening if he continued to believe that gardening was healthful exercise, but discovered that his gardening no longer pleased his wife, *and* whether he would continue gardening, if he ceased to believe that gardening was healthful exercise, but continued to believe that it pleased his wife, *and* whether he would continue gardening if he changed his beliefs on both points. That is to say, we need to know both what certain of his beliefs are and which of them are causally effective; and, that is to say, we need to know whether certain contrary-to-fact hypothetical statements are true or false. And until we know this, we shall not know how to characterize correctly what the agent is doing.

Consider another equally trivial example of a set of compatibly correct answers to the question 'What is he doing?' 'Writing a sentence'; 'Finishing his book'; 'Contributing to the debate on the theory of action'; 'Trying to get tenure'. Here the intentions can be ordered in terms of the stretch of time to which reference is made. Each of the shorter-term intentions is, and can only be made, intelligible by reference to some longer-term intentions; and the characterization of the behavior in terms of the longer-term intentions can only be correct if some of the characterizations in terms of

shorter-term intentions are also correct. Hence the behavior is only characterized adequately when we know what the longer and longest-term intentions invoked are and how the shorter-term intentions are related to the
longer. Once again we are involved in writing a narrative history.

Intentions thus need to be ordered both causally and temporally and
both orderings will make references to settings, references already made
obliquely by such elementary terms as 'gardening', 'wife', 'book', and
'tenure'. Moreover the correct identification of the agent's beliefs will be
an essential constituent of this task; failure at this point would mean failure
in the whole enterprise. (The conclusion may seem obvious; but it already
entails one important consequence. There is no such thing as 'behavior',
to be identified prior to and independently of intentions, beliefs and settings. Hence the project of a science of behavior takes on a mysterious and
somewhat outré character. It is not that such a science is impossible; but
there is nothing for it to be but a science of uninterpreted physical movement such as B.F. Skinner aspires to. It is no part of my task here to examine Skinner's problems; but it is worth noticing that it is not at all clear
what a scientific experiment could be, if one were a Skinnerian; since the
conception of an experiment is certainly one of intention- and belief-
informed behavior. And what would be utterly doomed to failure would
be the project of a science of, say, *political* behavior, detached from a study
of intentions, beliefs and settings. It is perhaps worth noting that when the
expression 'the behavioral sciences' was given its first influential use in a
Ford Foundation Report of 1953, the term 'behavior' was defined so as
to include what were called 'such subjective behavior as attitudes, beliefs,
expectations, motivations and aspirations' as well as 'overt acts'. But what
the Report's wording seems to imply is that it is cataloguing two distinct
sets of items, available for independent study. If the argument so far is correct, then there is only one set of items.)

Consider what the argument so far implies about the interrelationships
of the intentional, the social and the historical. We identify a particular
action only by invoking two kinds of context, implicitly if not explicitly.
We place the agent's intentions, I have suggested, in causal and temporal
order with reference to their role in his or her history; and we also place
them with reference to their role in the history of the setting or settings
to which they belong. In doing this, in determining what causal efficacy
the agent's intentions had in one or more directions, and how his short-
term intentions succeeded or failed to be constitutive of long-term intentions, we ourselves write a further part of these histories. Narrative history
of a certain kind turns out to be the basic and essential genre for the
characterization of human actions.

It is important to be clear now different the standpoint presupposed by the argument so far is from that of those analytical philosophers who have constructed accounts of human actions which make central the notion of 'a' human action. A course of human events is then seen as a complex sequence of individual actions, and a natural question is: How do we individuate human actions? Now there are contexts in which such notions are at home. In the recipes of a cookery book for instance actions are individuated in just the way that some analytical philosophers have supposed to be possible of all actions. 'Take six eggs. Then break them into a bowl. Add flour, salt, sugar, etc.' But the point about such sequences is that each element in them is intelligible as an action only as a-possible-element-in-a-sequence. Moreover even such a sequence requires a context to be intelligible. If in the middle of my lecture on Kant's ethics I suddenly broke six eggs into a bowl and added flour and sugar, proceeding all the while with my Kantian exegesis, I have *not*, simply in virtue of the fact that I was following a sequence prescribed by Fanny Farmer, performed an intelligible action.

To this it might be retorted that I certainly performed an action or a set of actions, if not an intelligible action. But to this I want to reply that the concept of an intelligible action is a more fundamental concept than that of an action as such. Unintelligible actions are failed candidates for the status of intelligible action; and to lump unintelligible actions and intelligible actions together in a single class of actions and then to characterize action in terms of what items of both sets have in common is to make the mistake of ignoring this. It is also to neglect the central importance of the concept of intelligibility.

The importance of the concept of intelligibility is closely related to the fact that the most basic distinction of all embedded in our discourse and our practice in this area is that between human beings and other beings. Human beings can be held to account for that of which they are the authors; other beings cannot. To identify an occurrence as an action is in the paradigmatic instances to identify it under a type of description which enables us to see that occurrence as flowing intelligibly from a human agent's intentions, motives, passions and purposes. It is therefore to understand an action as something for which someone is accountable, about which it is always appropriate to ask the agent for an intelligible account. When an occurrence is apparently the intended action of a human agent, but nonetheless we cannot so identify it, we are both intellectually and practically baffled. We do not know how to respond; we do not know how to explain; we do not even know how to characterize minimally as an intelligible action; our distinction between the humanly accountable and the merely natural seems to have broken down. And this kind of bafflement does indeed occur in a number of different kinds of situation; when we enter alien cultures or even alien social structures within our own culture, in our encounters with certain types of neurotic or psychotic patient (it is indeed the unintelligibility of such patients' actions that leads to their being treated as patients; actions unintelligible to the agent as well as to everyone else are understood—rightly—as a kind of suffering), but also in everyday situations. Consider an example.

I am standing waiting for a bus and the young man standing next to me suddenly says: 'The name of the common wild duck is *Histrionicus histrionicus histrionicus.*' There is no problem as to the meaning of the sentence he uttered: the problem is, how to answer the question, what was he doing in uttering it? Suppose he just uttered such sentences at random intervals; this would be one possible form of madness. We would render his action of utterance intelligible if one of the following turned out to be true. He has mistaken me for someone who yesterday had approached him in the library and asked: 'Do you by any chance know the Latin name of the common wild duck?' Or he has just come from a session with his psychotherapist who has urged him to break down his shyness by talking to strangers. 'But what shall I say?' 'Oh, anything at all.' Or he is a Soviet spy waiting at a prearranged rendez-vous and uttering the ill-chosen code sentence which will identify him to his contact. In each case the act of utterance become intelligible by finding its place in a narrative.

To this it may be replied that the supplying of a narrative is not necessary to make such an act intelligible. All that is required is that we can identify the relevant type of speech act (e.g. 'He was answering a question') or some purpose served by his utterance (e.g. 'He was trying to attract your attention'). But speech acts and purposes too can be intelligible or unintelligible. Suppose that the man at the bus stop explains his act of utterance by saying 'I was answering a question.' I reply: 'But I never asked you any question to which that could have been the answer.' He says, 'Oh, I know *that.*' Once again his action becomes unintelligible. And a parallel example could easily be constructed to show that the mere fact that an action serves some purposes of a recognized type is not sufficient to render an action intelligible. Both purposes and speech-acts require contexts.

The most familiar type of context in and by reference to which speech-acts and purposes are rendered intelligible is the conversation. Conversation is so all-pervasive a feature of the human world that it tends to escape philosophical attention. Yet remove conversation from human life and what would be left? Consider then what is involved in following a conversation and finding it intelligible or unintelligible. (To find a conversation intelligible is not the same as to understand it; for a conversation which

I overhear may be intelligible, but I may fail to understand it.) If I listen to a conversation between two other people my ability to grasp the thread of the conversation will involve an ability to bring it under some one out of a set of descriptions in which the degree and kind of coherence in the conversation is brought out: 'a drunken, rambling quarrel', 'a serious intellectual disagreement', 'a tragic misunderstanding of each other', 'a comic, even farcial miscontrual of each other's motives', 'a penetrating interchange of views', 'a struggle to dominate each other', 'a trivial exchange of gossip.'

The use of words such as 'tragic', 'comic', and 'farcial' is not marginal to such evaluations. We allocate conversations to genres, just as we do literary narratives. Indeed a conversation is a dramatic work, even if a very short one, in which the participants are not only the actors, but also the joint authors, working out in agreement or disagreement the mode of their production. For it is not just that conversations belong to genres in just the way that plays and novels do; but they have beginnings, middles and endings just as do literary works. They embody reversals and recognitions; they move towards and away from climaxes. There may within a longer conversation be digressions and subplots, indeed digressions within digressions and subplots within subplots.

But if this is true of conversations, it is true also *mutatis mutandis* of battles, chess games, courtships, philosophy seminars, families at the dinner table, businessmen negotiating contracts—that is, of human transactions in general. For conversation, understood widely enough, is the form of human transactions in general. Conversational behavior is not a special sort or aspect of human behavior, even though the forms of language-using and of human life are such that the deeds of others speak for them as much as do their words. For that is possible only because they are the deeds of those who have words.

I am presenting both conversations in particular then and human actions in general as enacted narratives. Narrative is not the work of poets, dramatists and novelists reflecting upon events which had no narrative order before one was imposed by the singer or the writer; narrative form is neither disguise nor decoration. Barbara Hardy has written that 'we dream in narrative, day-dream in narrative, remember, anticipate, hope, despair, believe, doubt, plan, revise, criticize, construct, gossip, learn, hate and love by narrative' in arguing the same point (Hardy 1968, p. 5).

At the beginning of this chapter I argued that in successfully identifying and understanding what someone else is doing we always move towards placing a particular episode in the context of a set of narrative histories, histories both of the individuals concerned and of the settings in which they act and suffer. It is now becoming clear that we render the actions of others intelligible in this way because action itself has a basically historical character. It is because we all live out narratives in our lives and because we understand our own lives in terms of the narratives that we live out that the form of narrative is appropriate for understanding the actions of others. Stories are lived before they are told—except in the case of fiction.

This has of course been denied in recent debates. Louis O. Mink, quarrelling with Barbara Hardy's view, has asserted: 'Stories are not lived but told. Life has no beginnings, middles, or ends; there are meetings, but the start of an affair belongs to the story we tell ourselves later, and there are partings, but final partings only in the story. There are hopes, plans, battles and ideas, but only in retrospective stories are hopes unfulfilled, plans miscarried, battles decisive, and ideas seminal. Only in the story is it America which Columbus discovers and only in the story is the kingdom lost for want of a nail' (Mink 1970, pp. 557-8).

What are we to say to this? Certainly we must agree that it is only retrospectively that hopes can be characterized as unfulfilled or battles as decisive and so on. But we so characterize them in life as much as in art. And to someone who says that in life there are no endings, or that final partings take place only in stories, one is tempted to reply, 'But have you never heard of death?' Homer did not have to tell the tale of Hector before Andromache could lament unfulfilled hope and final parting. There are countless Hectors and countless Andromaches whose lives embodied the form of their Homeric namesakes, but who never came to the attention of any poet. What is true is that in taking an event as a beginning or an ending we bestow a significance upon it which may be debatable. Did the Roman republic end with the death of Julius Caesar, or at Philippi, or with the founding of the principate? The answer is surely that, like Charles II, it was a long time a-dying; but this answer implies the reality of its ending as much as do any of the former. There is a crucial sense in which the principate of Augustus, or the taking of the oath in the tennis court, or the decision to construct an atomic bomb at Los Alamos constitute beginnings; the peace of 404 B.C., the abolition of the Scottish Parliament and the battle of Waterloo equally constitute endings; while there are many events which are both endings and beginnings.

As with beginnings, middles and endings, so also with genres and with the phenomenon of embedding. Consider the question of to what genre the life of Thomas Becket belongs, a question which has to be asked and answered before we can decide how it is to be written. (On Mink's paradoxical view this question could not be asked until *after* the life had been written.) In some of the medieval versions, Thomas's career is presented in terms of the canons of medieval hagiography. In the Icelandic *Thomas Saga* he is presented as a saga hero. In Dom David Knowles's modern biography the story is a tragedy, the tragic relationship of Thomas and Henry II, each of whom satisfies Aristotle's demand that the hero be a great man with a fatal flaw. Now it clearly makes sense to ask who is right, if anyone: the monk William of Canterbury, the author of the saga, or the Cambridge Regius Professor Emeritus? The answer appears to be clearly the last. The true genre of the life is neither hagiography nor saga, but tragedy. So of such modern narrative subjects as the life of Trotsky or that of Lenin, of the history of the Soviet Communist Party or the American presidency, we may also ask: To what genre does their history belong? And this is the same question as: What type of account of their history will be both true and intelligible?

Or consider again how one narrative may be embedded in another. In both plays and novels there are well-known examples: the play within the play in *Hamlet*, Wandering Willie's Tale in *Redgauntlet*, Aeneas' narrative to Dido in book 2 of the *Aeneid*, and so on. But there are equally well-known examples in real life. Consider again the way in which the career of Becket as archbishop and chancellor is embedded within the reign of Henry II, or the way in which the tragic life of Mary Stuart is embedded in that of Elizabeth I, or the history of the Confederacy within the history of the United States. Someone may discover (or not discover) that he or she is a character in a number of narratives at the same time, some of them embedded in others. Or again, what seemed to be an intelligible narrative in which one was playing a part may be transformed wholly or partly into a story of unintelligible episodes. This last is what happened to Kafka's character K. in both *The Trial* and *The Castle*. (It is no accident that Kafka could not end his novels, for the notion of an ending like that of a beginning has its sense only in terms of intelligible narrative.)

I spoke earlier of the agent as not only an actor, but an author. Now I must emphasize that what the agent is able to do and say intelligibly as an actor is deeply affected by the fact that we are never more (and sometimes less) than the co-authors of our own narratives. Only in fantasy do we live what story we please. In life, as both Aristotle and Engels noted, we are always under certain constraints. We enter upon a stage which we did not design and we find ourselves part of an action that was not of our making. Each of us being a main character in his own drama plays subordinate parts in the dramas of others, and each drama constrains the others. In my drama, perhaps, I am Hamlet or Iago or at least the swineherd who may yet become a prince, but to you I am only A Gentleman or at best Second Murderer, while you are my Polonius or my Gravedigger, but your own hero. Each of our dramas exerts constraints on each other's, making the whole different from the parts, but still dramatic.

It is considerations as complex as these which are involved in making the notion of intelligibility the conceptual connecting link between the notion of action and that of narrative. Once we have understood its importance the claim that the concept of an action is secondary to that of an intelligible action will perhaps appear less bizarre and so too will the claim that the notion of 'an' action, while of the highest practical importance, is always a potentially misleading abstraction. An action is a moment in a possible or actual history or in a number of such histories. The notion of a history is as fundamental a notion as the notion of an action. Each requires the other. But I cannot say this without noticing that it is precisely this that Sartre denies — as indeed his whole theory of the self, which captures so well the spirit of modernity, requires that he should. In *La Nausée*, Sartre makes Antoine Roquentin argue not just what Mink argues, that narrative is very different from life, but that to present human life in the form of a narrative is always to falsify it. There are not and there cannot be any true stories. Human life is composed of discrete actions which lead nowhere, which have no order; the story-teller imposes on human events retrospectively an order which they did not have while they were lived. Clearly if Sartre/Roquentin is right — I speak of Sartre/Roquentin to distinguish him from such other well-know characters as Sartre/Heidegger and Sartre/Marx — my central contention must be mistaken. There is nonetheless an important point of agreement between my thesis and that of Sartre/Roquentin. We agree in identifying the intelligibility of an action with its place in a narrative sequence. Only Sartre/Roquentin takes it that human actions are as such unintelligible occurrences: it is to a realization of the metaphysical implications of this that Roquentin is brought in the course of the novel and the practical effect upon him is to bring to an end his own project of writing an historical biography. This project no longer makes sense. Either he will write what is true or he will write an intelligible history, but the one possibility excludes the other. Is Sartre/Roquentin right?

We can discover what is wrong with Sartre's thesis in either of two ways. One is to ask: what would human actions deprived of any falsifying narrative order be like? Sartre himself never answers this question; it is striking that in order to show that there are no true narratives, he himself writes a narrative, albeit a fictional one. But the only picture that I find myself able to form of human nature *an-sich*, prior to the alleged misinterpretation by narrative, is the kind of dislocated sequence which Dr. Johnson offers us in his notes of his travels in France: 'There we waited on the ladies—Morville's.—Spain. Country towns all beggars. At Dijon he could not find the way to Orleans.—Cross roads of France very bad.—Five soldiers.—Women.—Soldiers escaped.—The Colonel would not lose five men for the sake of one woman.—The magistrate cannot seize a soldier but by the Colonel's permission, etc., etc.' (quoted in Hobsbaum 1973, p. 32). What this suggests is what I take to be true, namely that the characterization of actions allegedly prior to any narrative form being imposed upon them will always turn out to be the presentation of what are plainly the disjointed parts of some possible narrative.

We can also approach the question in another way. What I have called a history is an enacted dramatic narrative in which the characters are also the authors. The characters of course never start literally *ab initio*; they plunge *in medias res*, the beginnings of their story already made for them by what and who has gone before. But when Julian Grenfell or Edward Thomas went off to France in the 1914–18 war they no less enacted a narrative than did Menelaus or Odysseus when *they* went off. The difference between imaginary characters and real ones is not in the narrative form of what they do; it is in the degree of their authorship of that form and of their own deeds. Of course just as they do not begin where they please, they cannot go on exactly as they please either; each character is constrained by the actions of others and by the social settings presupposed in his and their actions, a point forcibly made by Marx in the classical, if not entirely satisfactory account of human life as enacted dramatic narrative, *The Eighteenth Brumaire of Louis Bonaparte*.

I call Marx's account less than satisfactory partly because he wishes to present the narrative of human social life in a way that will be compatible with a view of the life as law-governed and predictable in a particular way. But it is crucial that at any given point in an enacted dramatic narrative we do not know what will happen next. The kind of unpredictability for which I argued in Chapter 8 is required by the narrative structure of human life, and the empirical generalizations and explorations which social scientists discover provide a kind of understanding of human life which is perfectly compatible with that structure.

This unpredictability coexists with a second crucial characteristic of all lived narratives, a certain teleological character. We live out our lives, both individually and in our relationships with each other, in the light of certain conceptions of a possible shared future, a future in which certain possibilities beckon us forward and others repel us, some seem already foreclosed and others perhaps inevitable. There is no present which is not informed by some image of some future and an image of the future which always presents itself in the form of a *telos*—or of a variety of ends or goals—

towards which we are either moving or failing to move in the present. Unpredictability and teleology therefore coexist as part of our lives; like characters in a fictional narrative we do not know what will happen next, but nonetheless our lives have a certain form which projects itself towards our future. Thus the narratives which we live out have both an unpredictable and a partially teleological character. If the narrative of our individual and social lives is to continue intelligibly — and either type of narrative may lapse into unintelligibility — it is always both the case that there are constraints on how the story can continue *and* that within those constraints there are indefinitely many ways that it can continue.

A central thesis then begins to emerge: man is in his actions and practice, as well as in his fictions, essentially a story-telling animal. He is not essentially, but becomes through his history, a teller of stories that aspire to truth. But the key question for men is not about their own authorship; I can only answer the question 'What am I to do?' if I can answer the prior question 'Of what story or stories do I find myself a part?' We enter human society, that is, with one or more imputed characters — roles into which we have been drafted — and we have to learn what they are in order to be able to understand how others respond to us and how our responses to them are apt to be construed. It is through hearing stories about wicked stepmothers, lost children, good but misguided kings, wolves that suckle twin boys, youngest sons who receive no inheritance but must make their own way in the world and eldest sons who waste their inheritance on riotous living and go into exile to live with the swine, that children learn or mislearn both what a child and what a parent is, what the cast of characters may be in the drama into which they have been born and what the ways of the world are. Deprive children of stories and you leave them unscripted, anxious stutterers in their actions as in their words. Hence there is no way to give us an understanding of any society, including our own, except through the stock of stories which constitute its initial dramatic resources. Mythology, in its original sense, is at the heart of things. Vico was right and so was Joyce. And so too of course is that moral tradition from heroic society to its medieval heirs according to which the telling of stories has a key part in educating us into the virtues.

I suggested earlier that 'an' action is always an episode in a possible history: I would now like to make a related suggestion about another concept, that of personal identity. Derek Parfit and others have recently drawn our attention to the contrast between the criteria of strict identity, which is an all-or-nothing matter (*either* the Tichborne claimant *is* the last Tichborne heir *or* he is not; *either* all the properties of the last heir belong to the claimant *or* the claimant is not the heir — Leibniz's Law applies) and the psychological continuities of personality which are a matter of more or less. (Am I the same man at fifty as I was at forty in respect of memory, intellectual powers, critical responses? More or less.) But what is crucial to human beings as characters in enacted narratives is that, possessing only the resources of psychological continuity, we have to be able to respond to the imputation of strict identity. I am forever whatever I have been at any time for others—and I may at any time be called upon to answer for it—no matter how changed I may be now. There is no way of *founding* my identity—or lack of it—on the psychological continuity or discontinuity of the self. The self inhabits a character whose unity is given as the unity of a character. Once again there is a crucial disagreement with empiricist or analytical philosophers on the one hand and with existentialists on the other.

Empiricists, such as Locke or Hume, tried to give an account of personal identity solely in terms of psychological states or events. Analytical philosophers, in so many ways their heirs as well as their critics, have wrestled with the connection between those states and events and strict identity understood in terms of Leibniz's Law. Both have failed to see that a background has been omitted, the lack of which makes the problems insoluble. That background is provided by the concept of a story and of that kind of unity of character which a story requires. Just as a history is not a sequence of actions, but the concept of an action is that of a moment in an actual or possible history abstracted for some purpose from that history, so the characters in a history are not a collection of persons, but the concept of a person is that of a character abstracted from a history.

What the narrative concept of selfhood requires is thus twofold. On the one hand, I am what I may justifiably be taken by others to be in the course of living out a story that runs from my birth to my death; I am the *subject* of a history that is my own and no one else's, that has its own peculiar meaning. When someone complains—as do some of those who attempt or commit suicide—that his or her life is meaningless, he or she is often and perhaps characteristically complaining that the narrative of their life has become unintelligible to them, that it lacks any point, any movement towards a climax or a *telos*. Hence the pont of doing any one thing rather than another at crucial junctures in their lives seems to such person to have been lost.

To be the subject of a narrative that runs from one's birth to one's death is, I remarked earlier, to be accountable for the actions and experiences which compose a narratable life. It is, that is, to be open to being asked to give a certain kind of account of what one did or what happened to one or what one witnessed at any earlier point in one's life than the time at which the question is posed. Of course someone may have forgotten or suffered brain damage or simply not attended sufficiently at the relevant time to be able to give the relevant account. But to say of someone under some one description ('The prisoner of the Chateau d'If') that he is the same person as someone characterized quite differently ('The Count of Monte Cristo') is precisely to say that it makes sense to ask him to give an intelligible narrative account enabling us to understand how he could at different times and different places be one and the same person and yet be so differently characterized. Thus personal identity is just that identity presupposed by the unity of the character which the unity of a narrative requires. Without such unity there would not be subjects of whom stories could be told.

The other aspect of narrative selfhood is correlative: I am not only accountable, I am one who can always ask others for an account, who can put others to the question. I am part of their story, as they are part of mine. The narrative of any one life is part of an interlocking set of narratives. Moreover this asking for and giving of accounts itself plays an important part in constituting narratives. Asking you what you did and why, saying what I did and why, pondering the differences between your account of what I did and my account of what I did, and *vice versa*, these are essential constituents of all but the very simplest and barest of narratives. Thus without the accountability of the self those trains of events that constitute all but the simplest and barest of narratives could not occur; and without that same accountability narratives would lack that continuity required to make both them and the actions that constitute them intelligible.

It is important to notice that I am not arguing that the concepts of narrative or of intelligibility or of accountability are *more* fundamental than that of personal identity. The concepts of narrative, intelligibility and accountability presuppose the applicability of the concept of personal identity, just as it presupposes their applicability and just as indeed each of these three presupposes the applicability of the two others. The relationship is one of mutual presupposition. It does follow of course that all attempts to elucidate the notion of personal identity independently of and in isolation from the notions of narrative, intelligibility and accountability are bound to fail. As all such attempts have.

It is now possible to return to the question from which this enquiry into the nature of human action and identity started: In what does the unity of an individual life consist? The answer is that its unity is the unity of a narrative embodied in a single life. To ask 'What is the good for me?' is to ask how best I might live out that unity and bring it to completion. To ask 'What is the good for man?' is to ask what all answers to the former question must have in common. But now it is important to emphasize that it is the systematic asking of these two questions and the attempt to answer them in deed as well as in word which provide the moral life with its unity. The unity of a human life is the unity of a narrative quest. Quests sometimes fail, are frustrated, abandoned or dissipated into distractions; and human lives may in all these ways also fail. But the only criteria for success or failure in a human life as a whole are the critieria of success or failure in a narrated or to-be-narrated quest. A quest for what?

Two key features of the medieval conception of a quest need to be recalled. The first is that without some at least partly determinate conception of the final *telos* there could not be any beginning to a quest. Some conception of the good for man is required. Whence is such a conception to be drawn? Precisely from those questions which led us to attempt to transcend that limited conception of the virtues which is available in and through practices. It is in looking for a conception of *the* good which will enable us to order other goods, for a conception of *the* good which will enable us to extend our understanding of the purpose and content of the virtues, for a conception of *the* good which will enable us to understand the place of integrity and constancy in life, that we initially define the kind of life which is a quest for the good. But secondly it is clear the medieval conception of a quest is not at all that of a search for something already adequately characterized, as miners search for gold or geologists for oil. It is in the course of the quest and only through encountering and coping with the various particular harms, dangers, temptations and distractions which provide any quest with its episodes and incidents that the goal of the quest is finally to be understood. A quest is always an education both as to the character of that which is sought and in self-knowledge.

The virtues therefore are to be understood as those dispositions which will not only sustain practices and enable us to achieve the goods internal to practices, but which will also sustain us in the relevant kind of quest for the good, by enabling us to overcome the harms, dangers, temptations and distractions which we encounter, and which will furnish us with increasing self-knowledge and increasing knowledge of the good. The catalogue of the virtues will therefore include the virtues required to sustain the kind of households and the kind of political communities in which men and women can seek for the good together and the virtues necessary for philosophical enquiry about the character of the good. We have then arrived at a provisional conclusion about the good life for man: the good life for man is the life spent in seeking for the good life for man, and the virtues necessary for the seeking are those which will enable us to understand what more and what else the good life for man is. We have also completed the second stage in our account of the virtues, by situating them in relation to the good life for man and not only in relation to practices. But our enquiry requires a third stage.

For I am never able to seek for the good or exercise the virtues only *qua* individual. This is partly because what it is to live the good life concretely varies from circumstance to circumstance even when it is one and the same conception of the good life and one and the same set of virtues which are being embodied in a human life. What the good life is for a fifth-century Athenian general will not be the same as what it was for a medieval nun or a seventeenth-century farmer. But it is not just that different individuals live in different social circumstances; it is also that we all approach our own circumstances as bearers of a particular social identity. I am someone's son or daughter, someone else's cousin or uncle; I am a citizen of this or that city, a member of this or that guild or profession; I belong to this clan, that tribe, this nation. Hence what is good for me has to be the good for one who inhabits these roles. As such, I inherit from the past of my family, my city, my tribe, my nation, a variety of debts, inheritances, rightful expectations and obligations. These constitute the given of my life, my moral starting point. This is in part what gives my life its own moral particularity.

This thought is likely to appear alien and even suprising from the standpoint of modern individualism. From the standpoint of individualism I am what I myself choose to be. I can always, if I wish to, put in question what are taken to be the merely contingent social features of my existence. I may biologically be my father's son; but I cannot be held responsible for what he did unless I choose implicitly or explicitly to assume such responsibility. I may legally be a citizen of a certain country; but I cannot be held responsible for what my country does or has done unless I choose implicitly or explicitly to assume such responsibility. Such individualism is expressed by those modern Americans who deny any responsibility for the effects of slavery upon black Americans, saying 'I never owned any slaves'. It is more subtly the standpoint of those other modern Americans who accept a nicely calculated responsibility for such effects measured precisely by the benefits they themselves as individuals have indirectly received from slavery. In both cases 'being an American' is not in itself taken to be part of the moral identity of the individual. And of course there is nothing peculiar to modern Americans in this attitude: the Englishman who says, 'I never did any wrong to Ireland; why bring up that old history as though it had something to do with *me?*' or the young German who believes that being born after 1945 means that what Nazis did to Jews has no moral relevance to his relationship to his Jewish contemporaries, exhibit the same attitude, that according to which the self is detachable from its social and historical roles and statuses. And the self so detached is of course a self very much at home in either Sartre's or Goffman's perspective, a self that can have no history. The contrast with the narrative view of the self is clear. For the story of my life is always embedded in the story of those communities from which I derive my identity. I am born with a past; and to try to cut myself off from that past, in the individualist mode, is to deform my present relationships. The possession of an historical identity and the possession of a social identity coincide. Notice that rebellion against my identity is always one possible mode of expressing it.

Notice also that the fact that the self has to find its moral identity in and through its membership in communities such as those of the family, the neighborhood, the city and the tribe does not entail that the self has to accept the moral *limitations* of the particularity of those forms of community. Without those moral particularities to begin from there would never be anywhere to begin; but it is in moving forward from such particularity that the search for the good, for the universal, consists. Yet particularity can never be simply left behind or obliterated. The notion of escaping from it into a realm of entirely universal maxims which belong to man as such, whether in its eighteenth-century Kantian form or in the presentation of some modern analytical moral philosophies, is an illusion and an illusion with painful consequences. When men and women identify what are in fact their partial and particular causes too easily and too completely with the cause of some universal principle, they usually behave worse than they would otherwise do.

What I am, therefore, is in key part what I inherit, a specific past that is present to some degree in my present. I find myself part of a history and that is generally to say, whether I like it or not, whether I recognize it or not, one of the bearers of a tradition. It was important when I characterized the concept of a practice to notice that practices always have histories and that at any given moment what a practice is depends on a mode of understanding it which has been transmitted often through many generations. And thus, insofar as the virtues sustain the relationships required for practices, they have to sustain relationships to the past—and to the future —as well as in the present. But the traditions through which particular practices are transmitted and reshaped never exist in isolation for larger social traditions. What constitutes such traditions?

We are apt to be misled here by the ideological uses to which the concept of a tradition has been put by conservative political theorists. Characteristically such theorists have followed Burke in contrasting tradition with reason and the stability of tradition with conflict. Both contrasts obfuscate.

For all reasoning takes place within the context of some traditional mode of thought, transcending through criticism and invention the limitations of what had hitherto been reasoned in that tradition; this is as true of modern physics as of medieval logic. Moreover when a tradition is in good order it is always partially constituted by an argument about the goods the pursuit of which gives to that tradition its particular point and purpose.

So when an institution—a university, say, or a farm, or a hospital—is the bearer of a tradition of practice or practices, its common life will be partly, but in a centrally important way, constituted by a continuous argument as to what a university is and ought to be or what good farming is or what good medicine is. Traditions, when vital, embody continuities of conflict. Indeed when a tradition becomes Burkean, it is always dying or dead.

The individualism of modernity could of course find no use for the notion of tradition within its own conceptual scheme except as an adversary notion; it therefore all too willingly abandoned it to the Burkeans, who, faithful to Burke's own allegiance, tried to combine adherence in politics to a conception of tradition which would vindicate the oligarchical revolution of property of 1688 and adherence in economics to the doctrine and institutions of the free market. The theoretical incoherence of this mismatch did not deprive it of ideological usefulness. But the outcome has been that modern conservatives are for the most part engaged in conserving only older rather than later versions of liberal individualism. Their own core doctrine is as liberal and as individualist as that of self-avowed liberals.

A living tradition then is an historically extended, socially embodied argument, and an argument precisely in part about the goods which constitute that tradition. Within a tradition the pursuit of goods extends through generations, sometimes through many generations. Hence the individual's search for his or her good is generally and characteristically conducted within a context defined by those traditions of which the individual's life is a part, and this is true both of those goods which are internal to practices and of the goods of a single life. Once again the narrative phenomenon of embedding is crucial: the history of a practice in our time is generally and characteristically embedded in and made intelligible in terms of the larger and longer history of the tradition through which the practice in its present form was conveyed to us; the history of each of our own lives is generally and characteristically embedded in and made intelligible in terms of the larger and longer histories of a number of traditions. I have to say 'generally and characteristically' rather than 'always', for traditions decay, disintegrate and disappear. What then sustains and strengthens traditions? What weakens and destroys them?

The answer in key part is: the exercise or the lack of exercise of the relevant virtues. The virtues find their point and purpose not only in sustaining those relationships necessary if the variety of goods internal to practices are to be achieved and not only in sustaining the form of an individual life in which that individual may seek out his or her good as the good of his or her whole life, but also in sustaining those traditions which provide both practices and individual lives with their necessary historical context. Lack of justice, lack of truthfulness, lack of courage, lack of the relevant intellectual virtues—these corrupt traditions, just as they do those institutions and practices which derive their life from the traditions of which they are the contemporary embodiments. To recognize this is of course also to recognize the existence of an additional virtue, one whose importance is perhaps most obvious when it is least present, the virtue of having an adequate sense of the traditions to which one belongs or which confront one. This virtue is not to be confused with any form of conservative antiquarianism; I am not praising those who choose the conventional conservative role of *laudator temporis acti*. It is rather the case that an adequate sense of tradition manifests itself in a grasp of those future possibilities which the past has made available to the present. Living traditions, just because they continue a not-yet-completed narrative, confront a future whose determinate and determinable character, so far as it possesses any, derives from the past.

In practical reasoning the possession of this virtue is not manifested so much in the knowledge of a set of generalizations or maxims which may provide our practical inferences with major premises; its presence or absence rather appears in the kind of capacity for judgment which the agent possesses in knowing how to select among the relevant stack of maxims and how to apply them in particular situations. Cardinal Pole possessed it, Mary Tudor did not; Montrose possessed it, Charles I did not. What Cardinal Pole and the Marquis of Montrose possessed were in fact those virtues which enable their possessors to pursue both their own good and the good of the tradition of which they are the bearers even in situations defined by the necessity of tragic, dilemmatic choice. Such choices, understood in the context of the tradition of the virtues, are very different from those which face the modern adherents of rival and incommensurable moral premises in the debates about which I wrote in Chapter 2. Wherein does the difference lie?

It has often been suggested—by J. L. Austin, for example—that *either* we can admit the existence of rival and contingently incompatible goods which make incompatible claims to our practical allegiance *or* we can believe in some determinate conception of *the* good life for man, but that these are mutually exclusive alternatives. No one can consistently hold both these views. What this contention is blind to is that there may be better or worse ways for individuals to live through the tragic confrontation of good with good. And that to know what the good life for man is may require knowing what are the better and what are the worse ways of living in and through such situations. Nothing *a priori* rules out this possibility; and this suggests that within a view such as Austin's there is concealed an unacknowledged empirical premise about the character of tragic situations.

One way in which the choice between rival goods in a tragic situation differs from the modern choice between incommensurable moral premises is that *both* of the alternative courses of action which confront the individual have to be recognized as leading to some authentic and substantial good. By choosing one I do nothing to diminish or derogate from the claim upon me of the other; and therefore, whatever I do, I shall have left undone what I ought to have done. The tragic protagonist, unlike the moral agent as depicted by Sartre or Hare, is not choosing between allegiance to one moral principle rather than another, nor is he or she deciding upon some principle of priority between moral principles. Hence the 'ought' involved has a different meaning and force from that of the 'ought' in moral principles understood in a modern way. For the tragic protagonist cannot do everything that he or she ought to do. This 'ought', unlike Kant's, does not imply 'can'. Moreover any attempt to map the logic of such 'ought' assertions on to some modal calculus so as to produce a version of deontic logic has to fail. (See, from a very different point of view, Bas C. Van Fraasen 1973.)

Yet it is clear that the moral task of the tragic protagonist may be performed better or worse, independently of the choice between alternatives that he or she makes—*ex hypothesi* he or she has no *right* choice to make. The tragic protagonist may behave heroically or unheroically, generously or ungenerously, gracefully or gracelessly, prudently or imprudently. To perform his or her task better rather than worse will be to do both what is better for him or her *qua* individul and *qua* parent or child or *qua* citizen or member of a profession, or perhaps *qua* some or all of these. The existence of tragic dilemmas casts no doubt upon and provides no counter-examples to the thesis that assertions of the form 'To do this in this way would be better for X and/or for his or her family, city or profession' are susceptible of objective truth and falsity, any more than the existence of alternative and contingently incompatible forms of medical treatment casts doubt on the thesis that assertions of the form 'To undergo his medical treatment in this way would be better for X and/or his or her family' are susceptible of objective truth and falsity. (See, from a different point of view, the illuminating discussion in Samuel Guttenplan 1979-80, pp. 61-80). The presupposition of this objectivity is of course that we can understand the notion of 'good for X' and cognate notions in terms of some conception of the unity of X's life. What is better or worse for X depends upon the character of that intelligible narrative which provides X's life with its unity. Unsurprisingly it is the lack of any such unifying conception of a human life which underlies modern denials of the factual character of moral judgments and more especially of those judgments which ascribe virtues or vices to individuals.

I argued earlier that every moral philosophy has some particular sociology as its counterpart. What I have tried to spell out in this chapter is the kind of understanding of social life which the tradition of the virtues requires, a kind of understanding very different from those dominant in the culture of bureaucratic individualism. Within that culture conceptions of the virtues become marginal and the tradition of the virtues remains central only in the lives of social groups whose existence is on the margins of the central culture. Within the central cultural of liberal or bureaucratic individualism new conceptions of the virtues emerge and the concept of a virtue is itself transformed. To the history of that transformation I therefore now turn; for we shall only understand the tradition of the virtues fully if we understand to what kinds of degeneration it has proved liable.

16

From the Virtues to Virtue
and after Virtue

Near the beginning of this book I suggested that the interminable and unsettlable character of so much contemporary moral debate arises from the variety of heterogeneous and incommensurable concepts which inform the major premises from which the protagonists in such debates argue. In this conceptual *mélange* there are to be found, jostling with such modern concepts as those of utility and rights, a variety of virtue concepts, functioning in a variety of different ways. What is lacking however is any clear consensus, either as to the place of virtue concepts relative to other moral concepts, or as to which dispositions are to be included within the catalogue of the virtues or the requirements imposed by particular virtues. Within particular modern subcultures, of course, versions of the traditional scheme of the virtues survive; but the conditions of contemporary public debate are such that when the representative voices of those subcultures try to participate in it, they are all too easily interpreted and misinterpreted in terms of the pluralism which threatens to submerge us all. This misinterpretation is the outcome of a long history from the later middle ages until the present during which the dominant lists of the virtues have changed, the conception of individual virtues has changed and the concept of a virtue itself has become other than what it was. It could scarcely have happened otherwise. The two concepts which, as I have argued in the immediately preceding chapters, provide the necessary background for a traditional account of the virtues, the concept of narrative unity and the concept of a practice, were themselves displaced during the same period. Literary historians from Auerbach to John Gardner have traced the way in which the cultural place of narrative has been diminished and the modes of interpretation of narrative have been transformed until it has become possible for modern theorists as different as Sartre—whose views I have already discussed—and William Gass to understand the form of narrative, *not* as that which connects story-telling with the form of human life, but precisely as that which segregates narrative from life, which confines it to what is taken to be a separate and distinctive realm of art.

The contrast, indeed the opposition, between art and life, which is often in fact the premise rather than the conclusion of such theorists, provides a way of exempting art–including narrative–from its moral tasks. And the relegation of art by modernity to the status of an essentially minority activity and interest further helps to protect us from any narrative understanding of ourselves. Yet since such an understanding cannot be finally and completely expelled without expelling life itself, it continuously recurs within art: in the realistic novels of the nineteenth century, in the movies of the twentieth century, in the half-suppressed background plot line which lends coherence to the reading of each morning's newspaper. Nonetheless to think of a human life as a narrative unity is to think in a way alien to the dominant individualist and bureaucratic modes of modern culture.

Moreover the concept of a practice with goods internal to itself, understood as I have tried to understand it, is similarly removed to the margins of our lives. When I first introduced that notion I did so in terms of examples drawn from arts, sciences and games, remarking that the creation and recreation of human community in families, households, tribes, cities and kingdoms was taken to be in the same sense a type of practice in the ancient and medieval periods, but not in the modern world. Politics, as Aristotle conceives it, is a practice with goods internal to itself. Politics, as James Mill conceives it, is not. Moreover the kind of work done by the vast majority of the inhabitants of the modern world cannot be understood in terms of the nature of a practice with goods internal to itself, and for very good reason. One of the key moments in the creation of modernity occurs when production moves outside the household. So long as productive work occurs within the structure of households, it is easy and right to understand that work as part of the sustaining of the community of the household and of those wider forms of community which the household in turn sustains. As, and to the extent that, work moves outside the household and is put to the service of impersonal capital, the realm of work tends to become separated from everything but the service of biological survival and the reproduction of the labor force, on the one hand, and that of institutionalized acquisitiveness, on the other. *Pleonexia*, a vice in the Aristotelian scheme, is now the driving force of modern productive work. The means-end relationships embodied for the most part in such work–on a production line, for example–are necessarily external to the goods which those who work seek; such work too has consequently been expelled from the realm of practices with goods internal to themselves. And correspondingly practices have in turn been removed to the margins of social and cultural life. Arts, sciences and games are taken to be *work* only for a minority of specialists: the rest of us may receive incidental benefits in our leisure time only as spectators or consumers. Where the notion of engagement in a practice was once socially central, the notion of aesthetic consumption now is, at least for the majority.

Thus the historical process by and through which the aesthete, the bureaucratic manager—the essential instrument for organizing modern work—and their social kindred become the central *characters* of modern society (a process which I described even if too briefly in Chapter 3) and the historical process by which the narrative understanding of the unity of human life and the concept of a practice were expelled to the margins of modern culture turn out to be one and the same. It is a history one aspect of which is the transformation of forms of social life: the continuously re-established dominance of markets, factories and finally bureaucracies over individuals, themselves sometimes conceived of as independent, rational beings, prescribing their moral standpoint to themselves, and sometimes as anomic products of circumstances, whose happiness must be contrived for them. And it is a history another aspect of which is that very transformation of the virtues in conception and practice with which I am now concerned.

For if you withdraw those background concepts of the narrative unity of human life and of a practice with goods internal to it from those areas in which human life is for the most part lived out, what is there left for the virtues to become? That explicit and thoroughgoing rejection of Aristotelianism which was the counterpart at the level of philosophy to those social changes whose outcome was to deprive the virtues of their conceptual background made it impossible by the end of the seventeenth century to supply anything like a traditional account or justification of the virtues. Yet the praise and practice of the virtues still pervaded social life, often in highly traditional ways, even though there were quite new problems for anyone wishing to give a systematic account or justification of their place in that life. There was indeed one distinctively new way open to understand the virtues once they had been severed from their traditional context in thought and practice, and that is as dispositions related in either of two alternative ways to the psychology of that newly invented social institution, the individual. *Either* the virtues—or some of them—could be understood as expressions of the natural passions of the individual *or* they—or some of them—could be understood as dispositions necessary to curb and to limit the destructive effect of some of those same natural passions.

It was in the seventeenth and eighteenth centuries that morality came generally to be understood as offering a solution to the problems posed by human egoism and that the content of morality came to be largely equated with altruism. For it was in that same period that men came to be thought of as in some dangerous measure egoistic by nature; and it is only once we think of mankind as by nature dangerously egoistic that altruism becomes at once socially necessary and yet apparently impossible and, if and when it occurs, inexplicable. On the traditional Aristotelian view such problems do not arise. For what education in the virtues teaches me is that my good as a man is one and the same as the good of those others with whom I am bound up in human community. There is no way of my pursuing my good which is necessarily antagonistic to you pursuing yours because *the* good is neither mine peculiarly nor yours peculiarly—goods are not private property. Hence Aristotle's definition of friendship, the fundamental form of human relationship, is in terms of shared goods. The egoist is thus, in the ancient and medieval world, always someone who has made a fundamental mistake about where his own good lies and someone who has thus and to that extent excluded himself from human relationships.

For many seventeenth- and eighteenth-century thinkers however the notion of a shared good for man is an Aristotelian chimaera; each man by nature seeks to satisfy his own desires. But if so, there are at least strong reasons for supposing that a mutually destructive anarchy will ensue, unless desires are limited by a more intelligent version of egoism. It is in the context of the consideration of these grounds that a great deal of seventeenth- and eighteenth-century thinking about the virtues takes place. So David Hume, for example, has to distinguish between the natural virtues—virtues which are qualities useful or agreeable or both to the man whose passions and desires are normally constituted—and the artificial virtues which are socially and culturally constructed to inhibit the expression of those passions and desires which would serve what we usually take to be our self-interest in a socially destructive way. We naturally find useful and agreeable to ourselves generosity in others; we artificially inculcate in ourselves and others a regard for the rules of justice, even though to obey these rules may not always be to our immediate interest. But why should we find agreeable certain qualities in others which are not useful to us—Hume is sure that we do—and why should we obey rules on occasions when it is not to our interest to do so?

Hume's answers to these questions reveal the underlying weakness of his account. For he tries to conclude in the *Treatise* that it is to our long-term advantage to be just, when all that his premises warrant is the younger Rameau's conclusion that it is often to our long-term advantage that people in general should be just. And he has to invoke, to some degree in the *Treatise* and more strongly in the *Enquiry*, what he calls 'the communicated passion of sympathy': we find it agreeable that some quality is agreeable to others because we are so constructed that we naturally sympathize with those others. The younger Rameau's answer would have been: 'Sometimes we do, sometimes we do not; and when we do not, why should we?'

The importance of recalling in the form of objections to Hume's thesis those self-doubts which Diderot put into Rameau's mouth is not only however a matter of Hume's inability to transcend the eighteenth century's egoistic presuppositions. What they point to is a more fundamental weakness which becomes explicit when we consider Hume's attitude to rival tables of the virtues. One the one hand, Hume sometimes writes as if the knowledge of what is virtuous and what is vicious is a matter of simple reflection open to everyone: 'The final sentence, it is probable, which pronounces character and actions, amiable or odious, praiseworthy or blamable; that which stamps on them the mark of honor or infamy, approbation or censure; that which renders morality as active principle and constitutes virtue or happiness and vice or misery—it is possible, I say, that the final sentence depends on some internal sense or feeling which nature has made universal in the whole species' (*Inquiry* I). And so, when he considers how to determine what qualities to include in the catalogue of the virtues, he remarks: 'The quick sensibility which, on this head, is so universal among mankind, gives a philosopher sufficient assurance that he can never be mistaken in forming the catalogue or incur any danger of misplacing the object of his contemplation: he needs only enter into his own heart for a moment and consider whether or not he should desire to have this or that quality ascribed to him. . . . ' About the virtues apparently we cannot be mistaken. Yet who are *we?* For Hume also believes very strongly that some accounts of the virtues *are* mistaken. Diogenes, Pascal and others who uphold what he abhors as 'the monkish virtues' and the levellers of the preceding century all incur his severe censure.

Such examples Hume does *not* treat in terms of a general thesis to which he is otherwise committed: that apparent variations and differences in morality are to be explained entirely as the *same* human nature responding to *different* circumstances. A stubborn realism forces him to acknowledge the occurence of cases which cannot thus be dealt with. What he cannot acknowledge of course is that, within the limits imposed by his own understanding of the virtues, these cases can scarcely be dealt with at all. Why this is so emerges when we consider two incompatible attitudes which Hume adopts toward them.

For on the one hand Hume insists that there is nothing to judgments of virtue and vice except the expression of feelings of approval and disapproval. Thus there can be no criteria external to those feelings by appeal to which we may pass judgment upon them. Hume does recognize that Diogenes and Pascal held philosophical theories which led—or as he thinks, misled—them to believe that there is such a criterion. But his own theory has to exclude the possibility of such a criterion. Yet at the same time he wishes to condemn, sometimes in the harshest terms, those who hold certain alternative views of the virtues. We might perhaps have expected such condemnations to rest on an appeal to Hume's metaphysical views. In expressing his own moral preferences in a letter to Francis Hutcheson (Letter B of Sept. 17 1739 in Greig 1932) he wrote: 'Upon the whole I desire to take my Catalogue of Virtues from *Cicero's Offices* and not from the *Whole Duty of Man.*' His preference for Cicero over the Christian work clearly arises at least in the main from the fact that he takes central Christian beliefs to be false in a way and to a degree that Cicero's were not. And earlier in the same letter Hume had attacked any teleological view of human nature, thus explicitly dismissing any kind of Aristotelian view. But while the falsity of certain metaphysical views is necessary, if Hume's own position on the virtues is to be vindicated, that falsity is not sufficient. And Hume's problem about how 'ought' may be derived from 'is' denies him any overt appeal to his own understanding of the nature of things to supply that insufficiency. Hence, although Hume may find in what he takes to be the falsity of the Christian religion a ground for condemning the adherents of the monkish virtues—Hume condemns humility as useless, for example—his final court of appeal can be no more than the appeal to the passions of men of good sense, to a concurrence of feelings among the worldly.

Thus the appeal to a universal verdict by mankind turns out to be the mask worn by an appeal to those who physiologically and socially share Hume's attitudes and *Weltanschauung*. The passions of some are to be preferred to the passions of others. Whose preferences reign? The preferences of those who accept the stability of property, of those who understand chastity in women as a virtue only because it is a useful device to secure that property is passed only to legitimate heirs, of those who believe that the passage of time confers legitimacy upon what was originally acquired by violence and aggression. What Hume identifies as the standpoint of universal human nature turns out in fact to be that of the prejudices of the Hanoverian ruling elite. Hume's moral philosophy presupposes allegiance to a particular kind of social structure as much as Aristotle's does, but allegiance of a highly ideological kind.

Hume thus provides—and I am here repeating part of the argument of Chapter 4—an unsatisfactory underpinning for an attempt to claim universal rational authority for what is in fact the local morality of parts of eighteenth-century Northern Europe. It is scarcely surprising that rival attempts to achieve the same end multiply. Some of these—Diderot's, for example, and Kant's—I also noticed earlier. Others I shall draw attention to presently. But before doing so it is important to notice three features of Hume's treatment of the virtues which recur in other eighteenth-century and nineteenth-century moral philosophies.

The first of these concerns the characterization of particular virtues. In a society where there is no longer a shared conception of the community's good as specified by the good for man, there can no longer either be any very substantial concept of what it is to contribute more or less to the achievement of that good. Hence notions of desert and of honor become detached from the context in which they were originally at home. Honor becomes nothing more than a badge of aristocratic status, and status itself, tied as it is now so securely to property, has very little to do with desert. Distributive justice cannot any longer be defined in terms of desert either, and so the alternatives become those of defining justice in terms of some sort of equality (a project which Hume himself rejects) or in terms of legal entitlements. And justice is not the only virtue that has to be redefined.

Any conception of chastity as a virtue—in anything like the traditional meaning of the word—in a world uninformed by either Aristotelian or biblical values will make very little sense to the adherents of the dominant culture, and Hume's connection of female chastity with property is only the first of a series of desperate attempts to find some place for it. Other virtues fare a little better, although since utility becomes the hallmark of a virtue not only for Hume but also, for example, for Franklin, the vagueness and generality of the notion of utility infects any conception of 'doing good' and more particularly the new conception of the virtue of benevolence. Benevolence in the eighteenth century is assigned very much the scope which the Christian scheme of the virtues assigned to charity. But, unlike charity, benevolence as a virtue became a licence for almost any kind of manipulative intervention in the affairs of others.

A second feature of Hume's treatment of the virtues which recurs in later thought and practice is a quite new conception of the relationship of virtues to rules. I remarked earlier upon the degree to which the concept of a rule acquired a new centrality in modern individualist morality. Virtues are indeed now conceived of not, as in the Aristotelian scheme, as possessing a role and function distinct from and to be contrasted with, that of rules or laws, but rather as being just those dispositions necessary to produce obedience to the rules of morality. The virtue of justice, as Hume characterizes it, *is* nothing but a disposition to obey the rules of justice.

Hume will have many successors in this, among them both Kant and Mill; and a contemporary writer who is the heir of this modern tradition actually *defines* the notion of a virtue in terms of the notion of a moral principle: 'The virtues are sentiments, that is, related families of dispositions and propensities regulated by a higher-order desire, in this case a desire to act from the corresponding moral principles' (Rawls 1971, p. 192). It is no accident that the same writer divorces our commitment to both principles and virtues from any substantial belief in the good for man. (On this, see further Chapter 17.)

A third feature of Hume's treatment of the virtues which becomes even more salient later is the shift from a conception of the virtues as plural to one of virtue as primarily singular. As a linguistic phenomenon, this is a part of a general process whereby the moral vocabulary gradually came to be simplified and homogenized. Within the Aristotelian scheme 'moral virtue' was not a tautological expression; but by the end of the eighteenth century 'moral' and 'virtuous' have come to be used as synonyms. Later still 'duty' and 'obligation' came to be treated as largely interchangeable, and so did 'dutiful' and 'virtuous'. Where once the common language of morality, even in everyday speech, had embodied a set of precise distinctions which presupposed a complex moral scheme, there comes into being a kind of linguistic *mélange* which enables very little to be said. Within this trend there do of course emerge new linguistic distinctions of a more specialized kind: 'immoral' and 'vice' become associated in the nineteenth century with whatever threatens the sanctity of the Victorian marriage—that last refuge of those who, outside the domestic sphere, were quite prepared to be scoundrels—and hence acquired in some circles an exclusively sexual connotation. The Society for the Suppression of Vice did not have among its interests the suppression of either injustice or cowardice. What these linguistic twists and turns testify to is the way in which the moral vocabulary had become detached from any precise central context of understanding and made available to different competing moral groups for their special and differing purposes. But this fate was still in the future when 'virtue' became primarily a single noun. For initially this linguistic change was associated with one very precise moral direction.

I remarked in Chapter 13 that when teleology, whether Aristotelian or Christian, is abandoned, there is always a tendency to substitute for it some version of Stoicism. The virtues are now not to be practiced for the sake of some good other, or more, than the practice of the virtues itself. Virtue is, indeed has to be, its own end, its own reward and its own motive. It is central to this Stoic tendency to believe that there is a single standard of virtue and that moral achievement lies simply in total compliance with it. As recurrently in the ancient world, as in the twelfth century, so it is also with eighteenth-century Stoicism in all its versions. And this is not surprising since the background to Stoic ethics in the eighteenth century was a doctrine of nature similar to and indebted to the metaphysics of ancient Stoicism.

Nature for many writers becomes what God had been for Christianity. Nature is conceived of as an actively benevolent agent; nature is a legislator for our good. Diderot, who often thinks of nature in this way, is thereby forced to pose the problem of how nature, being so benevolent and powerful, can permit the occurrence of evils, in a way that precisely parallels the problem raised for Christian theologians by the occurrence of evils in a universe created and ruled by an omnipotent and benevolent deity. And in so doing Diderot reveals more plainly than do others the way in which nature itself has become a new deity. Nature harmonizes, nature orders, nature provides us with a rule of life. Thus even some Christians are apt to see what is crucial to their ethics as being the maxim to understand and to live in accordance with their nature. From this arises a peculiar blend of Stoicism and Christianity, most strikingly exemplified by Dr. Johnson.

In Johnson's writings the influence of Juvenal and Epictetus is modified by Johnson's judgment that the Stoics took too high a view of human nature, and yet in the sixth *Rambler* he nonetheless concludes that 'he, who has so little knowledge of human nature, as to seek happiness by changing everything, but his own disposition, will waste his life in further efforts, and multiply the griefs which he proposes to remove'. The cultivation of the virtues cannot issue in any further happiness. Consequently, when Johnson praises patience, the distance between his conception of patience and that of the medieval tradition is as great as the distance between Hume's concept of justice and Aristotle's. For the medievals the virtue of patience, as I pointed out earlier, is intimately related to the virtue of hope; to be patient is to be prepared to wait until the promise of life is fulfilled. For Johnson—at least so far as this life is concerned—to be patient is to be prepared to live without hope. Hope is necessarily deferred to another world. Once again the conception of a particular virtue is transformed in a way that corresponds to a change in the general understanding of the virtues.

A far more optimistic version of Stoicism is to be found in the writings of Adam Smith, a deist rather than a Christian; and Smith is explicit about his central debt to Stoic moral philosophy. For Smith the virtues fall into two classes. There are on the one hand those three virtues which, if they are perfectly possessed, enable a man to exhibit perfectly virtuous behavior. 'The man who acts according to the rules of perfect prudence, of strict justice, and of proper benevolence, may be said to be perfectly virtuous' (*Theory of Moral Sentiments* VI. iii. 1). Notice of course that once again to be virtuous had been equated with rule-following. When Smith comes to deal with justice, he makes it a charge against 'ancient moralists' that we do not find 'any attempt towards a particular enumeration of the rules of justice'. But on Smith's view knowledge of what the rules are, whether the rules of justice or of prudence or of benevolence, is not sufficient to enable us to follow them; to do so we need another virtue of a very different kind, the Stoic virtue of self-command which enables us to control our passions when they distract us from what virtue requires.

Smith's catalogue of the virtues is then not the same as Hume's. We have already reached a point at which rival and incompatible tables of the virtues have become more common. Nor is this degree and kind of variation restricted to moral philosophy. One source, in England at least, of knowledge about common beliefs about the virtues in the seventeenth and eighteenth centuries is the Church of England tombstone or memorial in church or graveyard. Neither Protestant dissenters nor Roman Catholics generally carried on this practice of funerary inscription in a systematic way in this period, so that what we learn from tombstones concerns only one section of the population, and one moreover ostensibly still committed by its religious allegiance to a Christian teleology. But this makes the degree of variation in funerary catalogues of the virtues all the more impressive. There are for example Humean inscriptions: the memorial to Captain Cook erected by Sir Hugh Palliser in 1780 on his own land speaks of Cook as possessing 'every useful and amiable quality'. There are inscriptions in which 'moral' has already acquired a highly-restricted meaning, so that to praise someone's virtues you must praise more than his or her morality: 'Correct in Morals, Elegant in Manners, Steady in Friendship, Diffusive in Benevolence,' says the tablet commemorating Sir Francis Lumm in St. James's Piccadilly in 1797, in a way that suggests that the Aristotelian ideal of the great-souled man still lives. And there are distinctively Christian inscriptions: 'Love, Peace, Goodness, Faith, Hope, Charity, Humility, Sincerity, Gentleness' are the virtues ascribed to Margaret Yates in the same church in 1817. We should take note that sincerity is a relative newcomer to this list of the virtues—for reasons which Lionel Trilling analyzed brilliantly in *Sincerity and Authenticity*—and that the memorial to Cook follows Hume (and of course Aristotle) in praising the intellectual virtue of practical judgment as well as the virtues of character, while Margaret Yates's inscription perhaps suggests that 'Be good, sweet maid, and let who will be clever' is one of the underlying maxims.

What is abundantly clear is that in everyday life as in moral philosophy the replacement of Aristotelian or Christian teleology by a definition of the virtues in terms of the passions is not so much or at all the replacement of one set of criteria by another, but rather a movement towards and into a situation where there are no longer any clear criteria. It is unsurprising that the adherents of virtue begin to look for another basis for moral belief and that various forms of moral rationalism and intuitionism reappear, articulated by philosophers such as Kant—who saw himself as the pre-eminent modern heir of the Stoics—and Richard Price, philosophers in whom the movement towards a morality exclusively of rules also continues to be clearly marked. Adam Smith did in fact allow for one moral area in which rules will not supply us with what we need: there are always borderline cases in which we do not know how to apply the relevant rule and in which niceness of feeling must therefore guide us. Smith attacks the whole notion of casuistry as a wrongheaded attempt to provide for the application of rules even in such cases. In Kant's moral writings by contrast we have reached a point at which the notion that morality is anything other than obedience to rules has almost, if not quite, disappeared from sight. And so the central problems of moral philosophy come to cluster around the question 'How do we know *which* rules to follow?' Virtue-concepts become as marginal to the moral philosopher as they are to the morality of the society which he inhabits.

There is however another source for that marginality. Those various eighteenth-century writers upon the virtues who define the virtues in terms of their relationship to the passions already treat of society as nothing more than an arena in which individuals seek to secure what is useful or agreeable to them. They thus tend to exclude from view any conception of society as a community united in a shared vision of the good for man (as prior to and independent of any summing of individual interests) and a *consequent* shared practice of the virtues, but they do not always and entirely so exclude it. Stoicism characteristically has a political dimension, and Adam Smith, for example, was a life-long republican. And the connection between Smith's preoccupation with virtue and his republicanism was not something peculiar to his own thought. Republicanism in the eighteenth century *is* the project of restoring a community of virtue; but it envisages that project in an idiom inherited from Roman rather than Greek sources and transmitted through the Italian republics of the middle ages. Machiavelli with his exaltation of civic virtue over both the Christian and the pagan virtues articulates one aspect of the republican tradition, but only one. What is central to that tradition *is* the notion of a public good which is prior to and characterizable independently of the summing of individual desires and interests. Virtue in the individual is nothing more or less than allowing the public good to provide the standard for individual behavior. The virtues are those dispositions which uphold that overriding allegiance. Hence republicanism, like Stoicism, makes virtue primary and the virtues secondary. The connection between eighteenth-century republicanism and eighteenth-century Stoicism is a loose one; many Stoics were not republican – Dr. Johnson was devoutly loyal to the Hanoverians – and many republicans were not Stoics. But they share an idiom, they use the resources of the same moral vocabulary, and it is unsurprising when we come across someone like Adam Smith who shares both allegiances.

Republicanism therefore represents an attempt at a partial restoration of what I have called the classical tradition. But it enters the modern world without either of the two great negative features which had so much to do with the discrediting of the classical tradition during the renaissance and in the early modern period. It did not, as I have just noticed, speak in an Aristotelian idiom and thus did not carry the burden of an apparent alliance with a defeated version of natural science. And it was not disfigured by the patronage of those absolute despotisms, both in the state and in the church, which at the very same time as they destroyed the medieval inheritance attempted to clothe themselves in the language of tradition, inventing such doctrines as that sixteenth- and seventeenth-century perversion, the doctrine of the absolute divine right of kings.

Republicanism by contrast inherited from the institutions of the medieval and renaissance republic what amounted to a passion for equality. 'The corporate ethos,' Gene Brucker has written, 'was fundamentally egalitarian. Members of the guild, political society (*parte*) or militia company (*gonfalone*) were assumed to possess equal rights and privileges, and to bear equal obligations to the society and their fellows' (Brucker 1977, p. 15). Equality of respect provided the ground for service to the corporate community. This is why the republican conception of justice was defined basically in terms of equality, but secondarily in terms of public desert, public merit, a notion for which once again a place has to be found. The Aristotelian virtue of friendship and the Christian love of the neighbor both contributed in the eighteenth century to the newly-named virtue of fraternity. And the republican concept of liberty was Christian too: '*Cui servire est regnare*', says the prayer about God, or as the English version has it, 'whom to serve is perfect freedom', and what the Christian said about God the republican says of the republic. There are a series of later writers – J.L. Talmon, Isaiah Berlin and Daniel Bell are examples – who see in this republican commitment to public virtue the genesis of totalitarianism and even of terror. Any short reply to their thesis will necessarily appear inadequate; but I am inclined to retort that I wish that any commitment to *virtue* were so powerful as to be able to produce of itself such stupendous effects. It was rather, so I would claim, the ways in which the commitment to virtue was institutionalized politically—I shall say a little more about this presently—and not the commitment itself which produced some at least of the consequences which they abhor; but in fact most modern totalitarianism and terror has nothing to do with *any* commitment to virtue. I thus take eighteenth-century republicanism to be a more serious claimant for moral allegiance than such writers suggest. And it is well worth exploring *its* catalogue of the virtues a little further as exemplified in, for example, the Jacobin Clubs.

Liberty, fraternity and equality were not the only Jacobin virtues. Patriotism and love of family were both important: the persistent bachelor was regarded as an enemy of virtue. So was the man who failed to do useful productive work or who failed to do good work. It was regarded as a virtue to dress simply, to live in a modest dwelling, to be—of course—regular in attending one's club and performing other civic duties, to be courageous and assiduous in the work given one to do by the revolution. The badges of virtue were long hair—visits to a barber were a form of vice, and so was overmuch attention to one's appearance—and the absence of a beard. Beards were associated with the *ancien regime* (see Cobb 1969). It is not difficult to see in this a remaking by societies of democratically inspired craftsmen and tradesmen of the classical ideal. In the Jacobin Clubs something of Aristotle—as well as a great deal more of Rousseau—lived, but with only the most limited cultural power. Why so? The true lesson of the Jacobin Clubs and their downfall is that you cannot hope to re-invent morality on the scale of a whole nation when the very idiom of the morality which you seek to re-invent is alien in one way to the vast mass of ordinary people and in another to the intellectual elite. The attempt to impose morality by terror—the solution of St. Just—is the desperate expedient of those who already glimpse this fact but will not admit it. (It is this and *not* the ideal of public virtue which, so I would argue, breeds totalitarianism.) To understand this is to be given the essential clue to the predicament of all those adherents of the older tradition of the virtues— some of whom cannot even recognize any more that that is what they are—who seek to re-establish the virtues. Consider briefly just two of them, William Cobbett and Jane Austen.

Cobbett—'the last man of the old England and the first man of the new', said Marx—crusaded to change the society as a whole; Jane Austen tried to discover enclaves for the life of the virtues within it. Cobbett looked backward to the England of his childhood, beyond that to England before the oligarchical settlement of 1688 and yet further to England before the

Reformation, seeing each stage as one in a decline towards his own day. Like Jefferson, Cobbett believed that the small working farmer is the social type of the virtuous man. 'If the cultivators of the land be not, generally speaking, the most virtuous and most happy of mankind, there must be something at work in the community to counteract the operations of nature' (*Political Register* xxxix, 5 May 1821). Nature constrains the farmer so that he has to be practically wise: 'The nature and quality of all living things are known to country boys better than to philosophers'. When Cobbett speaks of 'philosophers' it is usually Malthus and the Adam Smith of *The Wealth of Nations*, as that book had come to be read in the light of Ricardo's doctrine, to whom he is referring. Virtues which Cobbett particularly praises are lack of envy, love of liberty, perseverance and industry, patriotism, integrity and justice. The 'something at work in the community' which counteracts the tendency to produce a virtuous and happy community is the all-pervasive influence of *pleonexia* (although that is not Cobbett's word) in the form of the usury (that is Cobbett's word) inflicted on society by an individualistic economy and market in which land, labor and money itself have all been transformed into commodities. It is precisely because Cobbett looks back across that great division in human history towards the past before individualism and the power of markets, before what Karl Polanyi called 'the great transformation', that Marx saw Cobbett as possessing his peculiar significance for English history.

Jane Austen, by contrast, identifies that social sphere within which the practice of the virtues is able to continue. It is not of course that she is blind to the economic realities against which Cobbett railed. We learn somewhere in all her novels about where the money of the main characters comes from; we see a great deal of the economic self-seeking, of the *pleonexia* which is central to Cobbett's vision. So much so indeed that David Daiches once described her as a 'Marxist before Marx'. Her heroines must, if they are to survive, seek for economic security. But this is not just because of the threat of the outside economic world; it is because the *telos* of her heroines is a life within both a particular kind of marriage and a particular kind of household of which that marriage will be the focal point. Her novels are a moral criticism of parents and of guardians quite as much as of young romantics; for the worst parents and guardians—the silly Mrs. Bennet and the irresponsible Mr. Bennet, for example—are what the romantic young may become if they do not learn what they ought to learn on the way to being married. But why is marriage so important?

It is finally in the eighteenth century, when production has moved outside the household, that women no longer for the most part do work not very different in kind or work-relationship from that of men, but are instead divided into two classes: a small group of leisured women with no

work to fill the day and for whom occupations have to be invented—fine
needlework, the reading of bad novels and organized opportunities for
gossip, which are then thought of by both men and women as 'essentially
feminine'—and a huge group of women condemned to the drudgery of
domestic service or to that of the mill or factory or to prostitution. When
production was within the household the unmarried sister or aunt was a
useful and valued member of the household; the 'spinster', not surprisingly,
did the spinning. It is only at the beginning of the eighteenth century that
the expression becomes denigratory; and it is only then that the woman
who does not marry has to fear expulsion into drudgery as her characteristic lot. Hence to refuse even a bad marriage is an act of great courage,
an act that is central to the plot of *Mansfield Park*. A major emotion underlying Jane Austen's novels is what D.W. Harding called her 'regulated
hatred' of the attitude of society to unmarried women: 'Her daughter enjoyed a most uncommon degree of popularity for a woman neither young,
handsome, rich, nor married. Miss Bates stood in the very worst predicament in the world for having much of the public favor; and she had no
intellectual superiority to make atonement to herself or frighten those who
might hate her into outward respect. Her youth had passed without distinction and her middle of life was devoted to the care of a failing mother
and the endeavor to make a small income go as far as possible. And yet she
was a happy woman and a woman whom no one named without goodwill. It was her own unusual goodwill and contentment which worked
such wonders.' Miss Bates, you will note, is *exceptionally* favored because
she is *exceptionally* good. Ordinarily, if you are not rich or beautiful or
young or married, you will only gain outward respect generally by using
your intellectual superiority to frighten those who will otherwise scorn
you. As, we may guess, did Jane Austen.

When Jane Austen speaks of 'happiness', she does so as an Aristotelian.
Gilbert Ryle believed that her Aristotelianism—which he saw as the clue
to the moral temper of her novels—may have derived from a reading of
Shaftesbury. C.S. Lewis with equal justice saw in her an essentially Christian writer. It is her uniting of Christian and Aristotelian themes in a determinate social context that makes Jane Austen the last great effective
imaginative voice of the tradition of thought about, and practice of, the
virtues which I have tried to identify. She thus turns away from the competing catalogues of the virtues of the eighteenth century and restores a
teleological perspective. Her heroines seek the good through seeking their
own good in marriage. The restricted households of Highbury and Mansfield Park have to serve as surrogates for the Greek city-state and the medieval kingdom.

Much therefore of what she presents about the virtues and vices is thoroughly traditional. She praises the virtue of being socially agreeable, as Aristotle does, although she values more highly—in her letters as well as in her novels—the virtue of amiability, which requires a genuine loving regard for other people as such, and not only the impression of such a regard embodied in manners. She is, after all, a Christian, and therefore deeply suspicious of an agreeableness that conceals a lack of true amiability. She praises practical intelligence in an Aristotelian way and humility in a Christian way. But she does not ever merely reproduce the tradition; she continuously extends it and in extending it she has three central preoccupations.

The first I have already noticed. She is—indeed, given the moral climate of her times, she has to be—preoccupied in a quite new way with counterfeits of the virtues. Morality in Jane Austen is never the mere inhibition and regulation of the passions; although that is how it may appear to those such as Marianne Dashwood who have romantically identified themselves with a ruling passion and who make in a very unHumean way reason the servant of the passions. Morality is rather meant to educate the passions; but the outward appearance of morality may always disguise uneducated passions. And the waywardness of Marianne Dashwood is the waywardness of a victim, whereas the surface propriety of Henry and Mary Crawford, together with their elegance and charm, which do provide a disguise for morally uneducated passions, is apt to victimize others as well as themselves. Henry Crawford is the dissimulator *par excellence.* He boasts of his ability to act parts and in one conversation makes it clear that he takes *being a clergyman* to consist in *giving the appearance of being a clergyman.* Self is almost, if not quite, dissolved into the presentation of self, but what in Goffman's social world becomes *the* form of the self is still in Jane Austen's world a symptom of the vices.

The counterpart to Jane Austen's preoccupation with the counterfeit is the central place she assigns to self-knowledge, a Christian rather than a Socratic self-knowledge which can only be achieved through a kind of repentance. In four of her six great novels there is a recognition scene in which the person whom the hero or heroine recognizes is him or herself. 'Till this moment I never knew myself,' says Elizabeth Bennet. 'How to understand the deceptions she had been thus practising on herself, and living under!' meditates Emma. Self-knowledge is for Jane Austen both an intellectual and a moral virtue, and it is closely allied to another virtue which Jane Austen makes central and which is relatively new to the catalogue of the virtues.

When Kierkegaard contrasted the ethical and the aesthetic ways of life in *Enten-Eller*, he argued that the aesthetic life is one in which a human life is dissolved into a series of separate present moments, in which the unity of a human life disappears from view. By contrast in the ethical life the commitments and responsibilities to the future springing from past episodes in which obligations were conceived and debts assumed unite the present to past and to future in such a way as to make of a human life a unity. The unity to which Kierkegaard refers is that narrative unity whose central place in the life of the virtues I identified in the preceding chapter. By the time Jane Austen writes that unity can no longer be treated as a mere presupposition or context for a virtuous life. It has itself to be continually reaffirmed and its reaffirmation in deed rather than in word is the virtue which Jane Austen calls constancy. Constancy is crucial in at least two novels, *Mansfield Park* and *Persuasion*, in each of which it is a central virtue of the heroine. Constancy, so Jane Austen makes Anne Elliot agrue cogently in the latter novel, is a virtue which women are more apt to practise than are men. And without constancy all the other virtues to some degree lose their point. Constancy is reinforced by and reinforces the Christian virtue of patience, but it is not the same as patience, just as patience which is reinforced by and reinforces the Aristotelian virtue of courage, is not the same as courage. For just as patience necessarily involves a recognition of the character of the world, of a kind which courage does not necessarily require, so constancy requires a recognition of a particular kind of threat to the integrity of the personality in the peculiarly modern social world, a recognition which patience does not necessarily require.

It is no accident that the two heroines who exhibit constancy most strikingly are less charming than Jane Austen's other heroines and that one of them, Fanny Price, has been found positively unattractive by many critics. But Fanny's lack of charm is crucial to Jane Austen's intentions. For charm is the characteristically modern quality which those who lack or simulate the virtues use to get by in the situations of characteristically modern social life. Camus once defined charm as that quality which procures the answer 'Yes' before any question has been asked. And the charm of an Elizabeth Bennet or even of an Emma may mislead us, genuinely attractive though it is, in our judgment on their character. Fanny is charmless; she has only the virtues, the genuine virtues, to protect her, and when she disobeys her guardian, Sir Thomas Bertram, and refuses marriage to Henry Crawford it can only be because of what constancy requires. In so refusing she places the danger of losing her soul before the reward of gaining what for her would be a whole world. She pursues virtue for the sake of a certain kind of happiness and not for its utility. Jane Austen through Fanny Price rejects those alternative catalogues of the virtues that we find in David Hume or Benjamin Franklin.

Jane Austen's moral point of view and the narrative form of her novels coincide. The form of her novels is that of ironic comedy. Jane Austen writes comedy rather than tragedy for the same reason that Dante did; she is a Christian and she sees the *telos* of human life implicit in its everyday form. Her irony resides in the way that she makes her characters and her readers see and say more and other than they intended to, so that they and we correct ourselves. The virtues and the harms and evils which the virtues alone will overcome provide the structure both of a life in which the *telos* can be achieved and of a narrative in which the story of such a life can be unfolded. Once again it turns out that any specific account of the virtues presupposes an equally specific account of the narrative structure and unity of a human life and *vice versa*.

Jane Austen is in a crucial way—along with Cobbett and the Jacobins— the last great representative of the classical tradition of the virtues. It has proved easy for later generations not to understand her importance as a moralist because she is after all a novelist. And to them she has often appeared as not merely 'only' a writer of fiction, but a writer of fiction concerned with a very restricted social world. What they have not observed and what the juxtaposition of her insights with those of Cobbett and the Jacobins ought to teach us to observe is that both in her own time and afterwards the life of the virtues is necessarily afforded a very restricted cultural and social space. In most of the public and most of the private world the classical and medieval virtues are replaced by the meagre substitutes which modern morality affords. Of course when I say that Jane Austen is in a crucial way the last representative of the classical tradition, I do not mean to deny that she has *any* descendants. Kipling, in a short story now seldom read, with a good deal of insight made one of his characters say that she was the mother—he might better have said the grandmother—of Henry James. But James writes of a world in which—the progress of his own novels testifies to it—the substance of morality is increasingly elusive. That elusiveness alters the character of both private and public life. What it amounts to in public life particularly depends on the fate of the conception of one particular virtue, that of justice. To the question of what happened to our conception of justice I therefore now turn.

17

Justice as a Virtue: Changing Conceptions

When Aristotle praised justice as the first virtue of political life, he did so in such a way as to suggest that a community which lacks practical agreement on a conception of justice must also lack the necessary basis for political community. But the lack of such a basis must therefore threaten our own society. For the outcome of that history, some aspects of which I sketched in the preceding chapter, has not only been an inability to agree upon a catalogue of the virtues and an even more fundamental inability to agree upon the relative importance of the virtue concepts within a moral scheme in which notions of rights and of utility also have a key place. It has also been an inability to agree upon the content and character of particular virtues. For since a virtue is now generally understood as a disposition or sentiment which will produce in us obedience to certain rules, agreement on what the relevant rules are to be is always a prerequisite for agreement upon the nature and content of a particular virtue. But this prior agreement in rules is, as I have emphasized in the earlier part of this book, something which our individualist culture is unable to secure. Nowhere is this more marked and nowhere are the consequences more threatening than in the case of justice. Everyday life is pervaded by them and basic controversies cannot therefore be rationally resolved. Consider one such controversy, endemic in the politics of the United States today—I present it in the form of a debate between two ideal-typical characters unimaginatively named 'A' and 'B'.

A, who may own a store or be a police officer or a construction worker, has struggled to save enough from his earnings to buy a small house, to send his children to the local college, to pay for some special type of medical care for his parents. He now finds all of his projects threatened by rising taxes. He regards this threat to his projects as *unjust*; he claims to have a right to what he has earned and that nobody else has a right to take away what he acquired legitimately and to which he has a just title. He intends to vote for candidates for political office who will defend his property, his projects *and* his conception of justice.

B, who may be a member of one of the liberal professions, or a social worker, or someone with inherited wealth, is impressed with the arbitrariness of the inequalities in the distribution of wealth, income and opportunity. He is, if anything, even more impressed with the inability of the poor and the deprived to do very much about their own condition as a result of inequalities in the distribution of power. He regards both these types of inequality as *unjust* and as constantly engendering further injustice. He believes more generally that all inequality stands in need of justification and that the only possible justification for inequality is to improve the condition of the poor and the deprived—by, for example, fostering economic growth. He draws the conclusion that in present circumstances redistributive taxation which will finance welfare and the social services is what justice demands. He intends to vote for candidates for political office who will defend redistributive taxation *and* his conception of justice.

It is clear that in the actual circumstances of our social and political order A and B are going to disagree about policies and politicians. But *must* they so disagree? The answer seems to be that under certain types of economic condition their disagreement need not manifest itself at the level of political conflict. If A and B belong to a society where economic resources are such, or are at least believed to be such, that B's public redistributive projects can be carried through at least to a certain point without threatening A's private life-plan projects, A and B might for some time vote for the same politicians and policies. Indeed they might on occasion be one and the same person. But if it is, or comes to be, the case that economic circumstances are such that either A's projects must be sacrificed to B's or *vice versa*, it at once becomes clear that A and B have views of justice which are not only logically incompatible with each other but which—like the beliefs of the parties to the controversies which I discussed in Chapter 2—invoke considerations which are incommensurable with those advanced by the adversary party.

The logical incompatibility is not difficult to identify. A holds that principles of just acquisition and entitlement set limits to redistributive possibilities. If the outcome of the application of the principles of just acquisition and entitlement is gross inequality, the toleration of such inequality is a price that has to be paid for justice. B holds that principles of just distribution set limits to legitimate acquisition and entitlement. If the outcome of the application of the principles of just distribution is interference —by means of taxation or such devices as eminent domain—with what has up till now been regarded in this social order as legitimate acquisition and entitlement, the toleration of such interference is a price that has to be paid for justice. We may note in passing—it will not be unimportant later—that in the case of both A's principle and B's principle the price for one person or group of persons receiving justice is always paid by someone else. Thus different identifiable social groups have an interest in the acceptance of one of the principles and the rejection of the other. Neither principle is socially or politically neutral.

Moreover it is not simply that A and B advance principles which produce incompatible practical conclusions. The type of concept in terms of which each frames his claim is so different from that of the other that the question of how and whether the dispute between them may be rationally settled begins to pose difficulties. For A aspires to ground the notion of justice in some account of what and how a given person is entitled to in virtue of what he has acquired and earned; B aspires to ground the notion of justice in some account of the equality of the claims of each person in respect of basic needs and of the means to meet such needs. Confronted by a given piece of property or resource, A will be apt to claim that it is justly his because he owns it—he acquired it legitimately, he earned it; B will be apt to claim that it justly ought to be someone else's, because they need it much more, and if they do not have it, their basic needs will not be met. But our pluralist culture possesses no method of weighing, no rational criterion for deciding between claims based on legitimate entitlement against claims based on need. Thus these two types of claim are indeed, as I suggested, incommensurable, and the metaphor of 'weighing' moral claims is not just inappropriate but misleading.

It is at this point that recent analytical moral philosophy makes important claims. For it aspires to provide rational principles to which appeal may be made by contending parties with conflicting interests. And the two most distinguished recent attempts to carry through this project have a special relevance for the argument between A and B. For Robert Nozick's account of justice (1974) is at least to some large degree a rational articulation of key elements in A's position, while John Rawls's account (1971) is in the same way a rational articulation of key elements in B's position. Thus if the philosophical considerations which either Rawls or Nozick urge upon us turn out to be rationally compelling, the argument between A and B will have been rationally settled one way or another and my own characterization of the dispute will in consequence turn out to be quite false.

I begin with Rawls's account. Rawls argues that the principles of justice are those which would be chosen by a rational agent 'situated behind a veil of ignorance' (p. 136) such that he does not know what place in society he will occupy—that is, what his class or status will be, what talents and ability he will possess, what his conception of the good or his aims in life will be, what his temperament will be or what kind of economic, political, cultural or social order he will inhabit. Rawls argues that any rational agent so situated will define a just distribution of goods in *any* social order in terms of two principles and a rule for allocating priorities when the two principles conflict.

The first principle is: 'Each person is to have an equal right to the most extensive total system of equal basic liberties compatible with a similar system of liberty for all.' The second principle is: 'Social and economic inequalities are to be arranged so that they are both (a) to the greatest benefit of the least advantaged, consistent with the joint savings principle [the joint savings principle provides for fair investment in the interests of future generations], and (b) attached to offices and parties open to all under conditions of fair equality of opportunity' (p. 302). The first principle has priority over the second; liberty is to be restricted only for the sake of liberty. And justice generally has priority over efficiency. So Rawls arrives at his general conception: 'All social primary goods—liberty and opportunity, income and wealth, and the bases of self-respect—are to be distributed equally unless an unequal distribution of any or all of these goods is to the advantage of the least favored' (p. 303).

Many critics of Rawls have focussed their attention on the ways in which Rawls derives his principles of justice from his statement of the initial position of the rational agent 'situated behind a veil of ignorance'. Such critics have made a number of telling points, but I do not intend to dwell on them, if only because I take it not only that a rational agent in *some such* situation as that of the veil of ignorance would indeed choose *some such* principles of justice as Rawls claims, but also that it is *only* a rational agent in such a situation who would choose such principles. Later in my argument this point will become important. For the moment however I shall put it on one side in order to turn to a characterization of Nozick's view.

Nozick claims that 'if the world were wholly just' (p. 151) the only people entitled to hold anything, that is to appropriate it for use as they and they alone wished, would be those who had justly acquired what they held by some just act of original acquisition and those who had justly acquired what they held by some just act of transfer from someone else who had either acquired it by some just act of original acquisition or by some just transfer . . . and so on. In other words, the justifiable answer to the question 'Why are you entitled to use that seashell as you wish?' will either be 'I picked it up on the seashore, where it belonged to no one and where there were plenty left for everyone else' (a just act of original acquisition), *or* 'Someone else picked it up at the seashore and freely sold or gave it to someone . . . to someone . . . who freely sold or gave it to me' (a series of just acts of transfer). If follows from Nozick's view as he himself immediately notes that: 'The complete principle of distributive justice would say simply that a distribution is just if everyone is entitled to the holdings that they possess under the distribution' (p. 153).

Nozick derives these conclusions from premises about the inalienable rights of each individual, premises for which he does not himself offer arguments. As in the case of Rawls, I do not want to quarrel with Nozick's derivation of his principles from his premises; once again I shall want to stress instead that it is *only* from some such premises that such principles could be rationally derived. That is to say, in the case of both Nozick's account of justice and Rawls's account of justice. the problems that I want to raise do not concern the coherence of the internal structure of their arguments. Indeed my own argument requires that their accounts do not lack such coherence.

What I want to argue is threefold: first, that the incompatibility of Rawls's and Nozick's accounts does up to a point genuinely mirror the incompatibility of A's position with B's, and that to this extent at least Rawls and Nozick successfully articulate at the level of moral philosophy the disagreement between such ordinary non-philosophical citizens as A and B; but that Rawls and Nozick also reproduce the very same type of incompatibility and incommensurability at the level of philosophical argument that made A's and B's debate unsettlable at the level of social conflict; and secondly, that there is nonetheless an element in the position of both A and B which neither Rawls's account nor Nozick's captures, an element which survives from that older classical tradition in which the virtues were central. When we reflect on both these points, a third emerges: namely, that in their conjunction we have an important clue to the social presuppositions which Rawls and Nozick to some degree share.

Rawls makes primary what is in effect a principle of equality with respect to needs. His conception of 'the worst off' sector of the community is a conception of those whose needs are gravest in respect of income, wealth and other goods. Nozick makes primary what is a principle of equality with respect to entitlement. For Rawls how those who are now in grave need come to be in grave need is irrelevant; justice is made into a matter of present patterns of distribution to which the past is irrelevant. For Nozick only evidence about what has been legitimately acquired in the past is relevant; present patterns of distribution in themselves must be irrelevant to *justice* (although not perhaps to kindness or generosity). To say even this much makes it clear how close Rawls is to B and how close

Nozick is to A. For A appealed against distributive canons to a justice of entitlement, and B appealed against canons of entitlement to a justice which regards needs. Yet it is also at once clear not only that Rawls's priorities are incompatible with Nozick's in a way parallel to that in which B's position is incompatible with A's, but also that Rawls's position is incommensurable with Nozick's in a way similarly parallel to that in which B's is incommensurable with A's. For how can a claim that gives priority to equality of needs be rationally weighed against one which gives priority to entitlements? If Rawls were to argue that anyone *behind the veil of ignorance*, who knew neither whether and how his needs would be met nor what his entitlements would be, ought rationally to prefer a principle which respects needs to one which respects entitlements, invoking perhaps principles of rational decision theory to do so, the immediate answer must be not only that *we* are *never* behind such a veil of ignorance, but also that this leaves unimpugned Nozick's premise about inalienable rights. And if Nozick were to argue that any distributive principle, if enforced, could violate a freedom to which everyone of us is entitled—as he does indeed argue—the immediate answer must be that in so interpreting the inviolability of basic rights he begs the question in favor of his own argument and leaves unimpugned Rawls's premises.

Nonetheless there is something important, if negative, which Rawls's account shares with Nozick's. Neither of them make any reference to *desert* in their account of justice, nor could they consistently do so. And yet both A and B did make such a reference—and it is imperative here to notice that 'A' and 'B' are not the names of mere arbitrary constructions of my own; their arguments faithfully reproduce, for example, a good deal of what was actually said in recent fiscal debates in California, New Jersey and elsewhere. What A complains of on his own behalf is not merely that he is entitled to what he has earned, but that he *deserves* it in virtue of his life of hard work; what B complains of on behalf of the poor and deprived is that their poverty and deprivation is *undeserved* and therefore unwarranted. And it seems clear that in the case of the real-life counterparts of A and B it is the reference to desert which makes them feel strongly that what they are complaining about is injustice, rather than some other kind of wrong or harm.

Neither Rawls's account nor Nozick's allows this central place, or indeed any kind of place, for desert in claims about justice and injustice. Rawls (p. 310) allows that common sense views of justice connect it with desert, but argues first that we do not know what anyone deserves until we have already formulated the rules of justice (and hence we cannot base our understanding of justice upon desert), and secondly that when we have formulated the rules of justice it turns out that it is not desert that is in question anyway, but only legitimate expectations. He also argues that to attempt to apply notions of desert would be impracticable—the ghost of Hume walks in his pages at this point.

Nozick is less explicit, but his scheme of justice being based exclusively on entitlements can allow no place for desert. He does at one point discuss the possibility of a principle for the rectification of injustice, but what he writes on that point is so tentative and cryptic that it affords no guidance for amending his general viewpoint. It is in any case clear that for both Nozick and Rawls a society is composed of individuals, each with his or her own interest, who then have to come together and formulate common rules of life. In Nozick's case there is the additional negative constraint of a set of basic rights. In Rawls's case the only constraints are those that a prudent rationality would impose. Individuals are thus in both accounts primary and society secondary, and the identification of individual interests is prior to, and independent of, the construction of any moral or social bonds between them. But we have already seen that the notion of desert is at home only in the context of a community whose primary bond is a shared understanding both of the good for man and of the good of that community and where individuals identify their primary interests with reference to those goods. Rawls explicitly makes it a presupposition of his view that we must expect to disagree with others about what the good life for man is and must therefore exclude any understanding of it that we may have from our formulation of the principles of justice. Only those goods in which everyone, whatever their view of the good life, takes an interest are to be admitted to consideration. In Nozick's argument too, the concept of community required for the notion of desert to have application is simply absent. To understand this is to clarify two further points.

The first concerns the shared social presuppositions of Rawls and Nozick. It is, from both standpoints, as though we had been shipwrecked on an uninhabited island with a group of other individuals, each of whom is a stranger to me and to all the others. What have to be worked out are rules which will safeguard each one of us maximally in such a situation. Nozick's premise concerning rights introduces a strong set of constraints; we do know that certain types of interference with each other are absolutely prohibited. But there is a limit to the bonds between us, a limit set by our private and competing interests. This individualistic view has of course, as I noticed earlier, a distinguished ancestry: Hobbes, Locke (whose views Nozick treats with great respect), Machiavelli and others. And it contains within itself a certain note of realism about modern society; modern society is indeed often, at least in surface appearance, nothing but a collection of strangers, each pursuing his or her own interests under minimal constraints. We still of course, even in modern society, find it difficult to think of families, colleges and other genuine communities in this way; but even our thinking about those is now invaded to an increasing degree by individualist conceptions, especially in the law courts. Thus Rawls and Nozick articulate with great power a shared view which envisages entry into social life as—at least ideally—the voluntary act of at least potentially rational individuals with prior interests who have to ask the the question 'What kind of social contract with others is it reasonable for me to enter into?' Not surprisingly it is a consequence of this that their views exclude any account of human community in which the notion of desert in relation to contributions to the common tasks of that community in pursing shared goods could provide the basis for judgments about virtue and injustice.

Desert is ruled out too in another way. I have remarked upon how Rawls's distributive principles exclude reference to the past and so to claims to desert based on past actions and sufferings. Nozick too excludes that of the past on which such claims might be based, by making a concern for the legitimacy of entitlements the sole ground for taking an interest in the past in connection with justice. What makes this important is that Nozick's account serves the interest of a particular mythology about the past precisely by what it excludes from view. For central to Nozick's account is the thesis that all legitimate entitlements can be traced to legitimate acts of original acquisition. But, if that is so, there are in fact very few, and in some large areas of the world *no*, legitimate entitlements. The property-owners of the modern world are not the legitimate heirs of Lockean individuals who performed quasi-Lockean ('quasi' to allow for Nozick's emendations of Locke) acts of original acquisition; they are the inheritors of those who, for example, stole, and used violence to steal the common lands of England from the common people, vast tracts of North America from the American Indian, much of Ireland from the Irish, and Prussia from the original non-German Prussians. This is the historical reality ideologically concealed behind any Lockean thesis. The lack of any principle of rectification is thus not a small side issue for a thesis such as Nozick's; it tends to vitiate the theory as a whole—even if we were to suppress the overwhelming objections to any belief in inalienable human rights.

A and B differ from Rawls and Nozick at the price of inconsistency. Each of them in conjoining either Rawls's principles or Nozick's with an appeal to desert exhibits an adherence to an older, more traditional, more Aristotelian and Christian view of justice. This inconsistency is thus a tribute to the residual power and influence of the tradition, a power and influence with two distinct sources. In the conceptual *mélange* of moral thought and practice today fragments from the tradition–virtue concepts for the most part–are still found alongside characteristically modern and individualist concepts such as those of rights or utility. But the tradition also survives in a much less fragmented, much less distorted form in the lives of certain communities whose historical ties with their past remain strong. So the older moral tradition is discernible in the United States and elsewhere among, for example, some Catholic Irish, some Orthodox Greeks and some Jews of an Orthodox persuasion, all of them communities that inherit their moral tradition not only through their religion, but also from the structure of the peasant villages and households which their immediate ancestors inhabited on the margins of modern Europe. Moreover it would be wrong to conclude from the stress that I have laid on the medieval background that Protestantism did not in some areas become the bearer of this very same moral tradition; in Scotland for example, Aristotle's *Nicomachean Ethics* and *Politics* were the secular moral texts in the universities, coexisting happily with a Calvinist theology which was often elsewhere hostile to them, until 1690 and after. And there are today both black and white Protestant communities in the United States, especially perhaps those in or from the South, who will recognize in the tradition of the virtues a key part of their own cultural inheritance.

Even however in such communities the need to enter into public debate enforces participation in the cultural *mélange* in the search for a common stock of concepts and norms which all may employ and to which all may appeal. Consequently the allegiance of such marginal communities to the tradition is constantly in danger of being eroded, and this in search of what, if my argument is correct, is a chimaera. For what analysis of A's and B's position reveals once again is that we have all too many disparate and rival moral concepts, in this case rival and disparate concepts of justice, and that the moral resources of the culture allow us no way of settling the issue between them rationally. Moral philosophy, as it is dominantly understood, reflects the debates and disagreements of the culture so faithfully that its controversies turn out to be unsettlable in just the way that the political and moral debates themselves are.

It follows that our society cannot hope to achieve moral consensus. For quite non-Marxist reasons Marx was in the right when he argued against the English trade unionists of the 1860s that appeals to justice were pointless, since there are rival conceptions of justice formed by and informing the life of rival groups. Marx was of course mistaken in supposing that such disagreements over justice are merely secondary phenomena, that they merely reflect the interests of rival economic classes. Conceptions of justice and allegiance to such conceptions are partly constitutive of the lives of social groups, and economic interests are often partially defined in terms of such conceptions and not *vice versa*. Nonetheless Marx was fundamentally right in seeing conflict and not consensus at the heart of modern social structure. It is not just that we live too much by a variety and multiplicity of fragmented concepts; it is that these are used at one and the same time to express rival and incompatible social ideals and policies *and* to furnish us with a pluralist political rhetoric whose function is to conceal the depth of our conflicts.

Important conclusions follow for constitutional theory. Liberal writers such as Ronald Dworkin invite us to see the Supreme Court's function as that of invoking a set of consistent principles, most and perhaps all of them of moral import, in the light of which particular laws and particular decisions are to be evaluated. Those who hold such a view are bound to consider certain decisions of the Supreme Court inadequate in the light of these supposed principles. The type of decision which I have in mind is exemplified by the Bakke case, where two, at first sight strongly incompatible, views were held by members of the court, and Mr. Justice Powell who wrote the decision was the one justice to hold both views. But, if my argument is correct, one function of the Supreme Court must be to keep the peace between rival social groups adhering to rival and incompatible principles of justice by displaying a fairness which consists in even-handedness in its adjudications. So the Supreme Court in *Bakke* both forbade precise ethnic quotas for admission to colleges and universities, but allowed discrimination in favor of previously deprived minority groups. Try to conjure up a set of consistent principles behind such a decision and ingenuity may or may not allow you to find the court not guilty of formal inconsistency. But even to make such an attempt is to miss the point. The Supreme Court in *Bakke*, as on occassion in other cases, played the role of a peacemaking or truce-keeping body by negotiating its way through an impasse of conflict, not by invoking our shared moral first principles. For our society as a whole has none.

What this brings out is that modern politics cannot be a matter of genuine moral consensus. And it is not. Modern politics is civil war carried on by other means, and *Bakke* was an engagement whose antecedents were at Gettysburg and Shiloh. The truth on this matter was set out by Adam Ferguson: 'We are not to expect that the laws of any country are to be framed as so many lessons of morality . . . . Laws, whether civil or political, are expedients of policy to adjust the pretensions of parties, and to

secure the peace of society. The expedient is accommodated to special circumstances . . .' (*Principles of Moral and Political Science ii.* 144). The nature
of any society therefore is not to be deciphered from its laws alone, but
from those understood as an index of its conflicts. What our laws show
is the extent and degree to which conflict has to be suppressed.

   Yet if this is so, another virtue too has been displaced. Patriotism cannot
be what it was because we lack in the fullest sense a *patria*. The point that
I am making must not be confused with the commonplace liberal rejection
of patriotism. Liberals have often—not always—taken a negative or even
hostile attitude towards patriotism, partly because their allegiance is to
values which they take to be universal and not local and particular, and
partly because of a well-justified suspicion that in the modern world
patriotism is often a façade behind which chauvinism and imperialism are
fostered. But my present point is not that patriotism is good or bad as a
sentiment, but that the practice of patriotism as a virtue is in advanced
societies no longer possible in the way that it once was. In any society
where government does not express or represent the moral community of
the citizens, but is instead a set of institutional arrangements for imposing
a bureaucratized unity on a society which lacks genuine moral consensus,
the nature of political obligation becomes systematically unclear. Patriotism is or was a virtue founded on attachment primarily to a political and
moral community and only secondarily to the government of that community; but it is characteristically exercised in discharging responsibility to
and in such government. When however the relationship of government
to the moral community is put in question both by the changed nature
of government and the lack of moral consensus in the society, it becomes
difficult any longer to have any clear, simple and teachable conception of
patriotism. Loyalty to my country, to my community—which remains un-
alterably a central virtue—becomes detached from obedience to the government which happens to rule me.

   Just as this understanding of the displacement of patriotism must not
be confused with the liberal critique of moral particularity, so this necessary distancing of the moral self from the governments of modern states
must not be confused with any anarchist critique of the state. Nothing in
my argument suggests, let alone implies, any good grounds for rejecting
certain forms of government as necessary and legitimate; what the argument does entail is that the modern state is not such a form of government.
It must have been clear from earlier parts of my argument that the tradition of the virtues is at variance with central features of the modern economic order and more especially its individualism, its acquisitiveness and
its elevation of the values of the market to a central social place. It now

becomes clear that it also involves a rejection of the modern political order. This does not mean that there are not many tasks only to be performed in and through government which still require performing: the rule of law, so far as it is possible in a modern state, has to be vindicated, injustice and unwarranted suffering have to be dealt with, generosity has to be exercised, and liberty has to be defended, in ways that are sometimes only possible through the use of governmental institutions. But each particular task, each particular responsibility has to be evaluated on its own merits. Modern systematic politics, whether liberal, conservative, radical or socialist, simply has to be rejected from a standpoint that owes genuine allegiance to the tradition of the virtues; for modern politics itself expresses in its institutional forms a systematic rejection of that tradition.

18

After Virtue:
Nietzsche *or* Aristotle,
Trotsky *and* St Benedict

In Chapter 9 I posed a stark question: Nietzsche *or* Aristotle? The argument which led to the posing of that question had two central premises. The first was that the language—and therefore also to some large degree the practice—of morality today is in a state of grave disorder. That disorder arises from the prevailing cultural power of an idiom in which ill-assorted conceptual fragments from various parts of our past are deployed together in private and public debates which are notable chiefly for the unsettlable character of the controversies thus carried on and the apparent arbitrariness of each of the contending parties.

The second was that ever since belief in Aristotelian teleology was discredited moral philosophers have attempted to provide some alternative rational secular account of the nature and status of morality, but that all these attempts, various and variously impressive as they have been, have in fact failed, a failure perceived most clearly by Nietzsche. Consequently Nietzsche's negative proposal to raze to the ground the structures of inherited moral belief and argument had, whether we have regard to everyday moral belief and argument or look instead to the constructions of moral philosophers, and in spite of its desperate and grandiose quality, a certain plausibility—unless of course the initial rejection of the moral tradition to which Aristotle's teaching about the virtues is central turned out to have been misconceived and mistaken. Unless that tradition could be rationally vindicated, Nietzsche's stance would have a terrible plausibility.

Not that, even so, it would be easy in the contemporary world to be an intelligent Nietzschean. The stock characters acknowledged in the dramas of modern social life embody all too well the concepts and the modes of the moral beliefs and arguments which an Aristotelian and a Nietzschean would have to agree in rejecting. The bureaucratic manager, the consuming aesthete, the therapist, the protester and their numerous kindred occupy almost all the available culturally recognizable roles; the notions of the expertise of the few and of the moral agency of everyone are the presuppositions of the dramas which those characters enact. To cry out that the emperor had no clothes on was at least to pick on one man only to the amusement of everyone else; to declare that almost everyone is dressed in rags is much less likely to be popular. But the Nietzschean would at least have the consolation of being unpopularly *in the right*—unless, that is, the rejection of the Aristotelian tradition turned out to have been mistaken.

The Aristotelian tradition has occupied two distinct places in my argument: first, because I have suggested that a great part of modern morality is intelligible only as a set of fragmented survivals from that tradition, and indeed that the inability of modern moral philosphers to carry through their projects of analysis and justification is closely connected with the fact that the concepts with which they work are a combination of fragmented survivals and implausible modern inventions; but in addition to this the rejection of the Aristotelian tradition was a rejection of a quite distinctive kind of morality in which rules, so predominant in modern conceptions of morality, find their place in a larger scheme in which the virtues have the central place; hence the cogency of the Nietzschean rejection and refutation of modern moralities of rules, whether of a utilitarian or of a Kantian kind, did not necessarily extend to the earlier Aristotelian tradition.

It is one of my most important contentions that against that tradition the Nietzschean polemic is completely unsuccessful. The grounds for saying this can be set out in two different ways. The first I already suggested in Chapter 9; Nietzsche succeeds if all those whom he takes on as antagonists fail. Others may have to succeed by virtue of the rational power of their positive arguments; but if Nietzsche wins, he wins by default.

He does not win. I have sketched in Chapters 14 and 15 the rational case that can be made for a tradition in which the Aristotelian moral and political texts are canonical. For Nietzsche or the Nietzscheans to succeed that case would have to be rebutted. Why it cannot be so rebutted is best brought out by considering a second way in which the rejection of Nietzsche's claims can be argued. Nietzschean man, the *Übermensch*, the man who transcends, finds his good nowhere in the social world to date, but only in that in himself which dictates his own new law and his own new table of the virtues. Why does he never find any objective good with authority over him in the social world to date? The answer is not difficult: Nietzsche's portrait makes it clear that he who transcends is wanting in respect of both relationships and activities. Consider part of just one note (962) from *The Will To Power*. 'A great man—a man whom nature has constructed and invented in the grand style—what is he? . . . If he cannot lead, he goes alone; then it can happen that he may snarl at some things he meets on the way . . . he wants no "sympathetic" heart, but servants, tools; in his intercourse with men he is always intent on *making* something out of them. He knows he is incommunicable: he finds it tasteless to be familiar; and when one thinks he is, he usually is not. When not speaking to himself, he wears a mask. He rather lies than tells the truth: it requires more spirit and *will*. There is a solitude within him that is inaccessible to praise or blame, his own justice that is beyond appeal.'

This characterization of 'the great man' is deeply rooted in Nietzsche's contention that the morality of European society since the archaic age in Greece has been nothing but a series of disguises for the will to power and that the claim to objectivity for such morality cannot be rationally sustained. It is because this is so that the great man cannot enter into relationships mediated by appeal to shared standards or virtues or goods; he is his own only authority and his relationships to others have to be exercises of that authority. But we can now see clearly that, if the account of the virtues which I have defended can be sustained, it is the isolation and self-absorption of 'the great man' which thrust upon him the burden of being his own self-sufficient moral authority. For if the conception of a good has to be expounded in terms of such notions as those of a practice, of the narrative unity of a human life and of a moral tradition, then goods, and with them the only grounds for the authority of laws and virtues, can only be discovered by entering into those relationships which constitute communities whose central bond is a shared vision of and understanding of goods. To cut oneself off from shared activity in which one has initially to learn obediently as an apprentice learns, to isolate oneself from the communities which find their point and purpose in such activities, will be to debar oneself from finding any good outside of oneself. It will be to condemn oneself to that moral solipsism which constitutes Nietzschean greatness. Hence we have to conclude not only that Nietzsche does not win the argument by default against the Aristotelian tradition, but also, and perhaps more importantly, that it is from the perspective of that tradition that we can best understand the mistakes at the heart of the Nietzschean position.

The attractiveness of Nietzsche's position lay in its apparent honesty. When I was setting out the case in favor of an amended and restated emotivism, it appeared to be a consequence of accepting the truth of emotivism that an honest man would no longer want to go on using most, at least, of the language of past morality because of its misleading character. And Nietzsche was the only major philosopher who had not flinched from this conclusion. Since moreover the language of modern morality is burdened with pseudo-concepts such as those of utility and of natural rights, it appeared that Nietzsche's resoluteness alone would rescue us from entanglement by such concepts; but it is now clear that the price to be paid for this liberation is entanglement in another set of mistakes. The concept of the Nietzschean 'great man' is also a pseudo-concept, although not always perhaps—unhappily—what I earlier called a fiction. It represents individualism's final attempt to escape from its own consequences. And the Nietzschean stance turns out not to be a mode of escape from or an alternative to the conceptual scheme of liberal individualist modernity, but rather one more representative moment in its internal unfolding. And we may therefore expect liberal individualist societies to breed 'great men' from time to time. Alas!

So it was right to see Nietzsche as in some sense the ultimate antagonist of the Aristotelian tradition. But it now turns out to be the case that in the end the Nietzschean stance is only one more facet of that very moral culture of which Nietzsche took himself to be an implacable critic. It is therefore after all the case that the crucial moral opposition is between liberal individualism in some version or other and the Aristotelian tradition in some version or other.

The differences between the two run very deep. They extend beyond ethics and morality to the understanding of human action, so that rival conceptions of the social sciences, of their limits and their possibilities, are intimately bound up with the antagonistic confrontation of these two alternative ways of viewing the human world. This is why my argument has had to extend to such topics as those of the concept of fact, the limits to predictability in human affairs and the nature of ideology. And it will now, I hope, be clear that in the chapters dealing with those topics I was not merely summing up arguments *against* the social embodiments of liberal individualism, but also laying the basis for arguments in favor of an alternative way of envisaging both the social sciences and society, one with which the Aristotelian tradition can easily be at home.

My own conclusion is very clear. It is that on the one hand we still, in spite of the efforts of three centuries of moral philosophy and one of sociology, lack any coherent rationally defensible statement of a liberal individualist point of view; and that, on the other hand, the Aristotelian tradition can be restated in a way that restores intelligibility and rationality to our moral and social attitudes and commitments. But although I take the weight and direction of both sets of arguments to be rationally compelling, it would be imprudent not to recognize three quite different kinds of objection that will be advanced from three quite different points of view against this conclusion.

Arguments in philosophy rarely take the form of proofs; and the most successful arguments on topics central to philosophy never do. (The ideal of *proof* is a relatively barren one in philosophy.) Consequently those who wish to resist some particular conclusion are equally rarely without any resort. Let me hasten to add immediately that I do not mean to suggest by this that no central issues in philosophy are settlable; on the contrary. We can often establish the truth in areas where no proofs are available. But when an issue *is* settled, it is often because the contending parties—or someone from among them—have stood back from their dispute and asked in a systematic way what the appropriate rational procedures are for settling this particular kind of dispute. It is my own view that the time has come once more when it is imperative to perform this task for moral philosophy; but I do not pretend to have embarked upon it in this present book. My negative and positive evaluations of particular arguments do indeed *presuppose* a systematic, although here unstated, account of rationality.

It is this account—to be given to a subsequent book—which I shall hope to deploy, and will almost certainly need to deploy, against those whose criticism of my central thesis rests chiefly or wholly upon a different and incompatible evaluation of the arguments. A motley party of defenders of liberal individualism—some of them utilitarians, some Kantians, some proudly avowing the cause of liberal individualism as I have defined it, others claiming that it is misinterpretation to associate them with my account of it, all of them disagreeing among themselves—are likely to offer objections of this kind.

A second set of objections will certainly concern my interpretation of what I have called the Aristotelian or classical tradition. For it is clear that the account I have given differs in a variety of ways, some of them quite radical, from other appropriations and interpretations of an Aristotelian moral stance. And here I am disagreeing to some extent at least with some of those philosophers for whom I have the greatest respect and from whom I have learned most (but not nearly enough, their adherents will say): in the immediate past Jacques Maritain, in the present Peter Geach. Yet if my account of the nature of moral tradition is correct, a tradition is sustained and advanced by its own internal arguments and conflicts. And even if some large parts of my interpretation could not withstand criticism, the demonstration of this would itself strengthen the tradition which I am attempting to sustain and to extend. Hence my attitude to those criticisms which I take to be internal to the moral tradition which I am defending is rather different from my attitude to purely external criticisms. The latter are no less important; but they are important in a different way.

Thirdly there will certainly be a quite different set of critics who will begin by agreeing substantially with what I have to say about liberal individualism, but who will deny not only that the Aristotelian tradition is a viable alternative, but also that it is in terms of an opposition between liberal individualism and that tradition that the problems of modernity ought to be approached. The key intellectual opposition of our age, such critics will declare, is that between liberal individualism and some version of Marxism or neo-Marxism. The most intellectually compelling exponents of this point of view are likely to be those who trace a genealogy of ideas from Kant and Hegel through Marx and claim that by means of Marxism the notion of human autonomy can be rescued from its original individualist formulations and restored within the context of an appeal to a possible form of community in which alienation has been overcome, false consciousness abolished and the values of equality and fraternity realized. My answers to the first two kinds of critic are to some large degree contained, implicity or explicitly, in what I have already written. My answers to the third type of criticism need to be spelled out a little further. They fall into two parts.

The first is that the claim of Marxism to a morally distinctive standpoint is undermined by Marxism's own moral history. In all those crises in which Marxists have had to take explicit moral stances—that over Bernstein's revisionism in German social democracy at the turn of the century or that over Khruschev's repudiation of Stalin and the Hungarian revolt in 1956, for example—Marxists have always fallen back into relatively straightforward versions of Kantianism or utilitarianism. Nor is this surprising. Secreted within Marxism from the outset is a certain radical individualism. In the first chapter of *Capital* when Marx characterizes what it will be like 'when the practical relations of everyday life offer to man none but perfectly intelligible and reasonable relations' what he pictures is 'a community of free individuals' who have all freely agreed to their common ownership of the means of production and to various norms of production and distribution. This free individual is described by Marx as a socialized Robinson Crusoe; but on what basis he enters into his free association with others Marx does not tell us. At this key point in Marxism there is a lacuna which no later Marxist has adequately supplied. It is unsurprising that abstract moral principle and utility have in fact been the principles of association which Marxists have appealed to, and that in their practice Marxists have exemplified precisely the kind of moral attitude which they condemn in others as ideological.

Secondly, I remarked earlier that as Marxists move towards power they always tend to become Weberians. Here I was of course speaking of Marxists at their best in, say, Yugoslavia or Italy; the barbarous despotism of the collective Tsardom which reigns in Moscow can be taken to be as irrelevant to the question of the moral substance of Marxism as the life of the Borgia pope was to that of the moral substance of Christianity. Nonetheless Marxism has recommended itself precisely as a guide to practice, as a politics of a peculiarly illuminating kind. Yet it is just here that it has been of singularly little help for some time now. Trotsky, in the very last years of his life, facing the question of whether the Soviet Union was in any sense a socialist country, also faced implicitly the question of whether the categories of Marxism could illuminate the future. He himself made everything turn on the outcome of a set of hypothetical predictions about possible future events in the Soviet Union, predictions which were tested only after Trotsky's death. The answer that they returned was clear: Trotsky's own premises entailed that the Soviet Union was not socialist and that the theory which was to have illuminated the path to human liberation had in fact led into darkness.

Marxist socialism is at its core deeply optimistic. For however thoroughgoing its criticism of capitalist and bourgeois institutions may be, it is committed to asserting that within the society constituted by those institutions, all the human and material preconditions of a better future are being accumulated. Yet if the moral impoverishment of advanced capitalism is what so many Marxists agree that it is, whence are these resources for the future to be derived? It is not surprising that at this point Marxism tends to produce its own versions of the *Übermensch*: Lukacs's ideal proletarian, Leninism's ideal revolutionary. When Marxism does not become Weberian social democracy or crude tyranny, it tends to become Nietzschean fantasy. One of the most admirable aspects of Trotsky's cold resolution was his refusal of all such fantasies.

A Marxist who took Trotsky's last writings with great seriousness would be forced into a pessimism quite alien to the Marxist tradition, and in becoming a pessimist he would in an important way have ceased to be a Marxist. For he would now see no tolerable alternative set of political and economic structures which could be brought into place to replace the structures of advanced capitalism. This conclusion agrees of course with my own. For I too not only take it that Marxism is exhausted as a *political* tradition, a claim borne out by the almost indefinitely numerous and conflicting range of political allegiances which now carry Marxist banners—this does not at all imply that Marxism is not still one of the richest sources of ideas about modern society—but I believe that this exhaustion is shared by every other political tradition within our culture. This is one of the conclusions to be drawn from the arguments of the preceding chapter. Does it then follow more specifically that the moral tradition which I am defending lacks any contemporary politics of relevance and more generally that my argument commits me and anyone else who accepts it to a generalized social pessimism? Not at all.

It is always dangerous to draw too precise parallels between one historical period and another; and among the most misleading of such parallels are those which have been drawn between our own age in Europe and North America and the epoch in which the Roman empire declined into the Dark Ages. Nonetheless certain parallels there are. A crucial turning point in that earlier history occurred when men and women of good will turned aside from the task of shoring up the Roman *imperium* and ceased to identify the continuation of civility and moral community with the maintenance of that *imperium*. What they set themselves to achieve instead—often not recognizing fully what they were doing—was the construction of new forms of community within which the moral life could be sustained so that both morality and civility might survive the coming ages of barbarism and darkness. If my account of our moral condition is correct, we ought also to conclude that for some time now we too have reached that turning point. What matters at this stage is the construction of local forms of community within which civility and the intellectual and moral life can be sustained through the new dark ages which are already upon us. And if the tradition of the virtues was able to survive the horrors of the last dark ages, we are not entirely without grounds for hope. This time however the barbarians are not waiting beyond the frontiers; they have already been governing us for quite some time. And it is our lack of consciousness of this that constitutes part of our predicament. We are waiting not for a Godot, but for another—doubtless very different—St. Benedict.

19

Postscript to the Second Edition

The numerous critics of the first edition of this book have put me greatly in their debt and this in more than one way. Some have identified blunders—ranging from confusions over names to a factual error about Giotto; some have pointed out inadequacies in the historical narrative which supplies *After Virtue* with its argumentative continuity; some have disputed my diagnosis of the condition of modern and more particularly of contemporary society; and some have questioned in a number of ways both the substance and the method of particular arguments.

To criticisms of the first kind it has been easy to respond: all the mistakes so far identified have been corrected in this second edition. I am particularly grateful in this respect to Hugh Lloyd-Jones and to Robert Wachbroit. Responding to the other types of criticism is not only a more difficult task, but one which requires me to undertake a number of long-term projects directed towards the varying disciplinary concerns of my critics. For it is both a strength and a weakness of *After Virtue* that in writing it I had two overriding preoccupations: *both* to set out the overall structure of a single complex thesis about the place of the virtues in human life, even if to do so resulted in sketching rather than stating fully the subordinate arguments within that thesis; *and* to do so in a way that made clear how my thesis was deeply incompatible with the conventional academic disciplinary boundaries, boundaries which so often have the effect of compartmentalizing thought in a way that distorts or obscures key relationships, even if *that* entailed some large inadequacies from the standpoint of those immersed in each of the academically autonomous disciplines. I hope that some part at least of what is wanting will be supplied in my forthcoming interchanges with a variety of critics in the journals *Inquiry, Analyse und Kritik* and *Soundings* and that much more will be remedied in the sequel to *After Virtue*, on which I am now at work, on *Justice and Practical Reasoning*. But a number of critics have convinced me that some of the immediate dissatisfactions of the readers of *After Virtue* could be, if not removed, at least mitigated by a more adequate restatement of positions either central to or presupposed by the overall scheme of argument. There are perhaps three distinct areas where this need is most urgent.

1. The Relationship of Philosophy to History

'What bothers me is not distinguishing [history from philosophy]' wrote William K. Frankena (*Ethics*, 93, 1983: 500), 'or giving the impression that a historical inquiry can establish a philosophical point, as MacIntyre seems to do.' Frankena here speaks for what is still academic orthodoxy, although like other modern orthodoxies it is showing signs of strain. Philosophy is on this view one thing, history quite another. To the historian of ideas is assigned the task of recounting the rise and fall of ideas, just as to the political historian is assigned that of recounting the rise and fall of empires. The tasks reserved for the philosopher are twofold. Where subject-matters other than philosophy itself are concerned, such as morality, it falls to the philosopher to determine what the appropriate criteria for rationality and truth are in that particular area. Where philosophy has become its own subject-matter, it falls to the philosopher to determine by the best rational methods what is in fact true. It is this conception of the academic division of labor that Frankena seems to presuppose when he says of emotivism as a philosophical theory that 'I can, if I have the right conceptual equipment, understand *what* the view is without seeing it as the result of a historical development; and, so far as I can see, I can also assess its status as true or false or rational to believe without seeing it as such an outcome. Indeed MacIntyre's own arguments against emotivism are drawn from analytical philosophy; and his claim that modern attempts to justify morality *fail* and *had to fail* is a claim that can be established only by analytical philosophy, not by some kind of history' (loc. cit.).

Against this view I am committed to maintaining that although arguments of the kind favored by analytic philosophy do possess an indispensable power, it is only within the context of a particular genre of historical inquiry that such arguments can support the type of claim about truth and rationality which philosophers characteristically aspire to justify. As Frankena notices, I am not being original in so arguing; he names Hegel and Collingwood and he might have named Vico. For it was Vico who first stressed the importance of the undeniable fact, which it is becoming tedious to reiterate, that the subject matters of moral philosophy at least — the evaluative and normative concepts, maxims, arguments and judgments about which the moral philosopher enquires — are nowhere to be found except as embodied in the historical lives of particular social groups and so possessing the distinctive characteristics of historical existence: both identity and change through time, expression in institutionalized practice as well as in discourse, interaction and interrelationship with a variety of forms of activity. Morality which is no particular society's morality is to be found nowhere. There was the-morality-of-fourth-century-Athens, there were the-moralities-of-thirteenth-century-Western-Europe, there are numerous such moralities, but where ever was or is *morality as such?*

Kant of course believed that he had successfully answered that question. And it is important that both the analytic moral philosophy which Frankena defends and the type of historicism which I defend are in key part responses to criticisms of Kant's transcendental answer. For Kant's thesis that the nature of human reason is such that there are principles and concepts necessarily assented to by any rational being, both in thinking and in willing, encountered two distinct kinds of crucial objection. One, to which Hegel and subsequent historicists gave great weight, was that what Kant presented as the universal and necessary principles of the human mind turned out in fact to be principles specific to particular times, places and stages of human activity and enquiry. Just as what Kant took to be the principles and presuppositions of natural science as such turned out after all to be the principles and presuppositions specific to Newtonian physics, so what Kant took to be the principles and presuppositions of morality as such turned out to be the principles and presuppositions of one highly specific morality, a secularized version of Protestantism which furnished modern liberal individualism with one of its founding charters. Thus the claim to universality foundered.

A second set of objections were to the effect that the conceptions of necessity, of the *a priori*, and of the relationship of concepts and categories to experience that the Kantian transcendental project required could not be sustained: and the history of successive philosophical criticisms of the original Kantian positions, of their reformulation first by neo-Kantians and later more radically by logical empiricists, and of the criticism in turn of those reformulations, is central to the history of how analytic philosophy came to be what it is. The final recent subversion of the distinctions central to the Kantian project and to its successors at the hands of Quine, Sellars, Goodman and others has been chronicled by Richard Rorty, who has remarked upon how one effect has been to diminish to some large degree consensus in the analytic community as to what the central problems of philosophy are (*Consequences of Pragmatism*, Minneapolis, 1982, pp. 214-217). But this has not been the only or even the most important consequence.

For what the progress of analytic philosophy has succeeded in establishing is that there are *no* grounds for belief in universal necessary principles — outside purely formal enquiries — except relative to some set of assumptions. Cartesian first principles, Kantian *a priori* truths and even the ghosts

of these notions that haunted empiricism for so long have all been expelled
from philosophy. The consequence is that analytic philosophy has become
a discipline — or a subdiscipline? — whose competence has been restricted to
the study of inferences. Rorty puts this by saying that 'the ideal of philosophical ability is to see the entire universe of possible assertions in all their
inferential relationships to one another, and thus to be able to construct,
or criticize, any argument' (op. cit. p. 219). And David Lewis has written:
'Philosophical theories are never refuted conclusively. (Or hardly ever,
Gödel and Gettier may have done it.) The theory survives its refutation —
at a price. . . . Our "intuitions" are simply opinions; our philosophical theories are the same . . . a reasonable task for the philosopher is to bring them
into equilibrium. Our common task is to find out what equilibria there are
that can withstand examination, but it remains for each of us to come to
rest in one or another of them. . . . Once the menu of well-worked out
theories is before us, philosophy is a matter of opinion . . .' (*Philosophical
Papers*, Volume I, Oxford, 1983, pp. x-xi).

Analytic philosophy, that is to say, can very occasionally produce practically conclusive results of a negative kind. It can show in a few cases that
just too much incoherence and inconsistency is involved in some position
for *any* reasonable person to continue to hold it. But it can never establish
the *rational acceptability* of any particular position in cases where each of
the alternative rival positions available has sufficient range and scope and
the adherents of each are willing to pay the price necessary to secure coherence and consistency. Hence the peculiar flavor of so much contemporary analytic writing — by writers less philosophically self-aware than Rorty
or Lewis — in which passages of argument in which the most sophisticated
logical and semantic techniques available are deployed in order to secure
maximal rigor alternate with passages which seem to do no more than cob-
ble together a set of loosely related arbitrary preferences; contemporary
analytic philosophy exhibits a strange partnership between an idiom deeply
indebted to Frege and Carnap and one deriving from the more simple-
minded forms of existentialism.

What this outcome suggests to the historicist is first of all that analytic
philosophers, as represented by Rorty and Lewis and indeed by Frankena,
seem to be determined to go on considering arguments as objects of investigation in abstraction from the social and historical contexts of activity
and enquiry in which they are or were at home and from which they
characteristically derive their particular import. But in so doing the analytical philosopher is liable to inherit from his Kantian forebears those mis-
understandings which arose from the first of the two central objections to

Kant's own version of the transcendental project. For if for example we regard the principles and categories of Newtonian mechanics as satisfying the requirements of rationality-as-such, we shall obscure precisely that about them which rendered them rationally superior to their only available rivals in the actual context of physical enquiry in the late seventeenth and early eighteenth centuries.

What rendered Newtonian physics rationally superior to its Galilean and Aristotelian predecessors and to its Cartesian rivals was that it was able to transcend their limitations by solving problems in areas in which those predecessors and rivals could by their own standards of scientific progress make no progress. So we cannot say wherein the rational superiority of Newtonian physics consisted except historically in terms of its relationship to those predecessors and rivals whom it challenged and displaced. Abstract Newtonian physics from its context, and then ask wherein the rational superiority of one to the other consists and you will be met with insoluble incommensurability problems. Thus knowing how Newton and the Newtonians actually came to adopt and defend their views is essential to knowing why Newtonian physics is to be accounted rationally superior. The philosophy of physical science is dependent on the history of physical science. But the case is no different with morality.

Moral philosophies, however they may aspire to achieve more than this, always do articulate the morality of some particular social and cultural standpoint: Aristotle is the spokesman for one class of fourth century Athenians, Kant, as I have already noticed, provides a rational voice for the emerging social forces of liberal individualism. But even this way of putting matters is inadequate, for it still treats the morality as one thing, the moral philosophy as another. But any particular morality has as its core standards by which reasons for action are judged more or less adequate, conceptions of how qualities of character relate to qualities of actions, judgments as to how rules are to be formulated, and so on. Thus although there is always more to any particular morality than the philosophy implicit within it, there is no morality allegiance to which does not involve some philosophical stance, explicit or implicit. Moral philosophies are, before they are anything else, the explicit articulations of the claims of particular moralities to rational allegiance. And this is why the history of morality and the history of moral philosophy are a single history. It follows that when rival moralities make competing and incompatible claims, there is always an issue at the level of moral philosophy concerning the ability of either to make good a claim to rational superiority over the other.

How are these claims to be judged? As in the case of natural science there are no general timeless standards. It is in the ability of one particular moral-philosophy-articulating-the-claims-of-a-particular-morality to identify and to transcend the limitations of its rival or rivals, limitations which can be—although they may not in fact have been—identified by the rational standards to which the protagonists of the rival morality are committed by their allegiance to it, that the rational superiority of that particular moral philosophy and that particular morality emerges. The history of morality-and-moral-philosophy is the history of successive challenges to some pre-existing moral order, a history in which the question of which party defeated the other in rational argument is always to be distinguished from the question of which party retained or gained social and political hegemony. And it is only by reference to this history that questions of rational superiority can be settled. The history of morality-and-moral-philosophy written from this point of view is as integral to the enterprise of contemporary moral philosophy as the history of science is to the enterprise of contemporary philosophy of science.

It is, I hope, now clearer why Frankena and I disagree. He seems to hold that the methods of analytic philosophy are sufficient to establish what is true or false and what it is reasonable to believe in moral philosophy and that historical enquiry is irrelevant. I hold not only that historical enquiry is required in order to establish what a particular point of view is, but also that it is in its historical encounter that any given point of view establishes or fails to establish its rational superiority relative to its particular rivals in some specific contexts. In doing so many of the skills and techniques of analytic philosophy will be deployed; and on rare occasions these techniques may be sufficient to discredit a view. So when Frankena correctly says that on occasion I employ arguments drawn from analytic philosophy to establish that a particular theory or set of theories fails, he imputes to me nothing that is inconsistent either with my historicism or with my rejection of the view that analytic philosophy can never provide sufficient grounds for the assertion of any positive standpoint in moral philosophy.

Thus when we understand emotivism as a rejoinder to a particular historical conjunction of intuitionist moral theorizing with the exercise of a particular kind of moral judgment, we are able to understand its claims not only as a thesis about the timeless meaning of sentences used in moral judgments (a thesis with little plausibility), but also and more importantly as an empirical thesis about the use and function of moral judgments which may hold in a wider or a narrower range of historical situations. Hence making it intelligible how the theory came to be advanced and in what type of situation is relevant to both the understanding and the evaluation of the theory in a way that Frankena's sharp distinction between philosophical inquiry and history obscures.

To this the following rejoinder may be made. If we are able to write the kind of philosophical history that I have envisaged—and it is just this that I attempted to write in *After Virtue*—then in chronicling the defeats of one theory or the victories of another in respect of rational superiority, we the chroniclers must be bringing to that history standards by which the rational superiority of one theory to another is to be judged. These standards will themselves require rational justification, and *this* justification cannot be provided by a history which can only be written after a justification for these standards has been provided. Hence the historicist is covertly appealing to nonhistorical standards, standards which would presumably have to be provided with either a transcendental or an analytic justification, types of justification which I have rejected.

This rejoinder fails. For our situation in respect of theories about what makes one theory rationally superior to another is no different from our situation in regard to scientific theories or to moralities-and-moral-philosophies. In the former as in the latter case what we have to aspire to is not a perfect theory, one necessarily to be assented to by any rational being, because invulnerable or almost invulnerable to objections, but rather the best theory to emerge so far in the history of this class of theories. So we ought to aspire to provide the best theory so far as to what type of theory the best theory so far must be: no more, but no less.

It follows that the writing of this kind of philosophical history can never be brought to completion. The possibility has always to be left open that in any particular field, whether the natural sciences or morality-and-moral-philosophy, or the theory of theory, some new challenge to the established best theory so far will appear and will displace it. Hence this kind of historicism, unlike Hegel's, involves a form of fallibilism; it is a kind of historicism which excludes all claims to absolute knowledge. Nonetheless if some particular moral scheme has successfully transcended the limitations of its predecessors and in so doing provided the best means available for understanding those predecessors to date *and* has then confronted successive challenges from a number of rival points of view, but in each case has been able to modify itself in the ways required to incorporate the strengths of those points of view while avoiding their weaknesses and limitations *and* has provided the best explanation so far of those weaknesses and limitations, then we have the best possible reason to have confidence that future challenges will also be met successfully, that the principles which define the core of a moral scheme are enduring principles. And just this is the achievement that I ascribe to Aristotle's fundamental moral scheme in *After Virtue*.

That it was this type of historicist claim that I was and am making was not stated with adequate clarity; nor was the form of the argument which I was deploying in its favor adequately specified. For I was not merely claiming of what I called the Enlightenment project that it failed by its own standards, since its protagonists had never succeeded in specifiying a uniquely justifiable set of moral principles to which any fully rational agent whatsoever could not fail to assent, or of Nietzsche's moral philosophy that it too failed by its own standards; but also that the grounds for understanding those failures could only be provided out of the resources afforded by an Aristotelian account of the virtues, which, in just the way that I have described, turns out to emerge from its specific historical encounters as the best theory so far. But note that I did not assert in *After Virtue* that I had as yet sustained that claim, nor do I claim that now. What more has to be done?

Annette Baier has chided me for not understanding the strengths of Hume's position (in a paper forthcoming in *Analyse and Kritik*); Onora O'Neill has argued that my account of Kant is selective and simplified (in a paper forthcoming in *Inquiry*). I have a good deal of sympathy with both complaints for it is indeed the two very different accounts of practical reasoning advanced by Hume and Kant which present the central challenge to the Aristotelian scheme and to the account of practical reasoning embodied within it. And until the relationship of these three accounts has been clarified, the claim central to *After Virtue* will not have been established in the way that the historicist theory of knowledge presupposed by the argumentative narrative of *After Virtue* requires.

Finally a very different type of criticism of the way in which philosophy and history are related in *After Virtue* cannot be allowed to pass unnoticed. Frankena thinks me insufficiently appreciative of analytic philosophy: Abraham Edel thinks me still far too much of an analyst and accuses me of being no more than 'a heretic analyst whose heresy remains bound' by the cords of the analytic tradition (*Zygon*, 18, 1983: 344). The gist of his criticism is first that I focus too much attention upon the level of explicit theorizing, articulated concepts, and the stories told about their condition by various peoples and not enough on the actual social and institutional life of those peoples, and secondly that my partisanship leads me to distort the actual complex history of morality in the interests of my own Aristotelian point of view. Where Frankena sees me as an inadequate analytic philosopher with an additional, not entirely relevant interest in history, Edel sees me as an inadequate social historian who keeps needlessly dragging in analytic philosophy. Thus Edel's criticism is the mirror-image of Frankena's and not surprisingly.

For just as the kind of philosophical history that I wish to write breaks at certain points with the canons of analytic philosophy, so at others it violates those of academic social history and this perhaps in two ways. First from the point of view that I am taking theoretical and philosophical enterprises, their successes and failures, are far more influential in history than academic historians generally have taken them to be. The issues that need to be settled in this area are questions of fact concerning causal influence. They include such questions as the nature of the influence of the thinkers of the Scottish Enlightenment on British, French and American social, moral and political change. The answers to such questions depend upon enquiries into, for example, the social role and effectiveness of universities and colleges as bearers of ideas. And it may be that in the end historical enquiry will show my attention to explicit theorizing, articulated concepts and story-telling to be misplaced. But so far I remain unconvinced.

Secondly the narratives of academic social history tend to be written in a way that presupposes just the kind of logical distinction between questions of fact and questions of value that the account of narrative given in *After Virtue* commits me to denying. And the philosophical history which constitutes the central narrative of *After Virtue* itself is written from the standpoint of the conclusion which it itself reaches and sustains — or rather would sustain if its narrative were amplified in the way that I hope to amplify it in the sequel to *After Virtue*. So that the narrative of *After Virtue* is not accidentally or by default a partisan narrative with its own deliberate one-sidedness.

Yet Edel is of course right to some substantial degree in both his charges. A good deal of social and institutional history to which *After Virtue* at best makes oblique reference is in fact essential to the kind of narrative towards which I pointed in *After Virtue*, but which I did not yet succeed in writing; and the history of the interrelationship of the Aristotelian account of the virtues with other moral schemes from Platonism onwards to the present is of course vastly more complex than I allowed. Thus both Frankena and Edel have uttered salutary warnings both to me and to my readers by identifying issues to which I had at the very least paid insufficient attention. Their reviews have put me permanently in their debt.

2. The Virtues and the Issue of Relativism

Samuel Scheffler has raised important doubts about the account of the virtues which I advanced (*Philosophical Review*, 92, No. 3, July 1983) and so have Stanley Hauerwas and Paul Wadell (*The Thomist*, 46, No. 2, April 1982); Robert Wachbroit has suggested that one implication of that account is that some version of relativism is inescapable (*Yale Law Journal*,

92, No. 3, January 1983). Since it is only if I can respond successfully to the questions posed by Scheffler and by Hauerwas and Wadell that I will be able to reply adequately to Wachbroit's argument, their scepticisms about central points in my constructive argument can most effectively be considered together.

My account of the virtues proceeds through three stages: a first which concerns virtues as qualities necessary to achieve the goods internal to practices; a second which considers them as qualities contributing to the good of a whole life; and a third which relates them to the pursuit of a good for human beings the conception of which can only be elaborated and possessed within an ongoing social tradition. Why begin from practices? Other moral philosophers after all have begun from a consideration of passions or desires or from the elucidation of some conception of duty or goodness. In either case the discussion is all too apt to be governed from then on by some version of the means-ends distinction according to which all human activities are either conducted as means to already given or decided ends or are simply worthwhile in themselves or perhaps both. What this framework omits from view are those ongoing modes of human activity within which ends have to be discovered and rediscovered, and means devised to pursue them; and it thereby obscures the importance of the ways in which those modes of activity generate new ends and new conceptions of ends. The class of practices, defined as I defined it, is the class of those modes of activity and the shortest answer to the questions by Hauerwas and Wadell as to why some items are included in that class and others excluded (why, they asked, is architecture included, but not bricklaying?) is that those items excluded are not such modes of activity.

The importance therefore for beginnning from practices in any consideration of the virtues is that the exercise of the virtues is not only worthwhile for its own sake—it turns out that you cannot be genuinely courageous or just or whatever without caring for those virtues for their own sake—but has further point and purpose, and indeed that it is in grasping that point and purpose that we characteristically intitially came to value the virtues. Yet the virtues are not related to the goods which provide them with further point and purpose in the way in which a skill is related to the ends that its successful exercise procures or in the way in which a skill is related to those objects of our desire that its successful exercise may enable us to possess. Kant was quite right in supposing that moral imperatives are neither imperatives of skill nor imperatives of prudence, defined as he defined them. Where he erred was in supposing that the only alternative remaining is that they should be, in his sense, categorical imperatives. Yet this is just the conclusion to which one might move, without any of Kant's own additional reasons for so doing, if one tried to understand the virtues outside the context of practices. For the goods internal to practices which cannot be achieved without the exercise of the virtues are not the ends pursued by particular individuals on particular occasions, but the excellences specific to those types of practices which one achieves or fails to achieve, moves toward or fails to move toward in virtue of the way in which one pursues one's particular ends or goals on particular occasions, excellences our conception of which changes over time as our goals are transformed.

To understand this is a necessary preliminary to replying to Scheffler's objection to my thesis about the connection between virtues and practices; 'Although MacIntyre denies that it follows from this account that great chess players cannot be vicious, I am not entirely convinced that he is entitled to deny it, and in any case he does seem happy to say something that strikes me as hardly more plausible, namely that a great chess player who is vicious cannot achieve any of the internal goods of chess' (p. 446). Scheffler is quite correct in the views that he ascribes to me, but only of course if by 'internal goods' he means what I mean. Yet if one does mean what I mean, then the answer to Scheffler is clear.

Imagine an immensely skilled chess player who cares only about winning and cares for that very much. His skills are such that he ranks with the grandmasters. Thus he is a great chess player. But since what he cares about is only winning—and perhaps the goods contingently attached to winning, goods such as fame, prestige, and money—the good that he cares about is in no way specific to chess or to games of the same type as chess, as any good that is, in the sense in which I use the expression, internal to the practice of chess must be. For he could have achieved precisely the same good, that of winning and its contingent rewards, in any other field in which there is competition and there are victors, had he been able to achieve a comparable level of skill in those fields. Hence what he cares about and what he achieves *as his good* is not that kind of excellence which is specific to chess and the kind of enjoyment that supervenes upon such excellence, a good which far less skilled players may at their own level achieve. Hence Scheffler's objection fails; the relationship of virtues to practices, once it has been more clearly distinguished from the relationship of skills to practices than I succeeded in doing in my earlier account, does not entail the unfortunate consequences that Scheffler is inclined to impute to it.

Scheffler's objection seems also to owe something to another failure to be adequately clear on my part. For he says that on my view 'the virtues are provisionally characterized with reference to the notion of a practice, and this provisional account is then modified and supplemented at later stages' (p. 446). I ought to have made it clear that I did *not* intend to suggest—although I clearly did suggest—that the initial account of virtues in terms of practices provides us with an adequate conception of a virtue which is then merely enriched and supplemented by being connected with the notions of the good of a whole human life and of an ongoing tradition. Rather it is the case that no human quality is to be accounted a virtue unless it satisfies the conditions specified *at each of the three stages*. This is important because there are qualities which it is at least plausible to understand as satisfying those conditions which are derived from this notion of a practice, but which are not virtues, qualities which survive the tests of the first stage, but fail at the second or third.

Consider as an example such qualities as ruthlessness and relentlessness and distinguish them from the phronetic quality of knowing when to be ruthless or relentless. Clearly there are practices—the exploration of wilderness is one example—in which the ability to be ruthless and relentless in driving oneself and others may be a condition not just for achievement, but also for survival. Such an ability may require as a condition of its exercise the cultivation of a certain insensitivity to the feelings of others; caring about their feelings may get in the way of caring about their survival. Transpose that complex of qualities into participation in the practice of creating and sustaining the life of a family and you have a recipe for disaster. What seemed to be a virtue in the one context seems to have become a vice in the other. But this quality is in my account neither a virtue nor a vice. It is not a virtue, because it cannot satisfy the conditions imposed by the requirement that a virtue contribute to the good of that kind of whole human life in which the goods of particular practices are integrated into an overall pattern of goals which provides an answer to the question: "What is the best kind of life for a human being like me to lead?" It is of course possible that there are certain qualities which would succeed in satisfying that second type of requirement, but fail to satisfy the requirements of the third stage, at which the goods of particular lives have to be integrated into the overall patterns of a tradition informed by a quest for *the* good and *the* best.

It is partly the way in which I characterized this third stage in my account of the virtues which has seemed to more than one critic to provide grounds for an accusation of relativism. Robert Wachbroit (loc. cit.) has argued that my characterization of the human good in terms of the quest for the good, even with the constraints afforded by the first two stages of my account, is compatible with acknowledging the existence of distinct, incompatible and rival traditions of the virtues. And in this he is right. He' then attempts to impale my position on a dilemma. Suppose that two rival and incompatible moral traditions encounter one another in some specific historical situation where to accept the claims of the one is to be committed to conflict with the other. Then *either* it will be possible to appeal to some set of rationally grounded principles independent of each of the rivals *or* no rational resolution of their disagreements is possible. But if the former, then there is indeed a set of principles to which appeal can be made on fundamental moral issues the rational grounding of which is independent of the social particularities of traditions; and if the latter, there is no moral rationality which is not internal to and relative to some particular tradition. But in that case we can have no good reason for giving our allegiance to any one particular tradition rather than to any other. And since my rejection of the Enlightenment project commits me to deny what follows from the former of the two alternatives, it seems that I cannot avoid accepting these consequences of the latter alternative.

The force of this argument turns on whether this disjunctive statement of the alternatives is or is not exhaustive. It is not. For it is sometimes at least possible that one such tradition may appeal for a verdict in its favor against its rival to types of consideration which are already accorded weight in both the competing traditions. What types of consideration might these be?

If two moral traditions are able to recognize each other as advancing rival contentions on issues of importance, then necessarily they must share some common features. And since some kind of relationship to practices, some particular conception of human goods, some characteristics which arise from the very nature of a tradition will be features of both, this is unsurprising. Issues on which the adherents of the one tradition appeal to standards which are simply incommensurable with those appealed to by adherents of the rival tradition will not be and could not be the only kinds of issue to arise in such a situation. It will thus sometimes at least be possible for adherents of each tradition to understand and to evaluate—by their own standards—the characterizations of their positions advanced by their rivals. And nothing precludes their discovering that these characterizations reveal to them features of their own positions which had hitherto gone unnoticed or considerations which by their own standards they ought to have entertained, but had not. Indeed nothing precludes the discovery that the rival tradition offers cogent explanations of weaknesses, of inabilities to formulate or solve problems adequately, of a variety of incoherences in one's own tradition for which the resources of one's own tradition had not been able to offer a convincing account.

Traditions do on occasion founder, that is, by their own standards of flourishing and foundering, and an encounter with a rival tradition may in this way provide good reasons either for attempting to reconstitute one's tradition in some radical way or for deserting it. Yet it is also the case, as I noted earlier, that if in such successive encounters a particular moral tradition has succeeded in reconstituting itself when rational considerations urged upon its adherents either from within the tradition or from without so required, and has provided generally more cogent accounts of its rivals' defects and weaknesses and of its own than those rivals have been able to supply, either concerning themselves or concerning others, all this of course in the light of the standards internal to that tradition, standards which will in the course of those vicissitudes have themselves been revised and extended in a variety of ways, then the adherents of that tradition are rationally entitled to a large measure of confidence that the tradition which they inhabit and to which they owe the substance of their moral lives will find the resources to meet future challenges successfully. For the theory of moral reality embodied in their modes of thinking and acting has shown itself to be, in the sense that I gave to that expression, *the best theory so far*.

To this Wachbroit might well reply that I have not answered his objection. For nothing that I have said goes any way to show that a situation could not arise in which it proved possible to discover no rational way to settle the disagreements between two rival moral and epistemological traditions, so that positive grounds for a relativistic thesis would emerge. But this I have no interest in denying. For my position entails that there are no successful *a priori* arguments which will guarantee in advance that such a situation could not occur. Indeed nothing could provide us with such a guarantee which did not involve the successful resuscitation of the Kantian transcendental project.

It scarcely needs repeating that it is the central thesis of *After Virtue* that the Aristotelian moral tradition is the best example we possess of a tradition whose adherents are rationally entitled to a high measure of confidence in its epistemological and moral resources. But an historicist defence of Aristotle is bound to strike some sceptical critics as a paradoxical as well as a Quixotic enterprise. For Aristotle himself, as I pointed out in my discussion of his own account of the virtues, was not any kind of historicist, although some notable historicists, including both Vico and Hegel, have been to some greater or lesser degree Aristotelians. To show that there is no paradox here is therefore one more necessary task; but it too can only be accomplished on the larger scale that the successor volume to *After Virtue* will afford me.

3. *The Relationship of Moral Philosophy to Theology*

A number of critics have pointed out inadequacies in the argumentative narrative which is central to *After Virtue*. The most notable of these is the lack of anything like an adequate treatment of the relationship of the Aristotelian tradition of the virtues to the religion of the Bible and to its theology. Jeffrey Stout (in 'Virtue among the Ruins', forthcoming in *Neue Zeitschrift für systematische Theologie und Religions-philosophie*) has identified some unfortunate effects of this, one of overriding importance. From the moment that biblical religion and Aristotelianism encountered one another the question of the relationship of claims about the human virtues to claims about divine law and divine commandments required an answer. Any reconciliation of biblical theology and Aristotelianism would have to sustain a defence of the thesis that only a life constituted in key part by obedience to law could be such as to exhibit fully those virtues without which human beings cannot achieve their *telos*. Any justified rejection of such a reconciliation would have to give reasons for denying that thesis. The classic statement and defence of that thesis is of course by Aquinas; and the most cogent statement of the case against it is in an unduly neglected minor modern classic, Harry V. Jaffa's commentary on Aquinas' commentary on the *Nicomachean Ethics, Thomism and Aristotelianism* (Chicago, 1952).

By avoiding the issues that Aquinas' combination of theological allegiance to the Torah and philosophical allegiance to Aristotle raises I obscured or distorted a good deal that ought to have been central to the later part of my narrative: the complex and varying nature of Protestant and Jansenist reactions to the Aristotelian tradition and, in a later sequel, Kant's attempt to establish on a secular rational basis a morality of law which presupposes the existence of God, but entails not merely the rejection of Aristotelianism, but an identification of it as a prime source of moral error. So the content of my narrative once again requires addition and emendation in a number of ways if the central conclusions that I derive from it are to sustain their claim to rational justification.

Thus *After Virtue*, in this respect as in others, ought to be read as a work still in progress and if I can now proceed to carry that work further, it is in crucial part because of the generous and penetrating way in which so many philosophers—and sociologists and anthropologists and historians and theologians—have contributed to that work by their criticism.

Bibliography

This bibliography lists only works directly referred to or quoted in the text, except for classics of philosophy and the social sciences to which reference is made only when there is need to identify a particular translation or edition.

J.L. Ackrill, *Aristotle on Eudaimonia*, 1974
A.W.H. Adkins, *Merit and Responsibility*, 1960
S. Andreski, *Social Science as Sorcery*, 1973
G.E.M. Anscombe, 'Modern Moral Philosophy', *Philosophy*, 33, 1958
R. Aron, 'Max Weber' in *Main Currents in Sociological Thought*, trans. R. Howard and H. Weaver, 1967
Peter Berger, Brigitte Berger and Hansfried Kellner, *The Homeless Mind*, 1973
Egon Bittner, 'The Concept of Organization', *Social Research*, 32, 1965: 239-55
The Functions of the Police in Modern Society, 1970
Gene Brucker, *The Civic World of Early Renaissance Florence*, 1977
Tom Burns, 'Industry in a New Age', *New Society*, 31 January 1963
Tom Burns and G.N. Stalker, *The Management of Innovation*, 1968
Stephen R.L. Clark, Review of *The Aristotelian Ethics* by Anthony Kenny, *Philosophical Quarterly*, 1979: 352-5
Richard Cobb, 'The Revolutionary Mentality in France' in *A Second Identity*, 1969
James C. Davies, 'Towards a Theory of Revolution', *American Sociological Review*, 27, 1962: 5-13
Alan Donegan, *The Theory of Morality*, 1977
Ronald Dworkin, *Taking Rights Seriously*, 1976
Rosalind and Ivo Feierabend, 'Aggressive Behavior Within Politics, 1948-1962: A Cross-National Study', *Journal of Conflict Resolution*, 10, 1966: 249-71
M.I. Finley, *The World of Odysseus*, 1954
Hermann Fränkel, *Early Greek Poetry and Philosophy*, translated by M. Hadas and J. Willis, 1973

David Gadd, *The Loving Friends*, 1976
John Gardner, *The Life and Times of Chaucer*, 1977
William H. Gass, *Fiction and the Figures of Life*, 1971
Peter Geach, *The Virtues*, 1977
Bernard Gert, *The Moral Rules: A New Rational Foundation for Morality*, 1970
Alan Gewirth, *Reason and Morality*, 1978
Erving Goffman, *The Presentation of Self in Everyday Life*, 1959
  Encounters, 1961
  Interaction Ritual, 1957
  Strategic Interaction, 1969
J.Y.T. Greig, ed., *The Letters of David Hume*, vol. 1, 1932
Samuel Guttenplan, 'Moral Realism and Moral Dilemmas', *Proceedings of the Aristotelian Society*, 1979-80: 61-80
Barbara Hardy, 'Towards a Poetics of Fiction: An Approach Through Narrative', *Novel*, 2, 1968: 5-14
R.M. Hare, *The Language of Morals*, 1951
Philip Hobsbaum, *A Reader's Guide to Charles Dickens*, 1973
T. Irwin, Review of *The Aristotelian Ethics* and *Aristotle's Theory of the Will*, by A. Kenny, *Journal of Philosophy*, 77, 1980: 338-54
Herbert Kaufman, *Administrative Feedback*, 1973
Anthony Kenny, *The Aristotelian Ethics*, 1978
Walter Laqueur, 'A Reflection on Violence', *Encounter*, 38, April 1972: 3-10
Michael E. Levy, 'Constraining Inflation: Concerns, Complacencies and Evidence', *The Conference Board Record*, 12, October 1975: 8-14
R. Likert, *New Patterns of Management*, 1961
Hugh Lloyd-Jones, *The Justice of Zeus*, 1971
Louis Mackey, *Kierkegaard: A Kind of Poet*, 1971
Donald G.. Macrae, *Max Weber*, 1974
Gregor Malantschuk, *Kierkegaard's Thought*, translated by Howard V. Hong and Edna H. Hong, 1971
James G. March and Herbert A. Simon, *Organizations*, 1958
James Miller, *History and Human Existence*, 1979
Jeffrey S. Milstein and William Charles Mitchell, *Computer Simulation of International Processes: the Vietnam War and the Pre-World War I Naval Race*, 1968
Louis O. Mink, 'History and Fiction as Modes of Comprehension', *New Literary History*, 1, 1970: 541-58
Oscar Newman, *Defensible Space*, 1973

F. Nietzsche, *The Gay Science*, translated with commentary by Walter Kaufmann, 1974

The Will to Power, edited and translated by Walter Kaufmann, 1967

Robert Nozick, *Anarchy, State and Utopia*, 1974

J.A. Passmore, 'John Anderson and Twentieth-Century Philosophy', Introductory essay in *Studies in Empirical Philosophy* by John Anderson, 1962

K. Polanyi, *The Great Transformation*, 1944

W.V.O. Quine, *Word and Object*, 1960

John B. Rawls, *A Theory of Justice*, 1971

Lewis F. Richardson, *Arms and Insecurity*, 1960

P. Rieff, *The Triumph of the Therapeutic*, 1966

To My Fellow Teachers, 1975

Anne Righter, *Shakespeare and the Idea of the Play*, 1962

S.P. Rosenbaum, ed., *The Bloomsbury Group*, 1975

D.J.C. Smyth and J.C.K. Ash, 'Forecasting Gross National Product, the Rate of Inflation and the Balance of Trade: the O.E.C.D. Performance', *The Economic Journal*, 85, 1975: 361-4

Derek J. de Solla Price, *Little Science, Big Science*, 1963

Robert Solomon, ed., *Nietzsche: a Collection of Critical Essays*, 1973

C.L. Stevenson, *Ethics and Language*, 1945

Bas C. Van Fraasen, 'Values and the Heart's Command', *Journal of Philosophy*, 70, 1973: 5-19

S. Weil, 'The Iliad or the Poem of Force' in *Revisions*, edited by S. Hauerwas and A. MacIntyre, 1983

Index

Abelard, P., 168, 170-71
abortion, 6-7
Ackrill, J.L., 158, 175
Adkins, W.H., 133, 135, 138-39
Aeschylus, 142, 157
aesthetic attitude, 24-25, 40-41, 73
Alan of Lille, 171
analytical philosophy, 2-3, 20-21, 265-69
Anderson, J., 163-64
Andreski, S., 88
Anscombe, G.E.M., 53
Aquinas, 10, 53, 96, 142, 165, 171,
    177-80, 185, 200
Aristotle, 10, 15, 23, 52-54, 58, 81-82,
    105-20, 135, 142, 146-64, 165-69,
    175-87, 196-203, 213, 227-29, 232-33,
    236, 237, 240, 244, 252, 256-59, 268,
    270, 277 278
Arnold, T., 30, 72
Aron, R., 26
Ash, C., 89
Aubrey, J., 79
Auerbach, E., 226
Augustine, 175
Austen, J., 181-87, 239-43
Austin, J.L., 223
Ayer, A.J., 76, 107

Babbage, C., 95
Bach, J.S., 38
Bacon, F., 78
Baier, A., 271
Bakke case, 253
Barth, K., 170
Becket, T., 167, 172-73, 179, 203
Bell, D., 237
Benedict, 199, 263
Bentham, J., 62-63, 70, 198

Berger, P. and B., 117
Berkeley, G., 33
Berlin, I., 109, 237
Bismarck, O. von, 10
Bittner, E., 74-75, 90
Booth, C., 85
Bradley, F.H., 16
Brucker, G., 237
Buckle, H.T., 92
Burke, E., 221-22
Burns, T., 106
Bury, J.B., 99
Butler, J., 33

Calvin, J., 53
Carnap, R., 18, 76, 107
Chadwick, E., 64
characters, 27-31, 73
Chaucer, G., 176
Church, A., 94, 101
Cicero, 38, 167, 231
Clark, S.R.L., 158
Clausewitz, K. von, 10
Cobb, R., 237
Cobbett, W., 238-39, 243
Collingwood, R.G., 3, 4, 97, 265
Comte, A., 88, 92
Condorcet, Marquis de, 61, 87, 92
constancy, 183, 203, 242
Cook, J., 111, 235
courage, 122-25, 141, 155, 177, 192-93,
    199, 223

Dahrendorf, R., 204
Daiches, D., 239
Dante, 176, 243
Davies, J.C., 90
de Retz, Gilles, 175

de Solla Price, D., 95
Deutsch, K., 89
Diderot, D., 25, 40, 47-50, 51-52, 54-55, 61, 73, 87, 92, 119, 229-230
Dodds, E.R., 135
Donegan, A., 21
Douglas, M., 112
Duncan-Jones, A., 17
Dworkin, R., 69-70, 252-53

Edel, A., 271-72
emotivism, 11-14, 16-35
empiricism, 79-81
Engels, F., 110, 199, 213
existentialism, 4, 21

fact-value distinction, 57-59, 83-84
Feierabend, R. and I., 90
Ferguson, A., 37, 195-96, 253-54
Fichte, J.G., 10
Finley, M.I., 122
Forster, E.M., 156
Fortuna, 93, 105
Francis of Assisi, 199
Fränkel, H., 122
Frankena, W., 265, 267, 269, 271
Franklin, B., 181-86, 198-99, 232, 243
Freud, S., 72
Friedman, M., 7
friendship, 122-24, 134-35, 155-56, 158, 192-93
Fry, R., 16

Gadd, D., 16
Galton, F., 95
Gardner, J., 176, 226
Gass, W., 24, 226
Gauguin, P., 201
generalizations, 82-83, 89-91, 159
Geach, P.T., 179, 261
Gert, B., 21
Gewirth, A., 21, 66-67, 69
Giotto, 177, 189
Goffmann, E., 32, 35, 115-17, 204, 221
Goldmann, L., 110
Green, T.H., 10
Grieg, J.Y.T., 231
Guevara, C., 7
Guttenplan, S., 225

Handel, G.F., 38
happiness, 62-64, 148, 160, 198
Harding, D.W., 240
Hardy, B., 211-12
Hare, R.M., 20-21, 26, 113, 224
Hauerwas, S., 272-73
Hegel, G.W.F., 3, 4, 84, 261, 265, 270, 277
Helvetius, C.A., 92
Henry II, 167, 172-73, 179, 213
history, 3, 4
Hobbes, T., 61, 165, 196, 250
Hobsbaum, P., 215
Hofstadter, R., 4
Homans, G.C., 88
Homer, 121-34, 137-38, 166, 169, 181-87
Hume, D., 11, 23, 33, 37, 47-56, 61, 119, 161-63, 217, 229-33, 235, 242, 271
Husserl, E., 2
Hutcheson, F., 231
Huxley, A., 106

Ibn Roschd, 3
Irwin, T., 147
Isocrates, 136

Jacobin, clubs, 238, 243
Jaffa, H., 278
James, H., 24-25, 27, 125, 243
Jefferson, T., 61, 195, 239
John of Gaunt, 176
John of Salisbury, 167, 170
Johnson, S., 214-15, 234, 237
justice, 7, 134, 141, 153, 177, 192-93, 199, 202, 223

Kafka, F., 213
Kahn, H., 7
Kamehameha II, 112-13
Kames, Lord, 37
Kant, I., 10, 11, 23, 37, 43-47, 49-50, 51-52, 56, 62, 79, 82, 95, 113, 119, 140, 148-49, 154-55, 224, 232, 233, 236, 257, 266, 268, 271, 273-74, 278
Kaufman, H., 106
Kenny, A., 147
Keynes, J.M., 14, 16, 107

Kierkegaard, S., 25, 39-45, 49-50, 51-52, 54, 56, 73, 203, 241-42
Kipling, R., 243
Knowles, D., 213

Laqueur, W., 90
Lawrence, D.H., 72, 198
Lawrence, T.E., 201
Lee, R.E., 99
Lenin, V.I., 201
Levy, M.E., 89
Lewis, C.S., 185, 240
Lewis, D., 267
Likert, R., 27
Lipset, S.M., 4
Lloyd-Jones, H., 134, 264
Locke, J., 10, 33, 217, 250-51
Lowes Dickinson, G., 17
Luther, M., 95, 165, 167

Machiavelli, N., 61, 92-93, 105, 237, 250
Mackey, L., 42
Macrae, D.G., 26
Macrobius, 167
Maimonides, M., 53, 180
Malantschuk, G., 40
Malthus, T.R., 239
managerial attitudes, 26-27, 30-32, 74-78, 85-87
Mannheim, K., 110
March, J.G., 27
Maritain, J., 260
Marx, E., 199, 205
Marx, K., 10, 84, 85, 109-10, 215, 239, 252-53, 261-62
McCarthy, D., 14
meaning and use, 13-14, 68
Merleau-Ponty, M., 2
Merton, R.K., 4
Mill, J., 227
Mill, J.S., 11, 63-65, 70, 88, 92, 118-19, 137, 198-99, 233
Millar, J., 37
Miller, J., 115
Milstein, J.S., 99
Mink, L.O., 212
Mitchell, W.C., 99
Monboddo, Lord, 37

Moore, G.E., 14-16, 18, 23, 65, 72, 107, 112-13, 148
moral disagreement, 6-12
Mozart, W.A., 37-38

Namier, L.B., 4
Newman, O., 90
Newton, I., 81, 83, 268
Nietzsche, F., 21, 22, 26, 35, 110, 113-15, 116-20, 129-30, 137, 163, 256-59, 271
Nozick, R., 153, 246-52

Orwell, G., 106, 189

Parfit, D., 216
Parsons, K.P., 115
Pascal, B., 40, 54, 99
Passmore, J.A., 163
patience, 177, 202
Paul, 15, 184
Pericles, 136
personal identity, 33
phenomenology, 2, 3
Pindar, 136-37
Plato, 11, 23, 131, 140-45, 147, 157-58, 163, 169, 171, 195
Platt, J., 89
Polanyi, K., 239
Popper, K., 93-95
Porphyry, 147
practical reasoning, 23-24, 45-46, 161-62, 222-25
predictability and unpredictability, 93-106, 259
pragmatism, 65-66
Price, R., 236
Prichard, H.A., 18, 113
Prior, A.N., 57

Quine, W.V.O., 2, 72, 83-84, 266

Ramsey, F.P., 17
Rawls, J., 21, 119, 153, 233, 246-52
Rembrandt, 189
Ricardo, D., 238
Richardson, L.F., 99
Rieff, P., 26, 30-31
Righter, A., 143-44
rights, 66-70

Riker, W.H., 97
Rorty, R., 266-67
Rosenbaum, S.P., 14
Ross, W.D., 113, 153
Rousseau, J.J., 10, 237
Ruskin, J., 72
Russell, B., 42
Ryle, G., 13, 185, 240

Sartre, J.P., 21, 26, 32, 35, 205, 214, 221, 224, 226
Schelling, T., 102
Scheffler, S., 272-74
Scottish Enlightenment, 37, 272
self, the, 32-35, 61, 126-27, 216-22
Sellars, W., 266
Senghors, D., 89
Shakespeare, W., 143
Sidgwick, H., 16, 64-65, 198
Simon, H.A., 27
Skinner, B.F., 208
Smith, A., 10, 22, 37, 51, 54, 61, 234-35, 236, 239
Smyth, D.J.C., 89
Solomon, R., 115
Solzhenitsyn, A., 35
Sophocles, 131-32, 134-35, 142-45, 157, 163, 169, 179, 181
Spencer, H., 115
Stalker, G.N., 106
Steiner, F., 112
Stephen, L., 16
Sterne, L., 81
Stevenson, C.L., 12, 17, 19-20, 35, 72, 112-13

stoicism, 140, 168-70, 234-37
Strachey, L., 14, 16-17, 72
Strawson, P.F., 2
Strong, T., 115

Talmon, J.L., 237
Taylor, H., 199
therapeutic attitude, 30-31
Theresa, 199
Thring, E., 30
Trent, Council of, 170
Trilling, L., 235
Trotsky, L., 199, 262
truthfulness, 192-93, 223
Turing, A., 95
Turner, G.M.W., 191
Tylor, E.B., 112

utilitarianism, 14-16, 62-66, 70-71, 160, 198-99, 257, 260-61

Van Fraasen, B.C., 224
Verne, J., 93-94
Vico, G., 37, 216, 265, 277
Virgil, 167

Wachbroit, R., 264, 271-73, 277
Wadell, P., 272-73
Wampanoag Indians, 153
Weber, M., 26-27, 30, 74, 86, 109, 114-15, 143-44, 262
Weil, S., 127-28
William of Canterbury, 213
William of Conches, 167
Wittgenstein, L., 101, 189
Woolf, L., 16
Woolf, V., 14, 16

2